RACHELLE GILMOUR, Ph.D. (2010) from the University of Sydney,
is a post-doctoral research fellow at the Hebrew University, Jerusalem.

Representing the Past

Supplements

to

Vetus Testamentum

VOLUME 143

Representing the Past

A Literary Analysis of Narrative Historiography in
the Book of Samuel

By

Rachelle Gilmour

BRILL

LEIDEN • BOSTON
2011

BS
410
V452
vol.143

This book is printed on acid-free paper.

Library of Congress Cataloging-in-Publication Data

Gilmour, Rachelle.
  Representing the past : a literary analysis of narrative historiography in the book of Samuel / by Rachelle Gilmour.
     p. cm. — (Supplements to Vetus Testamentum ; v. 143)
  Includes bibliographical references (p.) and index.
  ISBN 978-90-04-20340-2 (hardback : alk. paper) 1. Bible. O.T. Samuel—Historiography. I. Title. II. Series.

  BS1325.6.H65G54 2011
  222'.4067—dc22

                                                                2010053577

ISSN 0083-5889
ISBN 978 90 04 20340 2

PRINTED BY DRUKKERIJ WILCO B.V. - AMERSFOORT, THE NETHERLANDS

In memory of my grandfather, John Knight

CONTENTS

ACKNOWLEDGEMENTS

This book was originally written for my doctoral dissertation at the University of Sydney, submitted in May 2010. Very special thanks are due to my dissertation supervisors, Assoc. Prof. Ian Young and Dr Noel Weeks. They have both taught me from the very beginning of my Hebrew study and I am indebted to each of them for many years of patient teaching and generous supervision. Their insights, ideas and encouragement throughout this project have always been perceptive, helpful and very welcome. I also thank Prof Graeme Auld, Dr Diana Edelman and Dr Robert Rezetko for reading either sections or the whole of this work and for their helpful suggestions for its improvement. I gratefully acknowledge Brian Taylor who made learning to read German an enjoyable process and for all his generous help in this regard. I am also grateful to Claire Willard for her providential and timely expertise in French.

I owe special thanks also to all my friends and colleagues at the University of Sydney, the Presbyterian Theological Centre and the wider community of biblical scholars and students in Sydney. Whilst they are too many to name, the interest, support and stimulating scholarship of all these people have been a wonderful provision to me as I have developed and shaped my own ideas over the years and learned so much from so many of them.

My family and friends have also played an indispensable role in shaping this book and bringing it to completion. In particular, my great thanks go to my father David Gilmour for always encouraging me to study what I was interested in, for his wonderful support over these years and especially for his careful proofing of my dissertation. Thanks also goes to Stephen Gilmour for his continual interest and encouragement. I am wonderfully blessed to have a family with whom I can discuss ideas and constantly rely on their enthusiasm for any project I undertake. A special mention also of Rosie Shorter for tirelessly making the tea, a very important contribution to any endeavour.

Finally, this book is dedicated to the memory of a man who deeply treasured and shared with others the words of the Hebrew Bible, my grandfather, John Knight. He is now with the Lord but the memory of showing him my completed dissertation is very precious to me.

LIST OF ABBREVIATIONS

ANES	*Ancient Near Eastern Studies*
BI	*Biblical Interpretation*
Bib	*Biblica*
BIOSCS	*Bulletin of the International Organization for Septuagint and Cognate Studies*
BWANT	Beitrage zur Wissenschaft vom Alten und Neuen Testament
CBQ	*Catholic Biblical Quarterly*
CJT	*Canadian Journal of Theology*
DJD	*Discoveries in the Judaean Desert*
FOTL	Forms of Old Testament Literature
HALOT	*The Hebrew and Aramaic Lexicon of the Old Testament.* By Koehler, Ludwig, Johann Jakob Stamm, M.E.J. Richardson, and Walter Baumgartner. Leiden: E.J. Brill, 1994
HTR	*Harvard Theological Review*
HUCA	*Hebrew Union College Annual*
JBL	*Journal of Biblical Literature*
JETS	*Journal of the Evangelical Theological Society*
JHS	*Journal of Hebrew Scriptures*
JNES	*Journal of Near Eastern Studies*
JNSL	*Journal of North West Semitic Languages*
JQR	*Jewish Quarterly Review*
JSOT	*Journal for the Study of the Old Testament*
JSS	*Journal of Semitic Studies*
JTS	*Journal of Theological Studies*
LXX	Septuagint
MT	Masoretic Text
NCBC	New Century Bible Commentary
NCOT	New International Commentary on the Old Testament
NLH	*New Literary History*
NLR	*New Left Review*
OTL	Old Testament Library
RSO	*Revista degli studi orientali*
SBL	Society of Biblical Literature

SBT	Studies in Biblical Theology
SJOT	*Scandanavian Journal of the Old Testament*
ST	*Studia Theologica*
TB	*Tyndale Bulletin*
TBC	Torch Bible Commentaries
TZ	*Theologische Zeitschrift*
VT	*Vetus Testamentum*
WBC	Word Biblical Commentary
WMANT	Wissenschaftliche Monographien zum Alten und Neuen Testament
WTJ	*Westminster Theological Journal*
ZAW	*Zeitschrift für die alttestamentliche Wissenschaft*

CHAPTER ONE

INTRODUCTION

There are many possible ways to describe the book of Samuel: literature, propaganda, entertainment, tragedy or theology. Most scholars would agree that historiography, or an interpretation of Israel's past, can be included amongst these descriptions. The book of Samuel is significantly different from modern historiography as there are literary devices and embellishments unimaginable in a modern work, and no statement of aims or explicit weighing of evidence or sources. Yet there are many similarities that make this description meaningful and worthwhile. The use of narrative to represent the past is as old as the concept of history itself but also at the forefront of modern historical theory. A return to the centrality of narrative in history in recent years has made literary embellishment and overt ideological interpretation more acceptable in a modern concept of historiography. They are now often considered inevitable and even desirable aspects of representation. They bring the past to life, offer an interpretation of its meaning and significance, and express the complexity of human experience and national events. Nevertheless, the rich characterisation, dramatic recreation of events and strong ideological bias throughout the book of Samuel remains a cause of difficulty for many attempting to understand the book from a modern historical viewpoint.

The purpose of this study is to analyse narrative historiography in the Masoretic Text version of the book of Samuel. We will examine how it conceives and presents historical information. More specifically, we will look at four aspects of its representation of the past, which are also important features in modern historiography: causation, ideological evaluation, meaning and significance, and coherence. We will look at the nature of these four characteristics of history, particularly how they are similar and different from the ideals of modern historiography. We will examine how narrative is used to represent the first three characteristics, paying close attention to literary devices that differ from modern conventions. In the final chapter, we will look at how the book of Samuel's conception of coherence and accuracy in historiography differs from modern requirements.

This study will demonstrate three main points about the nature of historiography in Samuel. Firstly, whereas modern historiography usually conveys causation, meaning and evaluation through explicit means, the historiography of Samuel uses an array of literary devices to convey these features. In particular, complex literary techniques communicate a complex depiction of the past. Secondly, the historiography of Samuel values different types of causation, meaning and ideological evaluation from the modern day. These include an emphasis on the Divine and the character of individuals within history, and an interest in patterns and cycles of people and events in the past. Thirdly, the extensive and creative literary devices, which appear in Samuel, affect the coherency and accuracy of the historiography by modern standards. Despite this, these inaccuracies and incoherencies contribute towards other aspects of the representation that are presented coherently throughout the book. This suggests that the interpretation of the past was more important than the accuracy of its details. To a modern eye, the historiography of Samuel is commonly regarded as unreliable, but for the ancient authors/redactors and readers/hearers it could be considered a legitimate rendering of the past.

By conducting this study, a contribution will be made primarily to the area of poetics in biblical narrative. Although certain literary features of the book have long been recognised, it is only in the last 40 years that these have become the subject of analysis within mainstream scholarship. Notably Alter, Berlin, Sternberg, Savran, Bar-Efrat, Gunn and Fewell, and Amit[1] have offered 'text book' guides to the literary devices used in Hebrew biblical narrative, identifying common features and demonstrating how they function in different texts. Fokkelman, Conroy, Gunn, Polzin, Eslinger, Jobling, Garsiel, Bodner, Green, Exum and Nicholson[2] among others have applied different types of literary

---

[1] Robert Alter, *The Art of Biblical Narrative* (New York: Basic Books, 1981); Adele Berlin, *Poetics and Interpretation of Biblical Narrative*, Bible and Literature Series (Sheffield: Almond, 1983); Meir Sternberg, *The Poetics of Biblical Narrative: Ideological Literature and the Drama of Reading* (Bloomington: Indiana University Press, 1985); George W. Savran, *Telling and Retelling: Quotation in Biblical Narrative* (Bloomington: Indiana University Press, 1988); Shimeon Bar-Efrat, *Narrative Art in the Bible*, JSOTSup. 70 (Sheffield: Almond Press, 1989); D.M. Gunn and Danna Nolan Fewell, *Narrative in the Hebrew Bible* (Oxford: Oxford University Press, 1993); Amit, Yairah, *Reading Biblical Narratives: Literary Criticism and the Hebrew Bible* (Minneapolis: Fortress Press, 2001).

[2] J.P. Fokkelman, *The Crossing Fates*, Vol. II of *Narrative Art and Poetry in the Books of Samuel: A Full Interpretation Based on Stylistic and Structural Analyses* (Assen: Van Gorcum, 1986); Charles Conroy, *Absalom Absalom! Narrative and Lan-*

analyses[3] directly to the book of Samuel and have shown convincingly that there is a high level of literary artistry in its final form. It is hoped that the close literary analysis in this study will offer a number of new readings or fresh perspectives on the narrative of Samuel and so add to these general works on its literary artistry. However, the expressed contribution of this book is to build on previous studies through particular attention to literary devices that convey the characteristics of history writing. We will examine not only how the techniques build characterisation, plot and theme, but also how they contribute to the causation of events, the evaluation of people in the past and the significance of the past. Literary devices can represent and interpret history, not merely tell a story and we will develop a portrait of the ways in which narrative is used in this particular historiography.

Secondly, our attention to Samuel as a work of narrative historiography, which is very different from modern historiography, is relevant to the recent, ongoing debate on how to write a history of ancient Israel.[4] Traditionally, histories of Israel tended to rely on the Bible as the primary source, using the historical critical methods to

---

guage in 2 Sam 13–20 (Rome: Biblical Institute Press, 1978); D.M. Gunn, *The Fate of King Saul: An Interpretation of a Biblical Story*, JSOTSup. 14 (Sheffield: JSOT Press, 1980), and D.M. Gunn, *The Story of King David: Genre and Interpretation* (Sheffield: JSOT Press, 1978); Robert M. Polzin, *Samuel and the Deuteronomist: A Literary Study of the Deuteronomic History; Part Two—I Samuel* (San Francisco: Harper and Row, 1989), and Robert M Polzin, *David and the Deuteronomist: A Literary Study of the Deuteronomic History; Part Three—II Samuel* (San Francisco: Harper and Row, 1993); Lyle M. Eslinger, *Kingship of God in Crisis: A Close Reading of 1 Samuel 1–12* (Decatur: Almond Press, 1985); David Jobling, *1 Samuel*, Berit Olam (Collegeville: Liturgical Press, 1998); Moshe Garsiel, *The First Book of Samuel: A Literary Study of Comparative Structures, Analogies and Parallels* (Ramat-Gan: Revivim, 1985); Keith Bodner, *David Observed: A King in the Eyes of His Court* (Sheffield: Sheffield Phoenix Press, 2005), and Keith Bodner, *1 Samuel: A Narrative Commentary* (Sheffield: Sheffield Phoenix Press, 2008); Barbara Green, *How are the Mighty Fallen? A Dialogical Study of King Saul in 1 Samuel*, JSOTSup. 365 (Sheffield: Sheffield Academic Press, 2003); J. Cheryl Exum, *Tragedy and Biblical Narrative: Arrows of the Almighty* (Cambridge: Cambridge University Press, 1992); Sarah Nicholson, *Three Faces of Saul: An Intertextual Approach to Biblical Tragedy*, JSOTSup. 339 (Sheffield: Sheffield Academic Press, 2002).

[3] Whilst most of these studies could be broadly termed 'poetics', there are a number of different approaches represented. Fokkelman's approach could be described as structuralist as he looks at the structural minutiae of the text. Polzin, Green and Bodner all draw on the work of Mikhail Bakhtin in their analyses. Nicholson looks at intertextuality and creative reinterpretation of Samuel in modern texts. Both Nicholson and Exum look at tragic elements in the text.

[4] For a recent analysis of current methodology for writing a history of Israel, see Megan Bishop Moore, *Philosophy and Practice in Writing a History of Ancient Israel* (New York: T&T Clark, 2006).

extract its history and archaeological evidence to supplement it. This approach has been challenged by so-called 'minimalists' who propose that the questionable and unverifiable historicity of the Bible render it an inappropriate source for writing a history of ancient Israel. These scholars are influenced by the *Annales* school which emphasises the role of sociology, archaeology and other scientific models in a multi-disciplinary approach for writing history.[5] The rejection of the biblical texts as a source for history has stimulated debate on how the biblical texts ought to be used in writing history[6] and heightened interest in the nature of the Bible as a source.[7] The purpose of this study is not to enter into the debate on how to write a history of Israel, but rather how to read the text of Samuel as ancient historiography. This will have implications for the debate because the way that the book is read will affect its usefulness as an historical source.

This debate has highlighted that, regardless of how reliable scholars believe the history of Samuel to be, some level of reconstruction of events must take place when writing a history of ancient Israel in the present day.[8] There are three main types of problems with using the Bible as a historical source, based on its differences from modern historiography. Firstly, it does not state its sources or show evidence of weighing up the accuracy of its sources. Secondly, it understands several key characteristics of history differently from modern histo-

---

[5] Major works which have written a history along these lines are: Philip R. Davies, *In Search of Ancient Israel*, JSOTSup. 148 (Sheffield: JSOT Press, 1992); Thomas L. Thompson, *Early History of the Israelite People: From the Written and Archaeological Sources* (Leiden: Brill, 1992); Niels Peter Lemche, *The Israelites in History and Tradition* (London: SPCK, 1998); Giovanni Garbini, *History and Ideology in Ancient Israel* (London: SCM, 1988).

[6] For example, the articles of Ahlström, Edelman and Miller in Diana Edelman, ed. *The Fabric of History: Text, Artifact, and Israel's Past*, JSOTSup. 127 (Sheffield: JSOT Press, 1991).

[7] See works of minimalist scholars cited above. On the other side of the debate, in favour of a broad understanding of what is history: Roger N. Whybray, "What Do We Know About Ancient Israel," in *Israel's Past in Present Research*, ed. V. Philips Long (Winona Lake, Ind: Eisenbrauns, 1999); K. Lawson Younger, Jr., *Ancient Conquest Accounts: A Study in Ancient Near Eastern and Biblical History Writing*, JSOTSup. 98 (Sheffield: JSOT Press, 1990), 25–58; Hans M. Barstad, "History and the Hebrew Bible," in *Can a 'History of Israel' Be Written?* ed. Lester L. Grabbe, JSOTSup. 57 (Sheffield: Sheffield Academic Press, 1997), and Jens Bruun Kofoed, *Text and History: Historiography and the Study of the Biblical Text* (Winona Lake: Eisenbrauns, 2005).

[8] For example, Iain W. Provan, Tremper Longman, and V. Philips Long, *A Biblical History of Israel* (Louisville: Westminster John Knox Press, 2003). They hold a high view of the reliability of the Hebrew Bible.

riography. For example, the ideology of Samuel is overt and often appears contradictory. Similarly, there are characteristics of causation, meaning and significance, and coherence in the book of Samuel that all violate the expectations of modern historiography. Thirdly, it uses literary devices in ways unaccustomed in modern historiography. In order to understand how (or if) Samuel can be used in modern historical reconstructions, we must understand in more detail the nature of these differences from modern historiography.[9] Past emphasis has tended towards what the text is *not* doing and so these features of Samuel's historiography are seen only as problems. However, we can also focus on what it *is* doing and so understand what its ancient conception of history was. It may not record the past in the same way as modern historiography, but this does not mean it has no value for studying the past at all, especially if we have an understanding of its ancient conventions, its notion of history, and the way it uses narrative to represent it. Philip R. Davies refers to three 'Israels': biblical Israel, historical Israel and ancient Israel.[10] Biblical Israel is the history presented by the Hebrew Bible, historical Israel is a history according to the standards of modern historiography and ancient Israel is 'what actually happened'. This study contributes towards understanding how to read 'biblical Israel' more satisfactorily.

The dominant response to the first problem of Samuel's sources has been to use historical critical methods for identifying the sources and extracting those elements of the text that are likely to have historical basis.[11] Recently, scholars have also begun to examine in greater depth what the source composition of Samuel reveals about the historians' conception of historiography. Halpern points out:

> To read Israel's historiography, we must allow that it stands on the far horizon of the Western tradition. The historians' idea of what leeway

---

[9] Green, *How are the Mighty Fallen*, 4, also highlights the importance of understanding how the Bible writes history for reconstructing the realities behind it.

[10] Davies, *In Search of Ancient Israel*, 16–18.

[11] Edelman describes a sophisticated and holistic approach to using literary criticism, including source criticism to reconstruct history. In effect, she is suggesting the use of literary criticism to address each of the four areas highlighted above and pointing to the need for the sorts of studies described below [Diana Edelman, "Doing History in Biblical Studies," in *The Fabric of History: Text, Artifact and Israel's Past*, ed. Diana Edelman (Sheffield: JSOT Press, 1991)]. She has also applied this approach to the reign of Saul in "Saul ben Kish in History and Tradition," in *Origins of the Ancient Israelite States*, ed. Fritz Volkmar and Philip R. Davies (Sheffield: Sheffield Academic Press, 1996), 142–59.

they enjoyed in presentation diverged from the standards of twentieth-century academic history, perhaps far more than their idea of what constituted evidence.[12]

His study, *The First Historians*, explores such differences, focusing on the use of evidence and the process for including sources in the historiography, often drawing on what we know of other ancient Near Eastern texts. He concludes that these ancient historians distinguished between myth and history but not always correctly.[13] Brettler also approaches the question of the nature of Israel's historiography from the perspective of how it was created. Using Chronicles as his starting point, he argues that the authors of the texts have used a number of different processes to reshape history: typologies, satire, creative reinterpretation and rhetorical devices.[14] His conclusion is that we cannot know what happened in Israel's history "beyond reasonable doubt" because of "the special blend of devices used by biblical historians."[15] Thus these scholars have addressed the first area in which we need to understand Samuel's conception of history: sources.

This study complements this previous research by responding to the second and third areas of problems raised in the debate about using the biblical historiography: a different conception of causation, ideological evaluation, meaning and coherence; and the extensive use of literary devices. A response to both of these problems can take a synchronic perspective of the text because they are the *result* of the process of creating the history rather than a part of it. By examining each of these issues in depth, we can analyse with greater specificity the ways in which the historiography of Samuel does not meet the ideals of modern historiography, but also understand what it offers as an alternative. By understanding how the book of Samuel writes causation, meaning, ideological evaluation and coherence, and what the role and extent of literary devices are, we are able to know what are the right questions to ask of the text and what we *can* discover in spite of the many differences from modern historiography.[16]

---

[12] Baruch Halpern, *The First Historians: The Hebrew Bible and History* (University Park: Pennsylvania State University Press, 1988), 276.

[13] Ibid., 269–70.

[14] Marc Zvi Brettler, *The Creation of History in Ancient Israel* (London: Routledge, 1995).

[15] Ibid., 144.

[16] For an article length introduction and discussion of some of these differences, see Claus Westermann, "The Old Testament's Understanding of History in Relation

To a certain degree we are also redressing the greater emphasis placed on discovering the diachronic processes of creating history rather than on analysing the nature of the result. However, both a diachronic and synchronic understanding of the nature of historiography in Samuel are ultimately important for scholars concerned with the debate on how to write a history of ancient Israel. This study will not address the historicity of the book of Samuel directly, but it will guide us as to its 'rules' of representing and interpreting the past.

Halpern's *David's Secret Demons*[17] is an example of a monograph that has used an understanding of how the author(s) of Samuel writes historiography to reconstruct a modern account of the past. Halpern describes his approach as an alternative view of David, as his enemies would have seen him. After looking at Assyrian display inscriptions and their use of 'spin', he analyses the likely use of 'spin' in II Sam 8, in order to discover a more negative depiction of David. He is establishing "David's reality"[18] which is more palatable for modern eyes than the Bible's literary creation of a king too good to be true. A similar approach is taken by McKenzie.[19] McKenzie follows McCarter's view that David's Rise and the Court History are apologetics for David[20] and then extracts biographical information from the texts. The use of this approach demands further research on the nature of Samuel as a work of historiography. We must expand our understanding beyond its use of sources and ideological slant, to its conception of the characteristics of history and its use of literary devices.

1.1 Historiography: A Representation of the Past

In order to understand how the book of Samuel functions as historiography, and to compare it with modern historiography, we need to examine more closely what historiography is. We will look at its essential and non-essential features and discuss which aspects are cultural

---

to That of the Enlightenment," in *Israel's Past in Present Research*, ed. V. Philips Long (Winona Lake: Eisenbrauns, 1999), 220–31.

[17] Baruch Halpern, *David's Secret Demons: Messiah, Murderer, Traitor, King* (Grand Rapids: Eerdmans, 2001).

[18] Ibid., xvi.

[19] Steven L. McKenzie, *King David: A Biography* (Oxford: Oxford University Press, 2000).

[20] Ibid., 27.

and which are not. Furthermore, there are many possible definitions
of historiography and so the definition used in our study needs to
be explained and justified. Our search is for a definition that is not
heavily biased towards modern Western ideas or ignores similarities
in texts from other cultures and times, but that is also not too broad
for it to be useful.

There are certain aspects of historiography that are non-controversial
and that are presumed, not stated, in our definition. Firstly, it is a
written representation. Although there are other legitimate ways of
representing the past, such as visual art, the Greek -graph- element in
the word 'historiography' means 'to write' and therefore it is logical
to restrict the meaning in this way. A second assumed aspect is that
the historiography contains causation.[21] According to Berkhofer, who
traces the idea through E.M. Forster back to Aristotle, "Chronicles
offer their readers 'one thing after another'; proper histories provide
their readers with 'one thing because of another'."[22] Causation is an
important feature of historiography in both modern and ancient cultures.[23] Thirdly, historiography conveys the meaning and significance
of the events in the past. In other words, the contents of the historiography are relevant either to the ongoing course of history or to the
present day. This is less a requirement of historiography and more an
inevitable feature. An author justifies the relevancy of the contents of
his/her work through a narrative link with the surrounding material,
explicit exposition or some other means. The consensus that causation, and meaning and significance, are fundamental to historiography
prompts their inclusion amongst the key features that we will examine
in the book of Samuel in the course of this study.

---

[21] We have presumed, not stated, causation in our definition because it is non-
controversial and it is preferable to keep the definition simple. However, we could
conceivably have made our definition more complex such as in Ferdinand Deist,
"Contingency, Continuity and Integrity in Historical Understanding: An Old Testament Perspective," in *Israel's Past in Present Research*, ed. V. Philips Long (Winona
Lake: Eisenbrauns, 1999), 380: "[History is] an explanation of the meaningful con-
nectedness of a sequence of past events in the form of an interested and focused
narrative."

[22] Robert F. Berkhofer, *Beyond the Great Story: History as Text and Discourse*
(Cambridge, Mass.: Belknap Press of Harvard University Press, 1995), 117.

[23] See the discussion on causation in ancient Greek historiography and the importance of asking 'why' in Peter Derow, "Historical Explanation: Polybius and his Predecessors," in *Greek Historiography*, ed. Simon Hornblower (Oxford: Clarendon Press,
1994), 73–90.

In addition to these assumed features of historiography, the definition of historiography in this study is that it is a *representation of the past*. The idea that it is representation is in contrast to the common idea that historiography must be an objective account of what happened and the criticism that texts with overt ideological intentions do not fit this category. This definition requires more rigorous justification than the features described above.

The principle that historiography should capture the objective past has its roots in positivism. This is a broad, multidisciplinary term that essentially signifies a reliance on the scientific method brought about through the Enlightenment. Within the study of historiography, it refers to the reduction of history to another form of science through which facts can be known from the past by means of unbiased method. A positivist history claims to be gaining access to past events as they actually happened[24] in a way that eliminates ideology and bias. An early proponent of positivism in the 19th century was Henry Thomas Buckle, who believed that history is deterministic and that regularity can be discovered in the past.[25] Finding generalisations in history was the method by which it could be made free from bias. There is a great deal of idealism in Buckle's formulation and it was criticised in his own time.[26] An alternative was offered by Ranke, who laid emphasis on the use of primary sources and proposed the goal of writing a universal[27] nationalistic history.

Many theorists of history, who were influenced by this modern scientific approach, have been aware of the problems involved with treating history as a purely scientific discipline.[28] However more recent theorists, influenced by postmodern thought, have challenged the idea that there is just 'one interpretation' of history and state that we can

---

[24] To steal a phrase from Ranke, *wie es eigentlich gewesen*.

[25] Fritz Richard Stern, "Positivistic History and its Critics: Buckle and Droysen," in *The Varieties of History: From Voltaire to the Present* (London: Macmillan, 1970), 124–5.

[26] See Droysen's response to Buckle also in Stern, *The Varieties of History*, 142.

[27] In a 'universal' history, all times and events are interdependent and connected. Although the study of details has its own particular interest, it will always be related to the greater context [Fritz Richard Stern, "The Ideal of Universal History: Ranke," in *The Varieties of History: From Voltaire to the Present* (London: Macmillan, 1970), 59].

[28] For example R.G. Collingwood, *The Idea of History* (Oxford: Oxford University Press, 1961), 205–82. Collingwood discusses the role of the imagination and interpretation in evaluating evidence and writing history.

never know the past in a single objective re-enactment. This broadens our idea of historiography from being 'what actually happened' to *an* interpretation or representation of what happened in the past that will vary among historians who hold different ideologies. Lowenthal[29] has given three factors that limit what we can know about the past: the immensity of the past; the distinction between past events and accounts of those events; and the inevitability of bias. We will discuss each of these factors and their implications for our definition of historiography.

(a) *The immensity of the past*

Lowenthal describes this problem:

> No historical account can recover the totality of any past events, because their content is virtually infinite. The most detailed historical narrative incorporates only a minute fraction of even the relevant past; the sheer pastness of the past precludes its total reconstruction.[30]

Historiography can never be an exact representation of the past because the past is infinite and unrepeatable. Only certain angles of the past can be captured in historiography which necessarily imposes a beginning and an end on the history and which selects events based on their significance for the chosen subject. Every possible cause and effect can never be taken into account or even known by an historian. Carr famously describes the infinite number of facts in history as "like fish swimming about in a vast and sometimes inaccessible ocean; and what the historian catches will depend, partly on chance, but mainly on what part of the ocean he chooses to fish in and what tackle he chooses to use."[31]

The limitation on an historian knowing all the facts is not a new idea and it was even recognised by Ranke in his quest for a 'universal history' that could transcend limits of time and geography on historiography. Although he believed in an ideal where all the particulars of events and their relation to their greater context can be discovered, he realised that the historian will fall short of this.[32] However, all the

---

[29] David Lowenthal, *The Past is a Foreign Country* (Cambridge: Cambridge University Press, 1985), 214–6.
[30] Ibid., 215.
[31] E.H. Carr, *What is History?* (London: Penguin Books, 1964), 23.
[32] See the extract from Ranke's work in Stern, "Ranke," 57.

implications of the immensity of the past are not recognised by those seeking to write history as it 'actually happened'. The first of these implications is that the necessary selection of events and facts from the past, and the imposition of a beginning and an end in historiography, will inevitably involve the ideology of the historian. This eliminates the possibility of objectivity in the historiography, an issue that will be explored further in a later section.

A second implication, particularly relevant to whether the book of Samuel ought to be considered historiography,[33] is that there will necessarily be gaps or leaps in any historiography. Not every detail can be told but rather the historian chooses them based on what he or she considers important. What a modern reader perceives as a gap in the historiography may not have appeared so for the ideological purpose of an ancient historian. The immensity of the past means that every historian is selective about what goes into his or her historiography and the narrative of the Bible ought not to be excluded from historiography because it selects events from the past based on different ideology and purposes to those held in the present. Thus, whilst modern readers perceive many gaps in the representation of the past in Samuel, this does not necessarily set it apart from other works of historiography.

(b) *The distinction between past events and accounts of those events*

Jenkins writes, "The past and history are different things. Additionally, the past and history are not stitched into each other such that only one historical reading of the past is absolutely necessary. The past and history float free of each other, they are ages and miles apart."[34] It is obvious that there is a distinction between past events and the accounts of those events but Lowenthal argues that it is highly relevant in the limitation of what we know of the past. The past no longer exists and so no account can be checked against it, only against other accounts. Although these other accounts can be anchored in reality, no historical account will strictly correspond with the events and so cannot be

---

[33] See for example Antony F. Campbell, *1 Samuel*, FOTL (Grand Rapids: Eerdmans, 2003), 14. He criticises the "existence of significant and unacknowledged leaps" in I Samuel.

[34] Keith Jenkins, *Re-thinking History* (London: Routledge, 1991), 4.

used for certain verification.[35] This again implies that there is no one authoritative account of the past but many possible representations.

(c) *Inevitability of bias*

Postmodernist critique of history has introduced a heightened awareness of the role of ideology in both the method and content of historiography. As we have seen, the selection of facts from the infinite array available is dependent on the historian's ideas about what is important and relevant to his/her history. Furthermore, a selection of facts on their own does not say anything; they need to be given context, related to other facts and placed in an order that is meaningful.[36]

More recently, Berkhofer has explored the inherency of ideology in historiography and shown that it has a role even in basic facts. He writes:

> The problem with historical facts, as with histories themselves, is that they are constructions and interpretations of the past. Evidence is not fact until given meaning in accordance with some framework or perspective. Likewise, events are not natural entities in histories, but constructions and syntheses that exist only under description.[37]

He illustrates his point by showing that even simple facts, such as George Washington's date of birth, can be challenged.[38] Berkhofer recognises that not all interpretations are equally valid and some can be eliminated. He concludes, "In the end, the quest for a single best or right interpretation denies multiple voices and viewpoints."[39] This perspective has made an impact on the discipline of history, which has begun to recognise the value of other voices in the past. These voices include those of women, lower classes and non-western cultures resulting in, for example, new feminist historiographies. No work of historiography can claim to be the one objective interpretation and works that do so, are either ignorant of or concealing the ideology which is shaping the historian's work.

---

[35] Lowenthal, *The Past is a Foreign Country*, 215.
[36] Described in these terms in C.L. Becker, *Detachment and the Writing of History* (New York: Cornell University Press, 1967), 53–55.
[37] Berkhofer, *Beyond the Great Story*, 53.
[38] Ibid., 53–55.
[39] Ibid., 50–53.

Ideology shapes the methodology for writing historiography as well as its content. For example, historians holding a modernist ideology will use scientific methodology for writing their historiography. Methodologies for writing historiography are constantly evolving, as is evinced in the current discussion, and so to define historiography based on any current ideology of history would be culturally exclusive and ignorant of the ideology inherent in the choice of methodology. There is no definitive method for writing historiography nor a definitive interpretation of events in the past. Thus it is problematic to include a particular type of causation or a modern idea of 'historical accuracy' in a definition of historiography.

An implication is that the Bible ought not to be rejected as historiography because of its overt ideology and lack of objectivity. The Bible is frequently described as religious propaganda[40] or parts of it as political propaganda[41] and this is placed in opposition to historiography. However, all historiography is a particular ideological interpretation on the past; the ideology of the Bible happens to be overt and in conflict with modern, secular ideology. There is an important difference between interpreting events so that their meaning and significance support your ideology and inventing events for the same purpose. It may not be obvious which of these are active in a text and this issue will be dealt with more fully shortly. Nevertheless, it is established that the presence of ideology in a text, even in the form of propaganda, is not a reason for dismissing classification of the text as historiography, because such interpretation is an inevitable aspect of all historiography. Indeed, as ideology is present in all historiography to some degree, the ideological evaluation of people and events in Samuel will be one of the key features of historiography that we will focus on in this study.

---

[40] For example, Ahlström writes that, as the Bible is concerned with religious propaganda, its ideology prevents it from rendering a faithful picture of history [Gösta W. Ahlström, "The Role of Archaeological and Literary Remains in Reconstructing Israel's History," in *The Fabric of History: Text, Artifact and Israel's Past*, ed. Diana Edelman (Sheffield: JSOT Press, 1991), 129].

[41] For example P. Kyle McCarter, Jr., "The Apology of David," *JBL* 99 (1980): 489–504, on the rise of David; Keith W. Whitelam, "The Defence of David," *JSOT* 29 (1984): 61–87, on I Sam 9–I Kgs 2; Tryggve N.D. Mettinger, *King and Messiah: The Civil and Sacral Legitimation of the Israelite Kings* (Lund: CWK Gleerup, 1976), on the History of David's Rise as a justification for David's dynasty sometime after the death of Solomon and the Succession Narrative, first a legitimation of Solomon, then also redacted as a legitimation of the Davidic dynasty.

Methodology for establishing the objective past

In its methodology for objective historiography, positivism relies on the premise that there is regularity in history and that it follows generalised laws. Thus scientific method is not only used for discovering history, but the subject of history can be reduced to a science about which generalisations and predictions can be made. It is important to discuss determinism because it is used as the grounds for claiming that objectivity can be achieved in historiography. Determinism, in its modern forms, tends to divide into two categories: genetic determinism and social determinism. A type of genetic deterministic method, which arises in modern historical scholarship, is 'analogy' where an historian's understanding of the present or the past in other cultures is a guide for evaluating the past.[42] This method is genetic because it assumes that the nature of human action and interaction in the present day is parallel to cultures distant in both time and space, on the basis of all peoples' shared humanity. Social determinism is the premise for using sociological theories to offer an objective investigation into history. Although Weber's own scholarship on ancient Judaism is largely ignored, his methods influenced Noth, whose theory of an early Israelite amphictyony had a profound impact on Biblical Studies.[43] Social determinism is also the foundation for form criticism, which is established on the premise that certain forms in literature arise in certain social conditions (the *Sitz im Leben*) and therefore we can learn about a *Sitz im Leben* based on the present form.

Sociology and analogy can be important and useful aspects of an historian's methodology but ultimately they are insufficient. Often the subjects chosen for historiography are precisely the unusual and the outstanding events in history.[44] Moreover, since the 1970s, it has become more accepted that the will of the individual is as important

---

[42] J. Maxwell Miller, "Reading the Bible Historically: The Historian's Approach," in *Israel's Past in Present Research*, ed. V. Philips Long (Winona Lake: Eisenbrauns, 1999), 357.

[43] See Martin Noth, *The History of Israel*, 2nd ed. (London: A. & C. Black, 1960), 85–109, for his analysis of the confederation of the twelve tribes of Israel. For example, see p. 86 for his belief that his method creates objectivity and p. 88 for comparisons with other tribal societies; for a critique of Noth's positivistic assumptions, see Provan, Longman, and Long, *A Biblical History of Israel*, 27–31.

[44] For the implications of this in writing a history of Israel, see Diane Banks, *Writing the History of Israel* (New York: T&T Clark, 2006), 9.

as the society for bringing about historical change.[45] Individuals cannot be generalised in the same way as societies and allowance must be made in historiography for the impact of the individual to generate the unusual and the profound, which frequently form the subject of our historiography. Ultimately however, determinism as a method requires ideology and interpretation. Otherwise, it underestimates the number of influences on any person, society or course of events in time and ignores the reality that these influences must necessarily be simplified before sociological theories or analogy can be applied. This simplification is subjective because it requires the historian to make value judgments about which influences are most important and which are less relevant. Thus, even so-called 'scientific' methodologies are insufficient for eliminating ideology and subjectivity from historiography.

Narrative in historiography and the use of literary devices

The postmodern critique by Lowenthal and others demonstrates the impossibility of an authoritative objective account of history and shows that all historiography is an ideological representation of the past. This highlights that historiography must use language to convey its representation. We have already referred to arguments within Biblical Studies that the use of complex narrative and literary devices in the Bible indicate it is 'story' rather than historiography. Such arguments suggest the influence of modern historians who reject narrative in history writing altogether and have even attempted to write historiography without imposing a beginning and end on their work.[46]

However, the value of narrative in historiography is once again being recognised within general historical theory. Appleby, Hunt and Jacob point to the human desire to impose beginnings and endings onto their representation of the past:

---

[45] Georg G. Iggers, *Historiography in the Twentieth Century: From Scientific Objectivity to the Postmodern Challenge* (Hanover, NH: Wesleyan University Press, 1997), 97.

[46] White lists Tocqueville, Burkhardt, Huizinga, and Braudel as having refused narrative in their work [Hayden V. White, *The Content of the Form: Narrative Discourse and Historical Representation* (Baltimore: Johns Hopkins University Press, 1987), 2]. See also Peter Burke, "History of Events and the Revival of Narrative," in *New Perspectives on Historical Writing*, ed. Peter Burke (Cambridge: Polity Press, 1991), 233–48. Burke argues that these 'structural' historians were justified in their rebellion against narrative and that narrative in modern historiography needs to be regenerated in a new form rather than just revived.

> The flow of time does not have a beginning, middle and end; only stories about it do. Yet lives share the structure of narratives, and perhaps a familiarity with their beginnings, middles, and ends predisposes people to cast their histories into narrative form.[47]

Lowenthal also argues:

> The contingent and discontinuous facts of the past become intelligible only when woven together as stories. Even the most empirical chroniclers invent narrative structures to give a shape to time. Unless history displays conviction, interest, and involvement, it will not be understood or attended to. That is why subjective interpretation, while limiting knowledge, is also essential to communication.[48]

Narrative can convey the complex causes, effects and significance of events which make up historiography in a way that uniquely interests and convinces a reader. Even historiography that avoids the use of narrative must use literary devices such as the repetition of key ideas, the careful choice of words and the imposition of structure in order to impress on the reader its particular interpretation.

Despite this, there is a perceived conflict between the use of narrative in historiography and the goal of 'what actually happened'. This conflict is exacerbated by the use of extensive literary devices and the role of imagination in the creation of narrative. However, the use of imagination does not necessarily imply that the text is further from conveying the past as it happened; in fact, it can bring the text closer. An example of this can be found in invented speeches in historiography. Even if an historian were to record the exact words of a speech, the intonation of the speaker, the emphasis on different words and the mood of the audience are not captured in the text. It still falls short of the ideal of 'what actually happened'. Indeed, an invented speech, whilst using different words to what were actually said, may capture the meaning of the speaker more precisely because the use of literary technique can incorporate the intonation, emphasis and mood of the speech into the text. Imagination is a necessary tool of the historian for discovering causation and significance in history, as these are not tangible or objective concepts. If imagination is employed for discov-

---

[47] Joyce Oldham Appleby, Lynn Avery Hunt, and Margaret C. Jacob, *Telling the Truth about History* (New York: Norton, 1994), 263.
[48] Lowenthal, *The Past is a Foreign Country*, 218.

ering these concepts, then its use can also be acceptable in the representation of them.[49]

Hayden White discusses in detail how narrative can represent reality and in particular he argues for the capacity of narrative to convey truth:

> Narrative historiography may very well, as Furet indicates, 'dramatize' historical events and 'novelize' historical processes, but this only indicates that the truths in which narrative history deals are of an order different from those of its social scientific counterpart. In the historical narrative the systems of meaning production peculiar to a culture or society are tested against the capacity of any set of 'real' events to yield to such systems. If these systems have their purest, most fully developed, and formally most coherent representations in the literary or poetic endowment of modern, secularized cultures, this is not reason to rule them out as merely imaginary constructions. To do so would entail the denial that literature and poetry have anything valid to teach us about reality.[50]

This is very relevant in the context of historiography in the Bible, where the ideology of the authors dictates that the 'historical processes' involved often include the activity of the Divine or the private and personal actions of individuals. The description of these processes is perfectly suited to narrative, which employs imagination for their reconstruction, even though it is impossible or unlikely for any evidence to remain of such causes or events.

Barstad, writing in the context of the discipline of Biblical Studies, has called for a shift in this discipline based on the postmodern concepts of multiple interpretations and representations. There needs to be recognition of different truths in history, and, in particular, we need to respect and understand that there exists narrative truth which, "is a different truth from that of conventional history, but it is *not* a lesser truth."[51] If it is acknowledged that narrative can convey truth, even when imagination is employed in its creation, then it

---

[49] Herodotus, the so-called father of history, has no qualms about including stories which take place in private situations and which are likely the product of his imagination. For example, Gyges watches the wife of Candaules in her bedroom in 1.10 and Darius is depicted lying in bed and discussing military strategies with his wife in 3.134 [Herodotus, *The Histories*, trans. Aubrey De Selincourt and John Marincola (London: Penguin Books, 2003), 6–7, 228.].

[50] White, *The Content of the Form*, 44.

[51] Barstad, "History," 51–53.

ought to be considered a vital tool for the representation of the past in historiography.

Causation and Divine Intervention

There is a common opinion in modern theories of historiography, and especially within Biblical Studies, that it should not contain references to divine causation and intervention. This approach to historiography is part of an overall secularisation of the discipline. It has been influenced by Marxist histories, which claim that all history can be explained in terms of economics and that religion has no part.[52] According to many definitions of historiography, it is not necessarily economic but political, social or a combination of forces that take precedence. For example, Ernest Nicholson compares the diverse causation found in Herodotus with the Bible. Although Herodotus refers to the operation of the gods, he does not do so consistently and draws on many other types of causes. By contrast, the Bible finds causes in the apostasy of Israel and the outworking of the divine will.[53] Nicholson believes, "there is no intellectually serious conception of history that resorts to divine agency as a mode of explanation."[54]

However, it is an imposition of modern western ideology to demand that all times and cultures understand their past in terms of political factors. If an author's ideology dictates that the Divine influences and intervenes in the events of history, then it is valid for that author to interpret this intervention as a source of causation in history. To state this more concretely, if, for example, miracles are within the worldview

---

[52] See E. Hobsbawm, "Marx and History," *NLR* 143 (1984): 39–50. Marx famously said that religion is the "opium of the people" and "man makes religion, religion does not make man." [Quoted in David McLellan, *The Thought of Karl Marx: An Introduction*, 2nd ed. (London: Macmillan, 1980), 22–23]. In other words, religion is only a construct that is used to subdue the people, not a force of history in itself. Note that this is a type of determinism that limits the sphere of influences to the economy. Compare also Martin Rose, "Deuteronomistic Ideology and Theology of the Old Testament," in *Israel Constructs its History*, ed. Albert de Pury (Sheffield: Sheffield Academic Press, 2000), 424. Rose comments that the term *ideologie* in German has become pejorative through the influence of Marx.

[53] Ernest Nicholson, "Story and History in the Old Testament," in *Language, Theology and The Bible*, ed. Samuel E. Balentine and John Barton (Oxford: Clarendon Press, 1994), 144–5. Nicholson writes that there is evidence of other types of causation in isolated narratives, e.g. II Sam, 9–20, but that the larger picture is not altered by this. Our own study of causation in Samuel will suggest Nicholson's reading is somewhat simplistic.

[54] Ibid., 137.

of an author, then the inclusion of miracles in his/her historiography is an accurate representation of how he/she interprets events.

There is diversity even within Western thought about the chief causes in history. For example, Marxist histories will emphasise economic factors and others will emphasise political. They are united in rejecting the religious, but political or economic causes are only ideological alternatives. In order to avoid cultural exclusivity, we will not specify a particular ideology of causation in our definition.

Primary sources and critical evaluation

Similar to Positivism, Leopold von Ranke in the 19th Century conceived of historiography as seeking to capture 'what actually happened', indeed it was his phrase *wie es eigentlich gewesen* that came to be synonymous with the search for objectivity in historiography. Ranke's contribution to modern methods of historical inquiry was his emphasis on eyewitness and primary sources.[55] Ranke writes in his preface to *Histories of the Latin and Germanic Nations from 1495–1514*:

> The basis of the present work, the sources of its material, are memoirs, diaries, letters, diplomatic reports, and original narratives of eyewitnesses; other writings were used only if they were immediately derived from the above mentioned or seemed to equal them because of some original information.[56]

Primary sources have become vital to historical method in modern historiography. However, secondary sources are also held in high regard provided they, in turn, are based on primary sources. Indeed, secondary sources or sources dated long after the event can provide perspective, which eyewitness accounts cannot, particularly if they have the advantage of multiple perspectives on their subject.[57]

The use of primary sources does very little to remove ideology or bias from the historiography. Eyewitness testimonies hold bias equal

---

[55] Ranke's formulation of historiography differed from positivism in a key way, as he did not agree that generalisations could be formed about history, rather he proposed the 'universal' history described earlier. Ranke also believed that political history was the universally relevant unit of history [Leonard Krieger, *Ranke: The Meaning of History* (Chicago: University of Chicago Press, 1977), 19].

[56] Stern, "Ranke," 57; See also Krieger, *Ranke*, 3. He notes that, whilst a critical attitude to sources dates back to Thucydides, Ranke turned it into a science.

[57] See Kofoed, *Text and History*, 42–43, for a discussion of the problems with both primary and secondary sources.

to, if not more than later accounts. Where there are discrepancies, it is the subjective task of the historian to decide between them.[58]

Primary sources (and secondary sources based on primary sources) are also considered an essential part of historiography because they are the means through which a high level of historicity can be achieved. We do not wish to argue with this proposition. Rather, we wish to show that *evidence* of the use of primary sources is not necessary in a text to classify it as historiography. The reason for this is that it is purely convention in modern historiography that sources are referenced. It is likely that sources were used in the Bible (and sometimes they are mentioned) but the conventions of the time and culture may not have required explicit reference every time a source was used.

It is not only the reference to sources, which is often used as criteria for historiography, but the critical use of sources. Herodotus is often called the father of history because he discusses where his sources came from and he prefers eyewitness accounts.[59] The Bible is criticised for using sources only because they were available, not because the writer had investigated their trustworthiness.[60] However, this judgment applies today's conventions for historiography to an ancient text. Conventions in ancient times may not have required discussion about why certain sources were selected. Halpern has suggested that a different type of source analysis is present in the Bible, where the

---

[58] Berkhofer, *Beyond the Great Story*, 74, describes the many different criteria by which the evaluation of histories could be judged and which could create argument between historians: intertextual agreement; how well it accords with how the world operates; the reader's aesthetic sense; or the reader's values and politics.

[59] Cf. Erhard Blum, "Historiography or Poetry: The Nature of the Hebrew Bible Prose Tradition", in *Memory in the Bible and Antiquity*, Wissenschaftliche Untersuchungen zum Neuen Testament 212, eds. L.T. Stuckenbruck, S.C. Barton & B.G. Wold (Tübingen: Mohr Siebeck, 2007), 32. He conceives of the difference between ancient historiography (including the Hebrew Bible) and ancient Greek and modern historiography as "the notion of an author who can be distinguished from his own work." In other words, there are discussions of sources in Greek historiography and modern historiography rather than an omniscient narrator.

[60] See for example Thomas M. Bolin, "History, Historiography, and the Use of the Past in the Hebrew Bible," in *The Limits of Historiography: Genre and Narrative in Ancient Historical Texts*, ed. C.S. Kraus (Leiden: Brill, 1999), 113–40. Bolin prefers to call the Bible 'antiquarian writing' rather than historiography for this reason. Of course, this distinction assumes that we can know whether the sources were evaluated by the author. See also Thompson, *Early History*, 372–5. He compares the Biblical texts with Herodotus and early Hittite texts which make claims of historicity and concludes that they are quite different from the fictive narrative traditions of the Bible.

authors juxtaposed sources in order to reconstruct history from them.[61] Although Halpern's proposed sources are much disputed, his theory offers an alternative to modern conventions of using sources. Licht also surmises about the conventions for combining sources in biblical literature and suggests that the writer has left the sources more or less as he found them but conveyed his solution through the narrative itself. Licht says, "this gentlemanly procedure has made the author look like a fool to his less civilised critics."[62] Therefore, the criteria that historiography must have explicit reference to primary sources or to the authenticity of secondary sources ignores the possibility that different cultures use different conventions for representing the past.

Thus, specifying the form of historiography, for example expecting it to reference its sources, is restrictive to one particular ideology and set of conventions in time. A definition based on form would be coherent and refer to a distinct set of texts but it would also be very restrictive. It gives priority to the currently accepted methodology for writing historiography and excludes all pre-enlightenment cultures from engaging in fully-fledged historiography. This is particularly undesirable in our study because the form of historiography is never static. The form, which is accepted now, may soon become outdated, making the definition of historiography also outdated.[63]

Historiography is best defined for our purposes by its function rather than by its form. Historiography's function is that it is a representation of the past. There are certain recognisable techniques, which are used for historiography, but these are conventions rather than inherent qualities of historiography. By referring to them as conventions, we recognise that they can change with time and cultural values. There is no definitively correct set of conventions because historiography is a subjective discipline in which different people will value different methods of interpretation based on their ideology.

---

[61] See Halpern's theory in practice on I Sam 8–12 in *The First Historians*, chapter 8.

[62] Jacob Licht, "Biblical Historicism," in *History, Historiography and Interpretation*, ed. Hayim Tadmor and Moshe Weinfeld (Jerusalem: Magnes Press, 1983), 108.

[63] Neville Morley, *Writing Ancient History* (Ithaca: Cornell University Press, 1999), 22, writes, "History has been practiced in different ways in the past, and it seems either naïve or arrogant to assume that our present methods will never be improved on in future. If we think of history purely in terms of its present form, we exclude from consideration a whole range of possible ideas about what history is and how it should be practised. It may turn out that this is the correct thing to do; conceivably our idea of history *is* far superior to that of earlier periods…I have my doubts about this, and it is certainly not something that we should take for granted."

Historical fiction, historiography and reality

Lowenthal and Berkhofer's critique of objective historiography reveals that there can be many interpretations and representations of history, each stemming from a different 'voice' or ideology. The goal of finding coherence, causation and significance in history adds to the difficulty of determining 'what actually happened'. Imagination plays a necessary and important role because it is used to fill in gaps and reconstruct the coherence, causation and significance. The past is in the past, it cannot be repeated and all historiographical accounts will be necessarily selective about what they include, shaping their depiction of the past based on ideology and intentions.

Ultimately, no historiography can represent history as it 'actually happened' and any definition of historiography that demands this draws a false distinction between texts which give the appearance of achieving objectivity and those which do not. Moreover, it is problematic for definitions to stipulate that historiography intends to give an objective account of 'what actually happened', even if they acknowledge that this is impossible. Objectivity is a culturally specific value and, as criterion for historiography, it excludes texts that are not ashamed of the ideology that is inherent in all works. Furthermore, because the nature of historiography is representation and interpretation, this can often be done more faithfully when imagination is employed in the process of the representation, rather than by a strict adherence to facts. In other words, the demand for objectivity and historicity in a definition of historiography is naïve about the complex correspondence between a representation of the past and the past itself and should not be included.[64] As we will see shortly, this does not imply that objectivity and historicity are irrelevant.

Indeed, one difficulty with this definition is that any text that has even the slightest connection to the past can be considered historiography. It eliminates any clear distinction between historical fiction and historiography. However, there is good reason for little distinction between these two categories. Morley examines the difference between historiography and fiction. He looks at the role of imagination and says that, although imagination is at home in fiction, it also "plays an

---

[64] Cf. Brettler, *The Creation of History*, 11, "Any understanding of history which depends on historicity cannot be profitably applied to the biblical corpus" because we know so little of the events standing behind it.

indispensable role in the interpretation of evidence."[65] The difference is that "historians are not supposed to let their imaginations get too carried away"[66] and this is reflected in conventions such as footnotes and justification for their reasoning. He concludes that, "the differences in form between history and fiction are a matter of convention and convenience, the differences in methodology are a matter of degree."[67] Historiography is on a spectrum with actual history and historical fiction/imagination at each of its extremes. We have already seen that a text can never be 'what actually happened'. Where a text includes ideological interpretation it uses the imagination to apply the ideology and so, in this sense, is fiction. Similarly, a text can never be entirely fiction or the imagination because all ideas originate in some real events.[68]

One suggestion in Biblical Studies for distinguishing between historiography and historical fiction, concerns the *intention* of the author. Amit has argued:

> We may therefore conclude that to qualify as a historiographic work it is only necessary for the author to be consciously seeking to describe the past. Whether or not it belongs to this specific genre is determined neither by its historical reliability nor by the degree of its objectivity.[69]

More specifically Halpern argues, after pointing out that historiography need not be comprehensively accurate, "Yet normally we would say that if the author does not *mean* to be accurate in representing the past ("as it really was"), if the author does not try to get the events right and to arrange them in the right proportion, the result cannot be history."[70] Thus, although accuracy itself is not an appropriate criterion, the intention of accuracy may be. One problem is that it is difficult to determine how strong this intention for accuracy ought to be, for example, whether it must extend to all details or just those considered important by the writer. As we will see in the final section of this study, there are some aspects of the historiography of Samuel

---

[65] Morley, *Writing Ancient History*, 32.

[66] Ibid.

[67] Ibid., 32–33.

[68] See Berkhofer, *Beyond the Great Story*, 67, for a similar description of the spectrum on which history, historical fiction and fiction lie. Berkhofer also suggests (p. 68) that the two genres can be differentiated by the claims of the author either for accuracy or imagination.

[69] Yairah Amit, *History and Ideology: Introduction to Historiography in the Hebrew Bible* (Sheffield: Sheffield Academic Press, 1999), 14.

[70] Halpern, *The First Historians*, 7.

that do not intend to be accurate in a modern historical sense and others that do. Brettler, in his formulation of a definition for history, also describes the criterion of 'intentionality' as problematic for ancient texts because of the difficulty of determining what that intention is.[71] In the case of Samuel, where there is no stated intention, such a criterion brings us no closer to discerning whether it is historiography rather than historical fiction.

Such a criterion creates more problems than solutions and, ultimately, a distinction between historical fiction and historiography is not necessary for the definition of historiography. The distinction between modern historiography and historical fiction is arbitrary and based on convention and, as we saw above, both descriptions lie on the same spectrum of actual history and fiction. Similarly, the definition does not distinguish between historiography and myth or legend. Brettler, who also defines historiography as "a narrative that represents the past," discusses why this distinction is not necessary. He argues that, within Biblical Studies, a representation of the past is all that is needed to delimit a "meaningful corpus of biblical texts which may be distinguished from other corpora, such as law, proverbs, psalms and (most of) prophecy."[72] In light of research already conducted on the historiography of the Bible, such distinctions could create a paradox in the classification of its books. It is possible that the authors/redactors may *intend* to represent the past accurately, yet draw on sources that are better described as myth or historical fiction.

The definition that historiography is a 'representation of the past' has great advantages and allows a meaningful and useful classification of texts. This definition attempts to avoid arbitrary and changing cultural conventions, as well as impossible and subjective ideals of accuracy. Instead it points to the fundamental similarity between texts from both modern and ancient cultures: these texts represent an interpretation of people, places and events in the past. Furthermore, in order to represent the past, there are a number of features, which frequently, if not always, occur: causation, ideological evaluation, significance and some degree of coherence. The commonality of these features further highlights the usefulness and legitimacy of this defini-

---

[71] Brettler, *The Creation of History*, 12.
[72] Ibid. See also D. Wyatt Aiken, "History, Truth and the Rational Mind: Why it is impossible to Separate Myth from History," *TZ* 47 (1991): 226–53.

tion and the group of texts it delineates. It is a broad definition that includes a wide variety of texts. However, the purpose of our study is to use this starting point to create a portrait of the nature, conventions and literary techniques of historiography in Samuel and so develop additional insights into its individuality as a work of historiography.

The relevance of historicity and modern scientific historical methods

A possible criticism of our definition is that it is too broad and that it does not take into account the reality that some histories are considered more useful or even 'better' than others in the modern day. The 'usefulness' of historiography as a description is that it groups together texts which have a fundamental similarity: the representation of the past. The label points to the similarity between the texts and does not make arbitrary discriminations or apply cultural bias. However, this does not imply that historicity and modern historical methods are irrelevant to our study of historiography. To the contrary, it is from the common platform of the description 'historiography' that we can proceed to analyse the differences between various ancient and modern works.

Firstly, a plurality of representations of the past does not imply that grades of accuracy or historicity do not exist. Postmodern theory demonstrates that there is not an all or nothing correlation between a work of historiography and 'what actually happened'. However, there are still texts that represent the past with greater or lesser accuracy.[73] Furthermore, texts that represent the past with greater accuracy will be more useful for the historian and so need to be identified. The level of accuracy can never be known with certainty but methods, such as comparison with other texts and plausibility of the interpretation, can give some indication. In the case of the book of Samuel, there is particular uncertainty about the level of connection between the historiography and the actual events and it is not a question we can answer through a final form analysis of the book. However, one of the aims of this study is to understand more deeply the conventions of Samuel's

---

[73] "It is possible to know some things more rather than less truly" [Appleby, Hunt, and Jacob, *Telling the Truth about History*, 194]. Berkhofer, *Beyond the Great Story*, 51, allows for the possibility that 'facts' can 'disprove' an interpretation but they cannot ever definitively 'prove' one. This is part of Berkhofer's argument that the fallacy of a best interpretation does not imply historiography cannot be written.

historiography so that others can determine its historicity or accuracy on the book's own terms. Furthermore, we can examine the coherency of the book and its level of variation between different versions. This will give an indication of which features it presents as accurate by a modern standard and which can be altered by literary devices in order to give a 'more true' representation. Thus accuracy will be the final feature of historiography that we will focus on in this study of Samuel.

Secondly, we have argued that our definition of historiography should not be biased towards modern ideology and conventions, yet this does not eliminate all differences between ancient and modern historiography, nor does it imply that modern ideologies of historiography should not have a special status. 'Scientific' history is valued by our modern Western society and so it is appropriate that there is a distinction made between it and the narrative historiography found in Samuel. It is an acknowledged modern convention that bias should be minimised, sources referenced and primary documents given special consideration. Texts that follow these conventions have a particular usefulness for modern scholars who wish to conduct historical investigation according to these ideals. Indeed, the very concepts of 'accuracy' and 'historicity' are shaped by our modern ideology. Therefore modern historical methods will also shape what we consider 'accurate' and it is important that these differences be taken into account in our analysis of Samuel. Once again, it is the purpose of this study to use the common description of historiography as a foundation from which we can determine the differences between the ancient and modern conceptions of representing the past.

However, all too often, the differences between modern and ancient historiography are emphasised and the similarities overlooked. There is significant overlap in the compositions of scientific and narrative historiography and there are texts that have characteristics of both types. For example, there are texts that draw on sources yet do not reference them. These share the nature of scientific historiography but not its form. Furthermore, many modern historiographies draw on narrative and artistic license whilst conforming to other important aspects of scientific historiography. This is particularly prevalent with the postmodern resurgence of narrative as a necessary and desirable means for representing the past.

In conclusion, historical fiction and history are not discrete categories but rather works of historiography lie on a spectrum between these two extremes. Nevertheless, historical accuracy, in contrast to imaginative reconstruction, is valued in modern scholarship and society and it is desirable to distinguish between texts that use different historical methods. Therefore the term historiography, according to the definition in our study, is better considered a description that can be applied to many different genres of texts, rather than constituting a genre of its own.[74] For example, it incorporates modern historiography, many modern works of historical fiction,[75] ancient propaganda texts and ancient Greek historiography. These categories of texts are diverse and should be considered different genres, even if they can be described more broadly as historiography.[76] Thus, although this study compares the historiography of Samuel with modern historiography, comparison could equally be made with modern historical fiction or other genres that fall under the description of historiography.

1.2   The Book of Samuel as Historiography

In our discussion, it has been assumed that the book of Samuel is a work of historiography according to the definition described here. It is often implicit in source critical discussions that the book is attempting

---

[74] There are many complications with discussing genres as they are fluid and therefore difficult to distinguish. According to Fowler, the difficulty of defining genres is that they often have no universally shared features or formal markers [Alastair Fowler, *Kinds of Literature: An Introduction to the Theory of Genres and Modes* (Oxford: Clarendon, 1982), 40]. He argues that they must be considered a *type* of text rather than a *class* which would have a set of common features. In contrast, a *type* can be compared to family resemblances where many features are shared within the group but there is not necessarily one that is universal to every member of the group [ibid., 41ff]. Fowler draws the corollary that genre must be looked at diachronically, an idea which is further developed by Cohen, then White, who both argue that the dynamic nature of genres is such that they will continue to eschew theory and so their study ought to be confined to an analysis of their history and their changing features over time [Ralph Cohen, "History and Genre," *NLH* 17 (1986): 203–18; and more recently on the development of Cohen's ideas, Hayden V. White, "Anomalies of Genre: The Utility of Theory and History for the Study of Literary Genres," *NLH* 34 (2003): 597–615]. However, even if we examine historiography diachronically as a genre, there remains the problem that many of the texts, which we wish to distinguish between, occur simultaneously, for example historical fiction and modern historiography.

[75] If historical fiction is considered a *type* of text (according to the theory of Fowler described above), it can be considered a genre. Some texts within the group will have features which represent the past and therefore can be described as historiography, whilst others do not contain these historiographic features.

[76] Cf. Diana Edelman, "Clio's Dilemma: The Changing Face of Historiography," in *Congress Volume, 1998* ed. A. Lemaire & M. Saebø, VTSup. 80 (Leiden: Brill, 1999), 253. She considers historiography a genre but preserves the distinction between modern and ancient historiography by subdividing the genre into these two additional categories. However, according to our definition many more subdivisions would be necessary and thus we prefer not to consider historiography a genre.

to represent the past. They appraise the historical nature of the sources under the assumption that the redactor combined them in order to create an orderly account of the past, even if the historian has failed to resolve all of the inconsistencies.[77] Campbell argues that the writer of I Samuel has amalgamated sources rather than adjudicated between them and for that reason it is not historiography.[78] However, he is evidently using a different definition of historiography. He concludes that the purpose of the book is to "articulate experience,"[79] and this description is consistent with the definition that historiography is a representation of the past. Similarly, Axel Knauf[80] does not consider Samuel history but this is also a question of definition. His reason for not considering books of the Hebrew Bible to be historiography is that they have nothing to do with 'what actually happened'. Furthermore, he considers Samuel 'novelistic' and argues that even the book of Kings presupposes factual history but does not recount it.[81] This demonstrates that he is using a more restrictive definition of historiography than 'a representation of the past' in his reasoning.

Furthermore, scholars who hold to a Deuteronomistic redaction usually suggest that the final redactor was representing the past. As Noth originally formulated it, the Deuteronomist brought together different sources in order to give an interpretation of the historical process by which Jerusalem fell.[82] According to many scholars, the Deuteronomic school shaped their source material to impose a Deuteronomistic theology on the events of the past.[83] Other propaganda

---

[77] Examples of this are: P. Kyle McCarter, Jr., *I Samuel*, The Anchor Bible (New York: Doubleday, 1980), (see his introduction); Ralph W. Klein, *1 Samuel*, WBC (Waco: Word Books, 1983), xxx.

[78] Campbell, *1 Samuel*, 13–14.

[79] Ibid., 15.

[80] Ernst Axel Knauf, "Does 'Deuteronomic Historiography' (DH) Exist?," in *Israel Constructs Its History: Deuteronomistic Historiography in Recent Research*, ed. Albert de Pury, Thomas Römer, and Jean-Daniel Macchi, JSOTSup. 306 (Sheffield: Sheffield Academic Press, 2000), 391–92.

[81] Ibid. Similarly, Collins argues that Biblical narratives ought not be considered history because its historical claims are not validated by historical criteria [John Joseph Collins, "The 'Historical Character' of the Old Testament in Recent Biblical Theology," in *Israel's Past in Present Research*, ed. V. Philips Long (Winona Lake: Eisenbrauns, 1999), 150–69]. This reason is also based on a stricter definition of historiography.

[82] Martin Noth, *The Deuteronomistic History*, JSOTSup. 15. (Sheffield: JSOT Press, 1981), 79.

[83] For example McCarter, *I Samuel*, 14–15; Barton suggests that it may have had a liturgical use [John Barton, "Historiography and Theodicy in the Old Testament," in

theories of the book[84] propose that the past is used to promulgate the authors/redactors' ideology. According to these theories, the book of Samuel is consciously guided by ideology and has a purpose apart from the representation of the past. Nevertheless, as it uses the past for its purposes, it can still be considered historiography according to our definition.

Similarly, the inclusion of legendary material in Samuel does not exclude its classification as historiography. Auld, in a departure from the usual understanding of the relationship between Samuel-Kings and Chronicles, suggests that each of these books was developed from a single shared source.[85] The nature of this source suggests "David and Solomon belong to the age of legendary beginnings rather than royal record."[86] Nevertheless, the process of expanding and rewriting the primary shared source and incorporating a number of other sources can still result in a representation of the past as interpreted by the editors of Samuel.

The concept that Samuel might contain intentional fiction has been introduced most prominently by literary studies on the book. Alter classifies the narrative in the Bible as 'sacred history' which he describes as "not strictly speaking, historiography but rather the imaginative reenactment of history by a gifted writer who organises his materials along certain thematic biases and according to his own remarkable intuition of the psychology of the characters."[87] Alter does not suggest that there is no historical basis for the narratives; to the contrary, he thinks they

---

Reflection and Refraction: Studies in Biblical Historiography in Honour of A. Graeme Auld, ed. R. Rezetko, T.H. Lim, and W.B. Aucker (Leiden: Brill, 2007), 27–33].

[84] E.g. Rost's succession narrative [Leonhard Rost, *The Succession to the Throne of David*, trans. Michael D. Rutter and David M. Gunn (Sheffield: Almond Press, 1982)] and the apology of David identified by McCarter ["The Apology of David," 489–504]. Whybray considers the succession document to be propaganda but adds to this a study of how it may also have functioned for wisdom teaching [R.N. Whybray, *The Succession Narrative: A Study of II Samuel 9–20; I Kings 1 and 2*, SBT (London: SCM, 1968)].

[85] Developed in the monograph, A. Graeme Auld, *Kings without Privilege: David and Moses in the Story of the Bible's Kings* (Edinburgh: T&T Clark, 1994).

[86] A. Graeme Auld, "Re-reading Samuel (Historically): 'etwas mehr Nichtwissen'," in *Origins of the Ancient Israelite States*, ed. Fritz Volkmar and Philip R. Davies (Sheffield: Sheffield Academic Press, 1996), 167.

[87] Robert Alter, "Sacred History and Prose Fiction," in *The Creation of Sacred Literature: Composition and Redaction of the Biblical Text*, ed. Richard Elliott Friedman (Berkeley: University of California Press, 1981), 16. See also his discussion on pp. 24–28, on Biblical narrative as 'historicised fiction', although he also suggests that 'fictionalised history' is perhaps more appropriate.

are largely based on historical facts.[88] The important difference is that the intention of the text is to use imagination of the past to capture theological truths rather than the past itself.[89] Essentially, it is the use of literary art, which Alter excels in analysing, that leads him to believe in the priority of imagination over the past in the text.[90] Gunn, in his study of King David, labels the text as 'story' for the sake of art and entertainment. He argues that the text does not hold up as history writing because of its use of private conversation, its meager treatment of public and political issues and its lack of interest in sources.[91]

In Gunn's discussion of II Sam 18, he admires the artistry and suspense of the description of David waiting for news of Absalom. He writes that this pericope adds no information for our understanding of the war or motivation of lead characters, nor does it teach us anything in particular. Rather it is for sheer entertainment.[92] Fokkelman agrees with this analysis and adds that it shows the emotional life of David and prepares for the rebuke of Joab in chapter 19.[93] By modern standards, the emotional life of David is not appropriate subject matter for historians. However, according to our definition of historiography, such subject matter does not exclude the narrative from being historiography. Similarly, political issues and quotation of sources are modern criteria. When Alter and Gunn argue that the book of Samuel is other than historiography, they appear to have a more nar-

---

[88] Ibid.

[89] Ibid., 24.

[90] Ibid., 16.

[91] Gunn, *The Story of King David*, 20. See also D.M. Gunn, "Entertainment, Ideology, and the Reception of 'History': 'David's Jerusalem' as a Question of Space," in *"A Wise and Discerning Mind": Essays in Honor of Burke O. Long*, ed. S.M. Olyan and R.C. Culley (Providence: Brown Judaic Studies, 2000), 153–61. Gunn suggests a possible reason why art/entertainment was included in the canon of sacred literature. Van Seters terms the stories of Samuel 'Saga' in the sense of Icelandic sagas which were based on written sources [John Van Seters, *The Biblical Saga of King David* (Winona Lake: Eisenbrauns, 2009)]. However, he also says that they were based on an older written historical record but extensive fictional details were added to make the "historical account more vivid and realistic" (p. 49). This would then conform to our definition of historiography. Note that in his earlier work, Van Seters does classify Samuel as historiography [John Van Seters, *In Search of History: Historiography in the Ancient World and the Origins of Biblical History* (New Haven: Yale University Press, 1983)].

[92] Gunn, *The Story of King David*, 45.

[93] J.P. Fokkelman, *King David*, Vol. I of *Narrative Art and Poetry in the Books of Samuel: A Full Interpretation Based on Stylistic and Structural Analyses* (Assen: Van Gorcum, 1981), 265.

row definition of historiography in mind than that argued for here.[94] Both scholars helpfully highlight that Samuel fully embraces imagination in its narrative and, on the basis of this observation, postulate a purpose for the narrative other than recording the past. However, it is possible that a text can have the purpose of entertainment yet use a representation of the past to achieve this entertaining quality. Historiography can be written for the fun of it. Alter and Gunn do not claim that Samuel does not use the past, but rather they emphasise that the artistic qualities of the book suggest a purpose other than didacticism or political propaganda.[95] Similarly, the success in applying a literary approach to the text does not imply that the work is fiction rather than historiography. As Hornblower writes regarding Greek historiography:

> Can we apply, to ancient historical writers, techniques of analysis successfully applied to poetry and fiction, without thereby committing ourselves to the view that the history is fiction? Put like that, the fallacy becomes obvious. By examining the techniques of historical presentation we do not necessarily imply that the subject-matter of the presentation is true or false.[96]

Finally, the book of Samuel could potentially be considered 'remembered' past rather than 'represented' past. This refers to the concept of 'cultural memory', which encompasses both rituals and texts used by a culture to communicate and perpetuate identity. Yerushalmi writes that the biblical appeal to remember the past has little to do with the impulse to record past events but rather to remember God's intervention. In other words, it is concerned with 'how' the past happened, not

---

[94] See for example Gunn, "Entertainment, Ideology, and the Reception of 'History'," 154, where he specifically states that our understanding of the relationship between history and entertainment will depend on what we understand by history.

[95] Gunn, *The Story of King David*, 61, clarifies that the entertainment found in Samuel is 'serious' entertainment and therefore is unlikely to have been regarded by the author as a work of fiction. The difference is that the stories in serious entertainment may be reshaped in tradition and still have been considered accurate whereas this would obviously not occur in modern historiography. Note that this description of serious entertainment falls within the broader definition of historiography argued for here. For a similar and more detailed theory of the growth of Samuel as oral tradition see Stanley Isser, *The Sword of Goliath: David in Heroic Literature* (Atlanta: SBL, 2003).

[96] Simon Hornblower, "Narratology and Narrative Techniques in Thucydides," in *Greek Historiography*, ed. Simon Hornblower (Oxford: Clarendon Press, 1994), 133.

what happened.[97] Assman, in a more general study of cultural memory,
draws not only on Yerushalmi but Halbwachs, Nietzsche, Freud and
Derrida to describe the nature and purpose of this type of memory.
Assman calls the social aspect of individual memories 'communicative
memory' and, in turn, cultural memory is the transmission of these
communicative memories throughout generations.[98] Cultural memories can take the form of rituals or memory techniques such as those in
Deuteronomy to ensure Israel will remember the exodus in their new
context settled in the land.[99] These memories thus have the function of
bonding a community together throughout changed circumstances.[100]
Written traditions are an important subset of cultural memories and
they differ from visible and oral memories by their potential to archive
large amounts of material.[101] This large amount of material and the
relative permanence of written compared to oral memories gives
scope for the written texts to be creative and to contain many voices
and viewpoints, some of which may be critical of the past.[102] In summary, "The past is needed because it imparts togetherness. The group
acquires its identity as a group by reconstructing its past togetherness,
just as the individual can use his memory to convince himself of his
membership in the group."[103] This description of cultural memory can
be convincingly applied to the book of Samuel. For example, as Assman suggests, if it was written throughout the exilic period, it would
have supplied the bonding memory of the united monarchy of Israel
to the now scattered Jewish people.[104] Furthermore, there is evidence
of different points of view and creative presentation in Samuel, which
Assman considers typical of written memories.[105]

---

[97] Yosef Hayim Yerushalmi, *Zakhor, Jewish History and Jewish Memory* (Seattle:
University of Washington Press, 1982), 8–11.

[98] Jan Assman, *Religion and Cultural Memory*, trans. Rodney Livingstone (Stanford: Stanford University Press, 2005), 3, 8.

[99] Ibid., 17. See pp. 18–19 for seven procedures of cultural memory in Deuteronomy.

[100] Ibid., 20.

[101] As Assman (p. 85) says, "All the evidence suggests that writing was invented as
a means of storage, not as a method of communication."

[102] Ibid., 27, 84–85.

[103] Ibid., 94.

[104] Ibid., 67–69.

[105] Cf. Joachim Schaper, "The Living Word Engraved in Stone," in *Memory in the
Bible and Antiquity*, Wissenschaftliche Untersuchungen zum Neuen Testament 212,
eds. L.T. Stuckenbruck, S.C. Barton & B.G. Wold (Tübingen: Mohr Siebeck, 2007), 15.
He writes that memory through literacy is inseparable from orality in Deuteronomy
and Joshua because the traditions were necessarily read aloud and memorised.

Understanding Samuel as remembered past does not therefore exclude it from also being represented past. All historiography is based on memory and so if a text represents the memory of a community rather than an individual or secondary sources, it can still be considered a representation of the past. Indeed, the emphasis on 'memory' highlighted by Yerushalmi in the Hebrew Bible has been interpreted by Amit as an indication that it was part of the ancient Israelite religion and ideology to write history not mythology for the purpose of teaching in the present.[106] A representation of the past can be used to form cultural bonds within a community and therefore a text such as Samuel can be simultaneously considered historiography and a type of cultural memory.

In summary, historical critical scholarship tends to assume that the book of Samuel is a represention of the past. Furthermore, literary approaches, which emphasise the artistic nature of the text, are compatible with this understanding. In addition to these arguments, this study will demonstrate that the book of Samuel contains three of the fundamental features of historiography described above, albeit in different forms to modern historiography: causation, meaning and significance, and ideology. As historicity does not feature in the definition of historiography, it is not necessary to demonstrate it here. Nevertheless we will also examine which features the book presents as coherent and with the appearance of accuracy.

Historiography is not the only description that can be applied to the book of Samuel—we have seen that many scholars also describe its propagandistic, theological, legendary and literary character. These descriptions are not mutually exclusive and the focus on historiography in this study does not imply that this description should even be considered primary. Rather, we examine it because of its relevancy to current debates and its interest for analysis of the book's poetics.

The text

In this study, we are analysing the final form of the book of Samuel rather than its various sources and earlier stages of redaction identified by historical critics. The concept of the final form is influenced by Brevard Childs' canonical criticism. He argued that, whilst historical criticism has much merit, it did not consider the canonical text as received by the religious community and did not relate it to the greater

---

[106] Amit, *History and Ideology*, 16.

context of the canon.[107] Thus he proposed 'Canonical Analysis', which focuses on the final form of the text and does not only use it as a source for other information or to reconstruct its historical development.[108] He believed that it is the final form which alone bears witness to the revelation to the authors at each stage of the development of the text and has ultimately influenced the faith community.[109]

Childs' emphasis on the value of the text before us has influenced our aim of understanding the historiography in the final form of the MT. In terms of our contribution to poetics, the final form has proved appropriate for such analyses because it is the text we read, which we want to appreciate more deeply from a literary point of view. Furthermore, the final form is the text that is used as the starting point for historical reconstructions of ancient Israel. There is immense value in understanding how to read this text as a whole, alongside other investigations.[110]

In contrast to Childs, who eschewed all historical critical analysis, this study of the final form of Samuel's historiography does not replace more traditional critical investigations into the text but rather complements it.[111] We have seen that previous studies on the nature of historiography in Samuel have used historical critical methods to look at the nature of its sources and the process through which the final form of the historiography came about. This study accompanies these by examining the final result of the processes.

---

[107] Brevard S. Childs, *Introduction to the Old Testament as Scripture* (Philadelphia: Fortress Press, 1979), 40–41.

[108] Ibid., 73.

[109] Ibid., 75–76.

[110] Another implication of this is that we will restrict ourselves to the parameters of I and II Samuel in the MT. Questions of book structure and patterns will be affected by how we define the parameters of the book.

[111] On the value of literary and historical criticism and the need for both, see John Barton, "Historical Criticism and Literary Interpretation: Is There Any Common Ground?," in *Israel's Past in Present Research*, ed. V. Philips Long (Winona Lake: Eisenbrauns, 1999), 427–38. He writes (p. 435), "Historical criticism may be able to tell us *how* the Pentateuch got put together; we may need help from literary critics if we are to understand *why*." See also the work of Serge Frolov, *The Turn of the Cycle: 1 Samuel 1–8 in Synchronic and Diachronic Perspectives* (Berlin: Walter de Gruyter, 2004). He argues that both synchronic and diachronic approaches have merit (p. 29) and suggests criteria by which the most appropriate method can be determined (pp. 27–36). Whilst he tends to favour synchrony, his study is important for its use of both methods [see Bill T. Arnold, "Review of 'The Turn of the Cycle'," *JBL* 124 (2005): 533–36].

Furthermore, historical critical studies highlight the problematic nature of referring to the author or intention of the final form of the book. They make us aware that multiple sources were used in the production of the book of Samuel and therefore the voices of many authors and redactors are likely to be found in the text. However, the final editors have retained these earlier voices and so to a certain extent, are responsible for them.[112] The editor may not be the origin of these voices nor have consciously intended them. If we consider the text as an entity in itself and as the sum of its authors and redactors, it will have an intention that more or less reflects the intention of the final editor. This assumes an intelligent editor who thought seriously about the text he/she/they were editing and who had the opportunity to omit or add what was necessary for Samuel to be a satisfactory work of historiography. In summary, as this study examines 'the book of Samuel's conception of history', we describe the collective and cumulative conception of the many authors and redactors of the book, which has been given conscious or unconscious approval by the final editor(s).

Moreover, at many points in this study it will be appropriate to review previous historical-critical research in order to avoid making other naïve assumptions and to understand the reasoning behind current scholarly views on certain passages. Our purpose will not be to arrive at a conclusion about the history of the text, although some evaluation will be inevitable, but rather to inform our synchronic study of the final form.

This study will examine the Masoretic text version because it represents a text that is read frequently and an actual rather than a reconstructed text. However there are a number of textual witnesses to the book of Samuel available. There are four fragmentary Hebrew texts from Qumran: 1QSam, 4QSam[a], 4QSam[b] and 4QSam[c];[113] the LXX

---

[112] As Noll writes, "It is reasonable to suppose that much of what various modern readers have discerned in the story was discerned also by Samuel's creator(s), who either intended those themes or at least chose not to rework the material another time." [K.L. Noll, *The Faces of David* (Sheffield: Sheffield Academic Press, 1997), 43].

[113] 4QSam[a] is the largest scroll [see Frank Moore Cross et al., *Qumran Cave 4: 1–2 Samuel*, vol. XII, *DJD* (Oxford: Clarendon Press, 2005), 4, for a list of its fragments], 4QSam[b] is but a scrap and 4QSam[c] contains only I Sam 25.30–32 and II Sam 14–15 [see Cross et al., *Qumran Cave 4: 1–2 Samuel*, 247]. 4QSam[a] and 4QSam[c] at many points agree with the readings of the LXX but there are also instances where it agrees with the MT and so should not be thought of as strictly corresponding to the Septuagint *Vorlage* [Philippe Hugo, "Text History of the Books of Samuel," in *Archaeology of*

witnesses: Codex Vaticanus (LXX[B]), Codex Alexandrinus (LXX[A]) and the Lucianic family of manuscripts (LXX[L]); the Peshitta, Targum Jonathan, the Old Latin and Vulgate. Amongst these textual witnesses, there are at least two ancient versions which are represented in the MT and the Old Greek (thought to correspond most closely to LXX[B], except for II Sam 10–24 where LXX[L] is thought to have closest resemblance).

We can only access the ancient historiography of Samuel through these witnesses and the number of variant readings between them indicates that there have been significant changes in transmission, including in the various Greek and Hebrew versions. However, despite these variants, we have chosen not to reconstruct a prior text of the MT version. The final form of the MT is a representation of the past and therefore can be considered a work of ancient historiography. It is an actual text that is used today, rather than a reconstructed text that is not universally accepted by modern scholars and that may never have existed. Therefore, as we are not reconstructing a more original or even preferable text, text critical considerations will be minimal. We will examine the MT with all its difficulties as a final form, using the other witnesses to illuminate rather than emend it. The purpose of our study is to understand how to read the text of Samuel, particularly for historians, and so it is important to use a text that is commonly read.

The conventions of historiography in the MT are likely to be similar to the conventions in the texts that preceded it, because of the proximity in time and culture. In the same way, the conventions will be similar to those found in the LXX version. Whilst this is a generalisation, their conventions were undoubtedly more similar to each other than to the modern day. In light of this, we will spend the first three chapters of this study looking exclusively at the conception of history in the MT. We will then broaden our study in the final chapter by comparing the MT with the LXX. There is a complex relationship between these versions and uncertainty about the direction of change between them. Although there is not complete consensus about which text is prior, comparison will shed light on the conventions of the cultural milieu spanning both of these texts. These conventions can then be applied to

---

the Books of Samuel: The Entangling of the Textual and Literary History, ed. Philippe Hugo and Adrian Schenker (Leiden: Brill, 2010), 2–3].

the MT of Samuel, based on the assumption that there was some level of uniformity within this period.

The Literary Approach

As the book of Samuel uses narrative to represent the past, a literary approach is an appropriate means of understanding the devices of its representation.

The literary approach is not a uniform theory of reading the Hebrew Bible. As referred to above, it generally represents all synchronic or final form studies of the text and their interpretation of it. It incorporates structuralist readings, New Criticism and deconstructionism, and other postmodern approaches. One approach to literary study that we will use here is commonly called 'poetics'. Barton describes poetics as, "an attempt to specify how literature 'works', how it enables us to perceive the meanings we do perceive in it...a poetics of the biblical text—or of any text—is interested in how the text is articulated, in how it comes to convey the meanings it does."[114] In other words, it is the study of art and literary devices in the text of the Bible.

In general biblical scholarship, poetics were brought to prominence by the work of Robert Alter. He describes the approach in the following way:

> By literary analysis I mean the manifold varieties of minutely discriminating attention to the artful use of language, to the shifting play of ideas, conventions, tone, sound, imagery, syntax, narrative viewpoint, compositional units and much else; the kind of disciplined attention, in other words, which through a whole spectrum of critical approaches has illuminated, for example, the poetry of Dante, the plays of Shakespeare, the novels of Tolstoy.[115]

Alongside Alter, there have been many more studies of the literary features or poetics used in biblical narrative. Berlin[116] looks at character types and the multiple points of view in narrative. Sternberg[117] examines ideology and persuasion in texts. Savran[118] analyses the function

---

[114] John Barton, *Reading the Old Testament: Method in Biblical Study* (Louisville: Westminster John Knox Press, 1996), 205.
[115] Alter, *The Art of Biblical Narrative*, 12–13.
[116] Berlin, *Poetics*.
[117] Sternberg, *Poetics*.
[118] Savran, *Telling and Retelling*.

of quotation and Bar-Efrat[119] and Amit[120] examine traditional categories such as character, plot and style in relation to the Hebrew Bible.
Gunn and Fewell[121] look at characters, plot and other aspects of language and how each of these techniques creates gaps waiting to be
filled by the reader.

One disadvantage of poetics is its subjectivity. A literary device to
one person may not have the same connotations, emphasis or effect
for another. One person feels the effect of particular word choice, repetition or juxtaposition whereas another will judge that the feature
detracts from the meaning and coherence of the texts. Separated as
we are in time and culture from the original author(s)/redactor(s), it
is impossible to know for certain what was considered by the ancient
Hebrew writers as good narrative technique and what is merely accident. However, there are ways to lessen this subjectivity. Firstly, the
function of a feature as a literary device can be confirmed by other
instances of its use throughout the Hebrew Bible. The literary studies of the scholars listed above are indispensable for understanding
which literary features recur in the narrative. Secondly, the effect of a
literary device can be substantiated by showing how it contributes to
the overall context and meaning of the text. When a number of features in a passage have a similar effect, there is a high probability that
they would all have been read in this way. Nevertheless, it will not be
certain that all these narrative techniques and effects are the specific
intention of the author or that they convey meaning to all readers.

These issues of subjectivity, author, text and audience come into
even greater focus when discussing the meaning of a text. Literary theories do not agree on where the meaning of the text lies, whether it is
in what the author intended, what the text itself conveys (this includes
both structuralism and New Criticism) or in the reader (deconstructionism and other postmodern approaches). Poetics looks at how
texts convey meaning but this approach is not incompatible with the
recognition that the author, text and reader each are important for
understanding the meaning of the text.[122] If the meaning of the histo-

---

[119] Bar-Efrat, *Narrative Art.*
[120] Amit, *Reading Biblical Narratives.*
[121] Gunn and Fewell, *Narrative.*
[122] On why all three of these are important, see Tremper Longman, *Literary Approaches to Biblical Interpretation*, Foundations of Contemporary Interpretation (Grand Rapids: Academie Books, 1987), 64–68.

riography in Samuel were the focus of this study, we would need to look more broadly at the author and the audience. However, we have chosen to limit our study to the workings of the text itself. This is a fruitful study because it improves our competence in reading for more holistic studies.[123]

One of the criticisms of poetics is that it is often used to argue for coherence and unity in the text in contrast to genetic approaches. However, overall unity is not necessarily a prior assumption for the study of poetics, as the final chapter on coherence in Samuel will demonstrate. There is some level of unity because we assume intelligent authors/redactors and because the book has been read coherently by many successive generations. This does not imply that *every* aspect of the book is intentional or has complete coherence, particularly for modern readers. Barton writes:

> But if we do not accept that Alter or Sternberg has shown older criticism to be mistaken in what it asserts—the fragmentary character of the text—we can still agree with them in rejecting what it denies: we can reject the idea that no sense can be made of the text as it stands. These scholars have shown that, on the contrary, much sense can be made of the biblical narrative, once we look for the right thing—narrative conventions—rather than the wrong one—historical coherence or the intentions of a single author.[124]

This is particularly relevant for our study of Samuel as a work of historiography. It has been, and is, read in its final form as a work of historiography and therefore we seek to understand its techniques for conveying the characteristics of historiography, and the nature of the history contained within it. Diachronic approaches search for the process through which the book of Samuel came about, this study will now analyse the literary text at the end of this process.

---

[123] For example, Green, *How are the Mighty Fallen*, which looks at the story of Saul using the insights of Mikhail Bakhtin and then applies what this would have meant for the context of the exile community.

[124] Barton, *Reading the Old Testament*, 208.

CHAPTER TWO

CAUSATION

Causation is a fundamental element of historiography that distinguishes it from annals and other lists of events or people in the past.[1] It creates continuity between discrete events and answers the question 'why'. The concept of scientific determinism first appeared to promise that causation in history could be reduced to a set of scientific physical explanations.[2] However, the complexity of history dictates that, even if this is held in principle, it is not possible in practice. Historians and philosophers have recognised that all the causes involved in history can never be investigated and the historian must select only those which he/she considers to be 'significant' forces.[3] Nevertheless, the 'New History' movement has influenced an expansion of the types of causes examined in modern historiography. These include the environment and sociological effects, alongside more traditional areas such as economics and politics.[4]

In contrast to the multitude of causation types in modern historiography, the historiography of Samuel is often thought to contain very limited variation in causation. Supernatural causation appears to dominate and other types are considered undeveloped, especially when compared to the Greek historians.[5] On the other hand, scholars have

---

[1] Robert F. Berkhofer, *Beyond the Great Story: History as Text and Discourse* (Cambridge, Mass.: Belknap Press of Harvard University Press, 1995), 117; Michael Stanford, *An Introduction to the Philosophy of History* (Malden: Blackwell, 1998), 85.

[2] See the discussion of positivism and determinism in chapter 1: Introduction.

[3] E.g. The historian Conkin writes, "Historians rarely claim any exclusivity for the necessary antecedents they identify. Even when, because of selective purpose, they give great emphasis to one cause, they are usually quite willing to acknowledge an unspecified and unknown number of other equally necessary even if not equally 'significant' antecedents" [Paul K. Conkin, "Causation Revisited," *History and Theory* 13 (1974): 3].

[4] Peter Burke, "Overture: The New History, its Past and its Future," in *New Perspectives on Historical Writing*, ed. Peter Burke (Cambridge: Polity Press, 1991), 18. He describes the number of new avenues as a "proliferation of sub-disciplines" that can be used to gain historical understanding.

[5] See Ernest Nicholson, "Story and History in the Old Testament," in *Language, Theology and the Bible*, ed. Samuel E. Balentine and John Barton (Oxford: Clarendon Press, 1994), 144–45. Nicholson builds upon the earlier opinions of James Barr.

marveled at the secularity of the Succession Narrative and other sections of the text, whilst agreeing that the earlier parts of Samuel rely on
supernatural explanations.[6] This study proposes that the text explores
multiple types of causation but these often differ sharply from modern ideas about what motivates history. Divine causation in Samuel
is the most evident of these differences; but two other tensions also
exist: the impact of public versus private causes; and the agency of the
group versus the individual.[7] These differences arise due to the ideology involved when the historian selects which causes he/she considers
to be most important.

Public and private causes

Modern historiography tends to focus on causation that is 'public' and
it is particularly interested in impersonal forces that act in history. The
emphasis of Ranke was on the political, Marx on the economic and
the 'New History' focuses on a multitude of causes related to the natural and sociological sciences. Economic and environmental causation
in the book of Samuel are minimal as even factors such as lightning
(I Sam 12) and plague (II Sam 24) are attributed to divine causation.
There are however many instances of political causation. The threat of
the Philistines is immanent throughout I Samuel; David is involved in
a struggle for power with Ishbosheth in II Sam 2–4; and Absalom is
similarly motivated by desire for political ascendency in II Sam 15–18.
The failure of the political system of the judges is largely attributable to
the corrupt politics of Eli and Samuel's sons in I Sam 2–8. Politics is
major subject matter in the book as Israel institutes its monarchy.

However, political forces are not the only causes for this political change in Israel. Private, personal causes for individuals are also
explored. Samuel is in a position to assume the leadership of Israel
because of a vow by his mother; David and Jonathan have an important alliance because of Jonathan's love for David; and civil war ensues
because of David's private sin with Bathsheba and his lack of control
over his family. There are many more examples throughout Samuel

---

[6] E.g. Gene M. Tucker, *Form Criticism of the Old Testament* (Philadelphia: Fortress
Press, 1971), 37.

[7] See Walter Brueggemann, *First and Second Samuel*, Interpretation (Louisville:
John Knox Press, 1990), 1–2. Brueggemann cites three main factors involved in
the transformation of Israel to a monarchy: firstly, political and social factors; secondly, the powerful personality of David; and thirdly, the direct and indirect part of
Yahweh.

where private matters influence the public sphere. Occasionally, the reverse takes place. For example, Uriah's public loyalty to his troops is a factor in the way that David deals with his personal problems in II Sam 11. The public and private are intertwined throughout Samuel, to the point where some scholars consider the influence of the private life on leaders to be a major theme of the book.[8]

The duality of public and private causation in Samuel has long been recognised in form critical studies and has been used as criteria for determining which sections of the text are saga and which are history writing.[9] Moreover, most form critics do not mean 'history' in the positivistic sense when they label large parts, particularly of II Samuel, as historiography. Tucker describes history writing as an attempt to make sense of the past by writing a "coherent and cohesive narrative of events;" but continues, "to be sure, the Old Testament contains no historical writing in the modern sense of the term."[10] On the other hand, form criticism tends not to regard saga as purely fictional but as having had some basis in real events and people. The difference between saga and history writing is that saga has undergone a long period of oral transmission and so has developed distinctive features such as an interest in private rather than public subject matter. These features obscure the real events to such an extent that saga is of most worth for understanding the social conscience (*Sitz im Leben*) that produced it rather than for stripping away supernatural elements to find an historical core.[11]

Such form critical analyses reflect a modern view of causation in history and this overview highlights that different ideology is used in the book of Samuel to select the 'significant' causes in history. However, not all modern historiographies eschew personal reasons as a type of causation in history. Stanford writes about the importance of

---

[8] E.g. Kenneth R.R. Gros Louis, "Difficulty of Ruling Well: King David of Israel," *Semeia* 8 (1977): 15–33.

[9] Gunkel sets out three criteria: 1) saga is transmitted by oral traditions whereas history writing is transmitted by written documents; 2) saga deals with private matters and history writing deals with great public events; 3) saga reports extraordinary events, such as the miraculous and the supernatural, and history writing contains credible events known to common experience [Hermann Gunkel, *Genesis*, trans. Mark E. Biddle (Macon: Mercer University Press, 1997), vii–xi]. See also Jay A. Wilcoxen, "Narrative," in *Old Testament Form Criticism*, ed. John Haralson Hayes (San Antonio: Trinity University Press, 1974), 60, and Tucker, *Form Criticism*, 35.

[10] Tucker, *Form Criticism*, 6.

[11] E.g. Klaus Koch, *The Growth of the Biblical Tradition: The Form-Critical Method* (London: A. & C. Black, 1969), 154.

feelings and emotions as causation. He says, "Sometimes we cannot understand why another did not do what seems to us the sensible thing in the circumstances. Only when we realise that he was pressed by a powerful emotion can we understand the action."[12] Such interest in emotions and other personal events features prominently in the book of Samuel and this is important for understanding how the book conveys causation in history.

The agency of the group or individual

Another modern dichotomy in causation is between the agency of the group and the individual. Burke describes this as one of the major differences between traditional Rankean history and the 'New History'. Traditional history, as he calls it, concentrates on the "great deeds of great men" whereas the 'New History' looks at trends and collective movements.[13] Causation in the book of Samuel focuses more on the individual than the collective as it follows closely the stories of four leaders of Israel: Eli, Samuel, Saul and David, and their impact on political events. However, significantly, it is not only these four men who are forces for change in history. At many stages of the narrative, women have an influence on the course of events, such as Hannah in I Sam 1, Michal in I Sam 19, Abigail in I Sam 25 and the woman of Tekoa in II Sam 14. Occasionally, the whole people of Israel are included as a factor, such as their persistent request in I Sam 8, their renewal of the kingship in I Sam 11, the transfer of Israel's support to David in II Sam 5.1–3 and their support of Absalom in II Sam 15. The historiography is not concerned with social trends and statistics in the way that modern historiographies often are, but the causation of all Israel and people of low social order are incorporated alongside the charismatic leaders.

Divine and secular causation

Divine causation is another criterion used by form critics to differentiate saga from history writing and it is a cause generally unacceptable

---

[12] Michael Stanford, *A Companion to the Study of History* (Oxford: Blackwell, 1994), 225.
[13] Burke, "Overture: The New History, its Past and its Future," 4.

in modern historiography.[14] Nevertheless the book of Samuel rarely, if ever, introduces supernatural events, only supernatural causes.[15] An exception to this is the speech of God, such as in I Sam 8.7–9, but such speech may be a stylistic representation of other types of divine speech, such as oracles, for which it is possible to give a rationalistic explanation. Invariably, divine causation is accompanied by secular explanations. For example, in I Sam 8, there are at least two causes given for the institution of the monarchy: the people's request for a king as a result of the corruption of Samuel's sons; and God's command to Samuel to obey their voice. The Divine is a very important factor in causation in Samuel but it is consistently associated with other secular explanations.

Causation through narrative

The primary method through which the book of Samuel conveys causation is narrative device. Rather than expounding causation through explicit statements, narrative techniques and literary devices are used to indicate connections and continuity in history. Causation is not just a feature of historiography, it is a component of all narrative, both fiction and non-fiction.[16] It is therefore appropriate to examine how the book of Samuel conveys historical causes using narrative techniques also found in fiction. The terms *plot* and *chain of historical causation* become virtually synonymous when we study Samuel.

There are three aspects of causation in narrative that are relevant to the book of Samuel. These are: chains of causation within an episode, chains of causation developed through a series of episodes and explicit causation through the speech of characters.

Firstly, causation is conveyed within individual episodes through a sequence of events which directly relate to each other. Plots can be conceived of as alternating periods of *equilibrium* when the situation of

---

[14] See Stanford, *A Companion to the Study of History*, 34–35. He compares divine causation in ancient texts with the role of chance and coincidence in secular terms.

[15] Observed in Baruch Halpern, *The First Historians: The Hebrew Bible and History* (University Park: Pennsylvania State University Press, 1988), 271. See also Yair Zakovitch, *The Concept of the Miracle in the Bible* (Tel Aviv: MOD Books, 1990). According to Zakovitch, it is literary formulation rather than the events themselves that determine whether something is portrayed as a miracle in the Hebrew Bible.

[16] See Brian Richardson, *Unlikely Stories: Causality and the Nature of Modern Narrative* (Newark: University of Delaware Press, 1997), 89–95. He argues that causality is a part of the definition of narrative.

the characters is stable; and *imbalance* when the situation of the characters is unacceptable and needs change.[17] Imbalance usually occurs because of a disruptive event, the first 'cause'; and it requires another 'cause' in order to return this imbalance to equilibrium. Therefore, an episode of narrative can correspond to one cycle of these causes: a shift from equilibrium to imbalance and back to equilibrium again. Bar-Efrat, in the context of biblical narrative, describes a similar pattern: "The plot develops from an initial situation through a chain of events to a central occurrence, which is the prime factor of change, and thence by means of varying incidents to a final situation."[18] In reality, pericopes are often less straightforward and there may be concurrent 'imbalances' in the narrative that require multiple causes and agents of change to restore them to equilibrium. However, defining the narrative in terms of its imbalances and equilibriums offers one way in which we can identify causation in Samuel. Indeed the causes, which shift the narrative through these cycles, form the fundamental chains of causation.[19]

Secondly, we look at how different episodes are brought together to create a holistic structure of causation in the narrative. The simplest way in which connections can be drawn is through the juxtaposition of episodes. Bar-Efrat describes a number of ways in which narratives are connected, three of which require juxtaposition of the episodes: the use of the *waw* conjunction (or consecutive); the phrase 'after this' (e.g. 2 Sam 13.1); or when a new episode starts with the same character as the previous episode ended (e.g. I Sam 15–16).[20] However,

---

[17] Todorov, Tzevetan, "Structural Analysis of Narrative" *Novel: A Forum on Fiction* (Fall 1969): 70–76, described in Emma Kafalenos, *Narrative Causalities* (Columbus: Ohio State University Press, 2006), 4–5.

[18] Shimeon Bar-Efrat, *Narrative Art in the Bible*, JSOTSup. 70 (Sheffield: Almond Press: 1989), 121. Bar Efrat (pp. 130–132) also describes a number of indicators frequently found in biblical narrative which mark the completion of an episode. These include, a statement saying that the characters returned home (e.g. I Sam 16.1–13), the separation of characters (e.g. I Sam 14.46) or the death of a protagonist.

[19] For an in-depth analysis of how such causal chains are constructed, see Kafalenos, *Narrative Causalities*, chapter 1. In particular, she describes the interpretive nature of the causal chain as different events can be given different functions within the narrative. For example, whether a person is given the protagonist function (i.e. the person who takes the decisive step in the narrative) will affect whether the reader perceives this person as the causal agent of the final situation. She writes (p. vii), "Interpretations of the causality of an event are contextual and depend on the other events in relation to which the event is perceived."

[20] Bar-Efrat, *Narrative Art*, 132–35.

not all narratives contain a linear causal chain of episodes. There are two other possibilities that occur in Samuel: distinct causal chains may intersect; or there may be a cumulative effect of unconnected episodes which transform the protagonist.[21] An example of the former is in II Sam 6 where David moves the ark to Jerusalem. Within the final form of Samuel this acts both as a conclusion to the ark narrative in I Sam 4–7 and David's rise throughout both books of Samuel. An example of the latter is in I Sam 9–11, which combines the cumulative and linear types of causation. Episodes that are not in a linear chain of progression use other methods for relating the events in the episodes, such as tracing the events of one character, using keywords, analogous plots or narrative threads. An example of this can be found in the series of narratives about David's interactions with Jonathan and Jonathan's sons.[22]

Thirdly, there are places in Samuel where causation is expounded explicitly through the speech of characters or the narrator. As we look at the speeches in II Sam 7, we will see that such exposition of causes can rarely be accepted by the reader in isolation but must be read in the context of the surrounding narrative and the reader's assessment of the characters.

Using this survey of narrative causation as a basis, this section will demonstrate how different types of causation are developed and combined: the public and private, group and individual, divine and secular. The narrative contains a complex web of causation and this encourages the reader to draw his/her own connections based on the evidence presented.

2.1   Samuel's Birth Story—I Sam 1

In a book that features the exploits and drama of four great leaders of Israel, it is remarkable that I Samuel begins with the poignant tale of an obscure, barren woman. This woman, Hannah, does not feature in the story again after I Sam 2.21 and, apart from being the mother

---

[21] Richardson, *Unlikely Stories*, 95–96. He also mentions two other possibilities which are less relevant for the book of Samuel: apparently unrelated incidents may be later brought into a causal chain; or there may be an ideological or aesthetic mode of connection, for example, an allegorical pattern.

[22] Bar-Efrat, *Narrative Art*, 135–40.

of Samuel, is otherwise unconnected with the events that shape this history of Israel. Yet the book opens with a spotlight on Hannah and gives a moving portrayal of her personal difficulties and their resolution.

This personal and domestic beginning to the historiography of Samuel is commonly thought to be an incorporation of a folktale into the story. Firstly, the birth story of Samuel contains a number of features that correspond to other birth stories in the Hebrew Bible. Comparisons are most often drawn with the birth story of Samson and with the patriarchs Isaac, Jacob and Joseph. The mothers of Samuel, Samson, Isaac, Jacob and Joseph are all barren but are given children through the intervention of Yahweh. The mothers of Samuel, Isaac and Joseph were in competition with another wife (or in Sarah's case, her maidservant Hagar) but in all of these narratives, the hero's mother was the one most loved by her husband. In the narratives of both Samuel and Samson, the mothers dedicate their sons to the Lord with a Nazirite vow.

Form critical studies of Samuel have concluded that such parallels indicate that these texts come from a common oral tradition of birth stories. Gunkel describes these birth stories as developing from a tradition of *Märchen* that contains the motifs of a barren mother who eventually gives birth to a son who in turn will later have a special role.[23] Furthermore, there are a number of features in I Sam 1 that have led scholars to believe the narrative was originally the birth story of Saul before it was appropriated for Samuel.[24] These include 1) the etymology of Samuel's name[25] and the wordplays on the root שאל through-

---

[23] Hermann Gunkel, *Das Märchen im Alten Testament* (Tübingen: Mohr, 1921), 113. See also Antony F. Campbell, *1 Samuel*, FOTL (Grand Rapids: Eerdmans, 2003), 43.

[24] Jan Dus, "Die Geburtslegende Samuels, I Sam 1: Eine traditionsgeschichtliche Untersuchung zu 1 Sam 1–3," *RSO* 43 (1968): 163–94; P. Kyle McCarter, Jr., *I Samuel*, The Anchor Bible (New York: Doubleday, 1980), 65. For arguments against, see Matitiahu Tsevat, "Die Namengebung Samuels und die Substitutionstheorie," *ZAW* 99 (1987): 250–54; Marsha White, "Saul and Jonathan in 1 Samuel 1 and 14," in *Saul in Story and Tradition*, ed. Carl S. Ehrlich and Marsha White (Tübingen: Mohr Siebeck, 2006), 119–38; R.P. Gordon, "Who Made the Kingmaker? Reflections on Samuel and the Institution of the Monarchy," in *Faith, Tradition, and History: Old Testament Historiography in its Near Eastern Context*, ed. Alan R. Millard, James K. Hoffmeier, and David W. Baker (Winona Lake: Eisenbrauns, 1994), 263–69.

[25] Cf. Yair Zakovitch, "A Study of Precise and Partial Derivations in Biblical Etymology," *JSOT* 15 (1980): 31–50. He argues that name derivations originally did not have a strong resemblance to the sounds in the name.

out the narrative;[26] 2) the similarity between I Sam 1.1 and I Sam 9.1; and 3) parallels with the Samson narrative, a figure who bears a closer similarity to Saul than Samuel.[27]

Although many scholars believe this story was not always connected with the figure of Samuel, it has the function of conveying causation in the final form of the historiography of Samuel. For the events of the narrative have an important conclusion—Samuel, a non-Elide, non-Levitical boy, is given to the priest Eli at the temple of Shiloh to serve there. As subsequent events will show, this position of Samuel will lead to his role as leader of Israel in place of Eli and his sons. Therefore, in this study, I will examine how narrative techniques and folktale elements are used to create a plausible causation for this important change in the politics of Israel. Crucially for our understanding of causation in Samuel, it provides an example of how private, personal and divine causes lead to political change.

A chain of causation: equilibrium and imbalance

I Sam 1 begins with a state of equilibrium. It describes the patrilineage of Elkanah and the names of his two wives. It is not until the last three words of v. 2 that an imbalance is described, ולחנה אין ילדים ('but Hannah did not have children').[28] The nature of this imbalance is developed throughout the following story, until the moment of change occurs in v. 20 and Hannah conceives. This is preceded by Hannah's prayer at Shiloh and her encounter with Eli the priest. However, this narrative is more complex than the simple pattern of equilibrium, imbalance and equilibrium. A second imbalance is created by Hannah's promise in v. 11 to give her child to the Lord and this second imbalance is dependant upon the resolution of the first imbalance. When the first imbalance is returned to equilibrium in v. 20, the story is not finished. There is no sense of resolution until Hannah brings Samuel to Shiloh in vv. 25–28 and the second imbalance is also resolved. Both of these imbalances and moments of change constitute the causation for the

---

[26] Cf. White, "Saul and Jonathan," 119–38. She demonstrates that the entire story is structured around the roots שאל and נתן which each appear seven times in the chapter. She also points out that the name Jonathan is based on the root נתן yet no one suggests that the birth story originally belonged to him.

[27] Although, as pointed out in White (p. 123), Samson's birth narrative is also thought to be a later addition to the stories about him.

[28] All translations of the Hebrew are mine unless otherwise indicated.

final equilibrium. From an historical point of view, the birth of a child
is not an event in history that usually requires causation, but his adop-
tion into the temple does necessitate explanation. In this case, Hannah's prayer and vow is the cause for Samuel's arrival at Shiloh.

In the chain of narrative causation in this chapter, it is primarily the
resolution of the first imbalance, Hannah's barrenness, which is reminiscent of other birth stories in the Hebrew Bible. However, its position in a chain of causes leading to the second imbalance, the promise
to take the child to Shiloh, makes it necessary for the final equilibrium.
As we examine the details of this chain of causation, we will see that
folktale elements contribute towards plausible and coherent causation
in the narrative. The recurrence of birth stories in Hebrew narrative
has been studied by Robert Alter who identifies the phenomenon as
a 'type scene', a concept borrowed from Homeric scholarship.[29] He
describes type scenes as "dependent on the manipulation of a fixed
constellation of predetermined motifs."[30] In particular, a type scene
conveys meaning when its conventions are broken in some way.[31]

Whilst such patterns in history are treated with suspicion by a modern historian, the inclusion of this story in Samuel reflects a different
ideology where patterns in history are searched for and even accentuated to convey meaning. Evidence for this hypothesis comes from
a number of literary devices that accentuate the parallels with other
birth stories. For example, the opening phrase ויהי איש אחד ('And
there was a certain man') is a functional means of introducing the story
but it has the additional advantage of paralleling the Samson narrative,
which is the only other place in the Hebrew Bible where it appears.[32]
Furthermore, Elkanah is introduced before Samuel in I Sam 1.1 and
this foreshadows a similar introduction to Saul's father in I Sam 9.1.

---

[29] Note that the type scene is an integral part of the oral formulaic nature in Homeric
studies but Alter says that it is a matter of conjecture whether the biblical narrator
was an oral storyteller or not [Robert Alter, *The Art of Biblical Narrative* (New York:
Basic Books, 1981), 52]. Nevertheless, showing that these 'oral' features function as
literary devices does not necessarily deny that they were developed through the oral
transmission of the story. Also see Robert Alter, "Samson Without Folklore," in *Text
and Tradition*, ed. S. Niditch (Atlanta: SBL, 1990). He writes that the Samson story is
based on folkloric materials but has recast them to give literary articulation.
[30] Alter, *The Art of Biblical Narrative*, 51.
[31] Ibid., 47–49.
[32] Lyle M. Eslinger, *Kingship of God in Crisis: A Close Reading of 1 Samuel 1–12*
(Decatur: Almond Press, 1985), 65–67. Note that the variant reading in LXX omits
'a certain' (ἄνθρωπος ἦν) and therefore does not contain the parallel.

It is possible that these verbal similarities have been added, or at least retained, by a redactor or author in order to highlight the patterns in the narrative with other birth stories.

The use of typical birth scene elements in I Sam 1 develops the initial imbalance of Hannah's childlessness. The presence of a second wife recalls the frequent element of rivalry within these stories, such as in the cases of Sarah and Rachel. Sarah provided her maidservant Hagar as a second wife for Abraham, but when Hagar looked on Sarah with contempt, Sarah dealt with her harshly.[33] Similarly Rachel envied her sister Leah after Leah bore four children and Rachel bore none.[34] The tradition of birth stories makes the audience sensitive towards Hannah's position as the barren wife, and this is heightened in v. 6 by the explicit remark that Peninnah would provoke her. Favouritism of the barren wife is another motif in birth narratives, for example, in the story of Rachel and Leah. Although Elkanah does not explicitly love Hannah more than Peninnah, it is implied through a series of suggestions. For example, it is suggested by the word order and choice of the words אחת and השנית in v. 2: ולו שתי נשים שם אחת חנה ושם השנית פננה ('And he had two wives: the name of one was Hannah and the name of the second was Peninnah').[35] Secondly it is implied in v. 5 where Elkanah gives Hannah some kind of special portion.[36] Furthermore, in v. 5, it is reported that Elkanah loved Hannah but there is no

---

[33] Gen 16.6.

[34] Gen 30.1.

[35] J.P. Fokkelman, *The Crossing Fates*, Vol. II of *Narrative Art and Poetry in the Books of Samuel: A Full Interpretation Based on Stylistic and Structural Analyses* (Assen: Van Gorcum, 1986), 16.

[36] The exact meaning of אפים in v. 5 is unknown. It literally means 'face' and so Hertzberg translates it as 'portion of face' or, in other words, a large portion [Hans Wilhelm Hertzberg, *I & II Samuel: A Commentary*, trans. John Stephen Bowden, OTL (London: S.C.M. Press, 1964), 24. McCarter, *I Samuel*, 52, argues that this does not work grammatically because of אחת between מנה and אפים. McCarter gives a number of other possibilities but favours restoring כפים and translating it as 'proportionate to', i.e. "A single portion equal to theirs." Aberbach suggests that it is derived from the root פים which is a weight found at Lachish equivalent to two thirds of a shekel and is also found in I Sam 13.21 [David Aberbach, "mnh 'cht 'pym (1 Sam. I 5): A New Interpretation," *VT* 24 (1974): 352]. Deist does not believe that Aberbach sufficiently deals with the א prefix on the root, making the theory unlikely [Ferdinand Deist, "'*APPAYIM* (1 Sam 1:5) < *PYM?*," *VT* 27 (1977): 205–09]. The point agreed however is that the word somehow indicates that Hannah received at least an equal portion to Peninnah, if not a greater one. Cf. Keith Bodner, *1 Samuel: A Narrative Commentary* (Sheffield: Sheffield Phoenix Press, 2008), 15. Bodner offers a significantly different reading and suggests that Elkanah gives Hannah 'only a single portion', implying that he would have gladly given her many portions if she only had children to eat them.

corresponding statement about Peninnah.[37] The frequency of a favoured wife in birth type scenes heightens the audience's perception of these suggestions. In turn, Elkanah's love for Hannah intensifies the pathos of her childlessness because she cannot fulfill this aspect of her wifely role. The familiarity of these 'typical' features from other birth narratives increases their plausibility as motivation for Hannah's despair.

In the chain of narrative causation, Hannah's response to her despair is not hostility towards the rival wife, but prayer to Yahweh. She breaks the convention of other stories representative of the birth type scene. Hannah is provoked just as Sarah was and she has a rival for her husband's affections just as Rachel did, yet she responds in a remarkably different way. When Peninnah provokes her, she does not react with envy or malice.[38] This is highlighted in the text by first reporting Peninnah's provocation in v. 6, using a *weqatal* verb וכעסתה, to which Hannah makes no response. It is then intensified in v. 7 by conveying that this happened year after year whenever they went up to Shiloh, the iterative sense of שנה בשנה strengthened by the use of the *yiqtol* יעשה. Again, Hannah makes no response to Peninnah and only increases in sadness in her own heart. The contrast between Hannah's reaction, and Sarah's and Rachel's, portrays Hannah as a woman of humility and integrity.

By both following and breaking the conventions of a type scene, the narrative creates a situation where Hannah plausibly promises her not-yet-conceived son to God. By following convention, the story demonstrates her desperation and by breaking convention, it reveals her remarkable integrity and piety. In turn, her desperation is the cause of her request and vow, and her integrity causes the fulfillment of her vow. Thus Samuel enters into the service of God at Shiloh, despite his non-Levitical background.

Alongside the personal causation in Hannah's situation, divine causation allows Hannah to conceive. It is explicitly stated in v. 19 that Yahweh gave Hannah the child and this is reinforced through the speech of characters (vv. 11, 17, 20, 27). God plays the role of hero

---

[37] McCarter, *I Samuel*, 60, notes the emphasis on Hannah in this verse through the placement of את־חנה ('Hannah') before אהב ('he loved') such that he translates the verse 'it is Hannah he loved'.

[38] There are similar observations in Shimeon Bar-Efrat, *Das erste Buch Samuel: Ein narratologisch-philologischer Kommentar*, trans. Johannes Klein, BWANT 176 (Stuttgart: Kohlhammer, 2007), 61.

who corrects the first imbalance of the narrative. However, it is Hannah who brings equilibrium to the second imbalance as she delivers the young boy Samuel to Shiloh. In this way, the personal causation of Hannah and the divine causation of Yahweh are interdependent. Yahweh acts in response to Hannah's request and Hannah fulfils her vow in response to Yahweh's action. These two types of causes cannot be separated from each other and together create the shift from equilibrium to imbalance to equilibrium in the chapter.

Preliminary causation for Samuel's future roles in Israel

The main chain of narrative causation in this chapter concerns Samuel's future role as the successor to Eli and leader over Israel. Not only is there a straightforward chain of causation for Samuel's entrance into the service of Eli, but there are more complex devices of causation for Samuel's other future roles in Israel.

Eli's primary role was priest, suggested by his location at Shiloh and his epithet in I Sam 1.9. However, priest is not the only role that is performed by Samuel in the book of I Samuel. Samuel is dedicated as a Nazirite in I Sam 1, established as a prophet in I Sam 3, a judge in I Sam 7 and a kingmaker in I Sam 10 and I Sam 16.[39] A complete explanation of the causes for all of these roles is not given in this chapter but each of them is foreshadowed to some degree. It is revealed in I Sam 4.18 that Eli's role included judging Israel and this implies that Samuel's succession to Eli, which is explained in I Sam 1, included the role of judge. Furthermore, the parallels created by the type scene link Samuel with his other future roles. Samuel's role as judge is foreshadowed through the strong allusions to the Samson story. Polzin suggests that the similarity of Hannah's vow to that of Jephthah also links this story to the Judges period.[40] The link to prophecy is perhaps less direct although Moses, the preeminent prophet before Samuel's time,[41] also has his birth story recorded. Whilst the stories are quite

---

[39] See Bar-Efrat (pp. 21–22), for a description of Samuel's roles as priest, prophet and judge. The multiplicity of Samuel's roles has long been observed by form critics who often consider them indicative of a number of different traditions which have been brought together. E.g. Georg Fohrer, *Introduction to the Old Testament*, trans. David Green (London: S.P.C.K., 1970), 226.

[40] They each sacrifice a child in order that God answer their prayers [Robert M. Polzin, *Samuel and the Deuteronomist: A Literary Study of the Deuteronomic History; Part Two—I Samuel* (San Francisco: Harper and Row, 1989), 23].

[41] Deut 34.10.

different, the importance attached to such birth narratives draws some level of parallel. Samuel's role as prophet will be developed in I Sam 3 where he hears the voice of the Lord calling to him. The comparison of Samuel with the patriarchs, God's chosen line, links with his role as kingmaker.

These allusions in the birth narrative connect Hannah's story to Samuel's multiple roles in Israel. Samuel's birth story sets him apart as a man chosen by God in the tradition of judges, prophets and now also kingmaker. The miraculous element of the birth story links with these traditions and so, in this sense, it is a statement of divine causation. However, in the case of judges and prophets, the general pattern is that men and women are raised up for these offices when a political or religious need arises, not merely as a divine whim. In the book of Judges, explanation of Israel's sin and an external military threat precede the narrative of each judge.[42] Similarly, prophets in the book of Kings appear in response to religious threats, such as Elijah in the time of Ahab's apostasy. The report of Samuel's remarkable birth contributes to the divine causation for these roles, but it will later be supplemented by other catalysts for them. The Philistine threat in chapters 4–6 necessitates Samuel's role as judge, Israel's request for a king causes him to become a kingmaker, and God's message of Eli's rejection (3.12–14) is placed closely in context with Samuel's confirmation as prophet (3.20). The divine causation of Samuel's miraculous birth will later be intertwined with religious, sociological and political causes.

Whilst the causes for Samuel's succession to Eli are important for the ongoing narrative in I Samuel, the causation for Samuel's dedication as a Nazirite appears less relevant because this role is not mentioned again in the book.[43] However, the Nazirite vow is not an end in itself but points to Samuel's other roles and to the depth of Hannah's commitment to her vow.

Firstly, we observe that the MT version of I Sam 1 does not state explicitly that Samuel is a Nazirite and, furthermore, it only mentions one of the three prohibitions associated with Nazirites.[44] This is in

---

[42] E.g. Jdg 3.7 relates Israel's religious disobedience, 3.8 relates the threat of the king of Mesopotamia and 3.9 reports the deliverance by Othniel.

[43] Dus, "Die Geburtslegende Samuels," 164.

[44] In I Sam 1.11 Hannah says she will not cut Samuel's hair. The other two prohibitions found in Num 6 are not drinking alcohol and not making contact with dead animals. The difficulty with applying the prohibitions from Num 6, is that it is possible that the concept of a Nazirite developed over time and, as part of the so-called

contrast to the LXX and 4QSamᵃ. The LXX adds the additional prohibition in v. 11, καὶ οἶνον καὶ μέθυσμα οὐ πίεται ('and he will not
drink wine or strong drink').[45] 4QSamᵃ is fragmentary in v. 11 but it
includes the term נזיר in v. 22 to make Samuel's designation explicit.[46]
However, regardless of which reading is earlier, we are examining the
MT in this study. According to Tsevat, it is an unjustified assertion
that Samuel is a Nazirite when the word נזיר does not appear in the
text and there is only one prohibition.[47] However, in discussion of
Nazirites in general, Diamond argues that not cutting the hair was the
primary prohibition because the essence of the vow was consecrating
hair at the altar as a symbol of offering oneself to the Lord. As the hair
was the symbolic offering, it could not be defiled by contact with the
dead[48] and the prohibition against drinking was a preparation for the
Nazirite's quasi-priestly status when he/she made the hair offering.[49]
If this is the essence of the vow, then the sole prohibition ought to
have been a sufficient allusion to the Nazirite vow. This allusion is
strengthened by the parallels to the Samson narrative where נזיר is
mentioned explicitly.

Exploring Diamond's understanding of the Nazirite vow further,
this allusion is less an introduction of an additional role for Samuel,
and more a predication of his other roles. Diamond argues that the
Nazirite in Num 6 is both the officiant and offering.[50] Thus, in the
Samson story, where the officiant (Samson's mother) and the offering

---

priestly code, these stipulations came into place after the story of Samuel's birth [for
an overview of these issues, see Stuart Chepey, *Nazirites in Late Second Temple Judaism: A Survey of Ancient Jewish Writings, the New Testament, Archaeological Evidence
and Other Writings from Late Antiquity* (Leiden: Brill, 2005), 2–6].

[45] It also uses a term δοτον which is understood by many to be a Nazirite. However,
this is a *hapax* and it is not used anywhere else to translate the term נזיר in the LXX.
Unless otherwise stated, all translations of the Septuagint are from Albert Pietersma
and Benjamin G. Wright, eds., *A New English Translation of the Septuagint* (New
York: Oxford University Press, 2007).

[46] Frank Moore Cross et al., *Qumran Cave 4: 1–2 Samuel*, vol. XII, *DJD* (Oxford:
Clarendon Press, 2005), 28–33.

[47] Matitiahu Tsevat, "Was Samuel a Nazirite?," in *"Sha'arei Talmon": Studies in
the Bible, Qumran, and the Ancient Near East Presented to Shemaryahu Talmon*, ed.
Michael Fishbane and Emanuel Tov (Winona Lake: Eisenbrauns, 1992), 200. He cites
examples in Jer 35.6 and Ezek 44.20, where there is one of the three prohibitions but
no mention of Nazirites.

[48] Num 6.9 [Eliezer Diamond, "An Israelite Self-Offering in the Priestly Code: A
New Perspective on the Nazirite," *JQR* 88 (1997): 5–6].

[49] E.g. The law against high priests drinking in Lev 10.9 [Ibid. 5–6].

[50] Ibid.: 4–5.

(Samson) are two different people, the prohibitions are separated between them.[51] The same principle can be applied in the MT of I Sam 1 to the lone prohibition applied to Samuel. Perhaps it is intended that the audience would presume Hannah would not drink or eat unclean food and so only Samuel's prohibition is stated. Diamond avers that being dedicated as a Nazirite is not a particular role within the religious structure of Israel[52] but rather is a dedication of an individual (usually the one who makes the vow himself according to Num 6) as an offering to the Lord. For Samson, the offering is that he will be a judge. The parallelism of prophet and Nazirite in Amos 2.11–12 suggests that some Nazirites had a prophetic role. In the case of Samuel, he begins by 'ministering' to the Lord in the presence of Eli the priest (והנער היה משרת את יהוה את פני עלי הכהן ;2.11). Later, he will perform prophetic functions, he will judge and he will be a kingmaker. His dedication as a Nazirite is thus an expression of his dedication to the Lord, and this encompasses all of the roles he performs in this capacity. The Nazirite vow is the causation for Samuel functioning in the Lord's service for his lifetime and performing each of the different roles.

Samuel's multifaceted role as priest, judge, prophet and subsequently kingmaker is indicative of the transitional period in which he figures.[53] His role as judge and priest ties with the past—the period of Judges and the succession to Eli the priest—and are the causes of his leadership of Israel. Prophet and kingmaker point to the future of kings and prophets and are the aspects of Samuel's leadership that cause change in the political structure of Israel. The significance of Samuel for transition in the system of leadership in Israel is conveyed by the embodiment of these leadership types in his own character.

Causation for the fall of Eli

There is one further aspect of causation in this chapter that lies outside the main narrative chain of causal events. The story uses the characterisations of Hannah and Eli in contrast with each other to emphasise

---

[51] Samson is forbidden from cutting his hair (Jdg 13.5) and his mother is forbidden from drink and eating anything unclean (13.4) [Ibid.: 8].

[52] Ibid.: 1–2.

[53] Willis points out that many talented people in human history have performed more than one role particularly in an unstable period such as when Samuel lived [John T. Willis, "Cultic Elements in the Story of Samuel's Birth and Dedication," *ST* 26 (1972): 41].

the piety of Hannah (already shown to be a factor in the basic chain of causation) and the inadequacies of Eli. The poignancy of Hannah's emotion and actions gives them realism, and the faults of Eli provide background for his later fall. The gradual introduction of Eli, alternating with the narrative of Hannah's plight, is a foreshadowing of chapters 2–3 where this device is further developed between Eli and Samuel himself.

The first suggestion of a comparison appears in v. 3 where Eli is introduced. Verse 2 ends with the terse statement ולחנה אין ילדים ('but Hannah had no children') which defines Hannah's identity in terms of her lack of children. In the verse immediately following, Eli is also defined in terms of his children, Hophni and Phinehas. We know nothing about Hannah except that she is married to Elkanah and does not have children, and we know nothing about Eli except that he has children and that they are priests. There has been significant discussion over this verse because of the peculiarity that Eli himself is not called a priest at Shiloh, only his two sons. The LXX has a variant reading of this verse, 'Eli and his two sons, Hophni and Phinehas' and it has been suggested that this reading be preferred.[54] In our study of the MT final form however, we also find some meaning. From this very early point in the narrative, there is a suggestion that Hophni and Phinehas are not under the control of their father but are effectively the priests at Shiloh in his place. Furthermore, just as Hannah is introduced only after the detailed introduction of Elkanah (such that the reader may initially expect Elkanah to be the hero of this story), so Eli's introduction is delayed by introducing him in relation to other people, even though he will feature more prominently than his sons. Eli and Hannah are introduced into the story using parallel devices in preparation for the more profound parallelism soon to come.

Eli is next mentioned in v. 9 followed by v. 12. His intermittent appearances heighten the drama as the audience is aware of his presence in the room. However it is not yet revealed that he is watching Hannah nor is any indication given of the significance that their interaction will hold. There is only a self-conscious awareness that while

---

[54] Smith also makes this suggestion but he discusses the alternative point of view that the narrator wished to bring Hophni and Phinehas to the forefront to prepare for the central role of their wickedness later on [Henry Preserved Smith, *A Critical and Exegetical Commentary on the Books of Samuel* (Edinburgh: T & T Clark, 1899), 6; Ralph W. Klein, *1 Samuel*, WBC (Waco: Word Books, 1983), 8].

Hannah is distressed, praying and weeping bitterly, there is another
presence. Apart from this dramatic function, Eli's presence allows a
contrast between Hannah and Eli. In vv. 7–8 Hannah is in a state
of depression over her barrenness, refusing to eat or drink, but, after
some kind words from Elkanah,[55] she steels herself for action. Verse
9 begins with ותקם ('and she arose') in an emphatic position to highlight her transition from inaction to action. This is complemented by
the prepositional phrases אחרי אכלה בשלה ואחרי שתה ('after eating
at Shiloh, and after drinking'). Presumably they occurred chronologically prior to Hannah arising but are indicative of her new efforts at
exertion.

The upright and active Hannah is juxtaposed in v. 9b with a station-
ary, sedentary Eli (ועלי הכהן ישב על־הכסא 'And Eli the priest was
sitting on the throne/seat'). The description of Eli is regal as he sits on
his throne[56] in his palace.[57] His passivity is highlighted by the contrast
to the string of verbs used of the activity of Hannah in vv. 10–11 and
her extended speech during which Eli recedes from view altogether.
Amongst these verbs, Fokkelman has noted the unusual use of על (lit:
upon) in the phrase ותתפלל על־יהוה ('and she prayed to the Lord').
He interprets this usage as implying that Hannah is not just praying
to God but she is praying for God himself to help her.[58] Whilst his

---

[55] There are differing interpretations of Elkanah's series of questions in v. 8, particularly his final question, הלוא אנכי טוב לך מעשרה בנים ('Am I not better to
you than ten sons?'). Fokkelman interprets Elkanah's words as an expression of his
own insecurity and a desire for Hannah to reassure him like a child [J.P. Fokkelman,
Vow and Desire, Vol. IV of *Narrative Art and Poetry in the Books of Samuel: A Full
Interpretation Based on Stylistic and Structural Analyses* (Assen: Van Gorcum, 1993),
29–30]. Polzin detects an underlying reproach as Hannah's own bitterness betrays
something of her own feelings towards Elkanah [*Samuel and the Deuteronomist*, 22].
Both these interpretations maintain that Elkanah's words also contain consolation,
whatever other feelings lie beneath them. Westbrook offers a neat explanation for why
Elkanah specifies ten sons by referring to a Sumerian dictionary from the library of
Ashurbanipal where there is an expression about an adopted son remaining the eldest
brother even if the adopter then has ten sons. Thus, Elkanah's point is that he, like an
adopted son, is worth more than 10 natural sons [Raymond Westbrook, "1 Samuel
1:8," *JBL* 109 (1990): 114–15]. Although it is doubtful that Elkanah would have been
familiar with this particular mode of usage, the Sumerian dictionary does demonstrate
that 10 is a common number used to describe a large family.

[56] כסא often means 'throne' rather than 'seat' as it is rendered in many translations.

[57] Again, whilst היכל can be used of the house of the Lord, it often refers to the
house of a king.

[58] Fokkelman, *Vow and Desire*, 35. However, note that the interchange of על and
אל is common within Samuel [see Robert Rezetko, *Source and Revision in the Narratives of David's Transfer of the Ark: Text, Language, and Story in 2 Samuel 6 and*

semantic explanation is plausible, the usage has the additional function of recalling that Eli sat *upon* (על) his throne, whilst Hannah is
praying *to* (על) God.

The physical contrast between Hannah and Eli is important because
it is developed throughout the narrative about Eli. There is a similar
contrast between Eli and Samuel in chapter 3. Eli lies down because of
his blindness (I Sam 3.2 ועלי שכב במקומו 'And Eli was lying down in his
place') and is associated with lying down by his repeated instructions to
Samuel to return to lying down (vv. 5, 6, שוב שכב, v. 9 לך שכב). However, as Samuel hears the voice of God, he persists in rising (vv. 6, 8, ויקם)
recalling the parallel action of his mother, Hannah, in chapter 1. These
physical descriptions of Eli culminate in his death where he falls from
his seat (I Sam 4.18, ויפל מעל־הכסא). The repetition of על־הכסא from
I Sam 1.9 demonstrates Eli's fall from leadership through complacency
and inaction.

The ensuing interaction between Hannah and Eli highlights the
distress of one and the inaccurate observation of the other. It begins
from Hannah's point of view with her vow in vv. 10–11. This is carefully crafted to evoke her distress and humble request to God. Biblical
narrative is notoriously economical with its language, yet in v. 10 the
verb תתפלל ('she was praying') is enclosed by two different ways of
expressing her distress, היא מרת נפש ('she was bitter of soul') and
בכה תבכה ('she was weeping intensely').[59] As Hannah begins to pray
we remember that this is the first time that she has spoken in the narrative, despite the provocation by Peninnah in v. 6 and the series of
questions from Elkanah in v. 8. Within the narrative world, Hannah
internalises her response to her situation until vv. 11–12. It has been
shown that her words in these verses include many features of laments
found in other parts of the Hebrew Bible[60] but it also has the quality
of being direct and artless. Alter observes that this is due to her avoidance of poetic symmetries and the reversal of the classic 'do et des'
formula.[61] The repetition of אמתך ('your maidservant') emphasises the

---

1 Chronicles 13, 15–16 (New York: T & T Clark, 2007), 93–94 n. 38], and therefore
there may be little significance.

[59] Compare for example the complete omission of Sarah's feelings about her barrenness in Gen 16–17; Rachel's emotions are conveyed in one phrase ותקנא רחל
באחתה in Gen 30.1.

[60] A.H. Van Zyl, "1 Sam 1:2–2:11—A Life-World Lament of Affliction," *JNSL* 12
(1984): 151–61.

[61] Alter, *The Art of Biblical Narrative*, 84.

humility in her request.[62] Hannah is a woman in distress who humbly seeks God for help.

As Eli reenters the scene, his metaphorical blindness becomes the focus of the narrative. The use of the *weqatal* of היה followed by כי to begin v. 12 והיה כי הרבתה להתפלל (lit: 'And it happened when she multiplied [her] praying') indicates a temporal clause and therefore most likely a disconnection with the preceding narrative.[63] This construction introduces a retelling of vv. 10–11 from Eli's point of view.[64] However, vv. 12–13 do not give a simple perspective of what Eli saw, but weave in reiterations of Hannah's grief with Eli's observations. This juxtaposes Hannah's heartfelt plea to God with Eli's misunderstanding, even though the overall effect is predominantly a comment on Eli.

The two threads of Eli and Hannah in vv. 12–13 are each a progression from the general to the specific. Hannah's point of view begins with her praying, followed by the more specific statement that she was speaking in her heart. Eli observes her mouth, then her lips and finally the stillness of her voice. Thus the narrative scrutinises both the internal and external aspects of Hannah simultaneously. Eli's sensitive observation of Hannah comes to an abrupt halt with the terse statement ויחשבה עלי לשכרה ('and Eli thought she was a drunken woman'). This statement enhances the depiction of Hannah's distress by comparing its intensity with drunkenness. Even more significantly, it shows that Eli does not understand Hannah's emotion despite his careful observation. In a sense he is blind.

Eli's blindness is an important theme that is developed throughout the narrative in I Sam 1–4. In 2.22, Eli 'heard' about what his sons were doing (וישמע את כל־אשר יעשון בניו לכל־ישראל, 'And he heard everything which his sons did to all of Israel') and his 'hearing' is further emphasised by the repetition of שמע ('to hear') in v. 23

---

[62] Again, compare this to the speech of Rachel to her husband Jacob in Gen 30.1 הבה־לי בנים ואם־אין מתה אנכי ('Give me sons or I will die').

[63] Williams chooses to read והיה as ויהי based on the Greek and renders it 'As she continued to pray'. This rendering is also used in the RSV [Ronald J. Williams, *Hebrew Syntax: An Outline* (Toronto: University of Toronto Press, 1967), 74, §445; McCarter, *I Samuel*, 50, 54]. Keeping the MT reading is important to the drama of the story and so the translation in Klein, *1 Samuel*, 'While she multiplied her prayers' is preferable. Note that both of these scholars do not translate the verb sequentially.

[64] On combining points of view, see Adele Berlin, *Poetics and Interpretation of Biblical Narrative*, Bible and Literature Series (Sheffield: Almond, 1983), 73. Even though Hannah is referred to in the third person, this does not exclude the narrative from taking her perspective [see Bar-Efrat, *Narrative Art*, 35].

and v. 24. Implicit in Eli's hearing about their wickedness is that he has been too blind to 'see' it and this is why it has continued unchecked. He could not 'see' the sins of his sons and becomes aware of them only by 'hearing' rumours. There is a subtle double meaning in 3.1 אין חזון נפרץ ('vision was infrequent') and 3.2 [ועיניו] ועינו החלו כהות לא יוכל לראות ('His eyes had begun to be faint and he could not see'): Eli is physically blind, morally blind and sees no prophetic visions. Furthermore, this is symptomatic of Israel as a whole.

Eli's faulty observation is further reinforced in his dialogue with Hannah and it foreshadows his oversight of moral laxity in his own household. He asks, not whether she is drunk, but how long she will continue being so. He does not consider that he might be mistaken. In Hannah's response, her use of שמך ('to pour') in ואשמך את-נפשי לפני יהוה ('and I have poured out my soul to the Lord') highlights that she has been doing the reverse: pouring out her soul not her drink.[65] The word בליעל ('worthlessness') will be recalled in 2.2 where Eli's sons are described in the same way. Firstly this emphasises the injustice that Hannah be associated with these immoral men, and secondly it is a subtle reminder of the later ramifications of Eli's faulty observation.

Finally, Eli's accusation against Hannah represents another distortion of the birth story type scene. In place of a typical annunciation of the birth of a child, he is uncomprehending and blind. As Alter writes:

> Eli is thus virtually a parody of the annunciating figure of the conventional type scene—an apt introduction to a story in which the claim to authority of the house of Eli will be rejected, and, ultimately, sacerdotal guidance will be displaced by prophetic guidance in the person of Samuel.[66]

---

[65] There is a discrepancy in the narrative here as the MT of v. 9 implies that Hannah ate and drank. There are many emendations that can be made to this verse [e.g. see McCarter, *I Samuel*, 53, for his emendations and justifications for this verse] but these are unnecessary because many plausible explanations can be made for the text as it appears in the MT (such as allowing for a time delay during v. 9 or assuming that it was only very little that she drank). Instead of justifying any one of these explanations, we note that this is an example where this kind of detail is irrelevant to the writer/redactor and he makes no attempt to explain it in the text. The meaning in v. 15 is clear despite v. 9.

[66] Robert Alter, *The David Story: A Translation with Commentary of 1 and 2 Samuel* (New York: W.W. Norton, 1999), 5.

Therefore, the complex characterisation of Hannah and Eli, which is developed through a structure of parallelism, accords the causal foundation for the end of the Elide priesthood and Samuel's succession to the leadership of Israel. This ancient historiography emphasises the role that one woman's piety, compared to one man's metaphorical lack of sight, can have on the futures of their children and, subsequently, the leadership of Israel. Furthermore, these personal causes are accompanied by divine causation. Yahweh responds to Hannah's piety with the birth of a son and to Eli's blindness with a rejection of his house as priests.

Causation beyond I Sam 1

These strands of causation are developed in the ensuing chapters until Samuel becomes the acknowledged judge, kingmaker, prophet and priest of Israel. In these chapters, the causation becomes more complex than the personal factors of Hannah, Samuel, Eli and the sovereignty of God in each of their situations. In chapter 2, the characters of Eli's sons, Hophni and Phinehas, are explored and their corruption in the temple is described. In 2.17, the failure of Eli to check their personal moral deficiency causes God to decree their downfall. Thus there are further personal and divine causes that build upon chapter 1.

Other types of causation are interwoven with the personal and divine. Social causes are suggested by the long description of Phinehas' and Hophni's sin in 2.13–16. Verse 13 states specifically that they violated the customs of the priests towards the people. Verses 13–14 describe how the priests stole from the people by using a fork to take meat whilst it was boiling and the extent of this sin against the people is highlighted by the phrase לכל־ישראל ('to all of Israel') in v. 14. Then in vv. 15–16, the narrative dramatises a second method of corruption by using dialogue between an unnamed worshipper at the temple and the נער הכהן ('young priest').[67] This exchange reveals the impact of the priests' corruption on the people: it did not go unnoticed and it directly affected and exploited the people in Israel. This contrasts with v. 26 where Samuel (also described as נער) grows in stature not only with the Lord but also with אנשים ('men'). The word expected here would be עם ('people') but this unusual word choice echoes the איש

---

[67] For a justification of this translation, see David Toshio Tsumura, *The First Book of Samuel*, NICOT (Grand Rapids: Eerdmans, 2007), 157.

('man') with whom the corrupt priest dialogued in vv. 15–16. Thus the text offers a social cause for the people of Israel's ready acceptance of Samuel in 7.3 after the sudden deaths of the Elide family. In addition to this social causation, there is more explicit political causation when Phinehas and Hophni, and subsequently Eli, die in the war against the Philistines. All of these causes are woven together in the first few chapters of the book to generate complex explanation for Samuel's rise to leadership in Israel.

2.2   THE ACCESSION OF KING SAUL—I SAM 9–11

In I Sam 9–11, we encounter another method of incorporating different types of causation. There is little indication in this section that the pericopes follow a chronological sequence. Rather, the text uses juxtaposition and the repetition of a pattern to give the momentous event both public and private perspectives. Let us examine firstly how causation is developed within each pericope and then how cumulative causation is developed throughout the section as a whole.

Causation in the pericopes of I Sam 9–11

I Sam 9–11 contains three narratives that contribute to the accession of Saul as king. Saul searches for lost asses but then meets Samuel and is anointed as king in 9.1–10.16, he is chosen publicly by lot in 10.17–27 and finally he is made king publicly after a military victory against the Ammonites in 11.1–15. These chapters have been the subject of extensive literary-critical discussion. The identification of pro- and anti-monarchial sources in these chapters will be analysed in detail in a later chapter. We turn here to form criticism's recognition of 'folklore' elements in the narrative of Saul searching for his donkeys. The folkloric identification was originally made by Gressman, who isolated the physical superiority of Saul, the anonymous seer and city in which he lives, the timelessness of the story and the setting in the realm of wonders as elements that indicate a prehistory of the story as a *Märchen*.[68] Scholars have since noted that these elements

---

[68] Hugo Gressmann, *Die älteste Geschichtsschreibung und Prophetie Israels (von Samuel bis Amos und Hosea): übersetzt, erklärt und mit Einleitungen versehen* (Göttingen: V & R, 1910), 26–27. He writes with certainty, "Nach dieser Analyse kann kein

do not extend throughout all of I Sam 9.1–10.16 and so have revised Gressman's form critical analysis.[69] There is now a widespread supposition that the earlier verses of chapter 9 represent an early folktale about Saul searching for asses but instead finding a seer, which was overwritten by the story of Saul being anointed king by Samuel.[70] One of the primary applications of this theory is that the folkloric elements in chapters 9–10 render it unlikely to be history in a modern sense. The more sober and plausible account of Saul rising up against the Ammonites is generally preferred as the true story of how Saul came to exert his kingship over Israel.[71] Gordon cites the attraction of this point of view as its "historical probability."[72]

Zweifel sein, daß wir es hier nicht, wie behauptet wird, mit einer Geschichtserzählung, sondern mit einer Legende zu tun haben."

[69] E.g. Bruce C. Birch, "Development of the Tradition on the Anointing of Saul in 1 Sam 9:1–10:16," *JBL* 90 (1971): 58.

[70] Klein, *1 Samuel*, 84; McCarter, *I Samuel*, 186; Campbell, *1 Samuel*, 106; John Van Seters, *In Search of History: Historiography in the Ancient World and the Origins of Biblical History* (New Haven: Yale University Press, 1983), 254–56; Birch, "Development," 55–68; J. Maxwell Miller, "Saul's Rise to Power: Some Observations Concerning I Sam 9:1–10:16; 10:26–11:15 and 13:2–14:46," *CBQ* 36 (1974); Ludwig Schmidt, *Menschlicher Erfolg und Jahwes Initiative: Studien zu Tradition, Interpretation und Historie in Überlieferungen von Gideon, Saul und David*, vol. 38, WMANT (Neukirchen-Vluyn: Neukirchener Verlag, 1970), 58–102; Dennis J. McCarthy, "Inauguration of Monarchy in Israel: A Form-Critical Study of 1 Samuel 8–12," *Interpretation* 27 (1973): 401–12. Although this theory is widespread, the exact divisions of the narrative between folktale and late rewriting vary among scholars. E.g. Birch (pp. 58–60) assigns 9.1–13, 9.18–19, 9.22–24, 10.2–44 to the early folktale and the remaining verses to the rewriting. In contrast, Miller (pp. 158–59) influenced by Schmidt but with modifications, considers 9.2b, 9, 13a, 14b–17, 20f, 22b–24a and 10.1, 5b, 9, 13–16 as the later additions. This has led some to assert that the exact divisions cannot yet be known with certainty.

[71] Klein, *1 Samuel*, 104; McCarter, *I Samuel*, 207. Whilst this viewpoint is common, it is not uniform. Scholars generally still accept that the story has historical foundation but several have doubted that it was part of Saul's accession to the throne and is more likely to have taken place later in his reign. E.g. van der Toorn suggests that it is unlikely that Saul would become king through a Transjordanian victory and considers that the victory is more likely to have been against the Canaanites as they were more central in Israel and would lead to the people recognising him as king [Karel van der Toorn, "Saul and the Rise of Israelite State Religion," *VT* 43 (1993): 525]. However, as van der Toorn does not consider I Sam 9–11 a unity, he overlooks that Saul was already acknowledged by the people in chapter 10, making it unnecessary for his military victory to be central in Israel. See also Diana Edelman, "Saul's Rescue of Jabesh-Gilead (1 Sam 11:1–11): Sorting Story from History," *ZAW* 96 (1984): 195–209.

[72] Robert P. Gordon, *1 & 2 Samuel: A Commentary* (Exeter: Paternoster, 1986), 29. Gordon (pp. 33–34) also warns not to be too hasty in assuming that chapter 11 is historical and reading into the text ideas about how Saul should have become king. He expresses doubt that the messenger from Jabesh Gilead would have gone directly to Gibeah.

These diachronic studies highlight the sharp difference in the type of causation that is developed in each section. It also draws our attention to the modern preference for political and public causation in contrast to the juxtaposition of such different types of stories in the historiography of Samuel.

9.1–10.16

The causation in I Sam 9.1–10.16 is private and explicitly incorporates the Divine. The first imbalance in the story is introduced in chapter 8, where God commanded Samuel to obey Israel's request for a king. That section closes with Samuel sending the people away but not acting on the request. Then chapter 9 begins, not by addressing this imbalance, but with a second imbalance, the need to find Kish's lost donkeys. It is in the process of restoring the second imbalance that Saul meets Samuel and the first imbalance, Israel's request for a king, is brought to equilibrium by the anointing of Saul.

Let us now examine the causation that restores each of these imbalances. Despite the unresolved conclusion to chapter 8, chapter 9 opens with what initially appears to be a new and disconnected narrative. The opening phrase of the chapter, ויהי איש ('there was a man') typically indicates a new beginning in the narrative and there is a sharp shift in the subject matter from a public assembly to the domestic scene of Kish and his son Saul. If the story had begun with the Lord's words to Samuel found in vv. 15–16, divine causation would have been immediately established and the connection between chapters 8 and 9 would have been clear. Instead the material is arranged in such a way that divine causation is revealed more subtly.[73] Indeed, the initial story does not cite any explicit divine intervention but demonstrates that it is a series of coincidences that lead to Saul meeting Samuel. At each point in the story, the agents of change who bring Saul closer to Samuel are anyone but Saul himself. It is his father who sends him to search for the donkeys. It is his servant who suggests visiting the seer and who solves the problem of no gift.[74] It is the women at the well

---

[73] Bar-Efrat, *Das erste Buch Samuel*, 151.

[74] Moreover, it has been suggested that the unusual passive construction used in v. 8, 'Behold, a quarter of a shekel of silver is found in my hand' (הנה נמצא בידי רבע שקל כסף), subtly implies that the silver appeared through divine sovereignty [McCarter, *I Samuel*, 185; Eslinger, *Kingship of God*, 295].

who point Saul towards the location of Samuel and encourage him to 'hurry' (9.12; מהר). This long suspenseful narrative depicts Saul as not only unwitting in this journey, but even, in v. 7, potentially hindering.[75] The causation is dominated by the private and personal concerns of Saul's father and servant, and is underlined by an implicit sense of divine guidance through coincidence.

Mid-way through Saul's journey, the first imbalance, Israel's request for a king, is again brought to the audience's consciousness through God's words to Samuel in vv. 15–17. Divine causation is stated explicitly but is also implied by the entire preceding narrative acting as a cause for the meeting between the two men. An explicit statement of Yahweh's agency is then repeated in 10.1[76] and the fulfillment of the signs concerning Saul in 10.2–13 is inescapably read in this light. However, compared to the passivity of Saul in the earlier part of the narrative, Samuel takes a more active role in Saul's anointing and therefore in restoring the imbalance. He gives Saul directions and performs the ceremony of anointing him with oil. This is again private and personal causation as Samuel overcomes his reluctance expressed in chapter 8 and is obedient to the command to make a king.

Whilst the divine causation in this section is unambiguous, the narrative does not present Yahweh's intervention in isolation from other causes. In the direct speech of 9.16, Yahweh cites both the threat of the Philistines and the insistence of the people as motivation for his intervention. As in I Sam 1, divine causation is not in isolation from other types of causes. Here it incorporates, and is a response to, the internal and external political issues in Israel at the time. However, overall, personal, private and divine causation are prominent in this section.

10.17–27

Despite the equilibrium brought to the question of Israel's leadership in 9.1–10.16, 10.17 remarkably opens with the same imbalance recur-

---

[75] For a more detailed study of the use of suspense in this narrative, see Rachelle Gilmour, "Suspense and Anticipation in I Sam. 9:1–14," *JHS* (2009).

[76] The LXX gives an even fuller statement of Divine causation with the additional words, καὶ σὺ ἄρξεις ἐν λαῷ κυρίου καὶ σὺ σώσεις αὐτὸν ἐκ χειρὸς ἐχθρῶν αὐτοῦ κυκλόθεν καὶ τοῦτό σοι τὸ σημεῖον ὅτι ἔχρισέν σε κύριος ἐπὶ κληρονομίαν αὐτοῦ εἰς ἄρχοντα ('And you shall reign among the people of the Lord, and you will save them from the hand of their enemies all around. And this shall be the sign to you that the Lord anoint you ruler over his heritage').

ring. The key difference is that I Sam 10.17 shifts to a public perspective, opening with Samuel calling the people together in Mizpah. In keeping with the shift to public events, the causation now has a primarily public nature. In 10.19, Samuel reminds Israel that they have requested a king and that the selection process is a result of their request. Thus the reader is reminded of the political agency of the people. The theme of internal pressure for a king is sustained throughout the two pericopes as the attitudes of the people are explored. In 10.26–27, there is concern that not all of Israel is in support of Saul, a problem which is resolved in 11.12–15.

Despite the prominence of these political causes, divine causation is equally a concern in this section. Although the direct speech of God is now formulaic and mediated through the mouthpiece of Samuel (10.18), the use of lots implies the guidance of the Lord in the selection.[77] Finally, the portrayal of Saul as non-complicit in his anointing in 9.1–10.16 is continued in 10.22 when he is found hiding in the baggage rather than taking an active part in Israel's choice of a king.[78]

11.1–15

This new section again opens with no recognition that Saul has been anointed king over Israel. The imbalance in the narrative is straightforward—Nahash the Ammonite has besieged Jabesh-Gilead—but essentially the imbalance is only secondary to the ongoing need of a king for Israel. However, in resolving the imbalance created by Nahash, the narrative also resolves the overarching imbalance of a king because Saul proves himself suitable. After this section, the imbalance is resolved permanently and the equilibrium achieved in the previous chapters is finally acknowledged in 12.1.

---

[77] Note that lots are not specifically mentioned in the MT. The verb used is וילכד ('and it was taken') and scholars have deduced that the process described must be lots [McCarter, I Samuel, 192]. The text apparently has little interest in explaining how the inquiries were made of the Lord, only the fact that they were and so it does not give details about any change in method of inquiry [cf. Hertzberg, I & II Samuel, 89, who postulates two sources based on the two methods of inquiry].

[78] Cf. Diana Edelman, King Saul in the Historiography of Judah, JSOT Supp. 121 (Sheffield: JSOT Press, 1991), 57. Edelman writes that Saul hiding in the baggage is a reflection of the requisite humility of a royal candidate and not his reluctance to become king. Nevertheless, even if his humility is not intended to be interpreted as authentic, he is depicted as acting passively in the process of his accession in this section.

Nahash the Ammonite, the cause of the imbalance, presents a public and political type of causation. This foreign political pressure is reminiscent of Israel's request in 8.20 for a king to fight their battles and in 9.16 where Yahweh says the king will save his people from the hand of the Philistines. The narrative in 11.1–11 explores foreign threats more deeply as a cause for the rise of Saul as king. In addition, the restoration of the imbalance introduces an element of internal political causation because Saul makes the politically significant move of uniting 'all' of Israel in the battle. Overall, this narrative corresponds more closely to modern expectations of public and political forces in causation in history.

Nevertheless, there are also traces of divine causation in this section. Saul's military victory displays the sovereign hand of God as the spirit rushes upon Saul (ותצלח רוח־אלהים על־שאול, 11.6) and fear of the Lord falls upon the people (ויפל פחד־יהוה על־העם, 11.7) so that they join Saul in battle. The divine causes are in response to a corresponding secular cause, the demand of Israel and the military threat of the Ammonites.

Cumulative Causation

Overall, there is a very different emphasis in causation between 9.1–10.16 and 10.17–11.15. The first story focuses on personal, private causation and overt divine causation whereas the second section is public and political with less intrusion of personal interests and the Divine. In addition to this shift in causation, there are a number of other discontinuities within I Sam 9–11. We have observed that each section begins as though the previous section had not taken place. Lots are needed in 10.17–27 to select the king when Samuel has already anointed Saul.[79] Then, even after he is publicly selected as king in 10.17–27 and the people say יחי המלך (10.24; 'long live the king'), his kingship is not fully established. When the Ammonite threat strikes in chapter 11, Saul is out farming with the oxen and the messengers from Jabesh-gilead do not go to find him in the field.[80] Finally, in 11.14, the people 'renew the kingdom' (v. 14; ונחדש שם המלוכה) but they also

---

[79] Klein, *1 Samuel*, 96.
[80] Ibid., 104.

'made Saul king' (v. 15; וימלכו שם את־שאול) as if for the first time.[81] In addition to this discontinuity, there is a conspicuous lack of time designations or other explanatory notes between the sections.[82] Both 10.17 and 11.1 begin with a *wayyiqtol* verb, suggesting that the sections may be sequential, but give no other information. A diachronic explanation for these discontinuities is that the sections are a number of different traditions, which have been placed side by side.[83] However, we wish to examine the effect of the juxtaposition of these stories in their final form.[84]

The relative independence of each episode suggests that they have been juxtaposed for cumulative effect rather than their strict sequential plot development. The pericopes form a pattern of accession that highlights the different angles of public and private causation. Thus it offers an example of cumulative causation.

Different structures of Saul's accession have been suggested in the past, particularly by comparing it with other accession narratives. Halpern, who looks only at 10.17–11.15, has identified a two-tiered pattern of divine designation and confirmation, inspired by the early

---

[81] See McCarter, *I Samuel*, 205, who argues that the renewal of the kingdom is an attempt to bring coherence to the arrangement of materials from separate traditions. Similarly, Klein, *1 Samuel*, 104, argues that the renewal of the kingship is a redactional attempt to harmonise 10.17–27 with chapter 11 and also to introduce Samuel into a story he probably did not take part in.

[82] See chapter 5: Coherence and Contradictions for further discussion of how patterns and juxtaposition of pericopes can take priority over clarity of chronology.

[83] Note that there are also those who argue for some level of continuity within this section. The reference to Saul and Samuel's secrecy, even from Saul's uncle in 10.16, is an appropriate segue into the need for a public election of Saul as king. Bodner points out that the question in v. 27, 'How can he save us' leads into the narrative of Saul's military victory [Bodner, *1 Samuel*, 101]. Fokkelman argues that the designation in 11.4 גבעת שאול ('Gibeah of Saul') implies that the messengers from Jabesh-gilead went there directly to find Saul. It is only implied in direct speech to the Ammonites in v. 3 that the messengers will go throughout all Israel [Fokkelman, *Vow and Desire*, 466]. Eslinger points out that the renewal of the kingship in 11.14–15 is appropriate as Israel accepts the king that God has chosen for them and finally makes him king [Eslinger, *Kingship of God*, 378–79]. Vannoy offers an argument for unity by asserting that it is the kingdom of God which is being renewed. He also points out (p. 87) that Saul was only designated as king at Mizpah, not actually made king [J. Robert Vannoy, *Covenant Renewal at Gilgal: A Study of I Samuel 11:14–12:25* (Cherry Hill: Mack Pub. Co., 1977)]. Whether these continuities are the result of unity of composition, a skilful editor or coincidence is beyond the scope of this study.

[84] As Edelman says, the author or editor "has arranged [the traditions] into a sequence which he felt would make logical sense to his audience" [Diana Edelman, "Saul ben Kish in History and Tradition," in *Origins of the Ancient Israelite States*, ed. Fritz Volkmar and Philip R. Davies (Sheffield: Sheffield Academic Press, 1996), 149].

Judges narratives and other ancient Near Eastern sources.[85] Edelman points out the importance of a 'testing' stage, also mentioned by Halpern but not included in his pattern, and suggests that it should therefore be considered a three stage process: designation, proof of worth by military deed and finally coronation.[86] Edelman suggests that the writer would have shaped the account to include the steps that his audience would have equated with the process of king-making. She writes, "He would have 'historicized' the familiar cultic rite to satisfy the cultural expectations of his audience."[87] This demonstrates one effect of using such a pattern to describe Saul's accession to the throne. The familiar pattern signals to the reader that an appointment is taking place and provides the corresponding emphases of causation expected by the audience: designation by God, military victory by Saul and confirmation by the people.

However, in our analysis of causation in these pericopes, we have identified a second pattern—first private then public causation. This observation allows us to build on the work of Halpern and Edelman and understand further how this three-stage accession pattern is being used in I Sam 9–11.[88] In particular, the three-stage accession process does not account for the double designation of Saul in both 9.1–10.16 and 10.17–27. As Edelman points out, when discussing the diachronic development of the account, the anointing of Saul in chapter 10 strongly implies that a military exploit should follow as confirmation.[89] However, in its current form, it is followed by a different sort of confirmation. 10.2–13 describes the confirmation of Saul through a series of signs. In particular, there is a rushing of the spirit in 10.10 that par-

---

[85] Baruch Halpern, *The Constitution of the Monarchy in Israel* (Chico: Scholars Press, 1981), 51–148.

[86] Edelman, "Saul's Rescue of Jabesh-Gilead," 198–99. See also her discussions in Edelman, *King Saul*, 30–32, and Edelman, "Saul ben Kish," 148–49.

[87] Edelman, *King Saul*, 31.

[88] Note that the recognition of one pattern in the narrative does not exclude the presence of other patterns using the same pericopes. That is, there can be more than one pattern occurring in the same chapters of narrative at once. This will become apparent when we examine the section of I Sam 8–12 and observe that there is also an alternation of public assembly and other events in these chapters. See also Edelman's description of four structuring devices and three patterns that overlap throughout the story of Saul [Ibid., 27–36].

[89] Edelman, "Saul's Rescue of Jabesh-Gilead," 200. She also mentions that the reception of the divine spirit adds to this implication and is a part of the designation stage. However, in 11.1–11, the rushing of the spirit is a part of the confirmation by victory account and so it can also be grouped in this category.

allels the rushing of the spirit in 11.6. Thus, rather than confirmation through the spirit and a military victory as expected after 10.1, Saul is confirmed by the spirit and a series of signs. This is a very fitting confirmation for the narrative of 9.1–10.1 considering the strong element of divine causation, the passivity of Saul and the private, non-political nature of the narrative.

Thus, the designation and confirmation stages of Saul's accession are repeated in the narrative: first in the private sphere in 9.1–10.16 and then in the public sphere in 10.17–11.13.[90] They are both concluded with a public installation scene in 11.14–15. In 9.1–10.16, Saul is chosen through the process of meeting Samuel and being anointed in 9.1–10.1. After this selection, Samuel explains to Saul that certain signs will take place (10.2–8) and then the narrative describes the enactment of those signs (10.9–13). This varies from the usual military victory but is appropriate to the private context and gives confirmation for the divine choice of Saul as king. The designation of Saul once again takes place in 10.17–25 where he is chosen by lot in the public assembly. Opposition to Saul in 10.26–27 suggests the need for confirmation of the choice. This takes place in 11.1–11 when Saul again receives the spirit and demonstrates that he is an answer to Israel's problems with foreign enemies. In both cases, the final equilibrium in the narrative chain is not reached until 11.15. In the former, because Saul's selection remains secret even from Saul's uncle[91] and in the latter, because of the hostility expressed by some of the people of Israel.

The juxtaposition of the two processes of designation and confirmation highlights that there are two processes of causation and two points of view on Saul's accession. Saul is appointed king both because of God's direct personal command to Samuel, and through the official

---

[90] Cf. Sarah Nicholson, *Three Faces of Saul: An Intertextual Approach to Biblical Tragedy*, JSOTSup. 339 (Sheffield: Sheffield Academic Press, 2002), 55–56. Discussing 10.1–16 and 10.17–27, she briefly describes a two step process for Saul's accession where the first stage is private and the second public.

[91] The sudden appearance of Saul's uncle (who is presumably either Abner or Ner, the father of Abner) is unexplained by the narrative. Ap-Thomas has suggested that the word דוד refers to the governor of the Philistine garrison [Dafydd R. Ap-Thomas, "Saul's 'Uncle'," *VT* 11 (1961): 241–45]. Although this is an attractive theory, there is no evidence in the text to confirm this meaning of דוד. Eslinger, *Kingship of God*, 334–35, suggests that there is no significance that Saul's uncle asked him (and thus the narrative sees no need to explain it) except that Saul's father would have known where Saul was and so did not need to ask. It may also be a play on the name of David (דָּוִד), a foreshadowing of the future.

avenues of the assembly, approval of the people and proof of his military prowess. The private and public processes are linked together by the common theme of divine causation and the common result of Saul established as king.

Moreover, the variation from the typical linear accession formula of designation, confirmation and installation is a powerful technique for conveying the significance of this particular accession. The separation of private and public causation disentangles what would otherwise be a very complex exposition of causation. It demonstrates that these are two discrete aspects of Saul's rise to the throne and initiates their interaction and conflict.[92] In addition to the cumulative causation of designation, confirmation and coronation, there is a cumulative causation of private and public events.

In summary, it has been demonstrated that the narrative in I Sam 9–11 uses juxtaposition and structure to expound the different types of causes for Saul's installation as king. Each pericope contains its own causation for shifting from equilibrium to imbalance to equilibrium, and these contain divine, personal and political causes to varying degrees. However, the duality of private and public causation for Saul's succession primarily receives expression through the cumulative effect of the predominantly private then public narratives.

---

[92] The dichotomy between the public and private lives of the king is maintained as a theme throughout the books of Samuel, with each leader's downfall occurring as the private intrudes on the public. Samuel is a successful public judge against the Philistines yet it is the intrusion of his private life—the corruption of his sons whom he also made judges—which motivates Israel to ask for a king (I Sam 8.1–5). Saul's military victories are interspersed with his personal weaknesses such as his rash vow which brings the death sentence upon Jonathan (I Sam 14). It is the intrusion of Saul's weak character into his public life in chapter 15 that leads to God's rejection of him as he fails to follow God's command. Moreover, his personal jealousy of David, which begins in private, eventually takes over his public life as pursuit of David becomes an obsession before his death in the war against the Philistines. The interplay of David's public and private lives has also been studied in detail in Gros Louis, "Difficulty of Ruling Well," 15–33. Therefore, as public and private causation continues to echo throughout Saul's life and the book of Samuel, the author valued private and public causation in the story of how he became king. These types of causation are described separately at the beginning of Saul's leadership but, as the narrative progresses, they intrude on each other more and more.

2.3   The Temple—II Sam 7

II Sam 7 ostensibly marks a state of equilibrium in David's reign to conclude the instability since his anointing in I Sam 16. II Sam 7 follows the joyous arrival of the ark in Jerusalem in chapter 6 and opens in v. 1 with David at home and at rest from his enemies. Furthermore, it concludes with David's praise to Yahweh for promising him a dynasty and is followed by three more chapters describing David's victories. This equilibrium is sustained until chapter 11 when another major imbalance occurs in the reign of David. Yet, within this overall equilibrium, an imbalance is created. David suggests that he should build a temple. This imbalance is resolved, not by God's blessing for a temple, but rather the promise of a different sort of house, David's dynasty. In this section, we will examine how II Sam 7 conveys causation for David *not* building a temple and for his dynasty.

II Sam 7 is dominated by direct speech and little narrative action. However, the speech is embedded in a narrative framework that shapes how this chapter is understood and interpreted. Despite the dominance of the divine speech, the divine causation incorporates a number of other types of causes. This complexity is highlighted by an examination of discontinuities in the passage which have been identified by historical critics. We will see that there are a number of literary techniques, such as juxtaposition and wordplay, employed to draw the connection between divine causation and other types of causation.

Why did David not build a temple?

The most explicit causation in this chapter for why David did not build a temple comes from the Divine. David makes a proposal to Nathan to build a temple, Nathan acquiesces, but Yahweh intervenes through an oracle. The first half of this oracle in vv. 5–7 directly addresses David's request and Yahweh states that he has never had a house in the past, nor has he ever asked for one. Thus a purely theological reason is given for not building a temple which, on the surface, does not incorporate any other causes relating to David or to Israel.

Despite the simplicity of Yahweh's reply, there are indicators in the text that point the reader to more complex causation. An examination of David's motivation for suggesting the temple points to a connection with the second half of Nathan's oracle and with the surrounding chapters in II Samuel. This context for Yahweh's words introduces

more complex meaning and a deeper understanding of the causes for
Yahweh's refusal of a temple and David's acceptance of this refusal.

There are two reasons in the text for David's initial proposal to build
a temple: firstly, it is the appropriate culmination to his rest from enemies; and secondly, he wanted to establish his dynasty.

a. 'Rest' and the fulfillment of the Deuteronomic covenant

The first motivation for David's speech in II Sam 7.1–2 is that the
temple is the appropriate culmination for the acquisition of rest in the
land. This is implied by v. 7.1b ויהוה הניח־לו מסביב מכל־איביו ('and
the Lord had given rest to him from all his surrounding enemies'). The
root נוח is strongly associated with Deuteronomistic theology, particularly the possession of the land.[93] 'Rest' is thus related to other themes
of the Deuteronomistic theology including the exodus and covenant[94]
and the establishment of a central place of worship. The association
between rest in the land and the building of a temple is particularly
close in Deut 12.10–11. 'Rest' (the root נוח) is specifically mentioned
in the protasis of Deut 12.10 and is fulfilled in the apodosis of v. 11
that they will sacrifice to God in the place (המקום) God chooses. The
connection between these ideas is later found in I Kgs 5 when Solomon builds the temple and, outside of the Deuteronomistic history,
in Ex 15.17.[95] Through this overt allusion to rest, and its association
with building a temple, the text implies that this connection formed
an important part of David's motivation.

However, source critical studies have observed that the presentation of rest in this chapter contains discontinuities. Whilst the chapter
begins with a statement of David's rest from enemies, many scholars
read vv. 10–11 as a promise to give rest from enemies in the future.
Furthermore, chapter 8 opens with the phrase ויהי אחרי־כן ('it happened after this'), implying chronological continuity with chapter 7,
before recommencing accounts of David's military exploits. This

---

[93] Moshe Weinfeld, *Deuteronomy and the Deuteronomic School* (Oxford: Clarendon Press, 1972), 343.

[94] See Weinfeld (pp. 326–30) for examples of this theme in the Deuteronomic history.

[95] For both Biblical and Mesopotamian examples of this association, see also Victor
(Avigdor) Hurowitz, *I Have Built You an Exalted House: Temple Building in the Bible
in Light of Mesopotamian and Northwest Semitic Writings*, JSOTSup. 115 (Sheffield:
JSOT Press, 1992), 330–31.

implies that David is not at rest from his enemies after all.[96] In light of these considerations, McCarter suggests that v. 1b should be deleted to resemble the parallel text in I Chron 17.1, although no other textual witnesses of Samuel share this deletion.[97] On the other hand, Anderson argues that the *weqatal* verb forms in vv. 9b-10 refer to God's dealings with David in the past rather than the future, such that these verses form an inclusio with v. 1b.[98]

Anderson's attention to the verbs in vv. 9b-10 raises a key difficulty for understanding the meaning of the passage. There are strong arguments on both sides for translating the verbs in the past or future. Loretz argues, on the basis of context, that the past tense is required. However, in our case, it is this very context that we are investigating. He shows that the *weqatal* is not purely a late feature in Hebrew and it is possible that this is a *waw* conjunctive with a perfect.[99] Furthermore, according to an interpretation of the Hebrew verb system as aspectual rather than tense oriented, a past translation is possible. The head verb in this case is a *wayyiqtol*, which refers to the past, and *weqatals* tend to be dependent on their head verb.[100] On the other side of the debate, it has been argued that the verbs are preceded by two *waw* consecutives with imperfects, and followed by two ordinary imperfects, and so

---

[96] Gordon, *1 & 2 Samuel*, 236, suggests that the solution lies in the chronology of chapter 7 belonging later than chapter 8. Van Seters suggests that the wars of chapter 8 belong to a different source than chapters 7 and they are a continuation of 5.17–25. Chapter 7 refers to a period late in David's life, establishing peace before Solomon builds the temple, and chapter 8 is a summary of David's reign [John Van Seters, *The Biblical Saga of King David* (Winona Lake: Eisenbrauns, 2009), 257–58]. However, within the world of the narrative, this alteration of chronology is not allowed by the opening phrase of chapter 8, which establishes that the chapters are sequential. Note also that Van Seters (p. 260) explains the internal contradiction in the chapter by suggesting that vv. 10b–11aα is a post-exilic interpolation applicable to the hope of restoration in this period. Without this section, these verbs can be read easily in the past tense.

[97] P. Kyle McCarter, Jr., *II Samuel*, The Anchor Bible (New York: Double Day, 1984), 191. Cf. Stephen Pisano, "2 Samuel 5–8 and the Deuteronomist: Textual Criticism or Literary Criticism?" in *Israel Constructs its History: Deuteronomistic Historiography in Recent Research*, ed. Albert de Pury, Thomas Römer, and Jean-Daniel Macchi (Sheffield: Sheffield Academic Press, 2000), 273. He points out that if the juxtaposing of this chapter with the wars of chapter 8 is an argument against including v. 1b in the text, the same argument also makes its later insertion incomprehensible.

[98] A.A. Anderson, *2 Samuel*, WBC (Waco: Word Books, 1989), 120.

[99] O. Loretz, "The Perfectum Copulativum in 2 SM 7, 9–11," *CBQ* 23 (1961): 294–6.

[100] See Rezetko, *Source and Revision*, 250–51, for a demonstration of this phenomenon with respect to 2 Samuel 6.22.

it is more natural to read the verbs of vv. 9b-10 as *waw* consecutives. This results in a future translation.[101]

There are a number of other examples in the Hebrew Bible where there are similar constructions and the future tense is forced more decisively by the context.[102] A third solution is offered by Murray. He argues that a change from *wayyiqtol* to *weqatal* forms, without a change in syntax, indicates a shift to some sort of future reference. However, he suggests that the verbs are future relative to the previous verbs, not to the viewpoint of the writer. Thus the *weqatals* express the consequence of the previous *wayyiqtol* verbs but still take place in the past relative to the speaker and hearer.[103] This question cannot be decided until some consensus is reached on the Hebrew verb system and therefore we will take both translations into account in our reading.

Even if it is proved that these verbs refer to the past, there remains tension between chapter 8 and the statement of v. 1b. Furthermore, a second problem arises: if God has given rest in the past, why does he not permit the building of the temple, in light of Deut 12.10–11, which connects rest with Yahweh establishing his sanctuary? Gordon suggests that rest in this chapter is only relative.[104] An examination of relative rest in the context surrounding chapter 7 explains God's intervention concerning the temple, and highlights a number of other causes in the narrative.

Juxtaposition with chapter 8
Although the narrative in chapter 8 resumes the accounts of David's wars from chapter 5, chapter 7 marks a change in the nature of these wars. David's position in the military conflicts shifts markedly from the defensive to the offensive.

Prior to II Sam 7, David must defend himself against the direct threats of his enemies. In I Sam 30, the Amalekites burn David's base in Ziklag and take his wives, and so he attacks them in order to regain his own property. In I Sam 31, Israel is under attack from the Philis-

---

[101] A. Gelston, "A Note on II Samuel 7[10]," *ZAW* 84 (1972): 92–94.

[102] Examples in Samuel include I Sam 17.36 and I Sam 15.28.

[103] D.F. Murray, *Divine Prerogative and Royal Pretension: Pragmatics, Poetics and Polemics in a Narrative Sequence about David (2 Samuel 5.17–7.29)*, JSOTSup. 264 (Sheffield: Sheffield Academic Press, 1998), 181–82.

[104] Gordon, *1 & 2 Samuel*, 237.

tines and the threat is not overcome until II Sam 5 when David finally defeats the Philistines. The offensive nature of the Philistines' attack against David is highlighted in 5.17 when they specifically search out David (ויעלו כל־פלשתים לבקש את־דוד). In the civil war between Israel, led by Ish-bosheth, and Judah, led by David, the text implies that Israel leads the offensive against David. In II Sam 2.12, Abner goes out[105] to Gibeon and Joab and the servants of David meet him in response. Even David's victory over Ish-bosheth in II Sam 4 is the result of traitors within Ish-bosheth's camp and not because of offensive activity on behalf of David.

Therefore, the ark is brought to Jerusalem and David receives the oracle from Yahweh in the context of David's convincing defense and defeat against the Philistines in II Sam 5. These chapters mark a change in the type of military activity in which David engages. In the wars of chapters 8 and 10, David is in the offensive position and, rather than defending his own territory, he makes vassals and takes land. In 8.1 he takes territory from the hand of the Philistines and in 8.2 the Moabites become his vassals. In 8.3 he defeats the king of Zobah and subsequently the Syrians who come to give aid.[106] Finally in 8.14, he puts garrisons in Edom. In chapter 10, although David's men suffer humiliation at the hands of Ammon, according to vv. 8 and 14 the fighting takes place in Ammonite territory not Jerusalem.

Chapter 7 also alludes to this subtle change in military engagement. In 7.1, the Lord had given David rest from all the enemies *around him* (מסביב) whereas in 7.11, the phrase מכל־איביך ('from all of your enemies') is repeated (with the appropriate change of pronominal suffix) without any qualification that it is those enemies who are around. Unlike the *weqatals* in v. 10, there is consensus that the *weqatals* of v. 11 refer to the future (as they follow two *yiqtol* verbs) and so והניחתי לך מכל־איביך ('And I will give you rest from all of your enemies') uncontroversially refers to a promise for the future. David has partial

---

[105] See Anderson, *2 Samuel*, 42, who notes the military connotations of the verb יצא ('go out'). Cf. McCarter, *II Samuel*, 94. He suggests that this military move is in response to David's friendly words to Jabesh Gilead. However, despite David provoking the attack, the military manoeuvre itself is initiated by Abner's side.

[106] See McCarter, *II Samuel*, 247, who points out that Zobah is north of Jerusalem and so it must be David who is on his way to the Euphrates not Hadadezer. Again David is initiating the campaign.

rest because he is no longer in the defensive position. However, he still has enemies as he extends his kingdom into further reaching lands.[107]

Chapter 6 is almost the first chapter in the entire book of Samuel where military conflict is not mentioned and the stabilising activities of a king in power can take place. Chapter 7 continues to explore the period of stabilisation but it suggests that rest is not fully complete as it is not yet time to build the temple. David must fight offensively in order to stabilise his kingdom further. Therefore the change from defensive to offensive in chapter 8 recognises that some degree of rest has been reached but that rest is not yet complete.

An understanding of incomplete rest illuminates Yahweh's oracle in vv. 5–7. God's ark was housed in a tent in the *past* and the time of David is in continuity with that past. It is not yet time to progress to the future when a permanent house for God is required. The rest promised in Deut 12.10–11 is not yet complete. All of Yahweh's statements in vv. 6–7 assert that there was no need for a temple in the past. In v. 6 he refers specifically to the period from the exodus to David (העלתי את־בני ישראל ממצרים ועד היום הזה), thus associating the age of David with all that preceded him. There are no statements in this verse about God's attitude towards a temple in general, only statements specific to Israel's past.[108] This implies that David is part of that past. Yahweh considers the rest, which has been sought after since the exodus, as incomplete.

Yahweh and David's different points of view on rest are further explored in the chapter through wordplay on בית ('house'). Yahweh redefines the word in order to overturn David's proposal that he has obtained rest and it is now time to build a temple.

The narrative introduces the logic of a house for David before a house for God through David's periphrastic remark in v. 2. Rather than asking directly for a temple, he merely points out the contrast between his own living conditions in a house of cedar and the ark of God dwelling in a tent. David's house of cedar is a symbol of the rest

---

[107] Notice the similar use of 'surrounding enemies' in Josh 23.1 where the ensuing speech also suggests that all conflict has not now ceased.

[108] Bar-Efrat also observes that these are not fundamental reasons for not building a temple, but rather an indication that the time is not yet ready [Shimeon Bar-Efrat, *Das zweite Buch Samuel: Ein narratologisch-philologischer Kommentar*, trans. Johannes Klein, BWANT 181 (Stuttgart: Kohlhammer, 2009), 74].

that he has achieved, a connection established in v. 1 where David's house and his rest are mentioned side by side. Although David is not explicit, he implies that his house and rest ought to be followed by a house for the ark of God. Chapters 5–6 foreshadow this logic because they relate in close succession the building of David's house in chapter 5 and his attendance to the ark in chapter 6.[109]

God responds to David's logic, yet he redefines it with a different interpretation of בית ('house').[110] This key word unites the themes of the oracle because it is used as a pun for both the physical house of David and of God (v. 2, 5–7) and then also the dynastic house of David (vv. 11, 16). In v. 13a, both meanings fit the context. As Craig has noted on David's words in v. 2, בית is used to describe his own house but it is strikingly absent to describe God's temple.[111] It is only in the oracle that the wordplay is introduced and it is through the wordplay that two contrasts can be conveyed. In vv. 5–7, בית is used to describe God's house. It is coupled with the verb ישב and later described as בית ארזים ('house of cedar') to further reinforce the parallel with David's words in v. 2 about his own house. Thus Yahweh takes David's logic, that David has a house of cedar and therefore he will build one for God, and he uses it to show that David is concerned with the wrong sort of house.

---

[109] David's defeat of the Philistines is inserted between these two events. Thus there is a progression where David's internal enemies are defeated (i.e. Ish-bosheth) and he is anointed king, then he builds for himself a house, then he brings peace from Israel's number one external enemy and finally he turns to the question of the ark. The importance of settling the Philistine threat before attending to the ark is a precondition set up by the final form of the narrative in I Sam 4–5.

[110] Compare Kenneth M. Craig, Jr., "The Character(ization) of God in 2 Samuel 7:1–17," Semeia, 63 (1993): 163. Craig also studies the redefinition of בית and redirection of David's desires. However, he focuses on the redirection of David's desire from temple to dynasty rather than the redirection of David's logic from a literal house to a dynasty indicating that rest has arrived. This is another function of the wordplay that we will examine further shortly.

[111] Ibid. This wordplay (or lack of wordplay!) gives an added reason for David's round-about-way of raising the topic of building the temple. A third reason might also be to hint at David's uncertainty about whether the time is yet right, supported by his unusual application to a prophet where he might ordinarily act on his own instinct [see Craig, "The Character(ization) of God," 165].

The third meaning of בית, introduced in v. 11, conveys the type of house needed to achieve rest: a dynasty. Once David has a dynasty, then it will be time to build a literal house for Yahweh and the state of rest will be complete. Thus the word בית parallels God's house with David's house, and David's literal house with his dynasty. Replacing the meaning of David's words redirects his logic. Furthermore, the logic of the oracle in vv. 11–13 follows the same logic of David in v. 2, inserting a new meaning of house. David has a house in vv. 11–12 and therefore God will also have a house in v. 13. We will discuss later how this is also a reversal of David's assumption that his own dynasty will be established through the building of a temple. By God's logic, David's dynasty is necessary for rest and therefore precedes the building of the temple.

The subtleties of the logic of David and the Divine, yet with a new definition of בית, are enhanced when the full flexibility of the word is recognised in each of its occurrences. Whilst the primary meaning of the word in each of its contexts is relatively clear, its other possible meanings are conjured up secondarily with every use of the word.[112] Thus, each time the word בית is used, the contrast between David's idea of a physical house, and Yahweh's reinterpretation of a dynasty is reinforced. This is particularly relevant in v. 13a where the use of בית is most ambiguous and either 'dynasty' or 'temple' fit the context, although 'temple' is perhaps a little more likely.

Thus divine intervention in this chapter is founded upon the divine prerogative. David is taking the initiative to build a temple when the time is not yet right and Yahweh overturns David's proposal. He overturns it by denying the request and re-defining the concept of 'house'. Yahweh indirectly censures David's presumption in a manner reminiscent of the ark episode in II Sam 6. In that episode, David took initiative in bringing up the ark to Jerusalem but did not follow Yahweh's laws concerning the appropriate treatment of the ark[113] and Uzzah was struck down. David's kingdom must be established on Yahweh's terms.

---

[112] Cf. Mark K. George, "Fluid Stability in Second Samuel 7," *CBQ* 64 (2002): 24–25. He raises this point in order to show how later redactors were inspired to reinterpret the oracle in their new situation.

[113] Anderson, *2 Samuel*, 102.

This reading of causation also introduces a political dimension to the divine intervention. The theological reason that God does not want a temple is connected to the incomplete political change from instability to stability under David's leadership. David is still connected with the political institutions of the judges that were characterised by internal and external unrest and an impermanence that made a temple unsuitable. This is reinforced by the context of II Sam 7, which demonstrates that rest is not yet achieved because peace is not yet complete. Furthermore, wordplay in the chapter highlights that rest is also not achieved because David's dynasty is not yet established. We will now explore further the importance of David's dynasty for causation in this chapter.

b. *David and Dynasty*

David's second motivation for building a temple is to establish his dynasty on the throne of Israel. The shift from the theme of temple to dynasty has suggested to many scholars that the chapter is composed of a number of sources. Rost was amongst the first to question the chapter's unity.[114] He divided up the oracle by excising v. 13 from the earlier text of vv. 8–17 and assigning it to a later redactor because it reintroduces the topic of the temple in a section otherwise exclusively concerning David's dynasty. He then argued that in vv. 8–17, only v. 11b and v. 16 can be considered the oldest stratum because of their references to David's 'house'. These were overlaid by vv. 8–11a, 12, 14, 15 and 17. These verses are unified in form and probably also content, and were a commentary on the older layer.[115] He also considered vv. 1–7 (or perhaps two sources, vv. 1–4a and vv. 4b–7) to be an ancient substratum, which was added by the author of vv. 8–17 because of the use of the word 'house'.[116] Similar theories have been

---

[114] Apart from the shift in theme, Rost also noted that the ark is mentioned in v. 2 but not mentioned again. In vv. 5ff, a house is built for Yahweh to dwell in but in v. 13 it is built for his name. Finally, there is a new start in v. 8 as the oracle is reintroduced [Leonhard Rost, *The Succession to the Throne of David*, trans. Michael D. Rutter and David M. Gunn (Sheffield: Almond Press, 1982), 35].

[115] Ibid., 42–46.

[116] Ibid., 52–55.

proposed by McCarter,[117] Schniedewind,[118] McKane, Mettinger,[119] and Anderson.[120]

Despite these discontinuities and their implications, the final form has meaning in the context of the ancient connection between temple and dynasty.[121] Herrmann made a comparison between the oracle

---

[117] McCarter, *II Samuel*, 221–25, also follows the method of using "identifiable thematic inconsistencies" to indicate diverse materials and he finds similar results to Rost. He considers v. 13a to be a later device to join the ideas of two older sources in vv. 4b–7 and 8–17. However he also conjectures a chronological order for these two older sources. He speculates that the first document consisted of David's intention to build a temple (vv 1–4a) and God's promise of a dynasty in return. The purpose of this document was to sanction the building of the temple in the time of Solomon and to show that it had been conceived of by David and approved by God (v 3). The second, later, document was negative towards the building of the temple and there was no mention that David's son would eventually take on that task. This was a prophetic document which was more negative about the monarchy and therefore did not wish to link the promised dynasty with David's suggestion to build the temple. The final document was edited by the Deuteronomist who added Deuteronomistic language to various points of the narrative (vv 1b, 9b–11a, 16) as well as v. 13a to link the two previous documents.

[118] Schniedewind also suggests that there were two sources that were bound together by v. 13a, although he does not order the sources chronologically [William M. Schniedewind, *Society and the Promise to David: The Reception History of 2 Samuel 7:1–17* (New York: Oxford University Press, 1999), 84]. He also differs from McCarter in that he believes v. 13a is the only addition certainly made by the Deuteronomist.

[119] Both McKane and Mettinger suggest that the Deuteronomist combined two unrelated oracles [William McKane, *I & II Samuel: Introduction and Commentary*, TBC (London: S.C.M. Press, 1975), 217–19; Tryggve N.D. Mettinger, *King and Messiah: The Civil and Sacral Legitimation of the Israelite Kings* (Lund: CWK Gleerup, 1976), 52–55].

[120] Anderson, *2 Samuel*, 115, assigns the temple rejection to an early exilic date when the temple lay in ruins. The Deuteronomist later added v. 13a to make God's rejection of the temple only temporary.

[121] Unity in the final form of this chapter has also been argued because of the editorial work of the Deuteronomist. Indeed, McCarter, *II Samuel*, 221, points out that his source division is provisional because of the heavy influence of the Deuteronomist in this chapter. This view is shared in Frank Moore Cross, *Canaanite Myth and Hebrew Epic: Essays in the History of the Religion of Israel* (Cambridge, Mass.: Harvard University Press, 1973), 249, and Van Seters, *In Search of History*, 276. They each rely on the study in Dennis J. McCarthy, "2 Samuel 7 and the Structure of the Deuteronomic History," *JBL* 84 (1965): 131–8. McCarthy highlights the large quantity of Deuteronomistic language in the chapter. Van Seters believes this unity eliminates the arguments made for dividing the oracle into sources, in contrast to Cross who makes an attempt despite the acknowledged difficulties. Another argument for unity is proposed by Tsevat. He argues for the unity of v. 13a with vv. 13b–16 in two articles. In Matitiahu Tsevat, "Studies in the Book of Samuel III: The Steadfast House: What was David Promised in II Sam. 7:11b–16," *HUCA* 34 (1963): 71–82, he bases his argument on the nature of the covenant and considers vv. 13b–16 to be the gloss because they convey the sense of an unconditional covenant in the context of a conditional covenant and are thus likely to be later in date. In "The House of David in Nathan's Prophecy," *Bib*

and ancient Egyptian *Königsnovellen*, in which a king would typically impart to his court a plan (either divinely inspired or because of his own divinity) to embark on a building project.[122] Importantly, the purpose of building the temple is for the king to legitimate himself and his kingship.[123] An argument against this parallel is that the relationship between the Egyptian king and the god is so close as to make refusal unthinkable[124] and therefore it cannot be used to argue for the original unity of the oracle in II Sam 7. Parallels with Mesopotamian building inscriptions have been more convincing,[125] although the perspective of these inscriptions is from the king as opposed to II Sam 7, where the perspective is from God through Nathan. Therefore these parallels do not allow an exact comparison to be drawn and, once again, they do not prove the oracle's original unity. However, they draw attention to the close link between building a temple and the legitimation of the throne in the ancient Near East. A building programme of a house and temple had a propagandistic element according to the Egyptian *Königsnovelle*[126] and the accounts of pious building programmes in the Assyrian royal apologies. In turn, propaganda was a way of establishing a dynasty and so the two were closely connected.[127] Thus, within

---

46 (1965): 353–6, Tsevat looks at unity in the text between the oracle and the prayer. He concludes that v. 13a is needed for the prayer of David to make sense.

[122] Siegfried Herrmann, "Die Königsnovelle in Ägypten und in Israel," *Wissenschaftliche Zeitschrift der Karl-Marx-Universität* 3 (1953): 57ff.

[123] Ibid.: 51.

[124] Erckhard von Nordheim, "König und Tempel: Der Hintergrund des Tempelbauverbotes in 2 Samuel vii," *VT* 27 (1977): 438.

[125] For parallels where the building project is refused, see Tomoo Ishida, *The Royal Dynasties in Ancient Israel: A Study on the Formation and Development of Royal-Dynastic Ideology* (Berlin: Walter de Gruyter, 1977), 94; Michiko Ota, "A Note on 2 Sam 7," in *A Light unto My Path: Old Testament Studies in Honor of Jacob M. Myers*, ed. Howard N. Bream, Ralph D. Heim, and Carey A. Moore (Philadelphia: Temple University Press, 1974), 403–7; and Hurowitz, *I Have Built You an Exalted House*, 139–165.

[126] Herrmann, "Die Königsnovelle," 51, shows that the purpose of Egyptian *Königsnovellen* is legitimisation of kingship.

[127] Tadmor points out that, whilst it is normally assumed that autobiographies of Babylonian kings were typically written early, the apologies of the Assyrian kings were not written until long after the succession and therefore the purpose was unlikely to have been to justify the king against his opponents [H. Tadmor, "Autobiographical Apology in the Royal Assyrian Literature," in *History, Historiography and Interpretation*, ed. Hayim Tadmor and Moshe Weinfeld (Jerusalem: Magnes Press, 1983), 37]. Rather they were written in the context of the appointment of the successor. See also the building inscription of Nebuchadnezzar II [quoted in Ishida, *The Royal Dynasties*, 90] where the connection between building a temple and the desire for the establishment of a dynasty are also combined.

the final form of the oracle, the two ideas can relate coherently. Furthermore, their juxtaposition in a single oracle implies that dynasty was an unspoken motivation for David suggesting a temple.

Evidence for this motivation can also be found in the text surrounding II Sam 7. Murray, in a study of II Sam 5.17–7.29, traces the theme of David's desire to manipulate God to fulfill his own royal pretensions. He also identifies these pretensions in II Sam 7.1–3 before they are transformed into deference in the course of the chapter.[128] These pretensions are particularly focused on a dynasty. This is implied by the close connection between David building a house in 5.11 and the report of his acquisition of concubines and wives and the birth of his children in 5.13–15. These verses suggest a close link between building a literal house for David and building his family.

The story of Michal's disapproval of David dancing before the ark of the Lord is even closer in proximity to chapter 7. The precise meaning and significance of this story is unclear to commentators and many disagree about the rightness or wrongness of Michal's rebuke of David.[129] Laying aside this difficulty, an examination of David's words to Michal reveals a reason for the juxtaposition of the story with chapter 7: it establishes David's concern with dynasty, particularly in vv. 20–23.[130] This is first hinted by the use of בית as the subject of ברך in 6.20, a context which implies a meaning of 'household' primarily

---

[128] Murray, *Divine Prerogative*, 162–67.

[129] E.g. Anderson, *2 Samuel*, 107, suggests that Michal is proud in her disapproval and is therefore reminded by David that it is he who is king. Polzin on the other hand sees Michal's criticism as the Deuteronomist's own voice presenting dishonour alongside glory for the house of David [Robert M. Polzin, *Samuel and the Deuteronomist: A Literary Study of the Deuteronomic History; Part Three—II Samuel* (San Francisco: Harper and Row, 1993), 70–1]. See overview in Rezetko, *Source and Revision*, 274–76. Rezetko concludes that there is no reason in the story to side with Michal and therefore her rebuke ought not to be taken as carrying the authority of the narrator. Finally, Bar-Efrat, *Das zweite Buch Samuel*, 64, points out that Michal and David have different understandings of honour. Michal sees honour reflected in outward behaviour but David sees honour in faith. In light of the silence of the narrator, the text allows any of these evaluations. Based on the observation of Bar-Efrat, I would judge that David's faith is commendable but Michal has a valid rebuke that he needs to preserve his dignity in the demonstration of that faith. Murray, *Divine Prerogative*, 109–10, also suggests that David's actions in this section are doubtful for the reader.

[130] In addition to the reasons given below for understanding David's motivation for building a temple to be tied to his desire for a dynasty, see also C.L. Seow, *Myth, Drama and the Politics of David's Dance* (Atlanta: Scholars Press, 1989), 137–39. Many of the roots in this chapter are used in KTU 1.41 where Athirat complains Ba'al has no temple and El gives permission for one to be built.

but does not exclude a secondary meaning of his physical house. The double meaning of the word, which will be key to chapter 7, is thus introduced. Thematically this shows that David has turned to the affairs of his household and structurally it links the story closely with chapter 7 where the theme of בית is expanded upon. The thematic and structural link is explored further when בית is repeated in David's words to Michal in v. 21, לפני יהוה אשר בחר־בי מאביך ומכל־ביתו ('it was before the Lord who chose me over your father and his house'). This implies that David is conscious of the end of the house of Saul and even suggests that the reason for his celebration is that the Lord has established him as king instead of Saul. However, as בי ('me') in David's words indicate, it is only David himself who has been chosen by God. He is yet to receive a promise indicating that his descendents have also been chosen.

Michal's position as a descendant of the rejected house of Saul is also emphasised throughout the passage. Three times she is given the epithet בת־שאול ('the daughter of Saul')[131] to remind the reader of her association with Saul. Moreover, David's use of the second person pronominal suffix on מאביך ('over your father') stresses that it is Michal's own father who has been replaced and this is coupled with ומכל־ביתו ('and over all of his house') a phrase which includes Michal herself because of her relation to Saul.[132]

The themes of 'house' and Michal as the daughter of Saul add significance and profundity to the final verse of chapter 6. The text does not specify whether Michal has no more children because of David, herself, or the intervention of God.[133] The text could have been more specific on this point but instead remains ambiguous. This shifts attention from the reason for her childlessness—the punishment of David or God—and spotlights the end of hope for Saul's house.[134]

---

[131] Verses 16, 20 and 23. For a discussion of how a series of epithets can be used to provide subtle commentary in narrative, see Meir Sternberg, *The Poetics of Biblical Narrative: Ideological Literature and the Drama of Reading* (Bloomington: Indiana University Press, 1985), 476.

[132] The similarity of sound between וּמִכָּל ('and over all') and מִיכַל ('Michal') reinforces David's connection of Michal with Saul in this speech.

[133] See Rezetko, *Source and Revision*, 268–73, for a survey of views on this gap in the narrative.

[134] As observed in Bar-Efrat, *Das zweite Buch Samuel*, 65, there are two levels of meaning to Michal's barrenness—the personal conflict with David and political significance. A child of Michal would have been the only hope of uniting the two houses of Saul and David.

The juxtaposition of this verse, which reinforces the end of Saul's house, with David's proposal for another house in 7.2 is very suggestive. This is enhanced by the wordplay on בית begun in 6.20, connecting a literal house and a dynasty.

These arguments demonstrate that there was a close connection between temple and dynasty in ancient Near Eastern cultures and in the narrative of Samuel. The context of II Sam 6 raises dynasty as a possible motivation for David, a suspicion confirmed by the course of the oracle from Yahweh. After Yahweh has told David that he did not ask for a temple in vv. 5–7, he describes in vv. 8–11 all the ways he has looked/will look after Israel and David. In light of David's concern with dynasty, a new interpretation of Yahweh's speech emerges: David does not need to build a temple to secure God's blessing of stability and a dynasty, for God looked after David in the past and will continue to look after him in the future. With this introduction, the transition to God's promises about David's dynasty in vv. 11b–16 is smooth and logical. David will not build a house for Yahweh but Yahweh will build a house for David.

Again, wordplay on בית highlights God's reversal of David's proposal. בית is redefined to convey God's adjustment of David's logic that a physical house indicates that it is time for a temple. The second level to the wordplay is that it is not David who will build a temple (בית) for God, but God who will build a dynasty (בית) for David. This is the corollary to the first wordplay because if David needs a dynasty before a temple can be built, he needs God to grant him the dynasty.

The opposition of pronouns throughout the oracle reinforces the meaning of the double wordplay. Many commentators have observed that the emphasis in 7.5 is on אתה ('you') because it is the first word in the sentence. There are a number of other pronouns that the narrative puts in contrast with 'you' in the oracle.[135] אתה is placed in opposition to the 1st person pronominal suffix (referring to the Lord) לי ('to me') in v. 5. In v. 11b, this is reversed and the 2nd person is the object (לך) and 'the Lord' is the subject. Thus these pronouns show that it is not David who will build God a house but God who builds David a house, and this corresponds to the second level of wordplay on בית. However אתה in v. 5 is also counterbalanced by the third person pronoun הוא

---

[135] McCarter, *II Samuel*, 198, attributes each of these contrasts to different stages of the redaction of the chapter.

in v. 13a to indicate that it is not David who will build God a temple but God will build his dynasty. The implication is that David must have a dynasty before a temple is built.

Thus the wordplay brings unity to the two halves of the oracle, and to the two themes of rest and dynasty. Their dual importance to David's request for a temple is reflected in his own prayer of thanksgiving. David's prayer curiously does not mention the temple, despite this being the original starting point for the oracle. Instead, the thanksgiving is concerned with David's two motivations for building a temple. After his initial words of praise in vv. 18–22, he reviews how God has brought Israel 'rest' (albeit incomplete) in vv. 23–24 through reviewing the Deuteronomistic covenant that is fulfilled in the attainment of 'rest' in the land. There is a concentration of Deuteronomistic language in vv. 23–24 such as פדית ('you redeemed'), ותכונן לך את־עמך ישראל ('and you established for yourself as your people, Israel') and הגדולה ונראות ('great and awesome deeds').[136] The tie between Deuteronomic covenant theology and 'rest' theology is reinforced by reference to the land in v. 23 (לארצך).[137] After this, David's words turn to his dynasty in vv. 25–29 and he uses the word בית five more times, usually in close association with עבדך ('your servant'). In this way, David's prayer betrays each of his main concerns lying behind his initial statement in 7.2.

By examining David's motivations of rest and dynasty, we discover a complex causation in this chapter. Firstly, David's motivation of rest is unfounded as Yahweh does not yet consider the rest to be complete. From the point of view of external politics, David has many more offensive campaigns ahead of him, even though his defensive activities are completed. From the point of view of internal politics, David's dynasty is not yet established. Secondly, building a temple is not the appropriate method for establishing this dynasty. As a dynasty is required for rest to be achieved, it must logically come before the temple not as a result of it.

Finally, David's prayer demonstrates his acceptance of Yahweh's answer, thus making the divine causation effective. David has received the promise of a dynasty in the future and so he no longer needs to

---

[136] See Weinfeld, *Deuteronomy*, 236–330, for the identification of these phrases as Deuteronomic.

[137] Only in MT. I Chron 17.21 has לגרש ('to drive out') and LXX has similar.

build a temple for this purpose.[138] Furthermore, his battles against
various nations in II Sam 8 demonstrate a realisation that rest is not
complete. The divine causation, which incorporates political causation,
influences the king who turns to attaining rest rather than building a
temple.

2.4   CONCLUSION

Causation in Samuel is a complex combination of divine, personal,
public, political and social factors. A key way that causation is conveyed is the narrative alternation between equilibrium and imbalance.
The agents of change, which bring imbalance to equilibrium, and
equilibrium to imbalance, are each fundamental causes for the final
equilibrium state in the pericope. For example, Hannah's barrenness
is a cause for Samuel to enter service at Shiloh in I Sam 1 because it
brings about the initial imbalance in this pericope. In II Sam 7, divine
intervention resolves the imbalance of whether David should build a
temple and is thus a cause for David not to embark on this building
project.

Our study of I Sam 1 has demonstrated that the changes from equilibrium to imbalance and back to equilibrium are not always straightforward. In this chapter, the imbalances compound: first, Hannah cannot
have a child; and secondly she promises that if she does conceive, she
will take the child to Shiloh. Two imbalances incorporate two causes—
her physical inability and her personal piety—and they require two
agents of change to restore them to equilibrium—divine intervention
and, again, her personal piety. In this way the number of connected
causes that are integrated into the narrative are multiplied.

The narrative of I Sam 1 also highlights how patterns and intertextuality add depth and complexity to the historiography. A pattern,
such as the births of important figures to barren women, will probably
appear coincidental or artificial to a modern historian. However, the
book of Samuel uses this pattern to help the reader quickly grasp the

---

[138] Cf. Murray, *Divine Prerogative*, 244. He interprets David's prayer as humble
deference to Yahweh's role for the king. This reading is compatible with our analysis,
although on its own it underplays the importance of a dynasty for David as fulfilling
his royal pretensions. The promise of a dynasty is undeniably a good outcome for
David, even if it is not quite as David would have had it, nor does it fulfill all of his
pretensions.

nature and significance of the current situation. Moreover, variations from the pattern highlight uniqueness in the events. Similarly, Deuteronomistic language in II Sam 7 connects the concept of rest with the temple and there is another type scene of an unwilling leader in I Sam 9.

Our examination of I Sam 9–11 offers an example of how causation is developed over a number of pericopes. The narrative in 9.1–10.16 focuses on private causation and 10.17–11.13 is limited primarily to public causes. Between the two sections of narrative, causes from both the public and private spheres are thoroughly expounded. Each narrative gives an account of Saul's designation then confirmation, which are connected by the common conclusion of Saul's installation in 11.14–15. Thus, a structure of pericopes, rather than a linear narrative progression, can develop complex causation.

Finally, the pericope of II Sam 7 is dominated by a divine oracle that is a major cause for David not building the temple. However, there are also a number of literary devices that add complexity to this causation. The repetition of keywords such as 'house' and 'rest' draws attention to the surrounding chapters and these give context to David's proposal to build a temple. His political motives are revealed and therefore the political dimension to the divine causation. In particular, juxtaposition with David's victories in II Sam 8 introduces an irony into II Sam 7 which, in turn, gives greater significance to its details. The juxtaposition of apparently unrelated passages is also effectively used in I Sam 8–9 to create suspense about the eventual choice of Saul as king. Whereas modern historiography tends to prefer to make the connection between adjacent pericopes explicit, the biblical narrative exploits discontinuity to create complexity in the situations.

CHAPTER THREE

MEANING AND SIGNIFICANCE

Historiography conveys the meaning and significance of events in the past, regardless of whether it claims to be objective. Events without meaning or significance are reduced to a collection of trivial details with little value for recording. It is not disputed that the book of Samuel conveys some sort of meaning. Its acceptance into the canon of Jewish and Christian scripture and its usefulness as an insight into ancient Israel has ensured that the book is considered a significant work. However, 'meaning and significance' are broad terms and it is not evident that Samuel conveys meaning and significance in a way comparable to modern historiography. A survey of some modern studies of historiography reveals two general senses of 'meaning and significance' in history: significance of the events for the course of history and significance of the events for the present day. We will look at each of these in turn and examine if, and how, the book of Samuel conveys such meaning and significance.

Meaning and significance for the course of history

In modern philosophies of historiography, there is a consensus that information about the past must be given context, order and be related together in order to constitute historiography.[1] For example, the meaning of David's anointing in I Sam 16 is dependent upon the context of Israel's request for a king, Samuel's role as kingmaker and God's rejection of Saul in the preceding narrative. It garners greater significance through subsequent events, such as the conflict between Saul and David and the eventual installation of David on the throne of Israel. Without this context, David's anointing is a random event in the past, which holds little interest in isolation.

---

[1] E.g. C.L. Becker, *Detachment and the Writing of History* (New York: Cornell University Press, 1967), 54–55; W.H. Walsh, "'Meaning' in History," in *Theories of History*, ed. Patrick Gardiner (New York: The Free Press, 1959), 297; John Tosh, *The Pursuit of History: Aims, Methods and New Directions in the Study of Modern History*, 3rd ed. (Harlow: Longman, 1999), 91.

In modern historiography, direct comments from the historian usually explain the significance of events,[2] but there is also a recognition that narrative can be used for this purpose. As Hayden White writes, "The narrative figurates the body of events that serves as its primary referent and transforms these events into intimations of patterns of meaning that any literal representation of them as facts could never produce."[3] Berkhofer conceptualises the process of transforming history into narrative as 'emplotment'. Narrative gives shape and patterning to events in the past that would otherwise be floating around in the empty space of time. By patterning events in what he calls the "presumably empty vessel of physical time," the historian is able "to give message and meaning to the (hi)story."[4] In the historiography of Samuel, there is a much greater reliance on narrative techniques than on explicit statements for conveying meaning and significance.

One way that events are given connection in history is through causation. However, when discussing meaning and significance, the emphasis is usually on consequences rather than causes. Ged Martin, in his discussion of significance in history writes, "Events become historically significant if we can reasonably assume that a markedly different outcome was plausible."[5] He is examining a 'counter-factual' approach where the historian hypothesises about what might have happened if that event had not occurred. Although he highlights the scope for inaccuracy with this method, it is illustrative of the need for details in history to have ramifications for the course of future events in order to be considered important. By examining causation, we also indirectly looked at consequences, as one is the reciprocal of the other.

The connection between events in a work of history can extend beyond this narrative cause and effect. Tosh differentiates between 'background causes' and 'direct causes'. He explains, "the former operate over the long term and place the event in question on the agenda of history, so to speak; the latter put the outcome into effect,

---

[2] See the examples in Marvin Levich, "Interpretation in History: Or What Historians Do and Philosophers Say," *History and Theory* 24 (1985): 44–61.

[3] Hayden V. White, *The Content of the Form: Narrative Discourse and Historical Representation* (Baltimore: Johns Hopkins University Press, 1987), 45.

[4] Robert F. Berkhofer, *Beyond the Great Story: History as Text and Discourse* (Cambridge, Mass.: Belknap Press of Harvard University Press, 1995), 115.

[5] Ged Martin, *Past Futures: The Impossible Necessity of History* (Toronto: University of Toronto Press, 1996), 212.

often in a distinctive shape that no one could have foreseen."[6] Often
background causes offer a more profound or accurate description of
the significance of history because they highlight connections that
transcend sequential or cumulative causal chains.

As Tosh explores these background causes further, he describes
the inadequacy of narrative for conveying this type of analysis. He
writes:

> Narrative is entirely inimical to this pattern of enquiry. It can keep no
> more than two or three threads going at once, so that only a few causes
> or results will be made apparent. Moreover, these are not likely to be the
> most significant ones, being associated with the sequence of day-to-day
> events rather than long-term structural factors.[7]

By structural factors he is referring to sociological, anthropological,
geographical, meteorological and other factors such as propounded in
the approach of Braudel and the *Annales* school. Whilst Tosh's specific
cross-disciplinary and scientific causes are not present in the book of
Samuel, comparable structures of meaning can be identified that place
the events of Samuel "on the agenda of history."

The first structures of meaning that we will look at in this section
are two points where the normal rules of narrative are broken: at
the beginning and end of Samuel. Both of these sections use poetry
alongside prose and contain explicit but generalised theological statements. Furthermore, the concluding four chapters of Samuel break the
approximate chronological adherence of the rest of the book and so
offer a view of the history that is not confined to the strict sequence
of events in the past.

Another way in which Samuel transcends sequential causation is
through the structure of the book as a whole. Structure provides a
framework through which all the different sections, pericopes and even
details of the text are connected. One possible structure of Samuel is
the repetitive pattern of the rise and fall of leaders. The cyclical nature
of this repetition suggests that history repeats itself and therefore its
message can be extrapolated beyond the events related in the book. The
patterns are created and underscored in the book through a number
of descriptive details. Therefore, these details gain significance through
their connection with the book's structural framework.

---

[6] Tosh, *The Pursuit of History*, 96.
[7] Ibid., 97.

Finally, as we search Samuel for significance, it will become evident that there is not only one meaning for episodes, events and details in the text. Just as events have many causes, they also have many consequences, and so their connections with the surrounding history are numerous.

This is illustrated through an example: the description of David in I Sam 16.12, והוא אדמוני עם יפה עינים וטוב ראי ('And he was ruddy with beautiful eyes and handsome appearance'). On one level this statement has no causal relevance to the story.[8] However, considering David's central role in the story, this extraneous material is justified as the reader searches for any additional information that will help interpret this enigmatic character. It may be a sign of divine favour[9] or an explanation for David's charismatic appeal. However, this is not the only significance of the description. A second arises through the context of I Sam 16. Earlier in v. 7, the Lord said to Samuel that he does not look on appearance but rather at the heart of a man, a statement which is recalled by the use of a noun based on the root ראה in both verses. It suggests the significance that, unusually, David bears both an attractive appearance and a heart that is pleasing to God.[10] Yet another level is added by comparison with the description of Saul's appearance in I Sam 9.2. This time the two verses are linked by the word טוב ('good'), used to describe appearance in each. From a positive angle David is attractive like Saul but, in addition, he has a heart pleasing to God. From a more negative angle, the description places David in parallel with Saul and so foreshadows his later failures. Finally, the use of טוב recalls I Sam 15.28 where Samuel says the Lord has taken the kingdom from Saul and given it to one הטוב ממך ('who is better than you'). Thus, this description further highlights David's superiority to Saul.[11] In these ways, many points of connection are created by the statement and the literary devices used within it: the personality of

---

[8] See Shimeon Bar-Efrat, *Narrative Art in the Bible*, JSOTSup. 70 (Sheffield: Almond Press, 1989), 50. He cites this as one of the few examples where a person's appearance is given but it does not have relevance to the plot.

[9] Robert P. Gordon, *1 & 2 Samuel: A Commentary* (Exeter: Paternoster, 1986), 151.

[10] See for example Walter Brueggemann, *First and Second Samuel*, Interpretation (Louisville: John Knox Press, 1990), 122–3, "What is valued and sought is a right heart, not appearance and stature. Yet David is handsome...Samuel and the narrator are dazzled."

[11] Meir Sternberg, *The Poetics of Biblical Narrative: Ideological Literature and the Drama of Reading* (Bloomington: Indiana University Press, 1985), 356.

David, his replacement of Saul, his later failure and his strengths as a charismatic leader. There are many layers of significance in this one small detail and, as we will see in this study, there are many layers of significance in the historiography as a whole.

Meaning and significance for the present

A second type of meaning and significance in modern philosophies of history is the relevance of the past for the present. This relevance may be as straightforward as a direct continuity between past events and the present. Tosh describes the significance of the application of steam power to cotton spinning as its contribution to the industrial revolution that has in turn directly shaped our modern economy and society. Significance, he says, is how we got from then to now.[12] Often this significance is closely linked with the significance of the events to the course of history, except that the present is included implicitly or explicitly in that course. However, there are also more subtle ways in which the past can be relevant, some of which are listed by Rüsen:

> It may be the realm of accumulated experiences without which no human orientation in real life is possible. It may 'teach' a lesson about the modes and consequences of human behavior. It may be a powerful tradition of life form. It may horrify people and push them into promising future-perspectives (or into the compulsion of repetition). It may be felt as a loss that is agonising to those who feel committed to it.[13]

In these ways, historiography relates themes that are important to the present as well as the past.

History can have significance for a nation in a more specific way by reflecting on that nation's identity. As George, inspired by Hayden White, writes:

> Histories are one way by which communities and nations construct their self-understandings and identities. Particular historical events are included in a community's history because those events are interpreted as significant (and therefore paradigmatic) in that community's history (and thus in its self-understanding or identity).[14]

---

[12] Tosh, *The Pursuit of History*, 8.
[13] Jörn Rüsen, "Introduction: What does 'Making Sense of History' Mean?," in *Meaning and Representation in History*, ed. Jörn Rüsen (New York: Berghahn Books, 2006), 2.
[14] Mark K. George, "Constructing Identity in 1 Samuel 17," *Interpretation* 7 (1999): 389–90.

Thus, he suggests, in the story of David and Goliath, each opponent metaphorically embodies their nation and the course of events reflects the cultural values of the historian's community.[15]

As we search for this type of significance in the book of Samuel, we encounter the problem that we do not know who the intended audience of the historiography was and, therefore, we are reduced to speculation about what the relevance of Samuel may have been to them. However, if we look for 'universal' themes of significance throughout Samuel, we can establish with some degree of certainty that these themes would also have been relevant for an intended audience. Furthermore, we assume that most readers of Samuel until the Christian era were a part of the Jewish community and so direct historical connection or identity building for that nation can be taken into account.

The meanings and significance in Samuel

There can be many meanings and aspects of significance for the book of Samuel, not a sole interpretation that should be argued for exclusively. Indeed, there are as many meanings and aspects of significance in the book as there are themes or points of wide ranging impact.[16] Many of these meanings may be unintentional or unconscious for the author(s)/editor(s) but together, in the final form, they contribute towards this work of historiography's significance.

Although we cannot posit one 'meaning' for the book of Samuel, we can place the many different meanings into one of three categories: political, theological or human significance. These categories allow us to discuss the relevance of the meanings for an intended audience. The demise of the era of the Judges and the rise of the monarchy forms an important political link in the Deuteronomistic history that extends to the exile and so would have held self-evident significance for any later Jewish community interested in the origins of their current political situation.[17] Secondly, theological meaning in the text is relevant for

---

[15] Ibid.: 390–94.

[16] Works worth reading have so many possible themes that you cannot announce just *one*, according to Wayne C. Booth, *The Rhetoric of Fiction* (Chicago: University of Chicago Press, 1961), 73.

[17] The self-evident nature of the political significance of Samuel is attested by the number of commentators who point to the rise of the monarchy as the book's key theme. See Brueggemann, *First and Second Samuel*, 1; Joyce G. Baldwin, *1 and 2 Samuel: An Introduction and Commentary*, Tyndale Old Testament Commentaries

all readers with religious belief in Yahweh and so this common belief connects the past and the present.[18] Finally, the text raises a number of themes about the 'character' of human leadership over Israel, which has significance both for the course of history and for the future. In many cases, the personal actions and decisions of Saul and David can be interpreted as moral lessons of how it is appropriate to conduct oneself in this position. Furthermore, the interest in biographies of political leaders, which continues in our day, further reinforces the significance that human nature obtains from such stories. Tosh writes:

> The rise and fall of statesmen and of nations or empires lends itself to dramatic treatment in the grand manner. Political power is intoxicating, and for those who cannot exercise it themselves, the next best thing is to enjoy it vicariously in the pages of a Clarendon or a Guicciardini.[19]

As we look at devices for conveying significance in Samuel, these three categories of meaning will constantly recur. They are also deeply interconnected as the example of the transition to monarchy will demonstrate. This change has political significance because it is the beginning of a new political system; theological significance because it is a result of Israel's rejection of Yahweh as their king; and human significance as the transition to a large degree hinges on the personalities of Saul and David. Rather than being discrete, independent categories demanded by the text, they organise our analysis of the innumerable meanings that could be identified in the text.

Techniques in Samuel for conveying meaning and significance

With these understandings of meaning and significance, we will now examine if and how they are conveyed in the book of Samuel. Despite the obvious significance that the book of Samuel has held for many

---

(Leicester: Inter-Varsity Press, 1988), 15; and Georg Fohrer, *Introduction to the Old Testament*, trans. David Green (London: S.P.C.K., 1970), 216.

[18] An example of this type of significance identified by commentators is that the book answers the question of why God rejected Saul but chose David. See Brueggemann, *First and Second Samuel*, 2, and D.M. Gunn, *The Fate of King Saul: An Interpretation of a Biblical Story*, JSOTSup. 14 (Sheffield: JSOT Press, 1980). Also McKane in a slight variation, sees this theological question as a preparation for the political significance that David's throne is established in the succession narrative [William McKane, *I & II Samuel: Introduction and Commentary*, TBC (London: S.C.M. Press, 1975), 29–31].

[19] Tosh, *The Pursuit of History*, 72.

generations of people, we do not assume that there is meaning and
significance derived from history in the sense in which modern histo-
riographers conceive of meaning.

The most basic way in which the book of Samuel conveys meaning
is through themes in the narrative. There are certain subjects, such
as the wayward sons of leaders or the threat of the Philistines, which
recur throughout the book. By continually revisiting these subjects, a
theme is developed where each occurrence gains significance through
its connection with the others. Often, themes are highlighted in the
text through the association of a *Leitwort* or motif. For example, the
root 'to anoint' (משׁח) appears many times throughout the book but
is concentrated around the narratives concerning Yahweh's choice of
Saul then David as king. Thus, the appearance of the word is associated with the divine selection of leaders and draws attention to this
theme by its repetition. An absent *Leitwort* can also draw attention to
a theme. In the story of Ishbosheth, he is not anointed by either God
or Israel and his kingship comes to a swift end. In the narrative of
Absalom, the word is used once when he has died and the subject of
the verb is conspicuously not the Divine (II Sam 19.11; ואבשׁלום אשׁר
משׁחנו מת במלחמה). The king must be the Lord's 'anointed' in order
to rule over Israel. Motifs[20] of objects also draw attention to themes in
the narrative. For example, the transfer of clothing is used repetitively
as symbolic of the transition of the kingdom from Saul to David.[21] The
motif of heart and eyes throughout the beginning of I Samuel highlights a theme about the qualities appropriate in a leader of Israel.[22]

Additionally, the book of Samuel contains a number of *structures*
of meaning that highlight the important themes and their intercon-
nections. They organise the multiple themes in the book and offer a
framework through which the significance of the whole work can be
understood. The structures of meaning and significance that we will
examine in this chapter are: the beginning and the end of the book; the

---

[20] H. Porter Abbott, *The Cambridge Introduction to Narrative*, 2nd ed. (Cambridge:
Cambridge University Press, 2008), 237, defines motifs as, "A discrete thing, image, or
phrase that is repeated in a narrative."

[21] E.g. I Sam 15.27–26, 17.38, 18.4, 24.4–11. For a study on the symbolic use of
clothing in Samuel, see O. Horn Prouser, "Suited to the Throne: The Symbolic Use of
Clothing in the David and Saul Narratives," *JSOT* 71 (1996): 27–37.

[22] Diana Edelman, *King Saul in the Historiography of Judah*, JSOT Supp. 121
(Sheffield: JSOT Press, 1991), 193.

pattern of the rise and fall of leaders; and comparative analogies. Each of these structures of meaning incorporate a large number of literary devices, so that the reader's attention is drawn to the structures and their significance is conveyed effectively. These literary devices include juxtaposition, repetition, motifs, poetry and ruptures in the narrative.

These structures of meaning incorporate many themes and offer a sophisticated exposition of the significance of the book. Yet, this exposition is through narrative devices, not explicit statements. We will see that a key feature of this mode of exposition in Samuel is that the structures of meaning are built upon the smallest details in the text. Conversely, the smallest details of the text have meaning because they contribute to the structures and therefore are related to the course of history and have relevance for the present.

3.1 The Beginning and End of Samuel

The book of Samuel is framed by two sections that lie outside of the main line of narrative in some way. The book opens with the story of the birth of Samuel and focuses on the emotional plight of his mother Hannah. Although this pericope is connected to the ongoing story line of Eli's, then Samuel's, leadership, the centrality of the woman Hannah sets the story apart from what follows. The only other mention of Hannah in the book is I Sam 2.18–21, and the plot of I Sam 1.1–28 is not dependent on any events surrounding it. Moreover, the shift to poetic form in the song of Hannah in 2.1–10 further distinguishes the opening story of Samuel. In a similar way, the book concludes with a collection of stories and poetry that are distinctive within the narrative. II Sam 21–24 breaks the chronological progress of the book in favour of a chiastic structure that spans an indefinite period of time. In this study we will explore, not only how these sections link thematically with the rest of the narrative, but also how they generalise the themes to give a simplified, abstract and concise presentation of the overall significance of the book. They create a structure of meaning because they introduce and conclude the thematic connections that unite the book.

Scholarship in the past has tended to focus on the separate origins of the beginning and end of Samuel, rather than their roles in introducing and summarising the themes of the book. The story of Samuel's birth is thought to have originally belonged to Saul because of the wordplay on his name.[23] It is also thought that Hannah's song has been artificially attributed to Hannah and inserted into the narrative at a later date.[24] There are a number of reasons for this supposition. McCarter highlights the anachronistic reference to the monarchy in 2.10,[25] and Hertzberg observes that 2.11 joins seamlessly with 1.28, giving the song the appearance of an insertion.[26] The subject matter of the song is largely unrelated to the story, because the only overlap is in 2.5 where Hannah refers to the barren bearing children. Furthermore, Hannah mentions seven children born to the barren whereas she herself has only six in 2.21.[27] Klein suggests the subject matter is unsuitable for a mother who has just given birth to her first child because it centres on the male-dominated sphere of warfare.[28]

Some of these points of disconnection can be explained.[29] Hannah's six children are not relevant because at the point in the story where Hannah sings the song, she has only had *one* child. It is more likely that the number seven holds a symbolic value of completion and fullness. Concerning Hannah's victory song, Watts demonstrates that the victory songs in Ex 15 and Jdg 5 are all in the mouths of women and are similar to I Sam 2. I Sam 18.6 also reveals that the tradition of victory songs was within the sphere of women.[30] Thus the poetry is disconnected rather than discordant with the immediate narrative.

Scholars have also questioned whether the conclusion of the book in II Sam 21–24 belongs in its present context. The six sections in these chapters break the chronology of the story of David and belong

---

[23] See chapter 2: Causation, pp. 48–49.

[24] Note also that Hannah's song is inserted in a different position in the MT, LXX[B] and 4QSam[a]. Watts argues that this and other small textual variations are a stronger argument for the later insertion of the song than the disconnections [James W. Watts, *Psalm and Story: Inset Hymns in Hebrew Narrative*, JSOTSup 139. (Sheffield, England: JSOT Press, 1992), 34–37]. However, the disconnections are more relevant for our current study of the final form.

[25] P. Kyle McCarter, Jr., *I Samuel*, The Anchor Bible (New York: Doubleday, 1980), 75.

[26] Hans Wilhelm Hertzberg, *I & II Samuel: A Commentary*, trans. John Stephen Bowden, OTL (London: S.C.M. Press, 1964), 29.

[27] E.g. Ralph W. Klein, *1 Samuel*, WBC (Waco: Word Books, 1983), 14.

[28] Ibid.

[29] Cf. J.P. Fokkelman, *Vow and Desire*, Vol. IV of *Narrative Art and Poetry in the Books of Samuel: A Full Interpretation Based on Stylistic and Structural Analyses* (Assen: Van Gorcum, 1993), 108. He suggests that the song was especially composed for this point in the narrative.

[30] Watts, *Psalm and Story*, 29. Note that Watts still considers it likely that the song of Hannah was a later addition despite his refutation of this point.

to different points in the period from Saul's reign (21.1) to David's last words (23.1). The different labels that have been attached to these chapters illustrate the different attitudes towards them. Scholars who believe they are a group of traditions disconnected from the main story line and purpose of the book have called the conclusion a 'conglomeration', 'miscellany', 'repository',[31] or 'appendices'.[32] Others, who find more coherence with the rest of the book, have termed it a 'coda',[33] 'special collection'[34] or more simply, the Samuel 'conclusion'.[35]

Although many consider II Sam 21–24 a collection of miscellaneous material, there is almost universal agreement that the pericopes are arranged in the form of a chiasm.[36] The first and last pericopes,

---

[31] P. Kyle McCarter, Jr., *II Samuel*, The Anchor Bible (New York: Double Day, 1984), 16.

[32] E.g. S.R. Driver, *Notes on the Hebrew text and the Topography of the Books of Samuel*, 2nd ed. (Oxford: Clarendon Press, 1966), 349, Hertzberg, *I & II Samuel*, 380, and A.A. Anderson, *2 Samuel*, WBC (Waco: Word Books, 1989), 248, among others. Driver, *Books of Samuel*, 349, writes that, because the appendix interrupts the continuous narrative of II Sam 9–20, I Kings 1–2, it must have been placed in its current position after the division of the books. However McCarter, *II Samuel*, 17, argues that it appears in the same position in LXX[L] where the division of books is between I Kings 2 and 3 and so it must have been placed there before the division. It is on this basis that McCarter asserts that the conclusion cannot be called an appendix.

[33] D.M. Gunn and Danna Nolan Fewell, *Narrative in the Hebrew Bible* (Oxford: Oxford University Press, 1993), 120–28.

[34] Antony F. Campbell, *2 Samuel*, FOTL (Grand Rapids: Eerdmans, 2005), 185.

[35] Herbert H. Klement, *II Samuel 21–24. Context, Structure and Meaning in the Samuel Conclusion* (Frankfurt am Main: Peter Lang, 2000). See also pp. 18–19, where he discusses the derogatory remarks made by other scholars concerning the Samuel conclusion. It is Klement's term that will be used here.

[36] However, it has been suggested that the chiasm was not intentional. Budde first proposed that 21.1–14 and 24.1–25 were initially placed at the close of the narrative as miscellaneous traditions. 21.1–14 was given this position because it was once a part of the succession narrative and 24.1–25 because of its connection to 21.1–14 expressed in 24.1. These two stories were then divided to insert the hero lists, which were in turn divided to insert the two poems [Karl Budde, *Die Bücher Samuel* (Tübingen: J.C.B. Mohr, 1902), 304]. In contrast, Carlson considers all six sections to have been inserted by the Deuteronomists. He suggests that the sections in 22.1–23.7, which are more positive towards David, were deliberately included to balance out the negative depiction of him in 21.1–14 and 24.1–25 [R.A. Carlson, *David, the Chosen King* (Stockhom: Almqist & Wiksell, 1964), 194–259]. Many scholars broadly agree with Budde's formulation but make some modifications. Hertzberg disagrees that 21.1–14 was once a part of the SN and reasons that it was a tradition known to the SN writer but not included by him. Otherwise the story would have been inserted before II Sam 9 and 16, which presuppose it. Furthermore, 21.1–14 and 24.1–25 were divided because 24.1–25 supplies the etiological legend for the location of the temple and so was placed as close as possible to the report of David's death [Hertzberg, *I & II Samuel*, 381, 416]. Both McCarter, *II Samuel*, 18, and Anderson, *2 Samuel*, 282, suggest that 21.1–14 was placed in its present position in order to answer Shimei's charge

21.1–14 and 24.1–25, are narratives about disasters affecting the people of Israel; 21.15–22 and 23.8–39 are lists of men and deeds with minimal narrative explanation; and 22.1–51 and 23.1–7 form the poetic core of the ring structure. Many scholars find a purpose or design, apart from diachronic accident, in placing this collection of stories at the end of Samuel. They have therefore demonstrated the conclusion's internal unity and numerous connections with the rest of Samuel.[37] In our study of the final form, these studies will be useful for showing how the conclusion conveys the themes and meaning of the preceding narratives.

Links with the rest of Samuel

The links between I Sam 1–2, II Sam 21–24, and the rest of the book of Samuel are so numerous and have been explored by enough scholars that only a summary will be offered here. Some of the most prominent links are between the poetry of I Sam 2 and II Sam 22.

---

against David in chapter 20. McCarter (p. 19) points out that it is more difficult to explain why the poetry was inserted in between the two lists and concludes, "the four units in 21:15–23:39 accumulated in random fashion after all."

[37] Gordon calls it "purposeful symmetry" which links David's success to Yahweh's patronage. This is an appropriate summation of David's life before the depiction of his old age in I Kings 1–2 [Gordon, *1 & 2 Samuel*, 45.]. Campbell also points to a number of characteristics that unify the stories, such as their concern with David, their neutral tone and unexpected themes. Therefore, although the stories remain a collection of miscellaneous material, they have been given a unity through their selection and placement in their current position [Campbell, *2 Samuel*, 185]. Polzin perceives both literary art and incoherencies. He highlights the artistic use of the numbers three and seven throughout the stories, but also believes that there are a number of features which cannot be explained [Robert M Polzin, *Samuel and the Deuteronomist: A Literary Study of the Deuteronomic History; Part Three—II Samuel* (San Francisco: Harper and Row, 1993), 208–09]. Klement, drawing on the work of Brueggemann, finds intentionality in the chiastic structure in II Sam 21–24, and proposes that it is an intentional contrast to another chiastic structure in II Sam 5–8 [Walter Brueggemann, "2 Samuel 21–24: An Appendix of Deconstruction?," *CBQ* 50 (1988): 383–97; Klement, *II Samuel 21–24*, 69]. He then expands on Brueggemann's work by suggesting that the entire book of Samuel can be divided into a series of chiasms. See the table in Klement, *II Samuel 21–24*, 157–59. Whilst Klement's work identifies a number of very helpful parallels when looking for these structures, in the words of one reviewer, "one may wonder whether there is not a tendency sometimes to discover chiasmus when it is not really there." [J.R. Porter, "Review of 'Second Samuel 21–24: Context, Structure and Meaning in the Samuel Conclusion'," *JSOT* 94 (2001): 67].

There are numerous key words overlapping between the two poems to create linguistic links. Simon lists 36 verbal links[38] and Fokkelman points out that therefore 40 of the 114 words in Hannah's song are also found in II Sam 22.[39] One such word is צור ('rock') in I Sam 2.2, also found in II Sam 22.3, 32 and 47 (twice). Moreover II Sam 22.2 uses a synonym, סלעי ('my rock'), establishing the theme of Yahweh as David's rock, at the beginning of the poem. Praise of Yahweh is prevalent throughout both poems and is the foundation for all their themes. As each poet is raised from a lowly position, he/she continually returns to God as the source of this salvation.

Furthermore, there are a number of words in the first verse of I Sam 2 that are also found in the opening verses of II Sam 22: קרן ('horn') in 22.3; איב ('enemy') in 22.4; and ישע ('to save') occurring three times in 22.3. Thus both poems open with the theme that God is the source of salvation over enemies. There is also striking similarity in the conclusions of the poems. They each have successive cola ending with מלכו ('his king') then למשיחו ('his anointed')[40] and they reflect on God's faithfulness to the king.[41]

Another common theme is reversal. In Hannah's song, the reversal of the powerful with the humble is conveyed as a series of opposites placed in both chiastic and parallel structures. For example, in v. 4, there is a chiasm of words with strong and weak semantic fields:

קשת גברים חתים
ונכשלים אזרו חיל

('the bows of the mighty become broken; but the weak bind on strength'). The pair of lines is balanced by the use of two words at beginning and end to describe strength (קשת גברים and אזרו חיל) circling the juxtaposition of single words each describing weakness (חתים and ונכשלים). This chiastic pattern is continued throughout v. 5 until v. 6 and v. 7 where weakness and strength are used in parallel

---

[38] László T. Simon, *Identity and Identification: An Exegetical and Theological Study of 2Sam 21–24* (Rome: Gregorian University Press, 2000), 247–48. See also Watts, *Psalm and Story*, 23, for a list of common words.

[39] J.P. Fokkelman, *Throne and City*, Vol. III of *Narrative Art and Poetry in the Books of Samuel: A Full Interpretation Based on Stylistic and Structural Analyses* (Assen: Van Gorcum, 1990), 254. The root רום is used three times and קרן twice in I Sam 2, giving a total of 40 words overlap.

[40] Fokkelman, *Vow and Desire*, 106, calls this a rhyming word pair.

[41] Paul Borgman, *David, Saul, and God: Rediscovering an Ancient Story* (Oxford: Oxford University Press, 2008), 194; Gordon, *1 & 2 Samuel*, 309.

and, finally, v. 8 is devoted to the reversal of fortune only for the poor. The poem in II Sam 22 has only one instance of a reversal in a chiastic pattern in 22.28. Similarly, there is a strength word and weakness word then weakness word and strength word:

ואת עם עני תושיע
ועיניך על רמים תשפיל

('An afflicted people you save; but your eyes are upon the proud you bring low'). There is a minor difference in structure as 22.28 reverses the order of the uplifting of the low and the humbling of the proud. Nevertheless, the chiastic word order of strength and weakness remains the same as in I Sam 2.4–7.

Although there is only one verse in II Sam 22 that contains a full reversal of the humble and mighty, there are many other verses that address the exaltation of David at the expense of his enemies (esp. 22.39–43) and the general exaltation of God. The significance of this overlap is illustrated by the series of key words relating to the concept of 'high', רום, גבה and עלה, which recur throughout I Sam 2, and the repetition of two of these words throughout II Sam 22.[42]

A final dominant theme in each poem is triumph and strength. Hannah's triumph is expressed in the first lines of her song:

עלץ לבי ביהוה
רמה קרני ביהוה

('My heart exalts in the Lord; My horn is lifted high because of the Lord'), and the song as a whole is often interpreted as a victory song. Although David's song begins with praise, he does not immediately address his own victory but gradually develops the theme from v. 17 until it reaches a crescendo in vv. 38–43. Whereas Hannah mocks her enemies in II Sam 2.1b, David pulverises them into dust in II Sam 22.43.

Not only are there links between these two works of poetry, but also numerous links between I Sam 1–2, II Sam 21–24 and the rest of the

---

[42] רום in 22.28, 47 and 49. עלה in 22.9. See Fokkelman, *Vow and Desire*, 103, for a study of these key words.

book of Samuel. The sheer quantity of connections and the limitations of space allow us only to list them here.[43]

Even amongst scholars who believe Hannah's song is a later insertion, there is consensus that the themes in the song are highly relevant for the themes of the whole book.[44] Reversal and the exaltation of the meek recur throughout the book as Saul and David rise from obscurity to become the first two kings of Israel. Conversely, Saul's fall from kingship and his debilitating jealousy of David illustrate the humiliation of the strong.[45] Hannah's closing statements about God's blessing on the monarchy offer a fitting introduction to another main theme of the book—the plight of the monarchy.[46] Bodner suggests that the repetition of קֶרֶן ('horn') in vv. 1 and 10, and also in II Sam 22.3, encapsulates the main story of Samuel. Just as Hannah's poem progresses from her own exalted horn to the horn of the king, so the book as a whole will progress from a barren woman to the exultant poem of the king himself.[47] This theme can be traced further by the use of קֶרֶן ('horn') of oil in the story of David's anointing and its absence in Saul's anointing where a פַךְ ('flask/vial') is used instead.[48] The horn motif alludes to the success of the Davidic dynasty in Israel.

These two themes can also be found in I Sam 1, although less prominently than their explicit articulation in I Sam 2. The unlikely birth of Samuel from a previously barren woman renders his leadership as unlikely as that of Saul or David. Furthermore, according to Polzin, there is a parallel between Hannah's request for a son and Israel's request for a king in I Sam 8.[49] Whilst Polzin's assertion that the story ideologically comments on Israel's request may not be evident for all

---

[43] See Klement, *II Samuel 21–24*, 165–227, for a more detailed study of connections between the Samuel conclusion and rest of the book of Samuel.

[44] E.g. McCarter, *I Samuel*, 76; Klein, *1 Samuel*, 14.

[45] Fokkelman, *Vow and Desire*, 110; Watts, *Psalm and Story*, 28; McCarter, *I Samuel*, 76.

[46] Watts, *Psalm and Story*, 22; Klein, *1 Samuel*, 14.

[47] Keith Bodner, *1 Samuel: A Narrative Commentary* (Sheffield: Sheffield Phoenix Press, 2008), 27–29.

[48] Cf. Ibid., 92–93. Bodner suggests that it is ominous that Saul is not anointed by a horn, particularly as Jehu is the only other king anointed with a vial.

[49] Robert M. Polzin, *Samuel and the Deuteronomist: A Literary Study of the Deuteronomic History; Part Two—I Samuel* (San Francisco: Harper and Row, 1989), 25.

readers, some attention is drawn to the parallel by the repeated use of the root שאל, which is a wordplay on the name Saul.[50]

The six sections of II Sam 21–24 yield numerous connections with their preceding narrative through both theme and motif. Klement and Noll[51] have each demonstrated ways in which the Samuel conclusion develops the theme of God's choice of David over Saul. Among the most explicit, are the narrative introduction to David's song in II Sam 22.1 and the slaughter of Saul's sons on account of Saul's bloodguilt in II Sam 21. Noll also draws a number of parallels and contrasts with David's song in II Sam 1 where he laments the death of Saul and Jonathan. Much of the vocabulary used in II Sam 1 to describe the loss of Saul and Jonathan is used in II Sam 22 to describe what David has gained. For example, Saul's shield was rejected on the heights in II Sam 1.19, 21 but Yahweh has become David's shield who places him on the heights (II Sam 22.31, 34, 36).[52] Thus these contrasts highlight that God took away the kingship from Saul and gave it to David.

Linked with Yahweh's choice of David, is his protection of David in battle throughout Samuel. This continues from the commencement of David's military career against Goliath until his final battle against Absalom. David's success through Yahweh is expressed explicitly in II Sam 22 and implicitly through the success of his mighty men in II Sam 21.15–21 and 23.8–39. Noll considers 22.44bα, תשמרני לראש גוים ('you have watched over me as a head of nations'), to be an allusion to God's protection of David in his relationship with King Achish in I Sam 27–29.[53] Moreover, in II Sam 22.7 David's distress (צר) links to I Sam 25.29 and II Sam 1.26 where the word צר is also used.[54]

Another connection, which draws attention to a positive aspect of David, is the loyalty of his men in II Sam 23.13–17. Klement describes the men's act of devotion and David's concern for their lives as exemplifying the relationship between David and his heroes.[55] The men's devotion is reminiscent of the loyalty to David from a number of

---

[50] See also Bodner, *1 Samuel*, 11–12. He comments that the frequency of this root indirectly introduces Saul.

[51] Klement, *II Samuel 21–24*, 165–66; K.L. Noll, *The Faces of David* (Sheffield: Sheffield Academic Press, 1997), 143–46.

[52] Noll, *The Faces of David*, 146.

[53] Ibid., 147.

[54] Polzin, *David and the Deuteronomist*, 205. He also mentions the link to another part of the Samuel conclusion in II Sam 24.23.

[55] Klement, *II Samuel 21–24*, 193–94.

different people throughout the story. In I Sam 19–20, Michal and Jonathan are devoted to David even against the wishes of their father; Joab is willing to commit murder for David in II Sam 11; and Hushai, Zadok and Abiathar, and Barzillai demonstrate loyalty as David flees Jerusalem in II Sam 15–17. However, David's concern for his men's lives is not a consistent theme in Samuel. Joab's rebuke of David in 19.1–8 is only a few chapters previous to the Samuel conclusion. Joab accuses David of excessive grief for a single rebellious son and neglect of the servants who saved his life and kingship. The narrator verifies this rebuke with the report in 18.7 that twenty thousand men of Israel died in the battle. In this context, David's act of pouring out the drink as an offering to God is an admirable expression of his concern for his men but also recalls his disregard for previous acts of kindness. The mention of Uriah in 23.39 and David's sin and need for repentance in chapter 24 also allude to negative aspects of David's character.

Finally, the references to David's house in II Sam 23.5 and to the site of the temple, the threshing floor of Araunah, in II Sam 24 recall the promise to David of a dynasty and temple in II Sam 7.[56] They are a reminder that David's successor and a permanent sanctuary for Yahweh are not yet established.

In addition to thematic links, there are also a number of motifs throughout Samuel that are completed in the Samuel conclusion. The lamp of Israel, first mentioned in I Sam 3.3, recurs in II Sam 21.17 to refer to God and in 22.29 to refer to David.[57] David's vocabulary in II Sam 22.2–3, צור ('rock'), סלע ('rock') and מצדה ('stronghold') are all also used of David's hiding places from Saul in I Sam 22.4–5, 23.25, 28 and 24.2, 23. In each of these stories, David's righteousness is a key theme, drawing another link with II Sam 22.25.[58] Klement traces a number of other motifs throughout Samuel such as famine and hunger (II Sam 21),[59] death of offspring (II Sam 21)[60] and thunder (II Sam 22.14).[61]

---

[56] Ibid., 184; Watts, *Psalm and Story*, 104–05.
[57] Klement, *II Samuel 21–24*, 188.
[58] Watts, *Psalm and Story*, 105, who cites E. Slomovic, 'Towards an Understanding of the Formation of Historical Titles in the Book of Psalms', *ZAW* 91 (1971), 368.
[59] Klement, *II Samuel 21–24*, 167.
[60] Ibid., 180.
[61] Ibid., 203–04.

Even this brief survey of the connections illustrates the saturation of links between I Sam 1–2, II Sam 21–24 and the body of the book of Samuel.

Another connection, which requires some justification, is the characterisation of David. Many scholars have understood the characterisation of David in this section as either solely positive or solely negative and therefore at variance with the complexity of David in the rest of the book. On one hand, there are those who consider the chiasm to be an attempt to legitimise David after the negative events described in the succession narrative. Whedbee identifies a number of modes of legitimisation in these chapters such as military conquest, diplomatic recognition and prophetic revelation.[62] On the other hand, a number of scholars have pointed out that, despite a generally positive presentation of David in the conclusion, there are certain points that undermine the whole and cast a shadow upon him.[63] In a similar vein, Brueggemann describes the conclusion as a 'deconstruction' of royal ideology, which acts as a counterbalance to the very positive account of David's rise to the throne in II Sam 5–8. Although David's image as a repentant sinner is maintained, the section also discredits David to some extent because it undermines the ideology of an infallible king.[64]

A reading of the stories in these chapters in isolation from the preceding narratives suggests that they are neutral or ambivalent about David's character, whilst the psalms are overwhelmingly positive.[65] However, in the context of the negative events in II Samuel, there are arguments in favour of a more cynical reading of the conclusion. The slaughter of potential rivals from the house of Saul in 21.1–14 is a convenient act for preventing challenges to his leadership. In 21.15–22 David is presented as a weary old king[66] and in 21.19 it is possible

---

[62] J. William Whedbee, "On Divine and Human Bonds: The Tragedy of the House of David," in *Canon, Theology and OT Interpretation*, ed. G.M. Tucker, D.L. Peterson, and R.R. Wilson (Philadelphia: Fortress, 1988), 162–63.

[63] Primarily Gunn and Fewell, *Narrative*, 120–28, and Robert M. Polzin, "Curses and Kings: A Reading of 2 Samuel 15–16," in *The New Literary Criticism and the Hebrew Bible*, ed. J. Cheryl Exum and David J.A. Clines (Sheffield: JSOT Press, 1993), 202–07.

[64] Brueggemann, "2 Samuel 21–24," 383–97.

[65] This is the judgment in Watts, *Psalm and Story*, 103, and Campbell, *2 Samuel*, 185. Cf. Robert Alter, *The David Story: A Translation with Commentary of 1 and 2 Samuel* (New York: W.W. Norton, 1999), 356. Alter finds David's character very flat by comparison with the rest of Samuel.

[66] Polzin, *David and the Deuteronomist*, 207.

that the narrative is undermining David's great victory over Goliath and attributing it to Elhanan.[67] David's claims to righteousness and divine favour in chapter 22–23 recall his sin in II Sam 11 and its consequences in II Sam 12–20.[68] The appearance of Uriah's name last in the list of 23.1–39 recalls David's sin and, finally, in chapter 24, a new failing of David is recounted as he conducts a census and is punished accordingly. These details in the narrative undermine a purely positive or legitimising reading of David in the conclusion. However they do not demand a completely negative reading either. Other negative points suggested by Brueggemann or Gunn and Fewell may occur to some readers but will not be revealed to all,[69] a subjectivity acknowledged by these scholars.[70]

Thus the conclusion of Gordon is most appropriate. He describes the Samuel conclusion as having a "familiar realism about the presentation of David as both saint and sinner."[71] The ambiguity of David, found throughout Samuel, is represented in the conclusion because he is both God's anointed and a man of many failings. The extent and seriousness of these failings are left for the individual reader to judge.[72] It is therefore unlikely that the Samuel conclusion is a final

---

[67] See chapter 5: Coherence and Contradictions, pp. 241–243.

[68] Polzin (p. 207) suggests that David's own statement in 22.28, that God will bring down the haughty, undermines his poem for the reader who remembers David's failings.

[69] For example, it is suggested in Gunn and Fewell, *Narrative*, 125, that the mention of David as a man of blood in 23.17 recalls the priests of Nob from I Sam 21–22, the murder of Uriah and the sons of Saul and that 23.24–39 is rich with allusions to the Bathsheba story with mentions of Eliam (her father), Nathan, Zobah and the Ammonites and Joab in addition to Uriah. An example in Brueggemann, "2 Samuel 21–24," 390, is that the list of the mighty men illustrates that David does not have the monopoly on greatness in the kingdom. This is a good example of Brueggemann's argument that the text is not necessarily deconstructing David's character but rather the royal ideology surrounding him.

[70] According to Brueggemann, "2 Samuel 21–24," 386, a suspicious reading is "not demanded exegetically." In Gunn and Fewell, *Narrative*, 123, there is also a reminder of the role of the individual reader in weighing up the evidence.

[71] Gordon, *1 & 2 Samuel*, 322.

[72] This view is also held by Klement, *II Samuel 21–24*, 228–29. Klement argues that, whilst David is not totally innocent, he is nevertheless chosen and favoured by God. Simon, *Identity and Identification*, 319, describes the 'kaleidescope' presentation of David and warns that the reader should not expect the ambiguities of David's character to be eliminated in this final section. Noll, *The Faces of David*, 120, describes the tension between the ideal David and his failings as being a tension between the viewpoint of the narrator and the implied author. Such a division between these entities is unnecessary in this case where they can be better understood as a complex whole.

attempt to legitimise David when the narrative of II Sam 11–20 depicts an anointed but flawed image of David. The complexity of David's character in the Samuel conclusion is a snapshot of the complexity developed over the course of the narrative. These final chapters capture both the positive and negative aspects of David and so present a summary of the character development in the whole book.

One of the foundational tensions in the book of Samuel is that Saul is rejected as king whilst David is forgiven for his sins. This tension is never resolved in the book and is often intensified by the sympathetic portrayal of Saul and the complex, often negative, portrayal of David.[73] Interestingly, the Samuel conclusion does not attempt to resolve this tension, as we might hope for in the conclusion to the book, but rather reinforces it. Firstly, the narrative in 21.1–14 provides further evidence for the finality of God's rejection of Saul and his house. His remaining descendants are slaughtered with the single exception of Mephibosheth, whose loyalty was ensured by David in II Sam 9. Furthermore, it is by the authority of Yahweh that the sins of Saul needed atoning (21.1) and the slaughter of his household proves effective. This echoes God's response to Saul's sin in I Sam 13 and 15, where he promises to take the kingdom away from Saul's house.

However, this story also contains elements that are sympathetic to Saul's family, such as those found in I Sam 13 and 15. The actions of the concubine Rizpah in the story highlight David's neglectful treatment of the bodies of Saul's sons, contrary to the Israelite law.[74] This adds to the complex picture of the weaknesses of David despite his replacement of Saul.

Yahweh's commitment to David despite his sin, and the contrast to the rejection of Saul, is expressed in chapter 24 of the Samuel conclusion. There are a number of parallels between the story of David in chapter 24 and the consequences of Saul's sin in chapter 21. In chapter 24, there is a disaster due to the sin of the king. Although the nature of David's sin is not made explicit, the parallel severity of punishment to Saul's sin in chapter 21 suggests that the sin is comparable.

---

[73] See Gunn, *The Fate of King Saul* for a full analyses of the rejection of Saul.

[74] See Deut 21.22–23. However, David's final actions are considered positive in Shimeon Bar-Efrat, *Das zweite Buch Samuel: Ein narratologisch-philologischer Kommentar*, trans. Johannes Klein, BWANT 181 (Stuttgart: Kohlhammer, 2009), 216–17. David retrieves the bones of Saul and Jonathan in addition to burying the most recently slaughtered sons.

Whereas Saul's sin was atoned for by the destruction of his house, Yahweh has mercy upon David and ceases the punishment of his own accord. Although David repents in v. 17 and offers a sacrifice according to the instructions of Gad, this pointedly follows Yahweh's prior decision to cease the punishment in v. 16. These two stories encapsulate the tension between Yahweh's destruction in response to Saul's sin and his mercy in response to David's sin.

Meaning and significance through I Sam 1–2

The significant thematic links between I Sam 1–2 and the rest of Samuel demonstrate how these chapters share in the thematic development of the book as a whole. The opening chapters introduce the main themes and provide a framework for understanding how the different parts of the proceeding narrative connect to one another. These chapters also establish the relevance of the ensuing history and show that it was worth recording. Many readers, it is expected, will not require much persuasion. I Sam 1.1 establishes that Elkanah was an Israelite through his homeland Ramathaim-zophim in Ephraim and his genealogy.[75] For a culture that understands theology through God's dealings with Israel, this introduction would be sufficient for many readers. However, it is not the only aspect of these stories that initiates the development of meaning in the history. There are more complex literary devices that, whether or not they intentionally have this effect, set a precedent for understanding the meanings of the book.

The first of these literary devices is the relative disconnection with the main plot of the book. This disconnection is not as great as that found between the Samuel conclusion and the book because I Sam 1–2 provides causation for the rise of the leader Samuel. However, there is a perceptible separation from what follows in the narrative. The prominent perspective in I Sam 1 belongs to Hannah and she is the common denominator to every scene in the story. There are details about her life and circumstances that play no future role in the story of the book of Samuel, giving the story some degree of independence from the rest of the book. I Sam 1.1–2.10 acts as an overture to the book

---

[75] Cf. Bodner, *1 Samuel*, 13. He suggests that the opening genealogy introduces themes such as sonship and succession in the narrative which will be developed later.

as a whole. It links thematically to the rest of the book but it is not as closely connected in plot as other more central stories in the book.

Polzin compares the beginning of Samuel to the 'synopsis' at the beginning of the book of Judges. He describes the entire book as answers to questions that are initiated in the first chapter.[76] In his analysis of the chapter Polzin suggests that Hannah's request for a son is intended to "introduce, foreshadow, and ideologically comment upon the story of Israel's request for a king."[77] Whilst Polzin makes a convincing case for the parallels between these two requests, an even more palpable parallel exists between God's sovereignty over Samuel's replacement of Eli and the succession of the other leaders throughout the book. This will be further discussed shortly.

Apart from disconnection, the other literary device used to introduce the significance of the ensuing narrative is poetry. Poetry makes concepts abstract and offers some of the few examples of explicit statements of meaning in the book. Furthermore, by conceptualising events in an abstract way, poetry has the ability to generalise experiences and make them appear timeless and universal.[78] This quality of poetry is relevant to I Sam 1.1–2.10. I Sam 1 tells a story of the reversal of a woman's fortune, from misery in her barrenness to joy at the birth of her child, and then the presentation of the child to Eli. The poem in 2.1–10 not only expresses Hannah's personal delight at God's role in her reversal of fortune,[79] but extends and generalises the reversal to become a theological paradigm. Hannah sings of an example similar to her own circumstances in 2.5, but she then extrapolates God's actions to many other spheres—the poor, the lowly and even the dead. Hannah's statements reverberate throughout the ensuing narratives, which do not contain explicit exposition of meaning.

In our survey of meaning and significance in history, we highlighted three categories of meaning in Samuel that can have relevance to future readers and are thus significant: politics, theology and the characters of leaders. All three of these categories appear within the microcosm of I Sam 1–2. Political change is alluded to by Hannah's anachronistic reference to the monarchy in 2.10. Furthermore, the service of Samuel,

---

[76] Polzin, *Samuel and the Deuteronomist*, 18.
[77] Ibid., 25.
[78] Similar comments concerning the poetry in II Sam 22 and 23 are made in Klement, *II Samuel 21–24*, 209, and Campbell, *2 Samuel*, 200.
[79] Hertzberg, *I & II Samuel*, 31.

a non-Levite, at the sanctuary at Shiloh implicitly points to the succession of leaders in Israel. Hannah's song effectively points to the role of Yahweh in the political change of Israel. As remarked above, the elevation of the lowly foreshadows the rise of Saul and David from obscurity; and the humiliation of the proud is reflected by the fall of Saul and David, although David's humiliation is not complete. Shortly in this chapter we will examine how the rise and fall of leaders is one of the governing structures of the book of Samuel. Hannah's song foreshadows this structure and establishes specifically that it is Yahweh who governs this process. Finally, the pious yet 'blind' character of the priest Eli in chapter 1 offers a glimpse of the complex characterisation of the leaders who form the structure of the book. Thus the dislocation of I Sam 1.1–2.10 from the ensuing narrative and the generalising medium of poetry establish the three major aspects of significance in Samuel. This introduction encourages the reader to follow these themes continually throughout the course of the book and offers a structure of meaning through which these themes can be understood.

Meaning and significance through II Sam 21–24

There are a number of ways in which II Sam 21–24 uses literary devices to highlight and summarise the main points of significance in the book. Firstly, the large number of thematic links listed above demonstrates how these themes are brought together and concluded very concisely in four chapters. The analyses of historical critical studies have also demonstrated the discontinuity between II Sam 21–24 and the preceding narrative in II Samuel. The primary cause for this disconnection is the chronological disruption between II Sam 20 and II Sam 21 and the lack of strict chronological order within the conclusion, in contrast to the linear progression of the rest of Samuel.[80]

The first effect of this disconnection is that it creates a bookend with I Sam 1–2. We have already seen how the introduction is separated from the rest of Samuel, although to a lesser extent than the Samuel conclusion. The link between this introduction and conclusion

---

[80] Cf. Klement, *II Samuel 21–24*, 97. He considers the whole of Samuel to be 'achronic', based on the structure of chiasms he identifies. Therefore they reflect an aspectual rather than linear view of history. Regardless, we observe that the break in linear chronology is more significantly pronounced in the conclusion as it leaps from David's last words in 23.1–7 to further narratives concerning his life in 23.8–24.25.

is strengthened by the large number of thematic connections between the poetry of I Sam 2.1–10 and II Sam 22. The bookends give the book a sense of completeness and reinforce theological and political significance through repetition.

Secondly, the chronological disruption between II Sam 20 and 21 gives the Samuel conclusion a degree of independence and introduces the achronic chiastic structure of the section. The chiastic structure incorporates a number of features that draw out the salient points of the preceding narrative. The paralleling of stories and lists in the rings of the chiasm highlights their points of comparison and the thematic development between them. Furthermore, a chiastic structure spotlights the centre which, in this case, is the poetry of 22.1–23.7. Poetry conveys timeless and universal statements of meaning and is an appropriate focus for this structure of significance.

An examination of the three areas of significance described earlier—political change, theological meaning and the characters of leaders—illustrates the ways in which these features of the Samuel conclusion come together. Firstly, the political changes of Samuel are summarised in these chapters. Although the progression from Eli to Samuel to Saul is not mentioned, the relationship between Saul and David is reviewed in chapters 21 and 22. Saul's failures are recalled in 21.1 through the reference to his bloodguilt for killing the Gibeonites. Although this incident is not mentioned elsewhere, it recalls the slaughter of the priests at Nob in I Sam 22 and possibly also his frequent attempts to kill the young David. Paradoxically it recalls his *not* putting to death the Amalekite king in I Sam 15, the pivotal point in Saul's kingship. Bloodguilt of one sort or another was a central part of Saul's life.

Furthermore, the slaughter of Saul's sons in II Sam 21 reinforces the end of Saul's dynasty and the transfer of kingship to David. Mephibosheth and the reference to David's covenant with Jonathan recalls the loyalty of Jonathan to David over his father in I Sam 20, another source of torment for Saul in rivalry with David. Finally, the psalm of II Sam 22 is set at a time when Yahweh delivered David from the hand of Saul (II Sam 22.1). This context allows the general statements of the poetry to be explicitly applied to Saul's relationship with David and draws out the theological implications of the succession. Yahweh defeated Saul in favour of David.

A second aspect of political change reflected in the Samuel conclusion is the shift from external to internal threats. This shift was analysed in the study of II Sam 7 and the surrounding narrative in our previous chapter. Here it is conveyed through the use of the ring structure. The stories of David and the Gibeonites and David and the census have much in common—there is a disaster averted by some sort of placation. These similarities are accentuated by the structure of the conclusion. Furthermore, the structure emphasises the development between the two stories. Whilst the first is concerned with finalising Israel's peace with its neighbours, the second only presents strife between Yahweh and Israel.[81] Indeed, the census in the second story highlights the vast extent of Israel's territory by the laborious details of place names in 24.5–7. Presumably one of the overtones of taking a census was military intent[82] of an offensive kind, which is in contrast to David's defensive appeasement of the Gibeonites in order to relieve the famine.

Another aspect of political advance throughout the reign of David, reflected in the Samuel conclusion, is the development of an organised state. The arrival of the ark in Jerusalem, the construction of David's palace and his efficient victories in II Sam 8 all describe a developed nation in contrast to Saul's strategy of sending parts of an ox around Israel in I Sam 11 to rally support. The development is conveyed through the ring structure of the chiasm with parallel lists in 21.15–22 and 23.8–39. In 21.15–22 the heroes are all victors in single combat against giants and there is no reference to a larger army. However in 23.8–39, the list of men is more extensive and is organised into units with three high commanders.

A final political change in the book of Samuel is the founding of David's dynasty, particularly in contrast to the end of Saul's. The second poem at the focus of the chiasm, II Sam 23.5, affirms God's covenant with David from II Sam 7. It is possible that the story of Araunah's threshing floor is an allusion to the future temple, although this is not made explicit in the text.

Theological meaning and the characters of leaders are closely intertwined in this section. We have already discussed the ambiguity about

---

[81] Although, as observed in Bar-Efrat, *Das zweite Buch Samuel*, 214, David also receives help from a foreigner, Araunah the Jebusite, in II Sam 24. However, in this story, David legally purchases the threshing floor in contrast to chapter 21 where the enemies need to be placated.

[82] Brueggemann, "2 Samuel 21–24," 392–3; Gordon, *1 & 2 Samuel*, 316; Klement, *II Samuel 21–24*, 177.

whether David is presented positively or negatively in the Samuel conclusion. His own words in 22.1–23.7 present him in the most positive
light whereas the remaining stories are more ambiguous or neutral.
The attitude of Yahweh is also mixed towards David. At the centre of
the chiasm, there are expressions of Yahweh's unfailing commitment
to David but the outlying stories in 21 and 24 involve punishment on
his kingdom. This reflects a tension found throughout Samuel that,
whilst Yahweh has favoured David over Saul and promised him a
dynasty, he demands obedience from him and will not withhold punishment. In the course of the book of Samuel, this theological significance is most explicit in II Sam 12 where God punishes David for his
sin but does not take away his rule as he did to Saul. It is also reflected
in the structure of David's rise through Yahweh's patronage, followed
by suffering and punishment in II Sam 13–20 as his family suffers the
consequences of his sin. Finally, the structure of the chiasm highlights
the theological conundrum that God rejects Saul but makes promises
to David, despite their parallel sins.[83]

3.2 PATTERNS

A key aspect of 'making sense' of the past is to find patterns in it. The
structure of history is a pattern or series of patterns that determine
the nature of the whole.[84] Thus, an overarching pattern connects all the
elements of the history and gives them significance. The patterns of
history in Samuel are not stated explicitly but are conveyed though the
patterns of the narrative itself. We have already observed the framing
structure of the book created by its beginning and ending. However,
as the book structure is implicit, it is possible that there are a number

---

[83] Cf. Alter, *The David Story*, 353. Alter believes the theology of chapter 24 to be
very different from the rest of Samuel. He writes, "The God of this story has the look
of acting arbitrarily, exacting terrible human costs in order to be placated." However,
Alter underplays the 'sinfulness' of holding a census and unnecessarily concludes that
there is "no discernable reason for God's fury against Israel." Furthermore, whilst he
may be justified in asserting that God's punishment is arbitrary to some extent, this
theological theme reverberates throughout the book of Samuel, particularly in the
comparison between David and Saul.

[84] Michael Stanford, *An Introduction to the Philosophy of History* (Malden: Blackwell, 1998), 81.

of structures that could feasibly be discerned.[85] One we will study here has a large number of other literary devices that all point to its prominence. This particular book structure is the parallel rise and fall of four leaders: Eli, Samuel, Saul and David.[86]

The focus on their leadership covers the entire book of Samuel with the questionable exception of the ark narrative in I Sam 4.2–7.2, which pertains to the mistakes of Eli and prepares for the deliverance by Samuel. Thus, every episode can be related to the leadership of one of these four men. Furthermore, the plot draws many similarities between the four men as they start their leadership, are rejected by God, then overlap with the next leader before their authority is passed on. The parallel is broken when David, despite falling from grace, is not rejected as the others were. The break from the pattern also highlights a circumstance of great significance.

However, the parallels extend beyond a basic similarity of events and there are a large number of details that highlight and deepen the comparisons. Many of these details are not very significant within the accounts of events themselves, but they find significance through their contribution to the overall book structure. Let us now look at the structure of parallels in detail and examine the devices that enhance its representation.

The choice of Samuel, Saul and David

The first parallel in the stories of Samuel, Saul and David is that they are each divinely chosen. The stories of the selection and anointing of Saul and David in I Sam 9–10 and I Sam 16.1–13 respectively contain the most parallels but there are also a number of similarities between their anointing and the call of Samuel in I Sam 3. These parallels are evoked through the presence of identical or similar plot points, which are developed through devices such as repeated word motifs and the similar narrative construction of the episodes.

---

[85] For example, for a structure of the reign of Saul, see W. Lee Humphreys, "The Tragedy of King Saul: A Study of the Structure of 1 Samuel 9–31," *JSOT* 6 (1978): 18–27.

[86] This pattern is also identified in Shimeon Bar-Efrat, *Das erste Buch Samuel: Ein narratologisch-philologischer Kommentar*, trans. Johannes Klein, BWANT 176 (Stuttgart: Kohlhammer, 2007), 11–13.

In all three narratives, the leader is appointed in juxtaposition with the rejection or displacement of the previous leader of Israel.[87] I Sam 3 opens immediately after the oracle to Eli, which foretells the downfall of his house because of the corruption of his sons. Saul's journey towards Samuel in I Sam 9 begins in juxtaposition with I Sam 8 where the people of Israel request a king because of the corruption of Samuel's sons (8.5). The anointing of David takes place in the chapter after Yahweh's final rejection of Saul. The verse immediately preceding the story of David's anointing states, ויהוה נחם כי המליך את שאול על ישראל (15.35; 'And the Lord regretted that he made Saul king over Israel').

Although the selection of each leader takes place immediately after the divine rejection of his predecessor, the actual leadership of Israel is not transferred until some time afterwards. Samuel does not take a public leadership role until I Sam 7.3; Samuel does not formally depart from leadership until I Sam 12, three chapters after he has anointed Saul; and David has a very long struggle for the throne that extends until II Sam 5. The private anointing takes place a significant period of time before there is public recognition of the new king.[88] The successions of the leaders are described in an overlapping structure, which allows scope for direct comparisons between the leader who is in decline and the leader who is rising to power.

Secondly, the divine choice of the leader is emphasised in a number of parallel ways throughout the passages, particularly through the explicit mention of divine intervention and the use of Yahweh's direct speech. In Samuel, divine speech occurs almost exclusively in passages where leaders are chosen and where they are rejected or chastised (Eli in I Sam 2.1–36, Samuel in I Sam 8, Saul in I Sam 15 and David in II Sam 12), making its appearance more significant and the parallel across the passages more pronounced.[89] Divine speech is repeated throughout I Sam 3 where Yahweh literally calls out to Samuel. Yahweh is not explicit that Samuel will replace Eli as leader of Israel but the repetition of his judgment upon Eli's house and the sending of his 'word' to Samuel, which according to v. 1 was rare, strongly implies

---

[87] As Garsiel puts it, "the setting of one star takes place as the next one rises" [Moshe Garsiel, *Biblical Names: A Literary Study of Midrashic Derivations and Puns* (Ramat Gan: Bar-Ilan University Press, 1991), 109].

[88] See chapter 2: Causation, pp. 63–72, for a detailed study of Saul's private and public accession to kingship.

[89] A significant exception occurs in II Sam 7.

that Samuel will replace Eli. In 9.16–17, Saul is selected through divine speech and this is confirmed by lots in 10.22–23. Yahweh also explicitly chooses David in 16.12. The act of anointing with oil by Samuel in both of these stories (10.1, 16.13) and the inevitable resemblance of the phrases ויקח שמואל את פך השמן (10.1; 'And Samuel took the flask of oil') and ויקח שמואל את קרן השמן (16.13; 'And Samuel took the horn of oil') adds to these parallels.

Furthermore, each of the leaders is given a passive role in the stories of their selection. The repetition of the root בחר ('to choose'), occurring in the early part of the stories of Saul[90] and David,[91] emphasises that these men were not volunteers for their new roles. The root is used to describe the men being chosen by God (10.24 and 16.8, 9, 10), chosen by the people (12.13 and 17.8) and for Saul, chosen in an abstract sense (9.2). Added to their status as 'chosen', all three leaders are depicted as young men. Samuel is explicitly called הנער ('the young man'[92]) in I Sam 3.1. Saul's youth is implied throughout 9.1–10.16 by the introduction of his father Kish who is still alive and by Saul's task of searching for his father's lost donkeys. David is referred to in I Sam 16.11 as הקטן ('the smallest') among הנערים ('the young men'). Along with other aspects of their passivity, the image of each leader's youth suggests a certain naivety as they are swept along by the selection process.

Another parallel, which contributes to this theme, is that all three leaders are given instructions by other people when they are chosen. Samuel is given instructions by Eli in 3.9, Saul receives advice from his servant in 9.6 and again from Samuel in 9.19–20, 27, and David must be called in from the sheep at the instruction of Samuel in 16.11–12.

---

[90] I Sam 9.2, 10.24 and 12.13.

[91] I Sam 16.8, 9, 10 and 17.8.

[92] נער is frequently translated as 'young man' but the range of ages that it can refer to is broad. According to Ludwig Koehler et al., *The Hebrew and Aramaic Lexicon of the Old Testament* (Leiden: E.J. Brill, 1994), (hereafter HALOT), the term can span from a lad or adolescent [Francis Brown, S.R. Driver, and Charles A. Briggs, "A Hebrew and English Lexicon of the Old Testament," (Massachusetts: Hendrickson, 2005),—even 'infant'] to a servant or attendant who presumably could be a fully-grown male adult. [See also John Macdonald, "The Status and Role of the *na'ar* in Israelite Society," *JNES* 35 (1976): 147–70, who argues it refers to a servant of high social status; and Hans-Peter Stähli, *Knabe-Jüngling-Knecht: Untersuchungen zum Begriff* נער *im Alten Testament* (Frankfurt am Main: Peter Lang, 1978), especially pp. 99–100, who concludes that it refers to the social status of dependant]. However, coupled with Samuel's behaviour in the rest of I Sam 3 where he continually runs to Eli to ask for directions, it seems that connotations of youth are intended here.

However, before each of the leaders is given instructions by other men, the narrative reveals that God has already chosen them. God has called to Samuel three times before Eli realises that Samuel must respond to Yahweh's voice. Samuel receives a revelation in 9.16–17 to inform him that God has settled on Saul as his choice. Finally Yahweh demonstrates his prior selection of David through his instructions to Samuel to go to Jesse in 16.1, followed by his rejection of Jesse's older sons in 16.6–10.[93]

Another similarity between the selections of Saul and David is the use of suspense in the narratives. Suspense is created in I Sam 3.4 by Yahweh's mysterious call to Samuel and is sustained by Samuel's repeated misunderstanding. As Eslinger observes, the audience is set on edge with the question, "Will Yahweh abandon the attempt to communicate with the duteous but obtuse Samuel?"[94] Tension is established in I Sam 8 when Israel asks for a king, which is then juxtaposed with the introduction of the young Saul in 9.1–2. Saul's journey is filled with hints about his meeting with Samuel (for example, his arrival in Zuph) and delays, which hinder the fulfillment of this meeting (for example, his lack of gift to bring the seer in 9.7).[95] Finally, it is established in 16.1 that the next king will come from among the sons of Jesse, yet the rejection of each successive son raises tension in the audience. This is further heightened in 16.11–12 as the audience waits with the household for the mysterious youngest son to appear.[96] The name of David is not revealed until after he is anointed in v. 13. The parallel use of suspense in these narratives highlights each leader's lack of knowledge before his selection. Furthermore, it generates a similar emotion in the reader each time. The repetition of apprehension and anticipation reminds the audience of the earlier moments in the narrative where they also felt this emotion. This, in turn, emphasises the cyclic nature of the rise and fall of each leader.

---

[93] The parallel between Saul and David in this regard is noted in Brueggemann, *First and Second Samuel*, 121. He writes, "In both cases, the new ruler is by the intention of God, not by historical accident or political stratagem."

[94] Lyle M. Eslinger, *Kingship of God in Crisis: A Close Reading of 1 Samuel 1–12* (Decatur: Almond Press, 1985), 150.

[95] For a detailed study of suspense in I Sam 9, see Rachelle Gilmour, "Suspense and Anticipation in I Sam. 9:1–14," *JHS* (2009).

[96] Brueggemann, *First and Second Samuel*, 122. He points particularly to the three-fold use of the phrase 'not choose' in combination with 'reject' to build suspense.

The parallels between the stories of these three leaders continue immediately after their selection. Firstly, the spirit Yahweh rushes upon both Saul and David following their anointing. The same root צלח ('to rush') is used in both 10.10 and 16.13, although the constructions are slightly different. There is no mention of the spirit coming upon Samuel, although the phrase in 3.19, ויהוה היה עמו ('And the Lord was with him') immediately following his selection story, similarly establishes God's presence with him. Following each of these accounts, the threat of the Philistines looms in 4.1, 13.3–4 and 17.1, although Saul also proved himself against the Ammonites in 11.1–11. The outstanding military victories of Saul and David in 11.1–11 and 17.1–54 confirm their designation as king in parallel ways. Thus, each king progresses through a lengthy process of designation and confirmation before their coronation and final acclamation as king.[97]

Finally, there are a number of other minor parallels between the stories, particularly between Saul and David, which create a sense of repetition.[98] In the stories of David and Saul, the anointing is associated with a sacrificial meal. Surprise is expressed at the choice of both Saul and David as Saul is from the smallest of tribes (9.21) and David is the youngest of his family. Neither of them is present during the selection process. Saul is on his journey when God speaks to Samuel in I Sam 9 and he is also hiding in the baggage when the selection takes place again in 10.22. David is with the sheep as Samuel surveys his older brothers. The signs, which are spoken of after Saul's anointing in 10.2–6, include the donkeys, bread, wine, a kid and the lyre and these items are echoed in 16.20–23 when David brings offerings to Saul carried by a donkey and containing bread, wine, a kid, and he then plays the lyre. Both men come to the attention of the previous leader through the intervention of a servant (נער). In 9.6, Saul's servant suggests he visits Samuel and, in 16.18, Saul's servant recommends David as court musician.[99] Both David and Saul are 'despised' (בזה) early in their careers in 10.27 and

---

[97] See chapter 2: Causation, pp. 69–72, on the pattern of designation, confirmation and coronation in these narratives.

[98] The following similarities are listed in Moshe Garsiel, *The First Book of Samuel: A Literary Study of Comparative Structures, Analogies and Parallels* (Ramat-Gan: Revivim, 1985), 114.

[99] Bar-Efrat, *Das erste Buch Samuel*, 231.

17.42.[100] Enquiries are made about each of their fathers in 10.12 and 17.55–58.[101]

We have observed the similarity between the suspense of the selection process in 9.1–10.16 and 16.1–13, but there are also many similarities between the public selection of Saul in 10.17–27 and the selection of David. First Mettinger and later McCarter have observed that the 'yes' and 'no' process of eliminating Jesse's sons in 16.1–13 is reminiscent of the casting of lots used to narrow down the tribe, family and person of Saul in 10.17–27.[102] Although these scholars use this similarity to argue for the dependency of 10.17–27 on 16.1–13, it is also significant from a literary point of view as the slow process of 16.1–13 recalls 10.17–27.

Parallels not only point to similarities between the two leaders but also highlight the differences. One such difference between Saul and David, which is made explicit in the text, is their appearance. Saul's appearance is described very favourably in 9.2, בחור וטוב ואין איש מבני ישראל טוב ממנו משכמו ומעלה גבה מכל העם ('he was choice and handsome and there was no one from Israel more handsome than he; from his shoulders and upward he was taller than all the people'). His impressive height is mentioned again in 10.23, ויגבה מכל העם משכמו ומעלה ('And he was taller than all the people from his shoulders upward'). Although it never states explicitly that the people were attracted to Saul's impressive height and looks, the juxtaposition of their support for the king in 10.24 with a reminder of Saul's height in v. 23 suggests that it was a factor. When David is anointed, an explicit statement is made in 16.7 that Yahweh is not looking for someone with an impressive outward appearance or height. In particular, there is repetition of the word גבה ('height'), which was earlier used in reference to Saul. Later in the pericope in 16.12, David's appearance is also described favourably and the adjective טוב recalls the earlier description of Saul. Yet this parallel is broken by the notable absence of the word גבה ('height') to describe David. The parallel makes the difference more conspicuous. David's smaller stature and youth are

---

[100] Bodner, *1 Samuel*, 186.
[101] A. Graeme Auld, "1 and 2 Samuel," in *Eerdmans Commentary on the Bible*, ed. James D.G. Dunn (Grand Rapids: Eerdmans, 2003), 223.
[102] Tryggve N.D. Mettinger, *King and Messiah: The Civil and Sacral Legitimation of the Israelite Kings* (Lund: CWK Gleerup, 1976), 176; McCarter, *I Samuel*, 277.

later of crucial importance[103] to the story of I Sam 17 where David's youth (נער) is commented on by Saul in v. 33 and he is taunted by Goliath in 17.42 for being a youth (נער) and for his handsome appearance. Without the height of Saul, he did not appear a fearsome warrior against Goliath but a young attractive boy. This will highlight God's role in David's victory over Goliath.

We have already looked at the parallel endowment of Yahweh's spirit upon Saul and David. Klein has suggested that the parallel shows David's endowment is superior to Saul's because David receives the spirit immediately after Samuel anoints him (16.13) whereas Saul does not receive the spirit until some time after.[104] As Saul receives the spirit before the end of the pericope in 9.1–10.16 and Samuel gives Saul instructions on when he will receive the spirit immediately after the anointing (v. 6), it is perhaps an insignificant contrast to draw between the two leaders. A more significant difference is revealed in the effect of the spirit on each man. For Saul, the rushing of the spirit results in uncontrolled prophesying that provokes wonder in those who knew him (10.10–12). Even in Saul's great victory over the Ammonites in 11.1–11, Saul is acting on impulse and as a result of his anger (11.6; ויחר אפו מאד) leading him to actions which, although successful, are eerily similar to the abhorrent events of Jdg 19. David, by contrast, has self-possession after the spirit rushes upon him. His own initial military success in chapter 17 is carefully calculated as he presents himself to Saul and carefully explains to Saul his credentials for fighting Goliath (17.34–36). He prepares himself for battle in v. 40 by selecting five smooth stones and placing them in his pouch. He does not rush into battle like Saul in chapter 11 but pauses to give Goliath a rather lengthy theological statement on the victory that is about to take place (vv. 45–47). David's self-control after he receives the spirit is further highlighted by the contrast with Saul in 16.14–23 who has now received an evil spirit. Saul is tormented and only the skillful lyre playing of David provides calm.

---

[103] Cf. Bar-Efrat, *Narrative Art*, 50. He mentions that David's appearance is one of the rare examples of description which is not relevant to the story. On the other hand, Sternberg, *Poetics*, 356, suggests that the use of טוב is a wordplay on Samuel's words to Saul in 15.28, ונתנה לרעך הטוב ממך ('And he has given it [the kingdom] to your neighbour who is better than you').

[104] Klein, *1 Samuel*, 162.

The failures and 'shadow side' of the reigns of Eli, Samuel,
Saul and David

Despite these promising beginnings, each of Israel's leaders fails in
some way and the future of their leadership is affected. For Eli, Samuel
and Saul, this results in the transfer of leadership to someone outside of their house. For David, the curse of the sword is placed upon
his dynasty. Common patterns emerge from the narrative as these
moments of failure are marked by the visit of a prophet and followed
by a period of overlap with each leader's successor.

Both Eli and Samuel have corrupt sons who cause the failure of their
leadership. The corruption of Eli's sons is narrated in extensive detail
(2.12–17) and the consequent removal of the priesthood from Eli's line
is appropriately dramatic. A man of God brings an extended oracle of
doom to Eli in 2.27–36 followed shortly by the death of Eli's sons and
finally Eli himself in 4.1–22. Unlike the other leaders, the account of Eli
is almost exclusively devoted to his failure and Yahweh's subsequent
judgment. The narrative intersperses the account of this judgment with
the call and rise of Samuel in 2.18–21, 2.26, 3.1–21, creating an overlap
period where Eli's leadership declines and Samuel's develops.

The details of Samuel's leadership are brief in 7.3–17 and so are
the details of his failure. The corruption of his sons is recorded in
only one verse, 8.3. The judgment on Samuel, that the leadership of
his house is ended, is pronounced not by God but by the people and
is merely affirmed by God as he commands Samuel to follow their
request. To some degree, Samuel's failure breaks the pattern of the
other leaders because he is not denounced specifically and there is no
special appearance of a prophet, although he himself is a prophet and
is forced to institute his own replacement. The remainder of Samuel's
life overlaps with the reign of Saul but entails some limited exercise of
Samuel's leadership. He also differs from the other leaders because the
rest of his life is not so dramatically marked by disgrace.

The patterns established by the first two leaders are echoed in the
narratives of Saul and David in even greater detail. Firstly, the failures
of Saul and David are each marked by the visit and condemnation
by a prophet. There are two accounts of Saul sinning in a way that
brings about his rejection as king in 13.8–15 and 15.1–35 and, in both
of these accounts, Saul is immediately reprimanded by the prophet
Samuel. Similarly, in terms of narrative time, the prophet Nathan
comes to David immediately after his sin against Uriah in II Sam 12,

although Bathsheba has borne a son in the intervening period (11.27) demonstrating that the juxtaposition is a narrative device.

Although the sins of Saul and David are different, there are similarities in the ways they are addressed by their respective prophets. The first similarity is that their sins are against God. In the case of Saul, this is self evident because of the cultic nature of his sins. First, he is over eager to sacrifice in chapter 13 and then he hesitates to sacrifice king Agag in chapter 15. In 13.13, Samuel states explicitly that it was God's command that Saul has disobeyed (לא שמרת את מצות יהוה אלהיך אשר צוך). In 15.11, 19 and 23, it is repeated three times that Saul has disobeyed God's commandment, voice and word. Saul himself echoes this verdict in v. 24. Nathan's statement that David's sin is a sin against God, מדוע בזית את דבר יהוה (12.9; 'why have you despised the word of the Lord') strengthens the parallel between the failure of Saul and David.[105]

Despite each man committing a different sin, their crimes are appropriate to earlier aspects of their respective narratives. Saul is appointed because of a request from the people and Yahweh's instruction to obey their voice in 8.7 (שמע בקול העם). Now, Saul's failures are attributed to weakness with respect to the people. In 13.11, Saul says the scattering of the people (עם) caused him to offer the burnt offering and, in 15.24, he spared Agag and the other spoil because he 'feared and obeyed the voice of the people' (יראתי את העם ואשמע בקולם). Not only does the repetition of עם ('people') in 15.24 recall 13.11, but the phrase ואשמע בקולם is reminiscent of 8.7.[106] Saul's crime was appropriate to his past history. David's sin also echoes events from the preceding narrative. Taking another man's wife recalls the incidents of I Sam 25 where David marries Abigail after Nabal dies and II Sam 3.12–16 where David demands back his wife Michal and she is followed by her weeping husband Paltiel. Although David obtains both of these wives legally, David 'takes' them from other men.[107] Secondly, David has been connected with a number of deaths

---

[105] Note particularly the repetition of the phrase את דבר יהוה from I Sam 15.23.
[106] McCarter, I Samuel, 270.
[107] For a study of this motif, see John Kessler, "Sexuality and Politics: The Motif of the Displaced Husband in the Books of Samuel," CBQ 62 (2000): 409–23. 'Taking' in these narratives is highlighted in Regina M. Schwartz, "The Histories of David: Biblical Scholarship and Biblical Stories," in Not in Heaven: Coherence and Complexity in Biblical Narrative, ed. Jason P. Rosenblatt and Joseph C. Sitterson (Bloomington: Indiana University Press, 1991), 203.

in the past although he has never before been directly responsible. These include the priests at Nob in I Sam 22.6–23, Nabal in I Sam 25, Abner in II Sam 3.26–30 and Ish-bosheth in II Sam 4. Furthermore, he almost kills Saul in I Sam 24 and 26 but restrains himself. Murder and taking other men's women are themes throughout David's life and his crime in II Sam 11 is a culpable extension of this.

These parallels highlight the key difference in severity of God's judgment between the two kings. However, even in the judgments delivered to Saul and David, there are certain similarities that draw a parallel between the two men's situations. Firstly, just as each crime was appropriate to the man, each punishment is appropriate to the crime. In both cases, this is conveyed through the repetition of a verbal root. In chapter 13, Saul did not do as God commanded him and so now God will command another to be prince over Israel. This is conveyed through the repetition of the root צוה ('to command') in v. 14, ויצוהו יהוה לנגיד על עמו כי לא שמרת את אשר צוך יהוה ('the Lord has commanded him as prince over his people because you have not kept what the Lord has commanded you').[108] In chapter 15, the wordplay is on the root מאס ('to reject'), which is repeated in 15.23 to similar effect (יען מאסת את דבר יהוה וימאסך ממלך, 'because you have rejected the word of the Lord, he has rejected you from being king'). David's punishment also fits his crime to the extent that there are two parts to his punishment just as there were two parts to his sin. David 'took' Uriah's wife (11.4, ויקחה), and now Yahweh will 'take' David's wives (12.11, ולקחתי את נשיך לעיניך) repeating the same root לקח ('to take') in both narratives. Then, just as David sent to Joab asking him to let Uriah die (11.15, ומת), now the child born to David and Bathsheba will die (12.14, הבן הילוד לך מות ימות) creating another wordplay on the root מות ('to die'). Another, more minor, parallel between I Sam 15.28 and II Sam 12.11 is that the punishment will be for the benefit of each man's neighbour (לרעך in I Sam 15.28 and לרעיך in II Sam 12.11).

Finally, the scope of each punishment is noticeably similar as it affects both the man and his dynasty. Klein interprets 13.14 as referring only to Saul's dynasty and so reads the punishments in chapters 13 and 15 as a two stage process of rejecting first Saul's dynasty and then Saul

---

[108] McCarter, *I Samuel*, 228.

himself.[109] Gunn, on the other hand, suggests that Saul's punishment in 13.14 is ambiguous. In the least, it means that he will not establish a dynasty and at most, his own kingship will come to an immediate end.[110] Samuel's words in 15.23 have no such ambiguity and pronounce that Saul himself has been rejected, and by extension, also his dynasty. The use of ממלכת in 13.14 supports Gunn's argument for ambiguity as it includes dominion, kingship, kingdom and, by implication, dynasty, within its semantic range.[111] However the language of 'establishing' (הכין) the kingdom in v. 13 suggests that Yahweh would have also secured Saul's dynasty. Therefore kingship, including a dynasty, is probably the primary meaning of ממלכת. Nevertheless, reading chapters 13 and 15 together reveals that Saul himself has been rejected as king and Yahweh will now anoint one who will not continue Saul's dynasty (13.14, 15.28). Similarly, David's punishment in II Sam 12 will affect him, the one who sinned, according to 12.11, הנני מקים עליך רעה מביתך ('Behold, I am raising up evil against you from your house'). It will also affect his whole house, not only through the immediate death of his newly born son, but forever into the future, ועתה לא תסור חרב מביתך עד עולם (12.10, 'And now, the sword will *never* turn away from your house').

As the judgments on Saul and David are fulfilled in the narrative, a number of other parallels are created between the two kings and, to a lesser extent, with Samuel and Eli. Borgman terms each man's reign after their failure as the 'shadow side' of their reign[112] and this description captures the significant change in their depictions. From I Sam 13–15 and II Sam 11 onwards, for Saul and David respectively, their weaknesses now tend to outweigh their strengths. They are both occupied with maintaining their position as king, rather than building their kingdom in a positive way. Apart from this general similarity, there are a number of specific ways that their depictions are similar.

Both Saul and David lack control over their children, a weakness which featured strongly in the stories of Samuel and Eli. David's conflict with his house was foretold in God's judgment upon him in II Sam 11 and the remaining narrative focuses on the dramas that unfold among David's children—Amnon's rape of Tamar, Absalom's

---

[109] Klein, *1 Samuel*, 127.
[110] Gunn, *The Fate of King Saul*, 67.
[111] See entry for ממלכת in HALOT.
[112] Borgman, *David, Saul, and God*, 125.

murder of Amnon and Absalom's attempted coup of the throne. In the
next chapter, we will explore the ways in which the narrative evaluates
David's own weaknesses as a cause for these events. In particular, by
neglecting to discipline Amnon and Absalom when they commit
crimes, he is partly responsible for the ongoing drama.

The narrative of the shadow side of Saul's reign also depicts Saul
with disloyal children whom he cannot control. I Sam 18–20 focus
on the loyalty of Saul's children to David rather than to their father.
A pattern is established where Jonathan expresses his love (using the
root אהב, 18.1–4)[113] towards David, followed by a pericope where Saul
becomes afraid (the root ירא, 18.12) of David. The sequence is then
repeated when Michal, Saul's daughter, also expresses her love (אהב,
18.20) for David, followed by events that confirm Saul's fear (ירא,
18.29).[114] After the repetition of this sequence, there are two further
narratives in chapter 19–20 in which Michal and Jonathan help David
escape from their father. In both stories, Saul's children deceive him
in some way. In the first, Michal pretends that David is sick (19.14)
and, when her pretence is discovered, she continues to deceive Saul
and claims that David threatened her (19.17). In chapter 20, Jonathan
also deceives Saul about David's whereabouts (20.28–29) but then he
openly expresses his support for David (20.32). Thus the narrative
emphasises, through the patterning of these three chapters, that Saul's
children have rebelled against him in favour of David. Neither Saul
nor David can control their children and they both experience this
political opposition in the shadow half of their reign. However, Saul is
not as culpable as David for his children's actions, nor are his children's
actions viewed negatively. Saul's children will all eventually be eliminated (II Sam 21) but this suffering befalls his house simply because
they are his children. In contrast, David's children directly contribute
to their own deaths.[115] Although Saul is the only leader without mor-

---

[113] The root אהב denotes both personal affection and political loyalty. It is probable
that both meanings are implied here through the use of the ambiguous term [J.A.
Thompson, "The Significance of the Verb Love in the David-Jonathan Narratives in
1 Samuel," VT 24 (1974): 334–38].

[114] See Walter Brueggemann, "Narrative Coherence and Theological Intentionality in 1 Samuel 18," CBQ 55 (1993): 225–43, for a more detailed literary analysis
of chapter 18. He remarks on the skilful use of narrative, not oracle, to pronounce
three judgments about David: he is loved, he is successful and Yahweh is with him
(pp. 239–40).

[115] Observed in J. Cheryl Exum, Tragedy and Biblical Narrative: Arrows of the
Almighty (Cambridge: Cambridge University Press, 1992), 70.

ally deficient children during his lifetime, any positive reflection on him as a father is undermined by their rebellion against him.

A second parallel in the shadow sides of Saul and David's reign is that they are each in constant conflict with a possible successor. The transfer of Saul's children's loyalty to David and Saul's reaction of fear underscores Saul's rivalry with David. This is intensified in I Sam 22–26 as Saul pursues David through the wilderness but is thwarted by David's own opportunities to kill him. One particular element of this rivalry is Saul's mixed feelings towards David. In I Sam 24.17–22, Saul speaks positively of David and even refers to him in v. 17 as בני דוד ('my son David'). He uses this tender address again in I Sam 26.16, 21 and 25.

Similarly David's shadow reign is dominated in II Sam 15–18 by the attempted coup of his son Absalom for the throne. An important feature of this narrative is David's loyalty towards the rebellious Absalom over his loyal troops. His cry in 19.5, בני אבשלום אבשלום בני בני ('My son, Absalom, Absalom, my son, my son') draws a considerable parallel to Saul's fatherly feelings towards his enemy and rival. However, once again, this degree of parallel highlights the important difference between the two men's struggle with their possible successor. David successfully replaces Saul, albeit after Saul's death, whereas Absalom is defeated and David is left with both his life and the opportunity to choose his own successor.

The dominance of these two issues—control over children and a successor—in each shadow reign is highlighted by the parallel absence of external military success for each king in this period. In the case of Saul, his attention turns to pursuing David. There is an exception in I Sam 23.28 where it is briefly reported that Saul went out against the Philistines, but no success is recorded. Finally, Saul dies in a disastrous military campaign against the Philistines in I Sam 31. Similarly, David's active military service ceases in II Sam 11. In 12.26–31, Joab calls David out to a siege so that he can take credit for Joab's success; and in the civil war against Absalom, David's men do not let him go out with them (II Sam 18.3) and so the military success belongs to others. Both men, despite their early impressive victories, become militarily impotent and this encapsulates their overall weak position in the shadow side of their reign.

Patterning as a structure of meaning

This study has demonstrated that the pattern of the rise and fall of leaders is emphasised in the book through the inclusion of many small and large parallels. Its prominence guides the reader's interpretation of events and directs the significance and meaning that he/she will find in the history.

Once again we return to two ways in which events in history have significance: through their connection with the course of history and their relevance to later readers. The pattern of the parallel rise and fall of leaders bestows both of these types of meaning upon the book of Samuel. Firstly, the pattern provides an overarching framework through which the whole book is linked together. Every section of the book holds a position within the pattern and is therefore linked with the entire course of history presented in Samuel. In particular, this book structure gives meaning and significance to many of the small details, which draw attention to the parallels but have little other purpose in the narrative.

Secondly, this pattern acts as a structure of meaning because it comments on the three categories of politics, theology and the character of leaders. In this case, the character of leaders is the most obvious category of significance as their reigns form the backbone to the structure. The repetition of the rise and fall pattern conveys the message of inevitable failure amongst human leaders. The theme of politics also features prominently, as the pattern incorporates the political rise of each leader, his succession and the conflict present in the transition between leaders. Political failure necessarily accompanies character failure. Finally, the intervention of God at the key moments of selection and rejection generates theological meaning. As the entire pattern is dependent upon these pivotal moments, it confers theological significance on the book as a whole. Moreover, the pattern is broken when David is not rejected as king and this rupture highlights the ongoing theological question of Yahweh's choice of David not Saul.

3.3   COMPARATIVE ANALOGIES

Complementary to the parallel pattern of the rise and fall of leaders, comparative analogies function as another structure of meaning in the narrative of Samuel. The movement of rising and falling is conveyed by comparing leaders with themselves at other stages of the narrative.

The period of conflict and contrast in fortunes between leaders is conveyed by comparisons between them. According to Garsiel, comparisons are how we understand things in everyday life and even the most basic descriptions are the result of a comparison with another object.[116] This technique of giving meaning to events and details in the narrative is used extensively in Samuel and is fundamental to the success of the overall book structure.

There have been a number of studies of the structures of comparison in the Hebrew Bible,[117] including two major studies in the book of Samuel by Garsiel and more recently, Borgman.[118] The comparisons are between people or events in the narrative and are given different labels by scholars depending on how they function: comparative analogies, narrative analogies, comparative structures or parallels. All of these structures are designed to create meaning in the text by relating details, events and characters to other parts of the history and to the overall structure of the book. As one example, Gordon has noted the role of chapter 25 as a 'narrative analogy' with the surrounding chapters. He writes, "Narrative analogy is a device whereby the narrator can provide an internal commentary on the action which he is describing, usually by means of cross-reference to an earlier action or speech."[119] Although the significance of the events is not explained explicitly, the structure of comparison itself can demonstrate the meaning of the action for the historiography as a whole.

As we examine examples of comparative structures in I Sam 24–26, there are two particular devices, which are used extensively to create comparison and which are rarely found in modern historiography: juxtaposition and repetition.

We have already looked at some of the effects of juxtaposition on causation in II Sam 7. Here we will see examples of the juxtaposition

---

[116] Garsiel, *The First Book of Samuel*, 16. He gives the example of simple adjectives such as 'big', 'wide', 'solid' or 'pretty' which only have meaning because at some stage the object has been compared with another.

[117] For an overview of the definition and history of scholarship of narrative analogies, see Joshua Berman, *Narrative Analogy in the Hebrew Bible: Battle Stories and Their Equivalent Non-Battle Narratives*, VTSup. 103. (Leiden: Brill, 2004), 1–17.

[118] Garsiel, *The First Book of Samuel*; Borgman, *David, Saul, and God*. See also Gordon who focuses on one particular analogy [Robert P. Gordon, "David's Rise and Saul's Demise: Narrative Analogy in 1 Samuel 24–26," *TB* 31 (1980): 37–64]; and the monograph, Klement, *II Samuel 21–24*, which focuses only on comparisons created by the use of chiasms.

[119] Gordon, "David's Rise," 42.

of different characters within a single pericope and the juxtaposition of whole pericopes, which draw out a contrast between the characters in each. In these cases, the stories may have little or no causal connection but they often have a strong thematic relation that is supplemented by other literary linkage techniques, such as verbal repetitions or other parallels.[120]

As Yair Zakovitch writes about the juxtaposition of stories more generally, "In this way, each story contained more than one meaning: one message when it was read independently of its context, another when read in conjunction with its neighbours."[121] Meaning and significance is accorded to these stories by placing them in a particular context that will draw attention to their connection with the other events. Juxtaposition is also a way in which the editors of the narrative were able to give an 'inner-biblical' interpretation of the stories. Rather than explaining explicitly what the stories meant, they used the arrangement of material to convey their interpretation.[122] Although we cannot speculate here how, when or by whom this editing took place, Zakovitch's concept of juxtaposition is important for our understanding of this narrative device as representing history. The history is not interpreted by explicit exposition of the events but by the arrangement of the stories.

A second device used for comparative structures in I Sam 24–26 is the repetition of plot elements. Other examples of this device in Samuel include the two stories where God rejects Saul in I Sam 13 and 15, and the two instances where David hears news of the death of his enemy and kills the messenger in II Sam 1 and II Sam 4. In these examples of plot repetition, there is often only a distant causal connection between the stories. However, the repeated elements create a different type of link between them. By drawing a comparison of the same leader in two very similar situations, the narrative accentuates

---

[120] For example, both Samuel and Eli's sons are in the service of the sanctuary in I Sam 2–3 but Samuel serves faithfully whilst Eli's sons are corrupt. In I Sam 28–30, Saul and David each seek the Lord's guidance. However, Saul resorts to necromancy in contrast to David who is successful in his use of lots [on the contrast created between these stories, see Bill T. Arnold, "Necromancy and Cleromancy in 1 and 2 Samuel," *CBQ* 66 (2004): 199–213].

[121] Yair Zakovitch, "Juxtaposition in the Abraham Cycle," in *Pomegranates and Golden Bells: Studies in Biblical, Jewish, and Near Eastern Ritual, Law, and Literature in Honor of Jacob Milgrom*, ed. David P. Wright, David Noel Freedman, and Avi Hurvitz (Winona Lake: Eisenbrauns, 1995), 510.

[122] Ibid., 509–11.

the small differences in their behaviour and in the circumstances surrounding the situations. These differences convey the character's development or degradation between the two stories and so contribute to the movement of rise and fall in the overall structure of the book.[123]

Primarily historical critical rather than literary studies have analysed the high degree of similarity between I Sam 24 and 26. Each of these stories describe a meeting between Saul and David in the wilderness and, although it is Saul who is pursuing David, it is David who is given the opportunity to take Saul's life. These similarities have suggested to many scholars that the two stories originated from the same event or tradition. In *The Growth of the Biblical Tradition*, Koch provides detailed form critical analysis of these chapters and proposes that each of the stories is a saga and the result of diverging oral traditions from one original story.[124] He believes I Sam 24 and I Sam 26 are independent from their context in Samuel as they each have their own climax and closing sentences. He speculates that the introductions were lost when the stories were inserted into their present context.[125] There are many elements in the stories that suggest they are sagas, such as the exaggeration of 3000 men, the identification of the landscape, lack of chronological dates and a sharp relief of characters.[126] There are also a number of anomalous features that suggest a new context has been given to these stories: David and his men return to the Ziphites after they had previously betrayed him; there is no mention in chapter 26 that a similar episode has happened before; and there are many verbal parallels between the two chapters.[127]

Koch's analysis has been influential and the single oral origin of the stories is accepted by many scholars.[128] However, alternative points of view do exist. McCarter believes that the differences between the

---

[123] On the development of Saul and David between these stories, despite the doubling, see David Jobling, *1 Samuel*, Berit Olam (Collegeville: Liturgical Press, 1998), 92, and Barbara Green, *How are the Mighty Fallen? A Dialogical Study of King Saul in 1 Samuel*, JSOTSup. 365 (Sheffield: Sheffield Academic Press, 2003), 374.

[124] Klaus Koch, *The Growth of the Biblical Tradition: The Form-Critical Method* (London: A. & C. Black, 1969), chapter 11.

[125] Ibid., 137–8.

[126] Ibid., 138–9.

[127] Ibid., 142.

[128] E.g. Klein, *1 Samuel*, 236; Antony F. Campbell, *1 Samuel*, FOTL (Grand Rapids: Eerdmans, 2003), 251; Baruch Halpern, "The Construction of the Davidic State: An Exercise in Historiography," in *Origins of the Ancient Israelite States*, ed. Fritz Volkmar and Philip R. Davies (Sheffield: Sheffield Academic Press, 1996), 62.

stories are too great and prefers the older literary critical explanation that the story in chapter 24 is a later, more tendentious retelling of chapter 26, which evolved exclusively through literary means.[129] Other scholars have also noted the differences between the stories and so maintained that the stories are the result of two different traditions or events.[130] These differences include the setting, the coincidence in chapter 24 versus the planned encounter by David in chapter 26, the address to Abner in chapter 26 where there is nothing comparable in chapter 24, and differences between the speeches in each story. The difficulty in analysing the similarities and differences is that they are both significant. Edenburg offers a unique suggestion that attempts to deal with this circularity. She believes that both events are based on II Sam 23 as their raw material but they have been composed by a single author who has intentionally devised textual links between the stories.[131] She gives compelling literary reasons for the doubling of the stories: to illustrate the hopelessness of David's position and the instability of Saul and to show that the two events did not happen by chance but by divine providence.[132]

Whilst our study is not concerned with the origins of these stories or with a reconstruction of 'what actually happened', this survey of historical critical studies is helpful for understanding some of the assumptions and conclusions of scholars on these chapters. Even if the characters in these chapters were polarised and one dimensional at an earlier stage in their history, a close examination of the text suggests that this is no longer the case. In terms of the structure of parallels that we have previously examined, these chapters lie within the section of narrative where Saul's fate is in decline and David is on the rise. Therefore, a superficial reading may suggest that Saul is depicted only negatively and David only positively. Not only does this assumption ignore many features in the text but recognition of the complexity of

---

[129] McCarter, *I Samuel*, 386–87 n. 1.

[130] Maunchline proposes that the two stories originated from different traditions but they each lost their individuality through the oral process, so that they came to resemble each other more than the original stories [John Mauchline, *1 and 2 Samuel*, NCBC (London: Oliphants, 1971), 173; Jakob Gronbaek, *Die Geschichte vom Aufstieg Davids (1 Sam. 15–2 Sam. 5)*, vol. X, Acta Theologica Danica (Copenhagen: Prostant Apud Munksgaard, 1971), 169–70].

[131] Cynthia Edenburg, "How (Not) to Murder a King: Variations on a Theme in 1 Sam 24; 26," *SJOT* 12 (1998): 81–82.

[132] Ibid.

Saul and David will prove important for understanding the complexity of comparison between the two men. Similarly, although the stories may have originally had identical themes and characterisation of each leader, there are now significant differences between them. Indeed, repetition with variation is a key device in these chapters for conveying meaning and significance. Furthermore, this review of the results of historical criticism is important because it highlights the unusual nature of these devices for writing history, compared to our modern ideology of historiography.

In the present study, we will first examine the comparative analogies of each leader with himself as he develops between the two pericopes. After this in-depth analysis of their characterisation, we will observe the comparisons made between Saul and David in these chapters.

The character and development of Saul

I Sam 24 and 26 are situated in the 'shadow' side of Saul's reign as king and, accordingly, many of Saul's weaknesses are highlighted in the text. Saul is in relentless pursuit of David. His intentions are revealed in I Sam 18.11, when he throws his spear at David twice, and I Sam 19, when Saul sends his messengers to David's house to kill him. The murder of the priests of Nob in I Sam 22 ensues and Abiathar's arrival at Keilah in chapter 23 is a reminder of this slaughter. Saul's repeated attempts to take David's life open up ironic contrast with David himself, who, despite being under constant threat from Saul, reiterates six times the sanctity of the Lord's anointed (24.7, 24.11, 26.9, 26.11, 26.16 and 26.23). David's restraint intensifies the depiction of Saul's pursuit.

One of the most disorientating aspects of the repetition between chapters 24 and 26 is that Saul changes his attitude so dramatically from the end of 24 to the beginning of 26. Saul repents of his pursuit of David in chapter 24 but then proceeds to pursue him again in chapter 26. However, this is consistent with the depiction of his 'madness' so far and marks an important culmination of Saul's inner torment. The primary way that Saul's changeability is conveyed is through the repetition of the plot line: he is put in a position of vulnerability before David; he realises that David means him no harm; and then he repents of his pursuit. However, there is other evidence that the text intends to convey Saul's confused state in chapter 24. Saul initially refers to David as 'my son' (v 17) but then asks David to promise to preserve his offspring (v 22). He himself is trying to kill David whom he sees as one of his own sons, yet his primary concern is to ask David not to harm his sons.[133] Moreover, contiguous to chapter 26, Saul takes away Michal from David in 25.44 and gives her to Palti and in this way strips David of his status as his son-in-law. This is juxtaposed with Saul's repetition of 'my son' three times in chapter 26. The message that Saul is disturbed and changeable in his attitude to David is thus a major concern in these narratives.

Whilst these circumstances present Saul in a negative way, closer analysis reveals many elements sympathetic to Saul. Garsiel writes:

> The comparative structure built upon the narrative triad of chapters 24, 25 and 26 admittedly establishes a clear contrast between Saul and David but at the same time it offers more that a simple black and white antithesis. Saul for his part admits his wrongdoing, speaks peaceably to him and remits his pursuit, so that he is by no means a symbol of abstract evil.[134]

Preston agrees that Saul's speeches in 24.18–22 and 26.21 generate sympathy for him and he adds that it is David who is suspect for publicising his mercy towards Saul.[135] A powerful element of David's speech is the rhetorical question in 24.20, וכי ימצא איש את איבו ושלחו בדרך טובה ('if a man finds his enemy, then will he send him on his way in peace'). This statement primarily refers to David's restraint from attacking Saul in the cave and highlights the contrast between David's restraint and Saul's constant pursuit of David in the previous chapters. However, Saul also lets David walk free after this meeting. Although Saul is alone in the cave, he has an army of 3000[136] men nearby, compared to David's 400 hundred men (22.2). If Saul were

---

[133] This becomes more ironic when the incident in I Sam 14 is considered because Saul is willing to let Jonathan die because of his oath. See also Robert B. Lawton, "Saul, Jonathan and the 'Son of Jesse'," *JSOT* 58 (1993). He theorises that David functions as Saul's son in place of Jonathan throughout the narrative.

[134] Garsiel, *The First Book of Samuel*, 123–4.

[135] Thomas R. Preston, "The Heroism of Saul: Patterns of Meaning in the Narrative of the Early Kingship," *JSOT* 24 (1982): 35–6. Preston generally takes a pro-Saul view of the narratives.

[136] This has frequently been considered an impossible number and a sign of the narrative becoming inflated through oral tradition. However, here we see that this large number holds a specific literary purpose in the narrative and it is plausible that it has been used to highlight this aspect of the story. For a more practical reading, we can also follow McCarter, *I Samuel*, 383, who understands it as three units of men not 3000 men. In that case, David would have four units of smaller size.

insincere, the audience would expect Saul to turn after David with his men and capture them shortly after this incident, but the narrative records no attempt to do so.[137] Although later hindsight reveals that Saul will eventually return to his pursuit of David, for the moment his acknowledgement of David's righteousness is genuine and this creates sympathy in the reader.

There are further elements of Saul's speech which indicate that Garsiel is correct in his evaluation of the complexity of Saul. There has been much discussion over Saul's response הקולך זה בני דוד (24.17 'Is this your voice, my son David?'), which also occurs in 26.17. The implications of the repetition and its suitability for this context will be discussed in more detail later. For now, we will note the tenderness of Saul's address, בני ('my son'), which is emphasised by the outpouring of emotion by Saul, highlighted in two parallel phrases in v. 17, וישא שאול קלו ('and Saul lifted his voice') and ויבך ('and he wept'). It is difficult to doubt the sincerity of Saul's response.

The sympathetic and ambiguous depiction of Saul continues in his speech in chapter 26. As with chapter 24, Saul addresses David as 'my son' in v. 17 and it is repeated for intensification in vv. 21 and 25. In this chapter the audience are also reminded that the Lord is against Saul in v. 12 when the narrator attributes the deep sleep to the Lord, כי תרדמת יהוה נפלה עליהם ('for sleep from the Lord fell upon them').[138] Saul's pursuit is futile because the Divine is acting against him. Whilst this situation could implicate Saul as unambiguously evil, David does not view it as such. In vv. 14–16, he begins his speech by accusing Abner not Saul. When he addresses Saul, he asks if it is God or men who have incited Saul to pursue David (v 19) but does not consider that it is Saul himself. From David's point of view, it is a force outside of Saul that is driving his actions and this reduced culpability can encourage the audience to take a similarly sympathetic view of him.[139]

---

[137] Cf. Edelman, *King Saul*, 222. There is a suggestion at the end of chapter 24 that Saul will go back on his word because he does not invite David back to his court.

[138] There is the possibility that the the divine name is used here as a superlative [see David Winton Thomas, "Consideration of Some Unusual Ways of Expressing the Superlative in Hebrew," *VT* 3 (1953): 209–24]. However, as with McCarter, *I Samuel*, 408, there is the implication that there is divine involvement in the sleep of Saul and his men.

[139] Cf. Borgman, *David, Saul, and God*, 89. He says that Saul's clearheaded confession 'I have been a fool', shows that the blame must fall squarely upon him. However, other evidence in the passage suggests that there is indeed divine power against him.

Alongside Saul's weakness is evidence of his decline between the two chapters. This decline is conveyed through physical means. In chapter 24, David discovers Saul squatting in the cave. It is humiliating for Saul to be caught in this vulnerable situation but it is the result of apparent coincidence rather than a fault of his own. At least he has consciousness even if he fails to notice David cutting the skirt of his robe. Moreover, as Fokkelman points out, there was an excuse for him not to have a bodyguard in this situation.[140] In chapter 26, Saul's vulnerability is increased. Now he is lying down asleep with no one watching over him. The narrative emphasises this vulnerability through the description in v. 5. Before his army is mentioned, there is a succinct statement שכב שם שאול ('Saul was lying there') that produces the image of Saul lying alone. The narrator only then reveals that Abner is near him and, further, that his entire army surrounds him.[141] The repetition of שאול שכב between these two additional facts intensifies the helplessness of Saul as he is lying asleep at the mercy of David. Not only does he not 'see', as in chapter 24, he is now not even awake. Furthermore, it is inexcusable that Saul does not have a watchful bodyguard in this situation, especially when a whole army surrounds him. Finally, the explicit intervention of God causes the audience to re-evaluate the coincidental meeting in chapter 24 and to suspect that Yahweh has been instrumental in both encounters. Saul's helplessness is intensified as God acts against him.

Saul's speeches also give evidence of his decline. Gordon has expressed surprise that Saul's speech in chapter 26 is unimpressive compared to chapter 24, considering it is the second time Saul has been placed in this position. He attributes this to the chapter's concern with the irreconcilability of David and Saul and David's imminent withdrawal to Philistia.[142] Certainly these are added elements in chapter 26; however an analysis of the speech in chapter 26 shows that each of its concerns is a result of the decline of Saul (and we will see later, the rise of David). Saul can barely defend himself. He repents of

---

As I will argue shortly, Saul's confession is a sign of his complete resignation to the fate that has been assigned to him.

[140] J.P. Fokkelman, *The Crossing Fates*, Vol. II of *Narrative Art and Poetry in the Books of Samuel: A Full Interpretation Based on Stylistic and Structural Analyses* (Assen: Van Gorcum, 1986), 540.

[141] Gunn, *The Fate of King Saul*, 102.

[142] Robert P. Gordon, "Word-Play and Verse-Order in 1 Samuel 24:5–8," *VT* 40 (1990): 59.

his actions but he no longer has the power to ask for David's protection over his family (cf. 24.22). He does not acknowledge a second time that David will become king because the preceding events have made this self-evident (cf. 24.21). Saul has reached his lowest point in his relationship with David, as is appropriate for their last meeting before his death.

These observations are supported by Garsiel's conclusion that chapter 26 is marked by distance and restraint by comparison with chapter 24.[143] The physical distance is emphasised in 26.13 where it uses three different ways to describe the space David puts between himself and Saul: ויעבר דוד העבר ('And David crossed to the other side'), ויעמד על ראש ההר ('and he stood afar on the top of the mountain') and מרחק רב המקום ביניהם ('a great space between them'). Garsiel also observes the psychological distance as David addresses himself to Saul's servants and Saul must interrupt.[144] Earlier it was suggested that this lent sympathy to the character of Saul because blame was placed on others not onto himself. However, it is also derogatory because Saul has lost the capacity to be responsible for his own actions.

The character and development of David

The character David is also surrounded by ambiguity. His depiction is largely positive because he overcomes temptation and refrains from harming Saul. In both stories, David's men describe Saul as 'your enemy' (24.5, 26.8), a description which is justified by the preceding narratives. Each time David changes Saul's description to 'the Lord's anointed' (24.7, 26.9) as he refrains from eliminating him. Yet, there are traces of complexity in David's actions in this chapter. In chapter 24, he suffers a twinge of guilt and chapter 26 contains elements that cast doubt over David's intentions.

Key to understanding the character of David in chapters 24 and 26 is the intervening story in chapter 25, which is linked through comparative analogy. The analogy is drawn primarily through the equation of the character Nabal with Saul.[145] Both of their families do not

---

[143] Garsiel, *The First Book of Samuel*, 126.

[144] Ibid.

[145] This equation has been identified by Gunn, *The Fate of King Saul*, 97–98; Garsiel, *The First Book of Samuel*, 129; Gordon, "David's Rise," 43; Klein, *1 Samuel*, 248; Alter, *The David Story*, 154, and Polzin, *Samuel and the Deuteronomist*, 211, among others.

support them,[146] they are both said to return good for evil,[147] Nabal has a 'king's banquet' in 25.36 (כמשתה המלך), both stories employ the terms 'son', 'servant' and 'Lord' to describe David's relationship with them[148] and the verb נגף ('to smite') is used of the men in 25.38 and 26.10. The equation of Nabal with Saul develops the common theme of David's restraint from violence against his adversary. On this level, it contributes to a positive picture of David.

On the other hand, David does not restrain himself in chapter 25 by his own initiative but because of Abigail's persuasion.[149] As he sets out to murder Nabal, another narrative analogy is developed. This equates David in chapter 25 with Saul in chapters 14 and 19 when he makes rash vows and needs to be warned about the shedding of blood.[150] There are two effects of this narrative on the reader's understanding of the surrounding chapters 24 and 26. Firstly, the reader glimpses David's violent side and so develops a certain level of distrust of his behaviour.[151] Secondly, the reader realises David's great depth of respect for the Lord's anointed, even though he is his greatest enemy, because he does not demonstrate this respect for Nabal. This series of comparative analogies demonstrate that David's behaviour towards Saul is exemplary compared to his behaviour towards Nabal, and Saul's behaviour towards David.

David's attack of guilt in 24.6 (ויהי אחרי כן ויך לב דוד אתו; 'And after this, David's heart smote him') has caused considerable discussion amongst interpreters. The narrative suggests that David's conscience was stricken because he cut off the corner of the robe, yet in v. 12 he holds up the corner to symbolise his restraint. Some commentators propose that, in order for the narrative to make sense, vv. 5b–6

---

[146] Saul's family in I Sam 19 and Nabal's servant in 25.17 and wife in 25.19, 25.
[147] Saul in 24.17 and Nabal in 25.21.
[148] David calls himself 'son' to Saul in 24.11, 'servant' in 26.18, 19 and Saul calls him 'son' in 24.16, 26.17, 21, 25. David calls himself 'your son' and 'your servant' to Nabal in 25.8. David also refers to Saul as lord in 24.8, 10, 26.17, 18 and 19.
[149] Biddle argues that David was the main threat to Nabal in these passages and that the chapter brings out the negative side of his character. Instead it is Abigail who is the real hero of the story [Mark E. Biddle, "Ancestral Motifs in 1 Samuel 25: Intertextuality and Characterization," *JBL* 121 (2002): 634–37].
[150] See Garsiel, *The First Book of Samuel*, 132–33.
[151] See Barbara Green, "Enacting Imaginatively the Unthinkable: 1 Samuel 25 and the Story of Saul," *BI* 11 (2003): 1–23. She argues that David's threat to Saul in chapters 24 and 26 is more serious than commonly recognised and that chapter 25 rehearses what almost happens in the surrounding chapters.

needs to be transposed to follow v. 8a so that David feels guilt for rising to take Saul's life. He then cuts off the corner as proof of his guilt then restraint.[152] McCarter rejects this based on the absence of textual witnesses, although he does concede that vv. 5b–6 and 12 are likely to be expansive.[153] On the other hand, Gordon favours the current location of these verses because it brings about a wordplay between the incident when David cuts Saul's robe in v. 5 (כרת 'to cut'), and the one when he 'clefts with words' his men in v. 8 (שסע, 'to cleave'). He argues that the literal must come before the metaphorical for this wordplay to be effective.[154] However, as the roots for the verbs in this wordplay are different, the force of this argument is somewhat weakened. In order to determine whether emendation is unavoidable, let us examine whether the cutting of Saul's robe was sufficient reason for David to experience guilt.

There are many reasons to suggest that David cutting Saul's robe was an act of violation against Saul. Firstly, David takes advantage of Saul when he is in an undignified condition. Secondly, the event recalls a similar situation in I Sam 15.27–28 when Saul snatches Samuel's cloak and it breaks. In this incident, Samuel tells Saul that the Lord has torn Saul's kingdom from him and given it to another. As Klein suggests, the tearing of the robe echoes this previous event and symbolises the snatching away of Saul's kingdom. He speculates that the possession of the royal robe implies that one is the legitimate heir.[155] Kruger explores the significance of clothing in the ancient Near East and shows that it was considered an extension of someone's personality and so its removal is "much more serious than a mere physical matter."[156] Based on this understanding, the removal of Saul's corner implies an inten-

---

[152] E.g. Driver, *Books of Samuel*, 193.

[153] McCarter, *I Samuel*, 384.

[154] Gordon, "Word-Play," 139–44.

[155] Klein, *1 Samuel*, 239. He uses the incident of Jonathan giving David his garment in chapter 18 as support for this theory. In addition, note the suggestion by Quinn-Miscall that it foreshadows the eventual tearing away of the kingdom from David's dynasty as well [Peter D. Quinn-Miscall, *1 Samuel: A Literary Reading*, Indiana Studies in Biblical Literature (Bloomington: Indiana University Press, 1986), 148].

[156] Paul A. Kruger, "The Symbolic Significance of the Hem (*kanaf*) in 1 Samuel 15:27," in *Text and Context: Old Testament and Semitic Studies for F.C. Fensham*, ed. W. Claasen (Sheffield: JSOT Press, 1988), 106. According to Kruger, the removal of clothing could mean that someone has been lowered in status, it could proclaim the dissolution of a relationship or it could serve as legal evidence in a court of contracts.

tion of harming Saul himself. This reading is supported by David's parallel removal of Saul's spear, the instrument with which Abishai threatens to take Saul's life.[157]

Drawing together these connotations, we conclude that the act of cutting off Saul's robe was an act of violation sufficient for David's heart to 'smite him'.[158] Nevertheless, the act was not comparable to actually taking Saul's life, and the narrative emphasises that David is innocent of this crime. David is a complex character who wrestles with temptation, takes a step too far, but his sense of guilt prevents him from performing an irrevocable act.

Another shadow is cast over David's character when he does not hesitate to publicise his restraint from harming Saul, despite his sense of guilt.[159] He has forced himself to spare Saul but he takes the opportunity to maximise his political advantage. In chapter 26, David's opportunism is even more marked, because he specifically seeks out Saul and then publicly announces his 'loyalty'.

The language used to narrate David's bold act in chapter 26 also creates ambiguity in his motives. The narrative describes each of David's actions—he sends out spies, then goes himself to the place where Saul is encamped and takes in the view of Saul and his army fast asleep around him. His intention to enter Saul's camp at all is only revealed indirectly in his direct speech in v. 6, when he asks who will go down with him to Saul's camp. The inner thoughts of David are not revealed and the audience must surmise. The tactic of two men entering an enemy camp alone recalls Jonathan and his army bearer in I Sam 14 in the camp of the Philistines when they killed 20 men between them. Moreover, David's determination to kill Nabal in chapter 25 lingers in the audience's consciousness as David again rises for action. Although David's intentions are not ultimately fatal to anyone in the

---

[157] A third suggestion in Gunn, *The Fate of King Saul*, 94–95, is based on the premise that the phrase כרת כרף ('to cut the skirt') is a euphemism for castration. Thus this is a metaphorical allusion to cutting off Saul's heirs. Whilst this initially seems far-fetched, it draws support from Saul's sudden request of David to preserve his heirs in v. 22. On the other hand, in v. 7 David refers to putting his hand against the Lord's anointed, not against his offspring, as the act that must be avoided.

[158] Fokkelman, *The Crossing Fates*, 458, points out the similarity in expressions when David's heart smites him in 24.6 (ויך לב דוד אתו) and Nabal's heart attack in 25.37 (וימת לבו בקרבו). He suggests that this was the effect on any person who opposes the Lord's anointed.

[159] As expressed in Green, *How are the Mighty Fallen*, 380–81, David cuts Saul's robe as a threat but then he rereads the act as a reassurance and uses it to his advantage.

enemy camp, these suspicions are raised. The narrative does not dispel them until the action has taken place. It is ambiguous, whether it was David's intention all along only to scare Saul or whether he originally had darker purposes in mind that he abandoned at the last moment. As Green observes, taking Saul's water supply in the dry wilderness is an aggressive act and, unlike chapter 24, David does not feel regret or guilt.[160]

At first glance the exchange between David and two of his men in v. 6 is unnecessary to the plot. Fokkelman offers several reasons for the inclusion of David's question, including the introduction of the sons of Zeruiah motif.[161] The exchange draws attention to Abishai, son of Zeruiah, as the one who accompanies David and tempts him in v. 8 to destroy Saul. In this chapter David has control over Abishai son of Zeruiah but in II Sam 4 he loses command over both Abishai and Joab when they murder Abner, another character who features in this narrative. David's lack of control over Joab, Abishai's brother, becomes a major weakness in the later years of his reign. Moreover, throughout the three narratives in chapters 24–26, there are a number of allusions to weaknesses in David's later life. In chapter 24, the issue of hastening on the succession to the king alludes to Absalom's coup. His marriage in chapter 25, whilst conducted honourably, bears resemblance to the dishonourable way he will obtain Bathsheba in II Sam 11. Finally, in chapter 26, there is allusion to Abishai and Abner. Whilst David is innocent of wrongdoing in these chapters, they allude to his later failings and give depth and complexity to his character.

David's character develops in a number of ways between chapters 24 and 26. His confidence increases such that he enters Saul's camp without waiting for coincidence to strike.[162] He is also more distant from Saul both physically and psychologically, as noted in the development of Saul. He removes the blame from Saul for the pursuit, assuming that he is acting under the influence either of his men or of the Lord. The distance is also indicated in 26.25 when David 'went his way' (וילך דוד לדרכו), even though Saul pleaded with him in v. 21 to return with him (שוב בני דוד) and promised that he would do him no

---

[160] Ibid., 388.
[161] Fokkelman, *The Crossing Fates*, 534.
[162] Bar-Efrat, *Das erste Buch Samuel*, 337; Borgman, *David, Saul, and God*, 86.

harm (לא ארע לך). David does not believe Saul's assurances because he has heard them before.

The analogy between chapter 25 and chapters 24 and 26 has implications for the development between these latter two chapters. The story of chapter 25 provides David with the revelation that God will avenge his enemies for him, when Nabal then dies of a heart attack (vv. 37–38). The narrative makes explicit that it was the Lord who struck down Nabal (v. 38) but it does not give a reason why God has done this. Thus it is established that David is innocent of taking Nabal's life but the audience must rely on David's own interpretation of events to determine that the Lord smote Nabal to avenge his insult to David (v. 39). Not only does this create ambiguity around David's character, it demonstrates that David himself is convinced of this reason for Nabal's death. Therefore, the development in David's character between chapters 24 and 26 is influenced by his belief that the Lord will bring about the destruction of his enemies on his behalf, because he has seen it occur in the Nabal incident.

Comparative analogy between David and Saul

The primary aspect of contrast between Saul and David is that whilst Saul grows weaker David grows stronger. The comparison is generated by the simultaneous development of these characters in opposite directions. The juxtaposition of David's rise with Saul's fall, within these two encounters, enhances the contrast and therefore gives greater emphasis to each. Borgman and Garsiel both suggest that the contrast between Saul and David, whilst softened by their complex characterisation, is difficult to miss.[163] These scholars have focused on the contrasts in each of the two stories individually, but the growth of the contrast between the two stories is also significant. As the character of Saul becomes more resigned and vulnerable, David becomes more bold and self assured. The increasing physical distance between the men symbolises the increasing contrast between them also. David's coolness of speech becomes more detached, in contrast to Saul's weeping and desire to extract promises of mercy for his children. As David's fortunes rise higher and higher, Saul's sink lower. This reaches a climax in the juxtaposition of stories in I Sam 30.16–31 and 31.1–13, where

---

[163] Borgman, *David, Saul, and God*, 90; Garsiel, *The First Book of Samuel*, 123.

David (after a series of setbacks) has decisive victory over his enemies and Saul finally succumbs to death and defeat.

There are two other significant contrasts between David and Saul in the narrative that form this comparative analogy. The first is the irony that David has the opportunity to kill Saul, when it is Saul who seeks David. This is achieved by the placement of the chapters within the overall plot of Samuel. They are the culmination of a long series of narratives where Saul is constantly pursuing, whilst David is fleeing. In chapters 19–23, words of 'escaping' and 'fleeing,' using the roots פטר, נוס, מלט and ברח, appear 15 times in reference to David[164] and words of 'hiding' are used 8 times.[165] In the same section, 'seeking' בקש and 'pursuing' רדף are used of Saul 9 times.[166] In chapter 24, David is hiding in a cave and Saul is once again 'seeking' him (24.3, וילך לבקש את דוד ואנשיו). Finally, Saul's pursuit of David is highlighted in both chapters 24 and 26 through explicit reference in the speeches of David (24.15, 26.18). Within this context, the irony that David is given the opportunity to kill Saul in both stories is apparent.

David's opportunity to kill Saul, instead of the reverse, is further emphasised by his theft of Saul's spear in chapter 26. Abishai offers to kill Saul with this spear in 26.8, saying, ולא אשנה לו ('and [I will] not [strike] him twice'), highlighting its threat. This recalls the narratives in 18.10–11 and 19.9–10, where Saul twice hurls his spear at David, and also 20.33, where Saul throws his spear at Jonathan on account of David.[167] David and Abishai now hold the power of this weapon in an ironic reversal.

The second contrast between Saul and David is also ironic: Saul is seeking to kill the Lord's anointed whilst David lets Saul live. This is foreshadowed in the preceding chapters through the juxtaposition of Saul murdering the priests at Nob in 22.6–23 and David rescuing the people of Keilah in 23.1–13. Then, in chapters 24 and 26, David repeatedly uses the rhetoric of the 'Lord's anointed' to explain his sparing of Saul. These demonstrate contrasting reactions to the presence of a rival anointed king. Saul seeks to kill whilst David considers it preferable to let Saul live.

---

[164] פטר: 19.10; נוס: 19.10; מלט: 19.10, 19.11, 19.12, 19.17, 19.18, 20.29, 22.1, 23.13; ברח: 19.12, 19.18, 20.1, 21.11, 22.17.

[165] סתר: 19.2, 20.5, 20.19, 20.24, 23.19; חבא: 19.2, 23.23 (twice).

[166] בקש: 19.2, 19.10, 20.1, 22.23, 23.10, 23.14, 23.15, 23.25; רדף: 23.28.

[167] Green, *How are the Mighty Fallen*, 386.

Observations on the devices of juxtaposition and repetition in comparative analogies

The success of the comparative analogies in these chapters is heavily reliant on two devices: juxtaposition and repetition. As stated above, juxtaposition in comparative analogies can work in two different ways. Either the two leaders are juxtaposed within the one pericope, or two pericopes are juxtaposed and comment on each other through their comparison. In these chapters, both types of juxtaposition can be identified. When the two leaders are placed side by side within the one story, such as in chapters 24 and 26, the comparison is most effective if they perform opposite actions. Thus, Saul seeks to kill the Lord's anointed at the same time that David spares the Lord's anointed. Saul's efforts to discover David are entirely unsuccessful whereas David discovers Saul without effort. Examples of this type of juxtaposition in comparative analogies can also be found in I Sam 14, where Jonathan's military success is in the same narrative as Saul's blundering, or I Sam 18–20, where the jealousy and plotting of Saul against David is contiguous to Michal and Jonathan's faithfulness and their actions to protect David. In each of these cases, the comparison relies on a common element between the characters that is manifested in opposite extremes.

The second type of juxtaposition is the placement of entire pericopes alongside each other, where there is no direct causal link. We studied the role of this type of juxtaposition for causation in I Sam 9–11 and observed that there was an absence of introductory joining statements or time designations at the beginning of each pericope. This feature can also be observed in chapters 24–26, and the comparative analogy between Samuel and Eli's sons in I Sam 1–4. In each case, the narratives for comparison are placed alongside each other with no explicit introduction announcing their relationship. Thus the comparison is revealed through other means. To some degree, the abrupt proximity of the passages alone has sufficient effect. Furthermore, the anomalous nature of chapter 25 wedged between chapters 24 and 26 invites the readers' reflection on its purpose and relationship with the surrounding chapters.

The effect of juxtaposition is aided by the device of repetition, which contributes to the comparative structure.[168] We have seen that rep-

---

[168] On the use of doublets to compare plot and characterisation, see also Sarah Nicholson, *Three Faces of Saul: An Intertextual Approach to Biblical Tragedy*, JSOT-

etition of plot elements between chapters 24 and 26 is essential for the comparative analogy between the two chapters. However, the plot repetition is enhanced by a number of more minor repetitions, such as motifs or phrases.[169]

An example of such repetition is the use of the phrase, הקלך זה בני דוד ('Is this your voice, my son David?') in 24.17 and 26.17. Its usage in chapter 24 has raised questions amongst commentators because it does not appear to fit its context. Campbell says that the event must be set in daytime because otherwise Saul had no need to come into the cave; but then in the daytime, there was no need for Saul to ask David if it was his voice.[170] It is difficult to disagree with this logic. There are a few possible alternatives, such as Saul could not see David for his tears, but this is implausible because the narrative says that he asked the question first and then he wept. Another is that David was bowed down (24.8) and so Saul could not see his face. Again this involves significant gap filling in the narrative. Instead, we argue, along with Campbell, that this question has entered the narrative based on the influence of chapter 26. Campbell attributes this to a common oral tradition,[171] but in the text's final form it also acts as a literary device to encourage the audience to associate the two stories and see that the history of Saul repeats itself. In particular, it highlights the repetition that Saul does not 'see'. Similarly, the phrase פרעש אחד ('a single flee') in 24.15 and 26.20 emphasises Saul's relentless pursuit. Each story begins with a formulaic introduction and a message to Saul in direct speech introduced by לאמר (24.2, 26.1). This is then followed by different locations, although both are designated by the description 'wilderness' (מדבר 24.2, 26.3). It is also repeated that Saul took 3000 'chosen' men. These linguistic repetitions are in addition to the repetitions of plot and characterisation already described in relation to Saul and David.

There are three discernable effects of this strong sense of repetition in the final form of the passages. The first is that doubling many elements of the story also doubles the strength of the message.[172] For

---

Sup. 339 (Sheffield: Sheffield Academic Press, 2002), 55–75.

[169] For a list of verbal similarities between these two chapters, see Bar-Efrat, *Das erste Buch Samuel*, 337.

[170] Campbell, *1 Samuel*, 252.

[171] Ibid., 251.

[172] Cf. Exum, *Tragedy and Biblical Narrative*, 30.

David to restrain himself from harming Saul not once, but twice, significantly increases the impact on the audience that he has performed a great moral action. For Saul to be caught in a vulnerable position twice emphasises his weakness and degradation.

The second is that it draws attention to chapter 25. Walsh demonstrates that within narratives, symmetry works to focus interpretive attention to the centre of the symmetrical structure.[173] Many commentators have argued that the purpose of these narratives is to show that David is innocent of any crime against Saul[174] and this message is emphasised in the text. However, the bracketing of chapter 25 puts this chapter in focus and David is depicted as violent and hasty.[175] This behaviour points to the future where his lack of control is the beginning of his own decline, an allusion which has already been demonstrated in the trio of chapters but which is most prominent in chapter 25.

The third effect of the repetition between chapters 24 and 26 is that it draws attention to where the repetition is broken. This was demonstrated in the analysis above as we observed the development of the characters of David and Saul. The close similarity between the stories created a platform from which the differences could be generated.

This use of repetition between the chapters suggests an approach to eliciting meaning in this historiography different from that used by modern historians. It suggests that repetition was looked for and valued by the historiographer of Samuel because of its usefulness for creating a structure of comparison and for emphasising certain points in the narrative. It was not viewed as an implausible or eerie repetition of events, but rather as significant and meaningful. The repetition of an event doubles its significance.

Comparative analogies as structures of meaning

As we discussed in the introduction to this chapter, an important aspect of conveying the significance of an event is to relate it to the his-

---

[173] Jerome T. Walsh, *Style and Structure in Biblical Hebrew Narrative* (Collegeville: Liturgical Press, 2001), 8.

[174] Gordon, *1 & 2 Samuel*, 178.

[175] This is particularly highlighted by the relative innocence of Nabal. By all means he is depicted as foolish but many commentators agree that the punishment David threatens is inordinate to the offense [e.g. Gunn, *The Fate of King Saul*, 101], particularly as it is implied that he never asked for the protection provided by David for his shepherds [Gordon, *1 & 2 Samuel*, 183].

tory as a whole. Often this is achieved through causation, but in I Sam 24–26 there is little significant causation for the following narratives. Chapter 25 explains how David married Abigail, but Abigail herself does not appear as a significant character again in the entire book of Samuel. Many scholars speculate that the story was included in order to exonerate David from the charge he stole another man's wife,[176] an understandable suggestion considering the disconnection with other stories. Moreover, David's encounters with Saul result in his fleeing to the Philistines but he had attempted to hide among them previously in 21.11–16, so this causation appears very complex for such unremarkable actions.

Therefore, as the causal chain of the book of Samuel does not entirely justify the inclusion of these stories, the narrative has used other devices to demonstrate their significance for the overall story. The claim of this study is that comparative analogies help to organise the themes and bestow a web of meaning upon the events.

Firstly, the comparative analogy relates the three chapters of I Sam 24–26 with each other and contributes to an understanding of how each fits within the course of history. In isolation, each chapter has little relevance for the greater plot of Samuel. However, the parallels between chapters 24 and 26 communicate the development in the characters of Saul and David and, in turn, this development can be understood in terms of the rise and fall of leaders. The isolated events are given meaning through connection with other events and together they form an important aspect of the book structure.

Moreover, the complexity of the characterisation of Saul and David allows for other layers of connection to the overall course of history. In particular, David's need to restrain himself from killing Saul, highlighted by comparison with his lack of restraint regarding Nabal, is connected by analogy to a later murder he will commit against Uriah. The characterisation of David includes not only a positive depiction

---

[176] Timo Veijola, *Die Ewige Dynastie: David und die Entstehung seiner Dynastie nach der deuteronomistischen Darstellung* (Helsinki: Suomalainen Tiedeakatemia, 1975), 53–54. Cf. Biddle, "Ancestral Motifs," 634–35. See also Jon D. Levenson, "1 Samuel 25 as Literature and as History," *CBQ* 40 (1978): 11–28, and J.D. Levenson and Baruch Halpern, "The Political Import of David's Marriages," *JBL* 99 (1980): 507–18. Levenson and Halpern suggest that the historical significance of the chapter is that David married the wife of a Calebite chief in a strategic political move towards taking the throne. They admit however that this is an historical reconstruction rather than a literary reading of the chapter.

of his rise, but also an ominous foreshadowing of his moment of failure.

Furthermore, the contrast between Saul and David connects these events to other parts of the book of Samuel. It is reminiscent of the contrast between Samuel and Eli's sons in I Sam 1–4. It links to the ongoing contrast between Saul and David initiated before David has even been introduced in I Sam 15.28 ('the Lord has torn the kingdom of Israel from you this day and has given it to a neighbour of yours, who is better than you'). The widening of the contrast between I Sam 24 and 26 links these two chapters together as an additional commentary on the rise of David and the fall of Saul.

The significance of a dynamic and contrasting rise of David and fall of Saul at this point in the book of Samuel has theological, human and political levels. It demonstrates the theological significance that Yahweh has chosen David and rejected Saul, and that this governs the success of all their endeavours. The analogies create a deep analysis of the characters of these leaders, particularly in reaction to each other, and this offers an insight into human behaviour. Finally, the two political strategies of Saul and David are contrasted as Saul seeks to eliminate his enemy and David allows him to survive. David's politically strategic actions to avoid association with the death of his enemies will also be explored at the death of Saul, Jonathan and Abner and this hints at the cause for success of the accession of David to the throne.

In these ways, comparative analogies can be considered a structure of meaning because they provide a link between disparate episodes and events apart from a causal chain. Furthermore, they expound the theological, political and human themes that have relevance for later audiences.

3.4 Conclusion

This section has demonstrated a number of ways in which meaning and significance are conveyed in Samuel. The main structures of meaning that we have analysed are: the opening and closing of the book, the structure of parallel leaders and comparative analogies. In many places in the narrative, the relation of events or details to the history as a whole or to the relevant themes of politics, theology and the character of leaders is not immediately obvious. These structures of meaning draw attention to the connections and add depth to other connections that the reader has already observed. In most cases, the ways in which these devices are developed in the historiography are different from the more explicit methods of modern historiography.

There are also similarities and differences between the book of Samuel and modern historiography in the way that meaning and significance is conceived. Our first reflection concerns the categories of significance that recur throughout the book: political meaning, theological meaning and the characters of leaders. It has already been observed in the introduction that political meaning is common in modern historiography. However, theological meaning and aspects of the characters of leaders, which do not directly relate to politics, are less often considered appropriate in the significance of the past. This is illustrated by the approach of an article by Jon Levenson on I Sam 25, which looks at the chapter in terms of both 'literature' and 'history'.[177] He offers a sensitive and insightful literary analysis of the chapter and shows its importance as a proleptic view of David's fall in II Sam 11–12. He then analyses the chapter from a modern point of view of history and speculates that David's marriage to Abigail was an important political move towards him becoming king in Hebron. His distinction between the Bible as literature (or in other words, the book of Samuel's own discovery of meaning in the past) and the history that can be gleaned from it (a modern search for political causes) is appropriate because it conforms to the ideology of modern scholarship for which he is writing. His search for political causes, in addition to the significance offered by Samuel itself, demonstrates that there is a considerable difference between ancient and modern conceptions of meaning and significance.

Another observation, which has been made in this section, is that the narrative devices of Samuel often accentuate repetition in history. This suggests that, to some degree, there was a conception of history as cyclical.

In the recent past, cyclic history has often been considered characteristic of 'primitive' cultures rather than modern historiography.[178] This was influenced by the Enlightenment belief in progress, where history is a constant process of change for the better. It is therefore an

---

[177] Levenson, "1 Samuel 25 as Literature and as History," 11–28.
[178] See for example, Mircea Eliade, *Cosmos and History: The Myth of the Eternal Return* (New York: Harper, 1959).

entirely linear view of history.[179] Both progress and degeneration have now fallen out of fashion in philosophies of historiography, yet the view that modern Western historiography should be linear rather than cyclical remains prominent in our thinking.[180] Nevertheless, there are also philosophies of history that encourage the combination of both cycles and linearity in history. As an example, Gould writes:

> Time's arrow and time's cycle is, if you will, a 'great' dichotomy because each of its poles captures, by its essence, a theme so central to intellectual (and practical) life that Western people who hope to understand history must wrestle intimately with both—for time's arrow is the intelligibility of distinct and irreversible events, while time's cycle is the intelligibility of timeless order and lawlike structure. We must have both.[181]

Similarly, Corfield writes that the 'return' in history can be taken too literally but that cycles do helpfully highlight patterns and rhythms in history.[182] She notes that, in the modern day, history tends to be viewed as 'open ended waves' rather than closed circles.[183]

Historiography in Samuel is not purely cyclical, but rather biblical narrative is often referred to as one of the earliest examples of linear history.[184] The linearity of history in Samuel is attested by our study of chains of causation in an earlier section of this book. Thus, there is a conception of both repetition and constant change in history in Samuel. This is also suggested by the overall structure of Samuel that consists of repetition of the pattern of leaders, which is then in some measure broken by David. Although the combination of these

---

[179] For a discussion of progress and its pessimistic counterpart, degeneration, as a linear view of history, see Tosh, *The Pursuit of History*, 12–14, and P.J. Corfield, *Time and the Shape of History* (New Haven: Yale University Press, 2007), 85–87.

[180] See for example, Stanford, *An Introduction to the Philosophy of History*, 74–75, who writes that a linear view of history is now obvious to us. In contrast, he gives a number of examples from Greek writers who saw time as a series of repetitions. Also, Tosh, *The Pursuit of History*, 24–25, writes that history does not repeat itself because conditions will never again be identical. He is however warning against such an extreme view of the cycles of history that it can be thought to predict the future.

[181] Stephen Jay Gould, *Time's Arrow, Time's Cycle: Myth and Metaphor in the Discovery of Geological Time*, The Jerusalem-Harvard lectures. (Cambridge, Mass.: Harvard University Press, 1987), 15–16.

[182] Corfield, *Time*, 53–54. She also notes (p. 55) that cyclical views of history are not limited to Eastern cultures as there have been relatively recent attempts in the modern western world to synthesise all of world history into cycles.

[183] Ibid., 56.

[184] E.g. Stanford, *An Introduction to the Philosophy of History*, 75; Gould, *Time's Arrow*, 12; Corfield, *Time*, 82.

two views of significance in history is not universally held amongst modern philosophies of history, there is now a tendency towards once again valuing cycles as well as linearity. Thus the conception in Samuel that patterns can be found in history is not so far removed from modern historiography, even though very different techniques are used to convey these patterns.

CHAPTER FOUR

MORAL, POLITICAL AND THEOLOGICAL EVALUATION

Interpretation and the influence of ideology are present in every facet of causation, and meaning and significance in history. Now we turn to a feature of the historiography of Samuel, which by its very nature is the expression of the authors/redactors' ideology: their moral, political and theological evaluation of people and events in the past.[1] An evaluation of the past looks at questions such as: Did these events have a positive or negative effect on the society, the politics, the future? What is a moral assessment of the individuals or groups who are the agents or actors in history? Were these actions and events condoned, tolerated or condemned by the Divine? Such evaluation is often a vehicle for presenting the ideology or theology of the author through the events, although this can be an unconscious as well as a conscious process. The historians' evaluation affects the way they present and colour the people and events but can also take the form of explicit comments and conclusions about the history.

Unlike causation and meaning, which are generally regarded as both desirable and necessary in all history, there has been significant debate about whether moral, political and theological evaluation has a place in modern historiography. Many have argued that it is inappropriate for historians to pass moral judgments, although the same arguments can be applied to political and theological evaluation. Objections against moral evaluation in history include: it compromises the objectivity of the historian; historians are not qualified and lack subtlety in such evaluations; it is problematic to judge dead people; judgment should be made against societies not individuals; the historian can never understand an historical agent well enough; and there is some difference between contemporary morals and those of the past.[2]

---

[1] The term 'ideology' is not used pejoratively here but rather, as a term encompassing the totality of the historian's beliefs and values concerning morality, politics and theology.

[2] See the overview of these reasons in Adrian Oldfield, "Moral Judgments in History," *History and Theory* 20 (1981): 262–66; and Richard T. Vann, "Historians and Moral Evaluations," *History and Theory* 43 (2004): 5–9.

However, ideology is inescapable in historiography and will manifest in the form of value judgments. In order to avoid moral judgments entirely, even such words as 'crimes' or 'murders' become problematic.[3] Both Oldfield and Vann argue that many of the other objections made against moral evaluations ought to be taken into consideration but are not necessarily reasons against evaluation altogether. For example, historians ought to be in dialogue with others, such as philosophers or the readers, when making their judgments. Furthermore, judgments are for the living rather than the dead.[4] Although, for some, moral judgments remain an inevitable but undesirable byproduct of the ideological influence on history, other modern scholars consider such evaluation to be a valuable characteristic.[5] Many modern historians believe that history ought to be used for learning lessons for the present and future[6] and evaluation of the past is an important step in this process. As Berkhofer points out regarding impartiality, "in this view the ultimate usefulness of history lies paradoxically in its lack of immediate or obvious utility."[7] The didactic purpose of history is not universally well regarded in modern history and historians generally seek to avoid reading their own ideologies into the past. Ultimately however, many will evaluate the tragedies and triumphs that have occurred in human history and in this way measure the past against a moral standard or against political or other ideology.

Despite the ambivalent modern attitude towards ideological evaluation in historiography, it is an important and central characteristic of the historiography of Samuel. In particular, theological evaluation is visible to modern eyes, probably because this is a type of ideology eschewed in modern historiography. There have been numerous stud-

---

[3] Vann, "Historians and Moral Evaluations," 12–16. Vann mentions an historian Hilberg, who attempted to eschew all such value-laden terms but found the practice untenable.

[4] Ibid.: 16, 17.

[5] Vann (p. 10), agreeing with an earlier work of Isaiah Berlin, writes of the necessity and propriety of evaluating human actions from a variety of viewpoints: moral as well as aesthetic and political.

[6] E.g. Neville Morley, *Writing Ancient History* (Ithaca: Cornell University Press, 1999), 137–59. He gives a number of reasons why history is important including: learning from the past [see also Michael Stanford, *A Companion to the Study of History* (Oxford: Blackwell, 1994), 40–41], understanding why there has been change since the past, understanding the present and evaluating the present.

[7] Robert F. Berkhofer, *Beyond the Great Story: History as Text and Discourse* (Cambridge, Mass.: Belknap Press of Harvard University Press, 1995), 140.

ies on ideology in the narrative of the Hebrew Bible and the book of
Samuel.[8] Although scholars debate whether the historiography of Samuel has a didactic or propagandist aim, evaluation of the past forms
the core of both these purposes. Thus, in this chapter, we will examine
the nature of this ideological evaluation and how it is conveyed using
narrative devices.

Methods of evaluation in Samuel

Berkhofer describes a number of ways in which modern historiography conveys conclusions about the past. First, there are explicit methods, where the historian's view is simply spelled out or he/she may use
adverbial praise and blame words such as 'rightfully' or 'wrongfully'.
Historians may also seek to correct explicitly what they consider to
be misunderstood lessons of the past.[9] Although there is consensus
that the historiography of Samuel is laden with ideological evaluation,
there are very few explicit judgment statements in the book.[10]

Berkhofer also refers to methods that are more subtle in their persuasion of the reader. For example, an historian may point to the paradox or contradiction "presented by the gulf between a society's ideals

---

[8] Examples, which approach the subject from many different angles, include:
Yairah Amit, *History and Ideology: Introduction to Historiography in the Hebrew Bible*
(Sheffield: Sheffield Academic Press, 1999); Marc Zvi Brettler, *The Creation of History
in Ancient Israel* (London: Routledge, 1995), chapter 6; Meir Sternberg, *The Poetics
of Biblical Narrative: Ideological Literature and the Drama of Reading* (Bloomington:
Indiana University Press, 1985); Giovanni Garbini, *History and Ideology in Ancient
Israel* (London: SCM, 1988); James Barr, *History and Ideology in the Old Testament:
Biblical Studies at the End of a Millennium* (Oxford: Oxford University Press, 2000).

[9] Berkhofer, *Beyond the Great Story*, 142.

[10] Bar-Efrat explains that the narrative does not give direct commentary on characters but judges them indirectly [Shimeon Bar-Efrat, *Das erste Buch Samuel: Ein
narratologisch-philologischer Kommentar*, trans. Johannes Klein, BWANT 176 (Stuttgart: Kohlhammer, 2007), 15]. He also argues that the covert means of evaluation are
more effective than the overt in narrative in Shimeon Bar-Efrat, *Narrative Art in the
Bible*, JSOTSup. 70 (Sheffield: Almond Press, 1989), 32. Eslinger performs a computer
analysis of explicit evaluation in the Deuteronomistic History and observes that it
occurs in spikes [Lyle M. Eslinger, *Into the Hands of the Living God*, JSOTSup. 84
(Sheffield: Almond Press, 1989), chapter 7]. However, none of these spikes in the book
of Samuel can be attributed to the narrator, rather to other characters. Schökel writes
that for a reader who shares a system of values with the author, cool reporting can be
more impressive that explicit emotion at events [Luis Alonso Schökel, "Narrative Art
in Joshua-Judges-Samuel-Kings," in *Israel's Past in Present Research*, ed. V. Philips
Long, (Winona Lake: Eisenbrauns, 1999), 273].

and practices."[11] Evaluation may also be conveyed through the voices
and viewpoints represented in the text.[12] Similarly, Oldfield observes
that constant appraisals of action throughout a work of historiography can be tedious and that "Historians can make clear their positions implicitly, in terms of the language they use, and in the tone
and style of composition."[13] These implicit methods predominate in
the book of Samuel. The past is evaluated within the structures of the
plot, characterisation and other features of its narrative. Despite the
unashamed ideology, people and issues are not presented in black and
white terms and the narrator often allows more than one opinion to be
heard and evaluated. A character may be depicted in an overall positive light, yet the narrator will not refrain from exploring that character's weaknesses. The sparseness of explicit comments in the text
allows the narrator flexibility to convey complex and therefore critical
interpretations of the events that otherwise could not be summed up
in a single statement.

As a foundation for examining these devices more closely, we shall
review a comprehensive list of methods of evaluation compiled by
Meir Sternberg. These are: (1) narratorial evaluation of an agent or
an action through a series of epithets; (2) through a single epithet;
(3) through a choice of loaded language; (4) explicit judgment left
ambiguous between narrator and characters; (5) as in the first three,
but judgment is relegated to characters; (6) judgment through a non-
verbal objective; (7) charged dramatisation, lingering over and thus
foregrounding plot elements designed for judgment; (8) informa-
tional redundancy; (9) direct inside view of characters; (10) the play
of perspectives; (11) order of presentation; (12) order of presentation
involving the displacement of conventional patterns; (13) analogical
patterning; (14) recurrence of key words along the sequence; (15) neutral or pseudo-objective narration.[14] Sternberg writes generally about
narrative in the Hebrew Bible but these categories can be applied to
Samuel. In the following discussion, each of these methods will be
referred to as (1), (2) etc.

(1) and (2) are the most overt of these evaluative techniques, yet they
appear rarely in Samuel. The sons of Eli are described in I Sam 2.12 as

---

[11] Berkhofer, *Beyond the Great Story*, 142.
[12] Ibid., 155–69.
[13] Oldfield, "Moral Judgments in History," 273.
[14] Sternberg, *Poetics*, 475–81.

בני בליעל (lit. 'sons of Belial' i.e. worthless men). Nabal and Abigail are given contrasting character traits in I Sam 25.3, והאשה טובת־שכל ויפת תאר והאיש קשה ורע מעללים ('And the woman was clever and beautiful and the man was harsh and mean'). Sheba is described in II Sam 20 as איש בליעל (lit. 'man of Belial') and the woman who delivers Sheba's head to Joab is described as אשה חכמה ('a wise woman'). These epithets are infrequent and, when they occur, they give a black and white evaluation of the characters. Yet closer analysis of the epithets reveals that they are often not as straightforward as they first appear. Each of these epithets describes a minor character in the narrative and, in each case, the straightforward evaluation has more complex implications for other characters. The turn of phrase, which passes judgment explicitly on Hophni and Phineas, implicitly suggests a negative judgment on Eli as the father of the sons of Belial. Nabal's meanness is important for the story's plot but it may also cast suspicion over why David sent to ask for provisions, making it a possibility within the text that he was deliberately provoking trouble.[15] The beauty of Abigail, who becomes David's wife by the end of the story, similarly adds another dimension to David's possible motives. The story of Sheba, a worthless man who leads a rebel people against the king, highlights David's loosening grasp over his kingdom and the ramifications of his weakness in handling the affairs of his children. The wise woman of Abel, who acts decisively to dispose of Sheba, is also in contrast with the weakness of David and so implicitly highlights his lack of wisdom in these matters. In essence, these overt judgments are used only where they highlight more complex issues at hand.

Nevertheless, when such overt comments or other direct information from the narrator occur, they have absolute authority in the text. Recent literary theory makes a distinction between the narrator and the implied author of the text such that the opinions expressed by the narrator are not necessarily those of the implied author. Noll has suggested both that this be applied to the book of Samuel and that the comments of the narrator are sometimes contradicted by the rest of the presentation by the author. He avers, "David's character

---

[15] E.g. Bodner suggests that it is almost as if David is expecting a rejection from Nabal [Keith Bodner, *1 Samuel: A Narrative Commentary* (Sheffield: Sheffield Phoenix Press, 2008), 261]. Edelman observes that David requires two hundred men to mind his supplies, suggesting that he already had plenty [Diana Edelman, *King Saul in the Historiography of Judah*, JSOT Supp. 121 (Sheffield: JSOT Press, 1991), 209–10].

emerges, at least partially, by means of the opposing perspectives provided by the narrator's and the implied author's differing evaluations of him."[16] This device is much more typical of modern literature and goes beyond the aims of the biblical text.[17] Furthermore, the narrator in Samuel is an omniscient impersonal observer. As there is no characterisation of the narrator, there is no basis for the reader to judge the reliability of his comments. Therefore, in this study we will assume that the opinions expressed by the narrator are those also of the implied author. Any incongruity between the overt comments of the narrator and the presentation of events, such as expressed by Noll, reflects the limited nature of the narratorial comments rather than an intentional disagreement between the two. The narrator's comments do not make conclusive statements of evaluation of the whole narrative but rather, remark on a small specific aspect of the characters or events. The narrator's full evaluation can only be gleaned from the narrative as a whole.

One of the covert methods of conveying evaluation in biblical narrative is through the play of perspectives (10). An example of how viewpoints work in Samuel is found in the two stories of Saul's death in I Sam 31 and II Sam 1. Two points of view, the first given authoritatively by the narrator and the second by the self-interested Amalekite, drive forward the plot. David acts on the second report to establish his loyalty to Saul, but the existence of the first report creates ambiguity in David's character as the reader questions David's ready acceptance of the story. Thus a clash of viewpoints gives the reader privileged access to this conflict and conveys significance in the second account.[18]

---

[16] K.L. Noll, *The Faces of David* (Sheffield: Sheffield Academic Press, 1997), 35.

[17] Yairah Amit, "'The Glory of Israel Does Not Deceive or Change His Mind': On the Reliability of Narrator and Speakers in Biblical Narrative," *Prooftexts* 12 (1992): 204. Bach also advocates contending with the viewpoint of the narrator but does so in the context of a feminist reading of the passage [Alice Bach, "Signs of the Flesh: Observations on Characterization in the Bible," *Semeia* 63 (1993): 63–69]. The concept of an unreliable narrator is more convincing in post-modern approaches rather than as the intention of the author in an ancient context. For an alternative description of the narrator in Samuel, see Eslinger, *Into the Hands*, 15–16, 21–23. He describes the narrator as exploiting his/her neutral and external narrative position to give an insight into the minds of characters.

[18] See also the studies on perspective in the wooing of Rebekah in Sternberg, *Poetics*, 131ff; and in Gen 37 in Adele Berlin, *Poetics and Interpretation of Biblical Narrative*, Bible and Literature Series (Sheffield: Almond, 1983), 48ff.

Ambiguity about judgment is often introduced through the mouths and thoughts of the characters (4), (5), and (9).[19] As Sternberg points out, the judgment of other characters is fallible since "the judging figures are themselves objects of judgment."[20] Therefore, at one end of the spectrum, where the characters have no alternative motives drawn, their judgments closely represent the viewpoint of the narrator. Examples include: the ransom of Jonathan by the people after Saul's rash vow in I Sam 14; and the refusal of Saul's servants to strike down the priests at Nob in I Sam 22. The judgment of spectators within the story is a persuasive verdict on the inappropriateness of Saul's actions. At the other extreme, the words of an enemy, such as Goliath in I Sam 17.42–44, lack persuasive authority because of his status as enemy of Israel. Characterisation is important for establishing how to read characters' judgments of situations and other characters.

Black and white characterisations tend to be reserved for minor characters in the narrative and the characters who are most vocal in their judgment of others are usually drawn with more complexity. There are many evaluations by characters within the story that are not as incontrovertible as they initially seem, because of their ambiguous motives or limited knowledge of the circumstances. For example, when it is reported that Jonathan loved David in I Sam 18.1, the obvious assessment is that this is a positive sign about David's character, particularly as it comes from the son of David's rival, Saul. Yet the reader may also reflect on the limitations of Jonathan's knowledge. Jonathan has only seen the public events of David's heroic feat against Goliath in 17.31–54, heard David's brief exchange with Saul in 17.55–58 (implied by 18.1) and would not know of David's particular interest in the reward in 17.12–30. The text allows for the possibility that Jonathan does not know David's full character or may be deceived about him, so that his assessment is not as conclusive despite its explicitness.

---

[19] Cf. Oldfield, "Moral Judgments in History," 271. He describes a similar method in modern historiography and writes, "If sympathetic understanding of the man of the past is required, then this can be conveyed with much more subtlety, and ultimately more effect, if the historian, instead of pronouncing his own moral judgments, speaks through the mouths of contemporaries, using their recorded thoughts and opinions as pieces of evidence much like any other. If he is skillful, the historian can still make us aware of his own moral position. But, because he is using contemporary utterances, he can also make us aware of the views and opinions of those whose moral positions diverge from his own."

[20] Sternberg, *Poetics*, 476.

Similarly, at least two interpretations are possible for Abigail's praise
of David and belief in God's protection in I Sam 25.28–31. It may
reflect the narrator's own positive assessment of David, evidenced
by the fulfillment of Abigail's prophecy in the narrative. However, it
may also be interpreted as motivated and shaped by her desire to win
favour with David through flattery.[21] The narrator plays an important
role in characterising the speakers of these viewpoints so that the audience is aware of their subjectivity. It is significant that complexity in
characterisation leads to complexity in understanding the ideology
that is being expressed by them. Ultimately, a cycle is created where
the characters, who express evaluations, are in turn evaluated by other
characters. This results in complexity of evaluation and characters, and
many layers of meaning within the text.

One character who holds a unique position in the narrative is the
Divine. He is an actor within the narrative like other characters, yet he
shares the omniscience of the narrator and his evaluations of events
and character hold particular importance.[22] However, God's moral
judgments on situations are rare, possibly only occurring in I Sam
15.35 and II Sam 11.27, each at major turning points for the leadership of Saul and David. Furthermore, other events in the narrative also
reveal that God has rejected Saul and that he is displeased with David,
making these explicit judgments somewhat redundant. In these two
situations, God's words or opinion are mediated through the narrator
but, in other situations, the words of the Lord are mediated through
a prophet. As the prophets, particularly Samuel, are often personally
involved in the narrative, their mediation is not as reliable as that
of the narrator. Occasionally there is cause to view the words of the
prophets with suspicion.

Often events are enacted, rather than stated, in the narrative to
imply the judgment of Yahweh. God withdraws his spirit from Saul,
he protects David from Saul's attacks and answers David's prayers for
protection when his kingdom starts to slip away from him. David may
sing in II Sam 22.21:

יגמלני יהוה כצדקתי
כבר ידי ישיב לי

---

[21] E.g. Bodner, *1 Samuel*, 266. See also Edelman, *King Saul*, 214, who suggests Abigail's desire is to become David's mistress.
[22] Bar-Efrat, *Narrative Art*, 19.

('The Lord has dealt with me according to my righteousness, according to the cleanness of my hands he rewarded me'), yet God himself never cites David's righteousness as his reason for supporting him.[23] Many times throughout the text God's favour is made explicit, yet his reasons are not given. For example, it is reported that God loved Solomon (II Sam 24) but not whether God has bestowed his love arbitrarily or because of some personal merit of Solomon.

These limitations in the presentation of God's moral and ideological judgments affect our assessment of whether his point of view is fallible. Most readers in history have assumed that God's judgment is infallible, although an exception to this is Gunn's fresh reading of the story of David where he questions the morality of David's child dying for his offence.[24] However, there are also points where the narrator's evaluation of events is more complex than the sparser judgments of God. In I Sam 24 and 26 there is some evidence of the narrator's sympathy towards Saul, despite Yahweh's intervention in favour of David. Similarly, the pivotal point in Saul's leadership, when he spares Agag in I Sam 15, contains traces of sympathy towards him, particularly in his repentance after the event.[25] In response to such observations, Sternberg says that God is concerned with man as a moral being whereas the narrator is interested in psychology and humanity. The difference in interests allows the narrator to complicate, but not undercut, God's point of view.[26] However, the narrator's study of the psychology of human motivations cannot be separated from his moral evaluation of them. Rather, there are very few explicit moral judgments from God and it is primarily his actions and final decisions that are reported in the text. This allows flexibility for the narrator to create a more

---

[23] The closest that he comes to this is in I Sam 13.14, בקש יהוה לו איש כלבבו ('The Lord has sought a man after/according to his own heart'). However, most commentators agree that this idiom means 'according to his own choosing' rather than indicating any like-mindedness [P. Kyle McCarter, Jr., *I Samuel*, The Anchor Bible (New York: Doubleday, 1980), 229; Robert P. Gordon, *1 & 2 Samuel: A Commentary* (Exeter: Paternoster, 1986), 134].

[24] D.M. Gunn and Danna Nolan Fewell, *Narrative in the Hebrew Bible* (Oxford: Oxford University Press, 1993), 88.

[25] Also, the complicity of the people in Saul's offence, his seeming conviction that he had followed God's commands and his insistence that he intended to sacrifice the best animals to God at Gilgal, further demonstrate a balanced account of Saul's actions. This evidence even leads Gunn to suggest that Saul's culpability in the whole affair is very minimal [D.M. Gunn, *The Fate of King Saul: An Interpretation of a Biblical Story*, JSOTSup. 14 (Sheffield: JSOT Press, 1980), 41–56].

[26] Sternberg, *Poetics*, 157–8.

complex picture of the events within this framework. For example, God's rejection of Saul does not necessarily imply that God considers his character to be wholly evil. It is the task of the narrator to give a more complex depiction, offering reasons for why it was a difficult but justified decision. Yahweh's judgment of events is the dominant cause for 'gaps' in the narrative, a phenomenon we will examine shortly. The narrator presents the reader with God's actions but uses other means of commentary to answer why these actions may have taken place.

Within the complexity of the narrative, there is a minority of events that imply a clear negative judgment on their agent (6). These occur at several turning points in the narrative such as: the corruption of Eli's sons, Saul's attempts to kill David, David's adultery with Bathsheba and murder of her husband, and the rape of Tamar. In several of these cases, other devices are used to intensify the evil of these actions. The redundancy of information (8) in II Sam 11.1, ויהי לתשובת השנה לעת צאת המלאכים ('It came to pass in the spring of the year, at the time the messengers[27] go out [to battle]'), highlights David's sin as he neglects his duty as king and wrongs one of his soldiers who is at battle. The lingering in the narrative (7) over David's efforts to have Uriah killed, compared to the terseness of his adultery with Bathsheba, emphasises how this deed greatly compounds his sin. The use of the *Leitwort* (14) 'sister' in II Sam 13 (it appears 8 times in the chapter) reminds the audience that not only has Amnon violated a young woman but his own sister, doubling the offence. In these passages of obvious moral corruption, the narrator often employs the most neutral language so that the deeds speak for themselves (15).

---

[27] Note that the LXX contains a variant reading favoured by most commentators and translators, εἰς τὸν καιρὸν τῆς ἐξοδίας τῶν βασιλέων ('at the time of the going out of kings'). This would carry an even more obvious negative evaluation of David. Although Alter prefers this variant reading [Robert Alter, *The David Story: A Translation with Commentary of 1 and 2 Samuel* (New York: W.W. Norton, 1999), 249], he points out (p. 250) that there is another contrast between David who is 'sitting' (יושב) and the messengers who 'went out' (צאת) in the same verse. The use of these antonyms also suggests that David is lax in fulfilling his responsibility. Polzin and Bodner prefer the *lectio difficilior* 'messengers' but point out that both are implied by the text anyway because of their similarity [Robert M. Polzin, *David and the Deuteronomist: A Literary Study of the Deuteronomic History; Part Three—II Samuel* (San Francisco: Harper and Row, 1993), 108–17; Keith Bodner, *David Observed: A King in the Eyes of His Court* (Sheffield: Sheffield Phoenix Press, 2005), 83–84]. Polzin describes the verse as 'deliciously ambiguous' (p. 108) and demonstrates that there is an ongoing theme of messengers throughout this section of the narrative.

Apart from these few pivotal events, most situations have greater ambiguity. The loaded language (3) that is used to describe David's reign in Israel in II Sam 8.15, ויהי דוד עשה משפט וצדקה לכל־עמו ('David administered justice and righteousness for all his people') is subverted in the next verse by the reference to Joab as the head of the army, despite his unlawful slaughter of Abner in II Sam 3. This order of presentation (11) highlights flaws in David's משפט ('justice').

In the moral and theological commentary in Samuel, many view-points are represented and complex assessments of the characters and events are developed. Yet, the text finds coherence within this complexity by means of its global structures. The analogy (13), which is drawn between Hannah and other barren women of Hebrew narratives, emphasises the piety of Hannah and the worthlessness of Eli in I Sam 1. The theme of blindness, which recurs throughout the stories of Eli and Saul, creates a coherent picture of weakness among these leaders. The implications of David's sin are explored through the ensuing chaos in his family and kingdom in the chapters that follow it. The patterning of stories in I Sam 18–20, which describe the loyalty of Saul's children and the people of Israel to David rather than Saul, highlights his lack of control over his children. This is reminiscent of Eli and Samuel and will soon be repeated in the story of David. These patterns in the narrative subtly reinforce certain evaluations of its characters.

Furthermore, analogy can be based upon contrast. By juxtaposing and interspersing the story of Samuel with the corruption of Eli's sons in I Sam 2–3, an analogy is drawn that highlights the difference between the two possible heirs to Eli's position. The calmness of David compared to Saul's lack of self-possession in I Sam 18–26 highlights the characteristics of each leader.

Complex Evaluation

Theoretically, these methods of conveying judgment and commentary combine in order to present a critical evaluation of the figures and events in history. However, historical critical studies of Samuel have highlighted that there are many places within the book where evaluations of situations contradict each other and ideologies clash, even within small sections of the text. In other words, devices, such as those enumerated above, offer opposing evaluations in close proximity to each other. Many scholars have reconstructed sources for the narrative based on this variation in ideology. Sections that express the same ideology are attributed to the same sources or redactions. A well-known example is I Sam 8–12, which was first proposed by Wellhausen to consist of two sources—one favourable toward the monarchy and the other unfavourable—in an attempt to account for the positive and negative attitudes found in the section. Scholars at various times have identified sources in Samuel corresponding to the Pentateuchal sources J, E and D;[28] they have proposed the role of the Deuteronomist in compiling various traditions;[29] and they have expanded this to include several Deuteronomistic redactors of a prophetic history compiled from a number of still earlier sources,[30] in order to identify strands with homogeneous ideologies. The large number of source theories for Samuel reflects the disagreement between scholars on what ideology or evaluation the text is conveying. This disagreement is not surprising considering the dominance of covert commentary techniques and the ambiguity created by many of them.

The use of covert commentary, rather than explicit statements, results in few direct contradictions within the evaluation. When these opposing viewpoints are juxtaposed, the ambiguity allows scope for their reinterpretation within the final form of the text. There are many pericopes that have clear ideological evaluation when viewed in isolation but that can be reinterpreted when placed within their overall context.

The final form achieves an overall complexity in evaluation of events by bringing together many different ideological viewpoints and this reflects the ambiguities of real life situations. It offers a number of different voices that must each be assessed in terms of the surrounding narrative. Whilst it is possible, or even probable, that these voices originated in different traditions, their position in the final form of Samuel contributes to an overall literary product that offers an insightful exploration of the issues and characters in the narrative. To some degree, 'contradiction of evaluation' and 'complexity of evaluation' are two labels for the same feature in the text. Therefore, we cannot expect every contradiction to be resolved.

---

[28] Karl Budde, *Geschichte der althebräischen Literatur* (Leipzig: Amelang, 1909), 59.
[29] Martin Noth, *The Deuteronomistic History*, JSOTSup. 15. (Sheffield: JSOT Press, 1981), 54–56.
[30] McCarter, *I Samuel*, 12–30.

Before analysing evaluation in specific passages of Samuel, we will examine two important (and related) concepts that emerge when the different viewpoints and modes of evaluation come together in the narrative: gaps and juxtaposition of opposing opinions.

The first of these occur when the narrative leaves a gap in the description of events that must be hypothetically reconstructed by the reader.[31] The reconstruction should be validated by features in the narrative, and is thus different to hypotheses about events to which the text does not give any support or even rules out.

The principle of leaving gaps in the narrative is found throughout the book of Samuel. The text does not state explicitly what the moral or theological significance of an event is but rather, leaves a gap for the reader to deduce this meaning. The narrator guides the reader with information for possible reconstructions of this ideology and so creates ambiguity and complexity in the people and events. Multiple reconstructions make the ideology multi-dimensional as each reconstruction can explore different aspects of the whole situation. Furthermore, although many readers will decide on one particular interpretation, the text itself does not force this decision, leaving the way open for some readers to view many aspects simultaneously, and others to develop further depth on each subsequent reading.

The concept of gaps is particularly important for understanding the characters' motivations, because their inner thoughts are rarely stated explicitly and the audience is left to judge by their words and actions. This creates realism not only because people rarely act from single motives but also because the audience is left to discern motives in the same way that they discern other people's motives in real life. External actions are observed and motivations inferred. The difference from real life, however, is that the text subtly controls the possible reconstructions of motives because it controls the evidence that is presented to the reader. This technique is also a succinct way of creating ambiguous and therefore complex characters. It compels the reader to contemplate a large number of possibilities whilst using only a few words.

The second concept of key interest in this study is the juxtaposing of opposite opinions. Sternberg relates this feature to gap filling and describes the effect as a discontinuity that begs for resolution by the

---

[31] The term 'gaps' to describe this feature is used in Sternberg, *Poetics*, chapter 6.

reader.[32] In other words, this type of juxtaposition creates a discord for the reader that compels him/her to ask a certain question and so find a resolution to the discord.[33] In our analysis of I Sam 8–12, we will see that this juxtaposition can come from two different characters expressing opposite opinions or, even more startling, it can come from the same viewpoint. In this latter case, the audience's attention is directed towards the subtle nuances of the character's position rather than being permitted to accept a caricature of them.

Types of evaluation

The ambiguity and complexity in the mode of conveying evaluation in Samuel makes the distinction between the types of evaluation even more difficult. In this section, we will examine moral, political and theological evaluation. Together, these three types encompass all the different aspects of ideology that scholars have identified at various times in the text. For example, there is moral evaluation of David's sin with Bathsheba, political evaluation of the institution of the monarchy and theological evaluation of David, not Saul, as the man after Yahweh's heart. Ultimately, however, these three categories are not completely distinct and often the first two are subsumed under the third. Within the world of the narrative, the evaluation of the Divine on any situation is taken as authoritative within the text. Thus a moral or political evaluation of an event will, in most cases, also be a theological one. There are exceptions to this. We will see that narrator expresses positive and negative arguments for a monarchy that lie outside of theological concerns.

4.1   THE INSTITUTION OF THE MONARCHY—I SAM 8–12

I Sam 8–12 has been a key focus of source critical debates in the book of Samuel. Wellhausen's division of the chapters into pro- and anti-monarchial sources initiated more than a century of debate over the

---

[32] Ibid., 242–47.
[33] Compare the similar use of oxymoron in poetry as described in W.G.E. Watson, "Hebrew Poetry," in *Text in Context*, ed. A.D.H. Mayes (Oxford: Oxford University Press, 2000), 277: "the apparent contradiction of *oxymoron* is an invitation to its resolution." The juxtaposition of opposite ideologies functions as a type of large scale oxymoron.

origins of the ideologies in these chapters.[34] He proposed that chapters 9–10.16 and 11 were in favour of the monarchy and so therefore should be dated to an early period when the monarchy was still popular. Chapters 7, 8, 10.17–27 and 12 were opposed to the monarchy and were written in a later period when Israel no longer had a king and theocracy was idealised.[35] Noth's revision of Wellhausen's theory has also had far reaching influence. He suggested that the Deuteronomist imposed his anti-monarchic account over a number of different Saul traditions that formed an earlier account of his rise to kingship.[36] The tendency since Wellhausen and Noth has been to question the homogeneity of the ideology in each of the pro- and anti-monarchial sources and so postulate more sources and traditions that constitute Wellhausen's original sources. Weiser, in a turning point from Wellhausen and Noth, points to the discrepancies within the sections supposed to be entirely the work of the Deuteronomist and so he postulates many older independent traditions in these sections.[37] In contrast, Crüsemann returns to the basic formulation of pro- and anti-monarchial sources but suggests that there are not as many anti-monarchy sources as previously supposed. He limits these to 8.1–3, 11–17, 12.3–5 and 8.7, 12.12, which he dates to an early period between Absalom's rebellion and the division of the kingdom.[38]

However, other scholars have argued that there is unity within the chapters, usually attributable to the Deuteronomist, even if this unity incorporates a number of tensions within the text. Such a position

---

[34] See overview in V. Philips Long, *The Reign and Rejection of King Saul: A Case for Literary and Theological Coherence*, SBL Dissertation Series (Atlanta: Scholars Press, 1989), 1766–180.

[35] Julius Wellhausen, *Prolegomena to the History of Ancient Israel* (Gloucester, Mass.: Smith, 1973), 253–55.

[36] Noth, *The Deuteronomistic History*, 49–53.

[37] Artur Weiser, *Introduction to the Old Testament* (London: Darton, Longman & Todd, 1961), 159–63.

[38] Frank Crüsemann, *Der Widerstand gegen das Königtum* (Neukirchen-Vluyn: Neukirchener Verlag, 1978), 54–84. There have been many other suggestions for source divisions in these chapters, which there is not room to survey here. For overviews, see Hans Jochen Boeker, *Die Beurteilung der Anfänge des Königtums in den deuteronomistischen Anschnitten des I. Samuelbuches* (Neukirchen-Vluyn: Neukirchener Verlag, 1969), 1–10; Crüsemann, *Der Widerstand*, 54–73; Ronald E. Clements, "Deuteronomistic Interpretation of the Founding of the Monarchy in 1 Sam 8," *VT* 24 (1974): 398–410; A.D.H. Mayes, "Rise of the Israelite Monarchy," *ZAW* 90 (1978): 1–19; Dennis J. McCarthy, "Inauguration of Monarchy in Israel: A Form-Critical Study of 1 Samuel 8–12," *Interpretation* 27 (1973): 405–6; Gordon, *1 & 2 Samuel*, 26–35.

requires an understanding of the ideology of the text that is more nuanced than the extremes of pro- or anti-monarchy. For example, Boeker proposes that the text is not anti-monarchial per se but rather it gives warnings about the dangers of kingship. Furthermore, it is not Saul that the text is criticising but the institution of kingship. Thus, positive views about Saul and negative warnings about kings stand side by side.[39] Clements explores further the position that the text is not against kingship as an institution. He argues that this complex ideological picture has come about because the Deuteronomist wished to include positive statements about King David. Therefore, he suggests that the text is condemning the precipitous request of the people of Israel and their rejection of Yahweh as their true king. Saul is depicted as a "futile and abortive monarch" and a result of Israel's hasty request.[40] Mayes draws attention to the role of chapter 12 in solving the problem of the rupture of the covenant created by Israel's request for a king. Again, he argues that the text is not against kingship but rather Israel's rejection of Yahweh as their king.[41] McKenzie also gives support to the view that the Deuteronomist is at worst ambivalent towards the monarchy and that it is the abandonment of Yahweh that is condemned.[42] McCarthy offers a slightly different reading where he suggests that kingship is depicted negatively in chapter 8, because Israel was looking for a war leader when Yahweh had always provided this. The depiction of Saul as a deliverer puts a negative spin on the otherwise positive stories that follow but this is resolved when Samuel returns as a judge in chapter 12 and Israel repents of their sin.[43] Most of these scholars still believe the text has multiple origins and many attempt to trace them. However, they also believe that these traditions have come together to create a complex ideological picture rather than a series of outright contradictions. They postulate that the

---

[39] Boeker, *Die Beurteilung der Anfänge des Königtums.*

[40] Clements, "Deuteronomistic Interpretation of the Founding of the Monarchy in 1 Sam 8," 406–7.

[41] Mayes, "Rise of the Israelite Monarchy," 1–19. See also Baruch Halpern, *The Constitution of the Monarchy in Israel* (Chico: Scholars Press, 1981), 158. Halpern conceptualises chapter 12 as embracing the new institution within the old covenant.

[42] Steven L. McKenzie, "The Trouble with Kingship," in *Israel Constructs its History: Deuteronomistic Historiography in Recent Research*, ed. Albert de Pury, Thomas Römer, and Jean-Daniel Macchi (Sheffield: Sheffield Academic Press, 2000), 303, 308.

[43] McCarthy, "Inauguration of Monarchy in Israel," 411–12

Deuteronomist has utilised older traditions, placing them side-by-side and giving them a new ideological standpoint.[44]

This vast body of research in historical critical studies provides the impetus for our study on the final form of I Sam 8–12. Their work highlights that the text is offering multiple opinions on the institution of the monarchy, many of which contradict each other. Some scholars maintain that the text remains a patchwork of these ideologies, whilst others have proposed that a new, more complex ideology or evaluation of the history emerges.[45]

Eslinger, and later Fokkelman and Long, who both advocate a uni-fied, coherent reading of these chapters, have pointed to the use of different character and narratorial viewpoints as accounting for the different ideological stances.[46] Eslinger, in particular, has detailed the

---

[44] E.g. Boeker, *Die Beurteilung der Anfänge des Königtums*, 1–10, 16–17; Mayes, "Rise of the Israelite Monarchy," 11; and McKenzie, "The Trouble with Kingship," 286. These scholars subscribe to Noth's basic analysis even though they believe the anti-monarchic source is more nuanced that Noth understood it and thus its ideol-ogy does not completely jar with the older material. McKenzie, "The Trouble with Kingship," 286–314, also examines more closely how the Deuteronomist has linked the various sources together using editorial verses at the end of each unit. McCarthy, "Inauguration of Monarchy in Israel," 401–12, accepts the role of the Deuteronomist but advocates a theory of change through constantly evolving traditions of oral lit-erature rather than in discrete moments. See also E.H. Scheffler, "Saving Saul from the Deuteronomist," in *Past, Present, Future*, ed. Johannes C. De Moor and H.F. Van Rooy (Leiden: Brill, 2000), 263–71. Following Karel van der Toorn, "Saul and the Rise of Israelite State Religion," *VT* 43 (1993): 519–42, Scheffler suggests that the Deuter-onomist has incorporated older pro-Saul traditions into a final work designed to vilify Saul. The reason he gives for the Deuteronomist to include material in favour of Saul is that he "set himself a difficult task" (p. 266).

[45] E.g. Bar-Efrat, *Das erste Buch Samuel*, 139, writes that there are two views of the monarchy in the same narrative, which demonstrate both its positives and negatives, and that opinions were divided. He offers the synthesis that the rule of the king does not replace the rule of God, but is in addition to it and dependent on it.

[46] Lyle M. Eslinger, "Viewpoints and Point of View in 1 Samuel 8–12," *JSOT* 26 (1983): 61–76; J.P. Fokkelman, *Vow and Desire*, Vol. IV of *Narrative Art and Poetry in the Books of Samuel: A Full Interpretation Based on Stylistic and Structural Analyses* (Assen: Van Gorcum, 1993), 320; Long, *The Reign and Rejection of King Saul*, 181. See also Sternberg's analysis of interpretations from different viewpoints in narrative in *Poetics*, 129–52; and Eslinger, *Into the Hands*, for a more general study on evaluation through points of view in Hebrew narrative. Cf. Antony F. Campbell, *1 Samuel*, FOTL (Grand Rapids: Eerdmans, 2003), 90–131. Similar to Eslinger and Fokkelman, Camp-bell sees the text as an artful juxtaposition of different points of view but still explains the origin of these points of view as being from different sources or traditions. Thus, reading the text such as Eslinger and Fokkelman do, does not eliminate the possibility that it is a compilation of sources. Long's study specifically addresses the division of this section into sources and argues that the literary coherence means scholars should be less certain of the source divisions.

separate viewpoints of different characters presented in the narrative. His study highlights that the voices of the narrator, God, Samuel and Israel are not in unison and this creates both pro- and anti-monarchy statements in the text. He is particularly insightful about the role of the narrator, who looks back at the events with a balanced view and gives only two direct evaluations (in 8.2–3 and 10.27). Most importantly, it is the role of the narrator to guide the reader through the many viewpoints and to give the controlling frame for understanding these voices.[47] In this study, we will use this premise to understand how commentary on the complex situation of the monarchy is conveyed. We will look at the different viewpoints present in these chapters and analyse how the narrator comments on the character and motivations of these viewpoints in order to guide the reader through them. Furthermore, there is another layer of complexity in chapters 8–12 because points of view coming from different characters are about different themes.[48] God and Samuel's opinions on the institution of the monarchy need to be distinguished from their opinions of Saul as the chosen first king. Not only must points of view be separated out in the text, but there also needs to be a nuanced look at what the objects of these points of view are. Multiple ideologies in the eyes of a modern reader also function as a complex assessment of history in Samuel.

An implication of covert evaluative techniques is that there is not just one 'correct' reading of the evaluation of the events. Due to its complexity, we must approximate the evaluation and the full intricacy is only available through the medium of narrative. Furthermore, the diversity of traditions and editorial work posited by scholars warns us against proposing one reading that is the intention of an author or final editor. Therefore, our reading of the evaluation is not a definitive exposition, but rather a demonstration of the devices and means by which the narrative shapes an audience's evaluation of the events. The most important principle in our reading is that we follow the cues of the final form of the text.

The Viewpoint of Samuel

We begin our study with the viewpoint of Samuel. Samuel has a dominating presence in three of the five pericopes in this section. This

---

[47] Eslinger, "Viewpoints," 68–9.
[48] Cf. Boeker surveyed above.

corresponds with the three 'assembly' narratives (chapter 8, 10.17–27, 11.12–12)[49] that are interspersed with two 'action' narratives (9.1–10.16, 11.1–11).[50] The narrative perspective favours Samuel in the assembly narratives and Saul in the action narratives.[51] Chapters 8, 10.17–27 and 12 each begins with Samuel as the subject of a verb and establishes that he will feature in the pericope. By contrast, chapter 9 begins with the introduction of Saul, whilst Samuel does not appear until v. 14. Furthermore, Samuel's characterisation in this chapter is comparatively flat as he obediently anoints Saul. Similarly, chapter 11 begins with the actions of Nahash the Ammonite as background, but quickly focuses on Saul as the hero of the story when he rescues Jabesh-gilead. Samuel's name is mentioned in v. 7 but he has receded into the background. Conversely, Saul is a minor character in chapters 8, 10.17–27 and 11.12–12.25 where Samuel dominates. The narrative alternates between focusing on the characterisations of Samuel and Saul and thus describes the transition between these two leaders. Observing this structure explains why Samuel's viewpoint dominates the three assembly narratives and why his characterisation in these chapters should receive close attention. As his viewpoint is more vocal in these chapters than other characters, his ideology can characterise the whole section for an inattentive reader who does not follow the narrator's cues for assessing it.

---

[49] Note that 11.12–15 is grouped with chapter 12 rather than with the rest of chapter 11 here because it is also an assembly. This section both completes the story in chapter 11 and introduces the assembly of chapter 12, as there is no indication in the text that chapter 12 takes place at a later stage. This position is also supported by Lyle M. Eslinger, *Kingship of God in Crisis: A Close Reading of 1 Samuel 1–12* (Decatur: Almond Press, 1985), 383–4; Gordon, *1 & 2 Samuel*, 250; and J. Robert Vannoy, *Covenant Renewal at Gilgal: A Study of I Samuel 11:14–12:25* (Cherry Hill: Mack Pub. Co., 1977), 9.

[50] For an analysis of the assembly and action structure of the section, see Matitiahu Tsevat, "The Biblical Account of the Foundation of the Monarchy in Israel," in *The Meaning of the Book of Job and Other Essays* (New York: KTAV, 1980), 77–99, and McCarthy, "Inauguration of Monarchy in Israel," 401–12, (who builds on the earlier Hebrew version of Tsevat's article). Tsevat (p. 84) points out that it is in the assembly sections that there appears to be the most diverse opinions on the monarchy. He attributes this to the nature of assemblies as places where different voices are heard. However, it can also be attributed to the prominence of Samuel in these sections, who adds his own vocal and divergent opinion to those around him. See also Bar-Efrat, *Das erste Buch Samuel*, 139. He highlights similar statements in the assembly narratives: 8.19, 10.19 and 12.12; and similar statements in the action narratives; in 9.2 and 10.23–24 and also in 9.16, 10.27 and 11.3.

[51] Cf. Fokkelman, *Vow and Desire*, 535, who considers the centre three pericopes as focused on Saul and the bookend chapters as focused on Samuel.

In chapter 8, Samuel's opinion about Israel's request for a king is conveyed authoritatively by the narrator, וירע הדבר בעיני שמואל ('But the thing was evil in the eyes of Samuel'). Samuel's speech about the ways of the king in vv. 11–18 is profoundly negative and the necessity for God to repeat his command to Samuel to obey the voice of the people (vv. 7, 21) demonstrates his unwillingness to anoint a king. What precisely was Samuel displeased about and why? These questions are not answered explicitly but can be assessed through the narrator's contextual frame and guiding commentary on the character Samuel. Analysis will reveal that there is a tension between piety and self-preservation in Samuel's motives. The reader must decide the extent to which he/she believes each of these motives has shaped Samuel's viewpoint and therefore determine the legitimacy of Samuel's evaluation of the monarchy.

The first reason for Samuel's displeasure is that he believes a monarchy would oppress Israel. Samuel's speech about a king in vv. 11–18 foresees burdensome and grievous consequences for Israel. Samuel's position as a prophet predisposes most readers to assume that he has unselfish motives for displeasure and that he genuinely believes his own negative depiction of kingship. This assumption is justified by the consistently positive characterisation of Samuel in I Sam 1–7, especially in contrast to the sons of Eli. Therefore, we may conclude that Samuel is displeased because he is concerned for the welfare of Israel and perhaps he perceives that the request reflects a rejection of Yahweh as king.

A second less disinterested reason for Samuel's displeasure is that he has been personally rejected as leader.[52] Yahweh's initial response to Samuel's prayer, that the people have not rejected Samuel but God, indirectly suggests that Samuel saw himself this way.[53] Furthermore,

---

[52] In addition to the scholars mentioned in the proceeding discussion, see also Robert M. Polzin, *Samuel and the Deuteronomist: A Literary Study of the Deuteronomic History; Part Two—I Samuel* (San Francisco: Harper and Row, 1989), 87; and McCarter, *I Samuel*, 87. Polzin, on the one hand, considers Samuel's self interest to run through all of the pericopes. McCarter, on the other, sees self interest but considers it justified by his prophetic position (particularly if written by a prophetic author.) Bar-Efrat, *Das erste Buch Samuel*, 139, also attributes Samuel's motives to both ideological and personal reasons.

[53] Green observes that it is obvious that Samuel is rejected but the word itself is not used until God introduces it in v. 7 [Barbara Green, *How are the Mighty Fallen? A Dialogical Study of King Saul in 1 Samuel*, JSOTSup. 365 (Sheffield: Sheffield Academic Press, 2003), 184].

the logic that Samuel is being rejected in favour of a king is established by the speech of the elders in v. 4. They do not say explicitly that Samuel's age and wayward sons are the reason for their request but their statement has this implication.[54]

A further indication of Samuel's personal displeasure is found in v. 6, הדבר...כאשר אמרו תנה-לנו מלך לשפטנו ('the thing...when they said, 'Give us a king to judge us'). Fokkelman describes this summary of the elders' speech as an embedding of Samuel's point of view that is used by the author to reveal what he was displeased about.[55] Firstly, although the statement is ambiguous, it suggests that Samuel is displeased about the act of asking for a king rather than kingship itself. This nuance is also expressed in his later speeches (e.g. 10.19, 12.17). Samuel's concern with the act of asking suggests that he is displeased by being replaced rather than because he has an ideological opposition to kings, although this will also be revealed in vv. 11–18. Secondly, Eslinger considers v. 6 a significant summary by what it leaves out. It repeats the first part of the request of the elders but omits their explanatory phrase, ככל-הגוים ('like all of the nations'). He argues that this phrase would indicate Samuel's concern about a breach of God's covenant and so self-interest is the only possible motive for displeasure.[56] Contra Eslinger, the omission of this phrase does not indicate that Samuel was entirely unconcerned with the rejection of Yahweh but it does suggest that this reason is not particularly emphasised in the text. Moreover, the inclusion of לשפטנו ('to judge us') in the reported speech highlights that the king will directly replace Samuel's role as judge and so alludes to Samuel's personal involvement in the issue.

Finally, Samuel's characterisation in chapter 8 also suggests that he disapproves of the monarchy for personal reasons. This is conveyed primarily through the narrator's background information in 8.1–3. Firstly, Samuel has appointed his sons to be שפטים ('judges'), normally a God given role and one that is not hereditary. Judges 9 is the only other example where the title of judge is passed from father to son and this has negative consequences.[57] Samuel is inappropriately

---

[54] Samuel's personal reasons for displeasure are also observed in Bodner, *1 Samuel*, 71–72.

[55] Fokkelman, *Vow and Desire*, 332–3.

[56] Eslinger, *Kingship of God*, 260.

[57] Although in the case of Gideon and Abimelech, Gideon did not appoint his son as judge and Abimelech took hold of the leadership of Israel by force. However, as the only exception to judges not passing from father to son, it gives a very negative view

retaining the role of judge in his family and this suggests that he is possessive of the position. Furthermore, the description in vv. 2–3 of the corruption of Samuel's sons indicates that Samuel is a weak father, either because he does not see their wickedness or he does not censure it.[58] This characterisation is intensified by the parallel with Eli's sons and the resulting demise of Eli's house. The weakness and blindness of Eli, which is characterised in I Sam 1–4, is now transferred to Samuel by analogy. Samuel is characterised as a flawed man who is unlikely to give up his role as leader of Israel willingly.

An implication of Samuel's self-interest is that the authority of his viewpoint is weakened. There is evidence that Samuel was also influenced by pious motives but his simultaneous self-interest makes the situation more complex. It will not necessarily be aligned with that of God or the narrator because he is personally involved and affected by the request of the elders. As Bodner writes, "While numerous scholars in the past have equated the opinions of Samuel with those of the Deuteronomist, such a merger may be imprudent. The words of a character in a story are not necessarily synonymous with the views of the implied author..."[59]

Apart from Samuel's personal involvement in the leadership of Israel, there is other evidence suggesting a distinction between the viewpoints of Yahweh and Samuel. Firstly, there is differentiation between God and Samuel as characters in the story. Samuel interacts with God, is corrected by him and responds to situations differently

---

of such a practice. See also David Toshio Tsumura, *The First Book of Samuel*, NICOT (Grand Rapids: Eerdmans, 2007), 245.

[58] Fokkelman, *Vow and Desire*, 329, even suggests that the significance of the sons being sent to Beersheba, the most southerly point in Israel, may be that Samuel had reservations about them and so kept them as far away as possible.

[59] Bodner, *1 Samuel*, 75. See also Eslinger, *Into the Hands*, 7, who describes the reading by historical critics of I Sam 8–12, "No matter whether it is Samuel, God, or the people speaking in the narrative, all statements are directly ascribed to a real author who stands immediately behind the voice in the narrative and voices his own dissenting views over against the other authors of this text, whose contrary voices are heard directly through the other characters or the narrator's own voice." Later (p. 185), he states, "the strategy of finding the narrator unreliable is out of the question." In discussion of II Sam 7, where Nathan and Yahweh do not agree, Bar-Efrat points out that this type of disagreement between the Divine and a prophet occurs a number of times in these passages, and also in I Sam 16 [Shimeon Bar-Efrat, *Das zweite Buch Samuel: Ein narratologisch-philologisch Kommentar*, trans. Johannes Klein, BWANT 181 (Stuttgart: Kohlhammer, 2009), 74].

from him.[60] God and Samuel function as autonomous characters in the narrative and so are able to hold independent viewpoints. Secondly, the structure of the passage highlights the friction between Samuel and Yahweh. Fokkelman has described the chapter as two cycles of a set pattern of interactions between God, Samuel and the elders of Israel. Each cycle begins with a question from the elders to Samuel (Q), then a consultation of Samuel with God (B), a response from God to Samuel (B') and an answer from Samuel to the people (A).[61] Samuel is the obstruction causing the cycle to repeat. Yahweh commands Samuel in v. 7 שמע בקול העם ('listen to/obey the voice of the people') but Samuel delays with his speech in vv. 11–18. The people resort to a second request in v. 19, resulting in God's second command to Samuel in v. 22 to listen to the voice of the people. The story concludes in this manner, with no indication that Samuel will heed the request of the people or the command of God.[62]

Samuel's obstruction in the cycle of the narrative is emphasised through the repetition of the phrase שמע בקול ('hear/obey the voice of…'). Yahweh uses it twice in his first speech (vv. 7, 9) to command Samuel to listen to the voice of the people. However, in vv. 10–18, Samuel speaks rather than listens and only fulfils the second half of Yahweh's command in v. 9, to show the people the משפט of the king. At the conclusion of Samuel's speech, it is reported in v. 19 that the people did not listen to Samuel's words, creating an ironic reversal of God's command to Samuel in v. 9. Samuel does not listen to the people or to Yahweh, and the people do not listen to Samuel. Finally in v. 21, the narrator grants that Samuel heard all the words of the people וישמע שמואל את כל־דברי העם, yet God's repeated command to hear their voice in v. 22 suggests that Samuel has somehow not heard their voice correctly. The wordplay on שמע, which can mean both 'to hear' and 'to obey',[63] suggests that Samuel heard the people in the sense 'to hear' but he has not yet obeyed them. The repetition emphasises the

---

[60] Cf. II Sam 12 where Nathan has no characterisation apart from his position as the messenger of Yahweh.

[61] Fokkelman, Vow and Desire, 324.

[62] Some scholars have read Samuel sending the people to their cities as outright disobedience [e.g. Eslinger, Kingship of God, 281] whereas others read it as ambiguous [e.g. Fokkelman, Vow and Desire, 354].

[63] Francis Brown, S.R. Driver, and Charles A. Briggs, "A Hebrew and English Lexicon of the Old Testament," (Massachusetts: Hendrickson, 2005), 1033–34.

cycle created by Samuel's obstruction to God's command and highlights the separation between their viewpoints in this chapter.[64]

Secondly, the prominence of Samuel's personal involvement in this
chapter can cause the audience to reconsider the legitimacy of his
concerns about a monarchy for Israel in vv. 11–18. His speech is not
conclusively undermined but there are a number of indications in the
text that support a suspicious reading. The main ambiguity concerns
whether Samuel is merely passing on the words of the Lord (and so
representing God's point of view and a legitimate fear) or whether he
is representing his own view, which suits his own political purpose. In
v. 10, Samuel tells the people 'all the words of the Lord', כל־דברי יהוה,
indicating their divine authority. These 'words' may refer to vv. 11–18
and this reading should not be ruled out. However, it is also grammatically possible for this statement not to include vv. 11–18. Fokkelman
points to the repetition of ויאמר in vv. 10 and 11 and suggests that the
repetition would be redundant if the speech of vv. 11–18 was included
among 'all the words of the Lord'. Furthermore, one would expect the
use of לאמר rather than the *wayyiqtol* form to indicate the continuation of one idea rather than a sequential event. Therefore, he sup-
poses that vv. 11–18 constitute the משפט המלך ('the ways/justice of
the king') from v. 9.[65] The ambiguity in these verses allows the reader
to interpret vv. 11–18 as Samuel's fulfillment of God's command to
show the ways of the king but not necessarily to interpret them as the
authoritative words of God himself. As Fokkelman also points out, the
narrator teasingly does not report whether God gave Samuel specific
instructions about the משפט המלך, further tempting the reader to
doubt if vv. 11–18 are God's words.[66] Eslinger offers an alternative
reading that Samuel misunderstands God's commands: he describes
the kingship rather than prescribes it as he was commanded.[67] Polzin
is willing to tolerate the ambiguity but argues that the narrator's selection of material allows the possibility that Samuel was disobedient.[68]

---

[64] Compare also the observation that in this story it is God who mediates between
Samuel and the people rather than the reverse [Fokkelman, *Vow and Desire*, 325;
Eslinger, *Kingship of God*, 258]. This further demonstrates that Samuel is the obstruc-
tion creating the cycle and that his viewpoint is distinct from that of Yahweh.

[65] Fokkelman, *Vow and Desire*, 345.

[66] Although Fokkelman (p. 346), concludes that v. 10 implies Samuel spoke in the
spirit of God's command.

[67] Eslinger, *Kingship of God*, 271.

[68] Polzin, *Samuel and the Deuteronomist*, 87. Polzin (pp. 82–3) points out that the
narrator does not dwell on what God says so that the ambiguity is created.

The subtle use of the phrase בקול שמואל ('the voice of Samuel') in
v. 19 immediately following this speech favours the stances of Polzin
and Eslinger because it implies that these words belong to Samuel and
not to God.[69]

Despite the ambiguous authority of Samuel's speech, the repetition
of משפט המלך in v. 11 strongly implies that this is his intended subject matter. However, if v. 10 does not apply to these words, it may not
be precisely the משפט המלך God intended. Samuel has the opportunity to give his own interpretation, and even spin, on the monarchy.
God's instructions to Samuel in v. 9, כי־העד תעיד בהם והגדת להם
משפט המלך ('however you should indeed testify against/warn them
and tell them the ways of the king') intensify the ambiguity because it
can be interpreted as either a positive or negative statement. The root
עיד suggests legal language[70] and can be translated either negatively as
'you shall solemnly warn' or positively as 'you shall testify in a legal
sense'. Similarly, משפט can be translated negatively as the harsh judgment coming from the king or even that the king is himself a judgment upon Israel. On the other hand, it can be translated positively as
the good judgment of the king, or neutrally as the practice of the king.[71]
Finally, it may be analogous to the משפט of the king in 10.25, which
refers to some sort of constitution.[72] Thus, it is possible that Yahweh
intended for Samuel to convey a neutral or even positive description
of the king but Samuel has placed a negative bias upon it.[73]

A close examination of Samuel's speech reveals how rhetoric is used
to paint a bleak picture of kingship and this offers additional support for an ambiguous reading of his viewpoint. The qualities listed
negatively by Samuel can be viewed from a more neutral or positive

---

[69] Further, note how the phrase coupled with the verb שמע ('to hear/obey') reverses
the oft repeated call to Samuel to listen to the voice of the people in vv. 7, 9, 21, 22.

[70] Tsumura, The First Book of Samuel, 252; McCarter, I Samuel, 157.

[71] See discussion in Tsumura, The First Book of Samuel, 252. HALOT lists five
meanings for משפט, three of which are possible here: 1. judgment/legal decision;
2. legal claims/rights (i.e. constitution; HALOT lists I Sam 8.9–11 here); 3. measure/
practice (i.e. manner).

[72] Polzin, David and the Deuteronomist, 82. Bodner, 1 Samuel, 74, also compares
Deut 17.17–18. Although the word משפט is not used in Deut 17.17–18, it appears
to be a comparable practice of writing down a constitution to which the king was
accountable.

[73] Cf. Fokkelman, Vow and Desire, 352. He suggests that Yahweh may have intended
for Samuel to describe the manner of the king but Samuel has chosen to interpret the
instructions as the harsh privileges of the king.

angle.[74] Israel has asked for a king to lead them into battle and so it is inevitable that the king will take their sons to fight these battles. Tithing is necessary for running an administrative government capable of conducting large-scale military operations. Furthermore, Samuel uses rhetorical devices that enhance the oppressive impact of the list. He repeatedly uses an inverted word order to emphasise the treasured possessions that the king will take.[75] The repetition of the third masculine singular suffix, in contrast with the second person plural pronoun, reinforces that wealth will be taken from the many and given to the one. The pattern is broken in v. 17, climaxing in the terse statement תהיו־לו לעבדים ('you will be his slaves'). The use of עבדים ('slaves') recalls Israel's bondage in Egypt and depicts kingship as a return to the oppression that God previously delivered them from. Yet in v. 14, Samuel has said that their fields, vineyards and orchards will be taken by the king to give to these same servants/slaves (ונתן לעבדיו). McCarter points out in a note on v. 14 that the title "'ebed hammelek' referred in ancient Israel not to menial functionaries but to a ranking member of the court.[76] This interpretation of עבד in v. 17, probably not intended by Samuel himself, offers a different perspective to these oppressions. Overall, there is evidence to suggest that Samuel has imposed negative connotations onto an otherwise neutral description of the king. Samuel may have genuinely believed the negative description of the monarchy and so it can still be considered a likely reason for Samuel's opposition to it. However, alongside these fears of oppression by the monarchy, the text highlights the political convenience for Samuel personally to foresee such bleak consequences.

In summary, Samuel disapproves of Israel's request for a king and has a negative view of a monarchy in Israel. His status as a pious judge and prophet in I Sam 1–7 endorses this viewpoint to some degree but his characterisation in chapter 8 simultaneously offers another possible reading. His displeasure may originate with his political pretensions for himself and his sons and therefore his depiction of the monarchy can be read as a biased re-interpretation of God's command. Although

---

[74] Eslinger, *Kingship of God*, 272. See also Polzin, *Samuel and the Deuteronomist*, 85, and Moshe Garsiel, *The First Book of Samuel: A Literary Study of Comparative Structures, Analogies and Parallels* (Ramat-Gan: Revivim, 1985), 68.

[75] Also observed in Green, *How are the Mighty Fallen*, 185.

[76] McCarter, *I Samuel*, 158. See similar discussion in Tsumura, *The First Book of Samuel*, 258, based on Ugaritic and Hittite texts.

there may be an overlap with the authoritative viewpoint of Yahweh, the characterisation of Samuel warns against making this uncritical assumption.

Samuel's viewpoint is next developed in detail in 10.17–27. Again, there is ambiguity over whether his view can be differentiated from Yahweh and whether it carries authority. Verse 18 carries the authority of Yahweh as direct reported speech but the narrator subtly changes the viewpoint in v. 19. God shifts from the first to the third person, subtly attributing the words in v. 19 to Samuel. He reminds the Israelites that they have rejected God and asked for a king but then finally proceeds to grant their request. Two readings are possible: the first is that the viewpoints of Yahweh and Samuel are distinguished grammatically but not ideologically. The reader may suppose that Samuel has abandoned his personal reservations and is acting only as God's loyal servant, a view suggested by his obedience in the intervening narrative. In the second possible reading, the ambiguity of Samuel's motivations in chapter 8 may be transferred to this chapter, generating further cynicism about Samuel's position. Perhaps he is now resigned to the reality that there will be a king but he believes he can maintain a need for his prophetic role in Israel, by reminding the people that their act of asking for a king was apostasy.

Amit, in a study of I Sam 15, suggests that once a character has been proved unreliable, he/she remains so for the reader. In I Sam 15.29, Samuel directly contradicts the words of God and the narrator in vv. 11 and 35. Amit observes that the narrator uses the same root נחם that Samuel uses in order to underline his unreliability.[77] This example encourages a suspicious reading of Samuel's speech despite his obedience in chapter 9. It demonstrates that the distinction between the viewpoints of God and Samuel is sustained later in the text. The evidence is not conclusive but this guidance from the narrator in the text allows the audience to form their own evaluation.

Aside from this ambiguity, another feature of Samuel's viewpoint in this pericope is that it concerns two different issues. This results in a sharp juxtaposition of opposites. In contrast to the negativity about the request for a king in v. 19, Samuel is overwhelmingly positive about Saul himself in v. 24. The phrase אין כמהו בכל־העם ('there is none like him amongst all the people') is a formula used of Moses in Deut

---

[77] Amit, "The Glory of Israel," 204, 209.

34.10–11 and Josiah in 2 Kgs 23.25 and so expresses astonishing praise for Saul.[78] The juxtaposing of Samuel's negative and positive opinions highlights the complexity of Samuel's position. The narrator does not offer a straightforward reason for Samuel holding both of these views but rather creates a gap in which the reader can infer the complex reasons. Several possibilities, or aspects of Samuel's reasoning, are offered by the text. Samuel states that the Lord has chosen Saul (בחר־בו יהוה). The people may have rejected their God but God has maintained the authority to choose their king for them and Samuel must support the choice of his patron. Whether Samuel has wholehearted support or reluctant support at this stage is left ambiguous. A second option springs from the depiction of Saul as a king with requisite humility in both 9.1–10.16 and in this pericope, when he is found hiding in the baggage. Even if his humility is a matter of form, at this point in the narrative he is yet to assert himself in any way. Perhaps אין כמהו בכל־העם ('there is none like him amongst all the people') ought to be read cynically and Samuel is looking down upon this humility. In its context, it most likely refers to Saul's height mentioned in v. 23. It is a possibility that Samuel intends a double meaning and refers also to Saul's act of hiding when he is chosen as king by lots. In other words, there is none like Saul in a negative sense. Such an ironic use of the phrase could either suggest that Samuel is a reluctant supporter of Saul or, as Polzin suggests,[79] that he supports Saul precisely because he can be easily kept under prophetic control. Samuel's characterisation in chapter 8, as a man eager to retain his power, increases the power of this suggestion. Nevertheless, it is left to the reader to fill this gap in understanding of Samuel's ideology and select from the alternatives left available by the narrative. Yet in the midst of this flexibility, it is firmly established by the narrative that Samuel is not wholly against the kingship and that there are nuances to his position.

In 11.12–12.25, Saul recedes into the background and Samuel is again prominent in the narrative. This is reflected in the absence

---

[78] Walter Brueggemann, *First and Second Samuel*, Interpretation (Louisville: John Knox Press, 1990), 80.

[79] Polzin, *Samuel and the Deuteronomist*, 104, says, "Saul appears to be exactly the kind of man whom Samuel would have every hope of molding into a compliant king who would least limit prophetic and judicial powers Samuel has been accustomed to exercise in the past and now sees threatened." See also Bar-Efrat, *Das erste Buch Samuel*, 151, 167, who points out that Saul has given every indication up to this point that he will submit to Samuel's control.

of any evaluation on the choice of Saul as king. In chapter 12, the appointed king is referred to neutrally and namelessly. Polzin suggests that Samuel's encouragement to the people, to renew the kingdom, prevented them from repenting. He considers the people's request in 11.12, to kill those who wanted to make Saul king, to be an attempt at repentance by the people. [80] Polzin bases this view on the phrase in I Sam 11.12, שאול ימלך עלינו. Most translations and scholars interpret this as a question, 'Shall Saul reign over us?' implying that the people wish to kill those questioning Saul's reign. Polzin interprets it as a statement and reads the verse as, 'Who is it that said, Saul shall reign over us? Bring us the men and we will kill them'. As the people make no threat against Saul or Samuel, and it is Saul who intercedes, it is unlikely that the people want to kill supporters of Saul. The rejoicing at the renewal in v. 15 also makes Polzin's scenario unlikely. However, in the absence of a definitive conclusion about the meaning of these verses, Polzin's suggestion cannot be dismissed. A suggestion of Samuel's hypocrisy may be intended by the narrator to add to the complexity of the situation.

Samuel's speech in chapter 12 offers a resolution to the two threads that recur in his point of view of Israel's request to this point: the position that a request for a king is a rejection of God; and that the institution of kingship threatens his own stronghold of power.[81] These are resolved (or partially resolved) respectively by the recommitment of Israel to God and the establishing of a new role for Samuel.

The first of these concerns is more palpable in Samuel's speech. Samuel seeks to establish his own integrity as leader of Israel in vv. 1–6, followed by the faithfulness of Yahweh in vv. 7–11.[82] In spite of this faithfulness, Israel has rejected God their real king (v. 12), and God's deliverer Samuel (v. 11), by asking for a king. This is Samuel's fullest account of how Israel has rejected God and it is followed, not by a call for repentance as one would expect when Israel acknowledges her sins (v. 18)[83] but by an exhortation to Israel to be obedient to God in the future. There are at least two possible readings of this. The first

---

[80] Polzin, *Samuel and the Deuteronomist*, 108–17.

[81] Cf. Campbell, *1 Samuel*, 120. He sees the positive and negative views of kingship as pulled together in this chapter.

[82] Samuel uses the cycle of sin, oppression, cry to Yahweh and deliverance, in order to emphasise the sinfulness of Israel's current request [Ralph W. Klein, *1 Samuel*, WBC (Waco: Word Books, 1983), 113, 120].

[83] E.g. I Sam 7.4 where Israel repents by reversing their sin of idolatry.

assumes that, once Saul was made king, it was too late to repent of this request. The second is that only Samuel, not Yahweh, was against the monarchy in principle and therefore it was not necessary to retract the request. In this case, repentance of the request would require revoking the king God himself has given to them.[84] These alternatives offer a resolution to the juxtaposition of Samuel's censure of Israel's request with his endorsement of Saul. Regardless of why Samuel does not encourage Israel to retract their request for a king, he charges them to future obedience as a resolution to their rejection of Yahweh.

The second thread in Samuel's viewpoint, his personal rejection, also finds resolution in Samuel's speech: he forges a new, vital role for himself as Israel's mediator. In light of the ambiguity established in chapter 8, Samuel's speech is more than a simple affirmation of his own innocence and Israel's need to obey Yahweh. One possible reading is that Samuel's innocence confirms his credentials for pleading on behalf of the people. However, elements of his speech suggest that his claims of innocence are responding to the elders' charges against his sons in 8.4 and his replacement as leader. Verse 2 infers that Samuel believes he has personally been replaced by the king through the parallelism of the king walking before the people in the present (conveyed through a participle מתהלך and the adverb עתה) and Samuel's role in the past (with a perfect verb התהלכתי). The contrast is further heightened by the use of the personal pronoun to emphasise Samuel (אני).

Furthermore, he formulates his claim to innocence in a way that implies his replacement was unnecessary. This is achieved by his very pointed and specific claims. He does not ask Israel generally whether he has been a good leader but specifies possible offences, which he has not committed, in a series of questions beginning with the particle מי ('who'). No one can answer these direct questions in the affirmative. Polzin describes the people's response as parroting Samuel,[85] an appropriate description for their responses, which answer Samuel's questions but add no further commendation.

---

[84] Cf. Polzin, *Samuel and the Deuteronomist*, 121–22. Polzin reads the absence of a call for repentance as Samuel leading the people astray. However, in Samuel's defense, he is calling for obedience to God and not to the king and so is not exactly promoting idolatry.

[85] Ibid., 118.

Samuel's description of himself in this chapter is designed to be in sharp contrast with his description of the king in chapter 8.[86] These verses recall Samuel's earlier list of a king's offences by its similarity in form and so imply that Samuel is preferable to a king as leader.[87] However, when his speech is examined more closely, apart from the taking of donkeys, a king as described in 8.11–18 would also be cleared of all the offences that Samuel mentions. This observation highlights Samuel's clever and persuasive use of rhetoric concerning the ways of the king in chapter 8 and his own conduct in chapter 12.

Furthermore, unlike the king, Samuel's sons would not be cleared of these offences according to 8.3 (although note that different vocabulary is used in 8.3 and 12.3). Samuel's sons make an awkward intrusion into Samuel's speech and commentators have offered different reasons for their mention without further explanation in 12.2.[88] Fokkelman avers that the reference to Samuel's sons subtracts from the effectiveness of Samuel's speech. Samuel was so hurt that he could not bring himself to mention their faults and so he insults the intelligence of the audience with their introduction.[89] On the other hand, Gordon suggests that Samuel wanted to highlight the contrast between himself and his sons[90] and Eslinger describes it as a defense tactic because Samuel pairs his sons with the king and suggests their camaraderie with the people through the use of אתכם ('they are with you').[91] Aside from Samuel's own purposes for his speech, the allusion to his sons functions as a reminder of this aspect of Samuel's characterisation. The reference reminds the reader of Samuel's self-interest and cautions against easy acceptance of his viewpoint.

Samuel's history of God's deliverance of Israel gives cause for further reservation about his viewpoint. In v. 12 he cites the catalyst for

---

[86] Garsiel, *The First Book of Samuel*, 69, and Fokkelman, *Vow and Desire*, 500, point to the use of the keyword לקח ('to take') and the mention of the asses as creating the rhetorical contrast. Also Gordon, *1 & 2 Samuel*, 127.

[87] Contra Tsumura, *The First Book of Samuel*, 318, who considers the absence of bribery, defrauding and oppression in chapter 8 to imply that no comparison is intended.

[88] In contrast to the literary explanations surveyed here, Klein, *1 Samuel*, 114, offers a source critical explanation and attributes it to another tradition or author who did not know of their corruption.

[89] Fokkelman, *Vow and Desire*, 496.

[90] Gordon, *1 & 2 Samuel*, 126.

[91] Eslinger, *Kingship of God*, 386.

Israel's request for a king to be the military threat of Nahash, the king of the Ammonites. Instead of crying to God for deliverance, as they did in the past, they asked for a king.[92] However, this depiction of events is contradicted by both Yahweh and the narrator at various stages. In 9.16, Yahweh says that he has heard the people cry out to him, implying that the request for a king was such a cry for help. Samuel's reference to Nahash the Ammonite is also in tension with the narrator's description of the approach of Nahash (chapter 11) after Israel's request for a king (chapter 8) within the sequence of chapters 8–12.[93] Samuel's subtle incongruence with God and the narrator suggests that he may be seeking to convict Israel of their sin through a representation of events that goes beyond those perceived by God or the narrator.

Through Samuel's characterisation and the details of his speech, the reader can assess the reasons for his call for obedience in 12.14–15. One aspect must be a desire for Israel to return their allegiance to Yahweh, their God. Another is that he is forging a resolution to his own sense of rejection as Israel's leader. This is suggested by Samuel's repeated emphasis on his continuing role as Israel's mediator. Samuel announces that he will plead with Israel before the Lord in v. 7, implying that he is mediating a message from the Lord to Israel. His history of Israel focuses persistently on mediators who have acted as deliverers for God, beginning with the most notable of mediators, Moses and Aaron, and concluding with himself in v. 11.[94] His invocation to the Lord to bring rain, and furthermore its effectiveness, demonstrates to Israel that his mediating role is fully functioning. The demonstration of God's power legitimates Samuel and acts as a warning to Israel. Samuel predicts the event in v. 17 and its result is that the people fear not only God, but also Samuel (ויירא כל־העם מאד את־יהוה ואת־

---

[92] Cf. Garsiel, *The First Book of Samuel*, 66. He shows that Samuel's speech in chapter 8 also depicts the cycle of service of God; crying out for salvation; and an answer from God. This is broken with the institution of kings.

[93] Other explanations of the inconsistency between Samuel and the narrator are possible when the problem is viewed from an historical or source critical angle. Chapter 12 is widely regarded as having a different origin to chapters 9 and 11. Also possible, Nahash was a threat to Israel before the attack on Jabesh Gilead thus prompting the request for a king [Tsumura, *The First Book of Samuel*, 323].

[94] Eslinger, *Kingship of God*, 395ff. Eslinger (p. 396) also points out that the only verb which God is the subject of is וישלח when he sent Moses and Aaron to show that the mediator is indispensible.

שמואל) even though the command of v. 14 was only to fear the Lord
(אם־תיראו את־יהוה). Furthermore, Samuel implies the precedence of
the prophetic mediator by associating the king with the rest of the
people. The king is under the blessings and curses of vv. 14–15 and, as
Brueggemann points out, he is an afterthought and rhetorically does
not merit his own treatment.[95] The king can be swept away (v. 25)
whereas the prophet is not explicitly subsumed under these conditions. Whilst Samuel is calling on Israel to be obedient to God, he is
also forging the importance of his own role and bringing resolution
to his own rejection.[96]

In summary, Samuel's point of view throughout these chapters
focuses on the sinfulness of Israel in asking for a king and the dangers of the monarchy itself. Samuel is characterised both as concerned
prophet and self-interested, rejected leader. This ambiguity is further amplified by the juxtaposing of opposites in the presentation of
Samuel's viewpoint. The combination of Samuel's full support for the
choice of Saul as king and yet his ongoing insistence on the sin of
Israel in their request compels the reader to contemplate the nuances
of his position and to search out a reason for him to hold both views.
The explanations for these tensions given in the above analysis are not
the only resolutions possible, but they demonstrate the methodology
through which readers look for indications in the text to guide them
towards such a solution.

The viewpoint of Yahweh

Whereas the viewpoint of Samuel is complex and multi-faceted, the
viewpoint of God is enigmatic. God makes opposing statements: Samuel should make Israel a king but Israel has sinned by rejecting God as
their king. The reader is not given direct access into the mind of God
but is presented with the experience of hearing God's words in order
to construct his/her own understanding. The narrator offers guidance
but no definitive answers.

---

[95] Brueggemann, *First and Second Samuel*, 93–4.
[96] Bar-Efrat, *Das erste Buch Samuel*, 179, states that chapter 12 is not a departure speech but rather, Samuel is establishing his influence in Israel. Each part of
the speech is designed to show the people the importance of the prophet in the new
arrangements for leadership.

In chapter 8, God's clearest statement of his opinion regarding Israel's request for a king is his response to Samuel, שמע בקול העם ('Obey/listen to the voice of the people'). He makes explicit that the anointing of a king is with his approval. However, this positive command is contradicted by his negative explanation introduced by the particle כי in v. 7. God describes Israel's rejection of himself in contrast to their rejection of Samuel, so the negative explanation is in the context of his persuasion of Samuel to obey his command. Yahweh's assessment that Israel has rejected him is in sharp tension with the other evidence that he is in support of the kingship. This tension creates a gap that can be filled by the reader in one of at least three ways. The first possibility is that God's understanding of Israel's rejection of him is more nuanced than is stated explicitly; the second is that God's support of the king is more nuanced; and the third is a combination of the above. The important theological principles of God's position are stated but it is left to the reader to resolve the tension and therefore attempt to understand each statement more fully. The large number of scholarly interpretations of this chapter, as well as a fresh reading of the text, will demonstrate a number of ways that the text allows this gap to be filled.

Let us first examine the nuances of God's viewpoint that Israel has rejected him as its king. The assumption made by most commentators is that Yahweh's words refer specifically to Israel's act of requesting a king. In other words, Yahweh states that Israel has rejected him by asking for another king just as they have long forsaken him for other gods.[97] This reading is justified in the text by the use of the word מלך ('king') in the phrase כי־אתי מאסו ממלך עליהם ('for it is me they have rejected as king over them'), which contrasts their request for a king with God's existing kingship.

A number of possible interpretations can be surmised through the wording of Israel's request and Yahweh's response. One such is that God objects to the request to be like other nations (v. 5; לשפטנו ככל־הגוים) but not to the monarchy itself. The desire to be like other nations, not the desire to have a king, is the act of rejection of God.[98]

---

[97] E.g. Eslinger, *Kingship of God*, 262; Tsumura, *The First Book of Samuel*, 243.

[98] Artur Weiser, *Samuel: Seine geschichtliche Aufgabe und religiöse Bedeutung* (Göttingen: Vandenhoeck & Ruprecht, 1962), 37–8, and Eslinger, *Kingship of God*, 255–59. Passages such as Ex 19.5–6 support this argument. However, Edelman points out that throughout the ancient Near East, the king was the national god's vice regent and,

Along a similar theme, Klein suggests that God is displeased the people want a king to go out before them in battle, as this replaces his own role of leading them into battle, such as in 7.10. Klein notes the use of the first person common plural pronominal suffix on מלחמתנו (v. 20; 'our battles'), which suggests Israel is now interested in fighting their own battles and no longer those of the Divine.[99]

There is yet another possibility for the reasoning behind God's standpoint that assumes another interpretation of his words in vv. 7–8. The grammar of these verses allows for the interpretation that God's claim of Israel's rejection does not refer specifically to their request for a king. מאסו ('they have rejected') is in the *qatal* tense/aspect signifying a change from the previous verb יאמרו ('they are speaking') in the *yiqtol*, which describes the request in the present.[100] The contrasting tenses/aspects suggest that they may not refer to the same action. This leads to the alternative interpretation that God is saying Israel rejected him before they asked for a king and thus the need for a king arose. The request itself was not apostasy but was the equivalent of a cry for help from a deliverer, a reading supported by 9.16. The phrases, מיום...ועד־היום הזה ('from the day…to this day') also suggest that he sees all the events which took place between the exodus and the present day as a rejection of him, not specifically the request for a king. Furthermore, this particular interpretation conforms neatly to later depictions of God's viewpoint. All of these interpretations are permitted by the narrator, so the reader can construct for him/herself a complex reasoning for God's viewpoint as a combination of these possibilities.

Another way of resolving the tension in God's viewpoint is to look for nuances in his position that Samuel should make Israel a king—is

---

therefore, this request is not implying that the king would break away from the commands of Yahweh [Diana Edelman, "Saul ben Kish in History and Tradition," in *Origins of the Ancient Israelite States*, ed. Fritz Volkmar and Philip R. Davies (Sheffield: Sheffield Academic Press, 1996), 39].

[99] Klein, *1 Samuel*, 78. See also McKenzie, Mayes and McCarthy surveyed earlier with similar views that the request is a rejection of Yahweh as military leader.

[100] This interpretation would make better sense of v. 8 כן המה עשים גם־לך ('thus they are also doing to you'), which has caused problems because of its contradiction with v. 7. The use of the participle in this phrase in v. 8 may suggest a reversion back to the present time when Israel is forsaking Samuel, compared to the past when they did not reject Samuel as they rejected God. For other ways of understanding this verse, see Fokkelman, *Vow and Desire*, 340, who offers a number of possibilities and Eslinger, *Kingship of God*, 265, who suggests an emendation of the text.

this wholehearted support or is it reluctant compromise? One reading is that God considers the request to be apostasy, yet he grants the
request out of his own graciousness.[101] The narrator's emphasis on the
evils of Samuel's sons in vv. 1–3 adds plausibility to this as it provides
a circumstance about which God is gracious in relieving his people.

A similar view is held by Bruggemann, except that he understands
God's granting of the request as a result of exhaustion rather than
graciousness. Yahweh knows better that a king will not answer Israel's
problems and so he commands Samuel to let Israel know the cost
of their naivety.[102] Bar-Efrat suggests that God is against the idea of
kingship but he does not wish to force his own rule upon the people.
He therefore compromises and takes the practical step of consenting
to their wish.[103] Eslinger points specifically to the use of אך כי in v. 9,
which he translates 'nevertheless', to indicate that God is relenting by
granting the request.[104] This interpretation allows the reader to accept
Samuel's point of view in vv. 11–18 as God's point of view also, because
it can be seen as an act of God to redefine kingship for Israel. Israel
wants a king to judge them and go out in battle before them. God
will grant them this, yet he also warns them of the negative aspects of
having a king. Although this aligns the viewpoints of God and Samuel
to a certain extent, it is still possible that Samuel has added his own
hyperbole to God's warning for Israel.

Instead of God's graciousness or exhaustion, the granting of Israel's request can be interpreted as an act of judgment. This reading is
dependent on the ambiguity of the term משפט in v. 9, which has been
alluded to above. Not only is there ambiguity in the meaning of the
term but also in the meaning of the construct chain. If we understand
the meaning of משפט as 'judgment', then the construct chain could
imply either that the judgment comes from the king or that the king
himself is the act of judgment against Israel because of his abuses of
power. In other words, God grants Israel a king, not as an act of graciousness, but as an act of judgment against Israel for rejecting him.[105]

---

[101] Tsumura, *The First Book of Samuel*, 243.
[102] Brueggemann, *First and Second Samuel*, 62–63.
[103] Bar-Efrat, *Das erste Buch Samuel*, 141–42.
[104] Eslinger, *Kingship of God*, 268.
[105] Cf. the phrase משפט מות found in Deut 19.6 and Jer 26.11, meaning the 'judgment of death', i.e. the death penalty. The second word in the construct chain is not
the source of the judgment but a description of it. A similar interpretation is offered
in Fokkelman, *Vow and Desire*, 324, who suggests that the use of the construct in

This latter meaning is a little more forced than the first and is best considered as a secondary wordplay in the text. The idea that the institution of the kingship is only a punishment on Israel does not cohere with God's later blessings and promises to King David, or with the lack of explicit fulfillment of the evils of the king in the near future. Nevertheless, the wordplay opens up leeway of interpretation that this is an aspect of God's reluctant granting of the request. This interpretation returns us to the ambiguity surrounding Samuel's words in vv. 11–18 and whether they represent the viewpoint of God as well as Samuel. Incidentally, even if the reader does not accept that God and Samuel evaluate the request for a king in the same way, this wordplay may be the basis for Samuel's reinterpretation of God's command to explain the מֹשׁפֹט of the king. The sort of king that Samuel describes may be the king he wishes upon Israel as punishment for rejecting him as their leader.

In the following chapters of this section, the words of God become even scarcer and his viewpoint is conveyed primarily through his actions and the authority of the narrator. These chapters give further evidence for how the reader is to understand the tension established in chapter 8. Earlier, we looked at divine causation for Saul becoming king. The implication of God's sovereignty in these events demonstrates that his viewpoint supports and enables Saul as his chosen king. However, supporting and enabling the anointing of a king does not necessarily imply that God is in favour of the institution of kingship and his choice of Saul does not immediately indicate that he is positive about Saul's character. They only show that God stands by his decision in chapter 8 to grant Israel a king and that Saul is his choice to fill that role.

The narrator also makes explicit at various stages of the narrative that God is intervening with his spirit to aid in the accession of Saul. His spirit comes upon Saul in 10.10, leading him to prophesy, and in 11.6, leading to his success in battle. Not only does the rushing of the spirit confirm that Saul is God's choice as king, the effects of the spirit indicate what sort of king God wants Saul to become. Significantly, the spirit transforms Saul firstly into a prophet and secondly into a

---

מֹשׁפֹט הַמֶלֶךְ shows that the king himself will be above justice and so therefore, this is an announcement of punishment in disguise.

judge-like figure,[106] thus granting Israel's request for a king to judge
them (8.6; לשפטנו). Both of these roles overlap with the domain of
Samuel, fulfilling Samuel's fears that the new king will replace him.[107]
God's willingness to grant Israel's request for a king who will take
over the duties of Samuel is in sharp contrast to the attitude of Samuel
himself, who, in chapter 12, wishes to retain a position of importance
within Israel.

There are two more instances of God's speech in these pericopes.
The first, in 9.15–17, has already been mentioned because it presents
a different picture of Israel's request for a king from that depicted
by Samuel. Yahweh communicates that he has already heard the cry
of Israel, presumably in their request for a king (כי באה צעקתו אלי;
'For their cry has come to me'). He attributes a saving role to the new
king (והושיע) that is linked to the Philistines (פלשתים), the recur-
rent enemy throughout the book of Judges and Samuel's early judge-
ship.[108] Therefore, similar to the implication of his spirit rushing upon
Saul, God intends for the new king to fulfill the function of a saviour
judge. God reveals a further glimpse of his view of the king in v. 17, זה
יעצר בעמי ('this is the man who will rule [lit. restrain][109] my people').
Unfortunately, because this meaning for the root עצר does not appear
elsewhere, it is difficult to determine its connotations. However, this
speech gives a further indication of God's viewpoint through its use
of עמי ('my people'), which has added emphasis because it is repeated
from v. 16. Although Saul will be ruling over Israel, they will remain
God's people within his covenant.[110] This suggests that God does not
consider his rule threatened by the appointment of a king, contrary to
Samuel's dire warnings.

---

[106] For parallels in Judges where the spirit rushes upon a judge leading to military
success, see Jdg 3.10, 6.34, 11.29, 14.19, 15.14.

[107] Note that Samuel's third role as priest is not subsumed by Saul until chapter 13
when Saul attempts to take on this duty and is severely reprimanded by Samuel for
it. It is interesting that in chapter 13 the condemnation of Saul comes only through
the words of Samuel reporting that God has rejected Saul but this report is not given
the authority of the narrator. Not until chapter 15, when Saul is indicted on another
offence, does God himself condemn Saul. Perhaps God is willing for Saul to take on all
the duties of Samuel as judge, prophet and priest and it is only Samuel in chapter 13
who objects in a desperate attempt to hold onto his last remaining unique position.

[108] See Jdg 3.31; 10.6–18; Samson in Jdg 13–16; I Sam 4–7.

[109] HALOT. Cf. McCarter's suggestion 'to muster', which would further add to the
depiction of God's approval of the king as military leader [McCarter, *I Samuel*, 179].

[110] See, for example, Ex 6.7 for the use of עמי in covenant language.

The second instance of Yahweh's speech is in 10.18, where he is quoted by Samuel rather than the omniscient narrator. The speech is used by Samuel to support his own viewpoint that Israel has rejected God by their request, by alluding to God's salvation of Israel in the exodus. They have responded to this salvation with rejection, adding further gravity to their sin. However, only Yahweh's short and oft repeated statement that he brought Israel out of the land of Egypt is reported by Samuel, not the implications of rejecting him. Thus Yahweh's speech reveals very little of his viewpoint at all because there is the possibility that it has been shaped and contextualised by Samuel.[111]

In summary, God's viewpoint in these chapters addresses the same two themes as Samuel: the institution of the monarchy and the choice of Saul as the first king. As with Samuel's viewpoint, God is explicitly in support of anointing Saul and Saul's position as God's choice is repeated throughout the chapters both by words and events. However, beyond confirmation that Yahweh has chosen Saul, no further information is given about his attitude towards him. Yahweh does not say whether he has chosen him because he is the most righteous and suitable man for the job, or whether it is for more complex reasons. A description of the chapters as 'pro-Saul' is misleading as they are more in favour of the *choice* of Saul rather than any particular qualities of Saul himself. Secondly, it is dubious whether the evaluations of Israel's request for a king by Yahweh and Samuel are the same. It is ambiguous whether Yahweh is saying that the request itself was apostasy or, contrary to this, he is stating that it was an act of crying out for deliverance.

Chapter 12 is dominated by the speech of Samuel that expresses his viewpoint. However, the chapter closes with a dramatic confirmation of Samuel by God through a thunderstorm at Samuel's request. Samuel explicitly states that the storm would be a sign that Israel has been wicked in asking for a king (v. 17). God's delivery of the sign would apparently give whole-hearted sanction to all of Samuel's words and, for the first time, God would be conveying that the request itself

---

[111] Cf. the similar speech in Jdg 6.8–10 by the unnamed prophet at the time of Gideon where God sends a saviour immediately after this review of God's salvation through the exodus [Peter D. Quinn-Miscall, *The Workings of Old Testament Narrative*, Semeia studies (Philadelphia: Fortress Press, 1983), 64]. This unnamed prophet reports from Yahweh the implications the deliverance in contrast to Samuel who conveniently ends the quote and commences his own analysis of the situation.

for a king was a form of apostasy. This is one interpretation allowed
by the narrator. However, in light of God's silence on the issue up to
this point, the reader may feel compelled to doubt Samuel's explanation of the significance of the sign. The non-verbal nature of the sign
makes other interpretations possible. Whilst undoubtedly the sign is
from God according to the narrator, the narrator does not necessarily
agree with Samuel's interpretation.[112] One suggested interpretation is
that it is a false sign, such as that described in Deut 13.1–5,[113] but this
is unlikely as the narrator authoritatively states that it was the Lord
who sent it, ויתן יהוה קלת ('and the Lord sent thunder'). A second
possibility is that the Lord requires the outcome to which this display
of power leads, namely a fear of the Lord by the people, but he does
not endorse Samuel's other words. It is significant that the explicit outcome of the lightning in v. 18 is that the people feared both the Lord
and Samuel. They do not withdraw their request for a king or act in
any other way that would suggest they have repented of asking for a
king. Neither Yahweh nor the narrator explains what the sign means,
so the reader is free to interpret it based on its outcome rather than
on Samuel's own interpretation.

The opinion of God throughout chapters 8–12 is consistently enigmatic. Yahweh wants Samuel to anoint a king and he chooses Saul.
Beyond these basic facts, the reader must observe God's interaction
in the events, as presented by the narrator, in order to recreate the
complex reasoning for this viewpoint. The viewpoint of Samuel can
be used to fill the gaps in God's viewpoint but it does not carry his
full authority.

The viewpoint of the people

The people give only one reason for their request for a king, although
they give a more extensive description of the king's function. The reason for the request is that Samuel is old and that his sons are corrupt

---

[112] As Green, *How are the Mighty Fallen*, 191, points out, the thunderstorm makes
clear that Samuel is in some way mediating between Yahweh and the people, but the
efficacy of that mediation is not vouched for. Thus, she also observes the ambiguity
of such a sign.

[113] Cf. Polzin, *Samuel and the Deuteronomist*, 122, interprets this passage as Samuel
leading the people away from God by not allowing them to repent of their request
for a king.

(v. 5), a circumstance which is emphasised through the repetition from vv. 1–3 of the key roots זקן ('old') and הלך with דרך ('walk in his/your ways'). The narrator's substantiation of these facts leads the audience to believe that this is a real problem. The locality of the sons in the remote city of Beersheba (v. 2) may cast some doubt for a reader over the extent to which Samuel's sons are a problem for all of Israel, although the age of Samuel suggests that the problem could soon become more widespread. The narrator does not reveal to us whether this is really the primary reason for Israel's request but he reveals that it is a valid one.

The first aspect of Israel's purpose for the king, לשפטנו ('to judge us'), further substantiates the reason for their request. The current judges (שפטים), Samuel's sons, are corrupt and so Israel desires a king who can perform this function in their place. The second half of Israel's description of the king is given in v. 20, where again they ask for a king to judge them like other nations, but add ויצא לפינו ונלחם את־מלחמתנו ('to go out before us and to fight our battles'). The narrative, which immediately precedes in chapter 7, confirms that there is no human leader who goes out before Israel in battle because Samuel stays behind and offers sacrifices (7.9) whilst the Lord frightens the Philistines away. Significantly, Samuel does not lead Israel as they pursue the fleeing Philistines (v. 10) and so the narrative substantiates that the Israelites did not have a human leader to go out before them in battle. Although there is a real deficiency, chapter 7 reveals that it is not a real need, because the Lord makes the decisive move that frightens away the Philistines. Furthermore, this defeat is final according to 7.13 and the hand of the Lord (יד־יהוה) is solely responsible for the victory. Israel's viewpoint is that God's victory for them in battle is not sufficient.

The additional phrase in Israel's request ככל־הגוים ('like all the nations') is ambiguous in what viewpoint it is expressing. As discussed above, some commentators consider it to be the phrase to which God primarily objects in Israel's request. It is possible that the phrase is used by Israel merely as an expression of the late development of the monarchy in Israel compared to other nations rather than a specific desire to cease being God's chosen people.[114] However its repetition in both vv. 5 and 20 suggests more is intended by it. In both cases it is

---

[114] Klein, *1 Samuel*, 75.

coupled with the verb שפט and so may be an expression of dissatis-
faction with Israel's judges rather than with Israel's God. Nevertheless,
asking for a king, a hereditary title, would be an illogical long-term
solution to the problem of leaders such as Eli and Samuel with corrupt sons.

Are the Israelite elders expressing a rejection of God in their request
for a king? A common understanding is that God is accepting of kingship but he wishes to redefine it as a theocratic model of the monarchy. This would imply that the Israelites were being apostate, even
if unwittingly.[115] However, Yahweh's response echoes the purpose of
the king asked for by the people. He intends to make the new king a
military leader (10.16, chapter 11), and the king takes on the judging
function of Samuel so that in chapter 12 Samuel needs to forge a role
for himself as a mediator. Furthermore, Yahweh's initial command to
Samuel in chapter 8 is to obey the voice of the people (שמע בקולם).
He does not tell Samuel to grant the request of a king but rather, to
obey their voice, implying that Samuel should obey all of their words.
This is reinforced in v. 7 by לכל אשר-יאמרו אליך ('according to everything which they say to you'). This can be interpreted as a command,
not only to listen to their request for a king, but also to their intended
role for him.

These observations demonstrate ambiguity in the text about whether
the people were asking for a form of monarchy that rejects Yahweh's
rule. On the one hand, their repeated phrase ככל-הגוים ('like all the
nations') would suggest they are. Other occurrences of similar phrases
referring to the nations (גוים) have negative connotations of God's
judgment against Israel or their worship of idols.[116] On the other hand,
a canonical reading of this passage in the context of Deut 17.14–20
implies that these connotations are not relevant here. Deut 17, which
uses the same phrase ככל-הגוים, suggests that God will permit Israel to
have a king, even a king like the nations, provided it is a king whom
God has chosen. This requirement is fulfilled by Israel's act of asking
God's representative, Samuel, to make them a king. Furthermore, they
approach Yahweh for the choice of king in 10.17–27, although the people's support of Saul after this point is mixed in 10.26–27. The people
also willingly accept the משפט המלכה ('way/rights of the kingdom'),
which is placed before the Lord in 10.25. Although there are worthless

---

[115] E.g. Fokkelman, *Vow and Desire*, 491; Eslinger, *Kingship of God*, 268.
[116] E.g. Deut 8.20, Ezek 20.32 and 25.8.

fellows who are not in support of Saul, their complaint in the direct speech, מה־יֹשִׁעֵנוּ זֶה ('how will this man save us') is directed at the choice of Saul and not at the constitution set up by Samuel. It is with minimum resistance that a theocratic monarchy is imposed, implying that the people may have desired this system from the beginning. In 12.19, the people confess that their request was a sin, although the reader wonders after Samuel's lengthy speech and impressive thunder and lightening, whether they are under his influence in this assessment.

In summary, there is uncertainty about Israel's motives and desires in their request for a king. Although the request is expressed as one voice in the narrative, perhaps the ambiguity reflects the range of viewpoints inherent in any large group of people. Such diversity of viewpoints among the people may also explain the complexity of Yahweh's response. However, it is significant that the complexity of the people's request is allowed to be heard in this presentation. The narrator has not caricatured the sinfulness of the people but represented to the reader both sides of the argument. This prevents the reader from making an unnecessarily harsh evaluation of them and brings balance to the narrator's overall evaluation.

The viewpoint of the narrator

In I Sam 8–12, the narrator makes few explicit comments about the rise of the monarchy. The two overt evaluations, which appear in 8.1–3 and 10.26–27, refer to peripheral issues that contribute to the characterisation and more subtle commentary about characters who express dominating viewpoints.

The narrator presents many different viewpoints of the situation and comments on each of the people who express them. The audience is presented with the viewpoints and steered by the narrator through a study of their motivations and reasoning, so that an informed opinion can be reached, albeit one that has been ideologically shaped by the narrator.

Samuel's viewpoint is the most dominant within the section, but there is also significant doubt cast over his character. The viewpoint of Yahweh, whose omniscience and moral righteousness gives him authority, is related least explicitly but with most complex inference.[117]

---

[117] Cf. Bar-Efrat, *Das erste Buch Samuel*, 142, who writes that, although the author lets all sides be heard, he ultimately sides with God. Whilst this is undoubtedly true,

One conjectures whether this is dictated by the limitations of knowledge of the author, the depth of the complexity of the viewpoint, or a
combination of the above.

One method for conveying such complexity, particularly from the
viewpoint of Yahweh, is through the juxtaposition of opposites. These
force the reader to consider how these aspects of the viewpoint can
stand side by side, adding nuance to the positions. The rise of the
monarchy is not a simple situation that produces only supporters and
detractors. Many issues are at stake, such as the reason the monarchy was requested, the person who will take the role, the constitution
of the monarchy and its imposition on the status quo—namely the
human leadership of Samuel and divine leadership of Yahweh. These
are issues that can be approached differently, even within a single
viewpoint, creating a multi-faceted effect.

It is claimed that the biblical writer has not adjudicated between
viewpoints in the biblical narrative[118] and, apart from guidance about
how and why the viewpoints are put forward, this is essentially correct.
Three explicit reasons are given by three different people for Israel's
request for a king: the narrator and the people say that it is because of
the corruption of Samuel's sons in chapter 8; Yahweh in 9.16 says that
it is because of the Philistine threat; and Samuel in 12.12 says that it is
due to the Ammonite threat. The juxtaposition of these three different
explanations presents a complex account with many different contrib-
uting factors and aspects. Thus our analysis of the rise of the monarchy
illustrates that adjudication is not possible in this complex issue. The
message of the chapters is that the institution of the monarchy was
neither completely positive nor completely negative but it had positive
and negative aspects that affected different people in different ways.

4.2   David—II Sam 13–19

As in I Sam 8–12, there is very little explicit commentary or evaluation in II Sam 13–19. Campbell describes meaning in these chapters
as "more than usually elusive" because of the multitude of causes and

---

the enigmatic nature of Yahweh's viewpoint means that the narrator's viewpoint must
ultimately draw on the other views represented in the narrative also.
   [118] E.g. Campbell, *1 Samuel*, 13–14.

unanswered questions alluded to in the narrative.[119] The lack of a clear ideological point of view in these chapters has long been praised as objective storytelling in contrast to the more overt ideologies of other sections. Not only is the narratorial viewpoint generally considered more subtle than other sections, scholars have not identified conflicting ideologies within individual pericopes to the same extent as we saw in earlier passages. Rost's thesis of a unified Succession Narrative extending through II Sam 9–20 and I Kgs 1–2[120] has largely been accepted among scholarship, albeit with significant variations of start and end points. Some scholars have disagreed with Rost's proposal that the narrative serves solely to legitimise Solomon,[121] yet many of these give alternative, literary reasons for believing that there is unity in the text.[122] The unity of the text is not universally agreed upon,[123] but the section has not undergone intense source criticism like other parts of Samuel.

Considering this contrast between I Sam 8–12 and II Sam 9–20, it is of interest whether the techniques for conveying complex critical evaluation found in I Sam 8–12 also apply in the less controversial section. This analysis will focus upon the evaluation of David in II Sam 13–19: his culpability or innocence in the sequence of events. We will see that there are a number of viewpoints, each incorporating some sort of tension, that offer commentary on David's role in the sequence

---

[119] Antony F. Campbell, *2 Samuel*, FOTL (Grand Rapids: Eerdmans, 2005), 135–37.

[120] Leonhard Rost, *The Succession to the Throne of David*, trans. Michael D. Rutter and David M. Gunn (Sheffield: Almond Press, 1982), passim.

[121] E.g. Whybray argues that it is wisdom as well as propaganda because of the interest in psychological insights [R.N. Whybray, *The Succession Narrative: A Study of II Samuel 9–20; I Kings 1 and 2*, SBT (London: SCM, 1968), 56]. Bar-Efrat, *Das zweite Buch Samuel*, 93–94, argues that the central theme is the sins of David and their consequences and the rights and boundaries of the king's powers. The political aspects of the events are not explored in detail. Some other scholars who disagree that the Succession Narrative is about succession are Charles Conroy, *Absalom Absalom! Narrative and Language in 2 Sam 13–20* (Rome: Biblical Institute Press, 1978), 101ff; D.M. Gunn, *The Story of King David: Genre and Interpretation* (Sheffield: JSOT Press, 1978), 21–26; and Kiyoshi K. Sacon, "A Study of the Literary Structure of 'The Succession Narrative'," in *Studies in the Period of David and Solomon and Other Essays*, ed. Tomoo Ishida (Winona Lake: Eisenbrauns, 1982), 53–54.

[122] Whybray, *The Succession Narrative*, 56.

[123] Examples of scholars who have postulated sources are Sophia Katharina Bietenhard, *Des Königs General: Die Heerführertraditionen in der vorstaatlichen und frühen staatlichen Zeit und die Joabgestalt in 2 Sam 2–20; 1 Kön 1–2* (Freiburg, Schweiz: Universitätsverlag, 1998); and James W. Flanagan, "Court History or Succession Document: A Study of 2 Samuel 9–20 and 1 Kings 1–2," *JBL* 91 (1972): 172–81.

of events. The narrator's complex characterisation of David through other literary devices is read in conjunction with these viewpoints to offer a complex and often ambiguous critical evaluation of David.[124]

The Viewpoint of God

In I Sam 8–12 two observations were made about the viewpoint of God. Firstly, two apparently contradictory views are expressed and secondly, these views did not necessarily constitute a moral judgment but rather, a commandment or decision based on God's evaluation. There are also two contradictory views in this section on David's culpability for the sequence of event. The events are portrayed both as the fulfillment of God's judgment on David in II Sam 12 and, ultimately, as an act of God's deliverance. There is no direct speech from Yahweh in this section and so perhaps what follows here should not technically be termed God's viewpoint. It represents what the narrator implies is the evaluation by God of David throughout these events.

Firstly we examine how the events of II Sam 13–19 are portrayed as a punishment from God.[125] In II Sam 12, Nathan rebukes David for his sin with Bathsheba and murder of Uriah. The formula used in 12.7 and 11, כה אמר יהוה ('thus says the Lord'), along with the use of the first person pronouns and verbs in vv. 7, 8, 11, 12, indicate that these words have come directly from Yahweh and Nathan's role as mediator is minimal. After this chapter, Yahweh does not raise the subject of David's sin or punishment again. However, a number of other devices demonstrate that the ensuing events are a fulfillment of this punishment.[126]

---

[124] The focus of complex evaluation on the character David is probably why the multiple 'ideologies' or opinions presented in the text have not been a cause of concern for most historical critics. Most scholars have postulated that the main theme of the section is the succession of Solomon and, on this subject, the ideology is uniformly against the other contenders. The complexity of evaluation surrounds David not Solomon, a feature which is less surprising in a propaganda document for Solomon than for David. Cf. Flanagan, "Court History or Succession Document," 176. He proposes that there was an early court history which was positive about David, but which was reworked into a succession document. He suggests that the change of interest to Solomon created the willingness for the inclusion of David's faults, namely the narrative of David and Bathsheba.

[125] Parallels and an overall causal chain are also argued in Bar-Efrat, *Das zweite Buch Samuel*, 114. He describes it as the measure for measure principle.

[126] This is studied closely in Polzin, *David and the Deuteronomist*, 131; and J.P. Fokkelman, *King David*, Vol. I of *Narrative Art and Poetry in the Books of Samuel: A Full Interpretation Based on Stylistic and Structural Analyses* (Assen: Van Gorcum,

The first aspect of the judgment in 12.10 is that the sword (חרב) will never depart from David's house. The violence of Absalom against Amnon, the threat of Absalom against his own father and finally the death of Absalom at the hand of Joab (David's nephew[127] and close military general) all fulfill this. It is further confirmed in the narrative in 15.14, where David explicitly uses the word 'sword' to describe Absalom's threat against David and his supporters (-והכה העיר לפי חרב; 'and he struck the city with the edge of the sword').[128] The second aspect of God's judgment in 12.11 is that he will raise up evil against David from his own house. Absalom's attempt at a coup for the kingship fulfils this judgment, although the rape of Tamar and Joab's insubordination towards David are also examples of evil that originate from members of David's own family. The final punishment, that Yahweh would give David's wives to his neighbour in full view of Israel, is fulfilled explicitly in 16.21–22 when Absalom sets up a tent on the roof and goes in to his father's concubines.[129] Even David's own verdict for the parable in 12.6, 'he shall restore the lamb fourfold' (ואת־הכבשה ישלם ארבעתים) is fulfilled as four of David's sons die between that

---

1981), 157ff. Fokkelman describes the fulfillment as *karma* (p. 159). Long describes it thus, "One may say that the private actions of David and Bathsheba set in motion a series of events, brought forth like caricatured offspring" [Burke O. Long, "Wounded Beginnings: David and Two Sons," in *Images of Man and God: Old Testament Short Stories in Literary Focus*, ed. Burke O. Long (Sheffield: Almond Press, 1981), 34]. See also Bietenhard, *Des Königs General*, 168–72, who shows how the phrase הדבר הזה ('this matter') is used as a *Leitwort* to describe the sins of David, Amnon and Absalom in II Sam 11.25, 13.20, 13.33.

[127] This family relation is not made explicit in the books of Samuel. It is only from I Chron 2.16 that we learn that Zeruiah, Joab's mother is David's sister. Nevertheless, the unusual designation of these three men in terms of their mother, rather than father, suggestions that the family connection is assumed.

[128] Anderson suggests Amnon's rape of Tamar was motivated by rivalry with Absalom rather than lust for Tamar [A.A. Anderson, *2 Samuel*, WBC (Waco: Word Books, 1989), 172]. This would imply that the rape of Tamar was also a result of the conflict within David's house. However, Amnon's illness, which comes about explicitly because of his sister (בעבור תמר אחתו), would appear to make his lust the primary motivation for his actions and there are no other clues in the text that this is his motivation. Thus Anderson's suggestion is not a prominent concern of the narrator.

[129] Alter, *The David Story*, 295, even suggests that it is the same roof from which David looked upon Bathsheba. Hill looks for a reason why David leaves his concubines behind in Jerusalem when they will be at risk [Andrew E. Hill, "On David's 'Taking' and 'Leaving' Concubines (2 Samuel 5:13; 15:16)," *JBL* 125 (2006): 129–50]. His chain of links to Egyptian diplomatic practice is a little tenuous but the article highlights the anomaly that David would leave them undefended. Regardless of David's logic behind the action, the episode functions in the narrative as a stark fulfillment of Nathan's prophecy.

point and the end of I Kgs 2.[130] Nathan's rebuke foreshadows all of the
key events in II Sam 13–19, conveying the connection between them.

The parallel is also highlighted through structure in the narrative.
Jensen demonstrates that there is a pattern of desire, rivalry and violence in the stories of David, Bathsheba and Uriah, then Amnon,
Tamar and Absalom and finally Absalom in his desire for the throne.[131]
Campbell focuses on slightly different aspects in the stories and recognises a cycle of rape, murder and then parable.[132] This pattern occurs
in II Sam 11–12 and is repeated in chapters 13–14. The pattern begins
again when Absalom rapes David's concubines and Ahithophel gives
Absalom advice to murder David in 17.2–3.[133] At this point the events
depart from the pattern, because Absalom does not succeed in the
battle against David. The rupture in the cycle indicates an act of God's
deliverance that we will discuss shortly. However, its repetition highlights that the sin in David's house is even greater than David's own.
As Gunn demonstrates, Amnon's crime against Tamar is narrated
with much greater emphasis on his emotions than David's. Furthermore, whereas David left the enemy to kill Uriah, Absalom murdered
Amnon blatantly.[134] The cycle of David's sin is being repeated among
his sons at a progressively greater intensity.

Scholars have observed many more elements of the story of David,
Bathsheba and Nathan that are repeated or reversed in II Sam 13–19,
forming a commentary on these latter events.[135] Many have pointed to
the irony that David is the unwitting messenger for his sons' wrongdo-
ings in the same way that he sent Uriah as the messenger of his own
death warrant.[136] David conveys Amnon's request for Tamar to come

---

[130] Fokkelman, *King David*, 413–4; and Alter, *The David Story*, 258–59. Ackerman
adds that there are further parallels to the metaphor of the lamb as Absalom murders
Amnon at a sheep shearing festival and Absalom has long hair that is cut and weighed
each year [James S. Ackerman, "Knowing Good and Evil: A Literary Analysis of the
Court History in 2 Samuel 9–20 and 1 Kings 1–2," *JBL* 109 (1990): 49–50]. These
parallels are less obvious but it is possible they are intentional.

[131] Hans Jürgen Lundager Jensen, "Desire, Rivalry and Collective Violence in the
'Succession Narrative'," *JSOT* (1992): 39–59.

[132] Campbell, *2 Samuel*, 127.

[133] Ibid., 152.

[134] Gunn, *The Story of King David*, 100.

[135] A more minor parallel is the appearance of the *Leitwort* שכב ('to lie down') in
both narratives. The verb appears six times each in II Sam 11 and II Sam 13 and has
both literal and euphemistic meanings [Bar-Efrat, *Das zweite Buch Samuel*, 106, 125].

[136] Gunn, *The Story of King David*, 99, and Brueggemann, *First and Second Samuel*,
287. Ackerman, "Knowing Good and Evil," 40, also points out how the verb 'to send'
(שלח) features in each of these situations.

and make him cakes in 13.7 and then he gives permission for Amnon to accompany Absalom to the sheep shearing in 13.24–27. The narrative time of this latter exchange between Absalom and David far exceeds the short description of Amnon's actual death in 13.29, which takes place in only seven words, highlighting the narrator's particular interest in David's role.

David's change of roles from culprit to messenger is captured further in Polzin's analysis of Nathan's parable to David in 12.1–7.[137] The most natural reading of the parable is that David is the rich man who takes the lamb (Bathsheba) from the poor man (Uriah).[138] However, a closer reading suggests that there are other layers of meaning possible in the parable. When Nathan says 'you are the man' (אתה האיש) in 12.7, he does not specify to which man in the story he is referring. Furthermore, in the most obvious reading, the character of the wayfarer has no apparent parallel. Therefore, Polzin suggests that the parable can also be interpreted with God in the role of the rich man who takes the kingship and women[139] (the lamb) from Saul (the poor man) and gives it to David (the wayfarer). The parable may also refer to the future when David becomes the poor man whose kingship and concubines (the lamb) are taken from him by God (the rich man) and given to Absalom (the wayfarer). This reading by Polzin demonstrates the irony that David's role has been reversed from the one who exploits to the exploited in this repetition of the pattern of his affair with Bathsheba.

Hagan has also drawn attention to the recurrence of deception in this section. There is a pattern of deception in order to obtain a woman

---

[137] Polzin, *David and the Deuteronomist*, 122–26.

[138] Cf. the reading in J.W. Wesselius, "Joab's Death and the Central Theme of the Succession Narrative (2 Samuel IX–1 Kings II)," *VT* 40 (1990): 346–8, esp. note 15. He interprets the poor man to be Bathsheba's family and the lamb to be Uriah. He cites 11.3 where Bathsheba is called the daughter of Eliam as well as the wife of Uriah and so concludes that Uriah was the weaker party and is represented by the lamb. As Bathsheba's father otherwise does not appear in the narrative, it seems unlikely that this is supposed to be the most natural reading. Wesselius continues this theme with the later connection that Ahithophel was Bathsheba's grandfather and that his advice to Absalom was an act of revenge on David. However, again the text does not make this connection obvious (Eliam is not said to be the son of Ahithophel until 23.34), making it at most a secondary consideration in this story.

[139] Polzin, *David and the Deuteronomist*, 124, suggests that Saul's women could include his wives as well as Michal his daughter. He argues that David is likely to have taken Saul's wives when he became king but, as this is not made explicit anywhere in Samuel, it seems less likely that this is being alluded to. Certainly the kingship and Michal is sufficient for the parable to make a close fit.

or the kingship, followed by counter deception, such as the parables, to restore order.[140] The pattern is begun by David's affair with Bathsheba and is repeated among his children with the alteration that David is now the one who is being deceived.[141]

The exchange of roles for David from rich man and deceiver to poor man and deceived produces a number of other ironies in the text. Joab was the instrument for Uriah's death to the benefit of David but later he becomes the instrument for Absalom's death, generating immense grief for David.[142] This reversal is intensified through the lengthy parallel scenes where Joab sends a messenger to tell David the news of each death (11.19–25 and 18.19–19.1). In both cases, David's suspense is unnecessarily prolonged and there is considerable narrative time spent on these episodes. However, in the second case, David is no longer able to answer philosophically as he did in 11.25 that 'the sword devours now one, now another' (כי־כזה וכזה תאכל החרב), because 'the sword' has now been turned on his own family, according to God's punishment. A final reversal (or attempted reversal) is the irony that David wishes to fight in battle against Absalom in 18.2, in contrast to 11.1 where the narrator pointedly remarks that David stayed at home when he ought to have been at battle.

These parallels in the narrative between II Sam 11–12 and II Sam 13–19 demonstrate that the events of Amnon and Absalom are a result of God's judgment on David. However, in tension with this, there is evidence of the alternate viewpoint that God delivers David in the battle with Absalom. God's support for David suggests a more positive evaluation of him.

God's deliverance and support for David is conveyed most plainly through the answer to David's prayer in 16.31. As Campbell points out, this prayer is only six words long yet it touches on the core of the narrative because the rejection of Ahithophel's advice by Absalom will eventually bring about the victory of David.[143] The prayer is a turning point in the fortunes of David because, from that moment onward, many more of the events begin to work in David's favour. Hushai appears with an offer of help, Ziba brings him supplies, Absalom takes

---

[140] Harry Hagan, "Deception as Motif and Theme in 2 Sm 9–20; 1 Kgs 1–2," *Bib* 60 (1979): 301–26.

[141] Ibid.: 322.

[142] Brueggemann, *First and Second Samuel*, 320.

[143] Campbell, *2 Samuel*, 149.

Hushai's advice and eventually Absalom is defeated in battle. Even the episode in 16.5–14, where Shimei curses David, ends with refreshment for David (וינפש שם) in a reversal of his weariness (עיפים).

On the other hand, David's prayer is immediately followed by his strategic action to bring about its answer, as he commissions Hushai to return to Absalom and send word via the sons of Zadok and Abiathar.[144] Yet the narrative also gives a number of indications that the change of fortune is ultimately the work of Yahweh in support of David. The immediacy of the appearance of Hushai is emphasised in v. 32 by the inclusion of the information that David was only just approaching the top of the mount of Olives (ויהי דוד בא עד־הראש) when Hushai arrived. This must be in close proximity of time to David's prayer, when he made the ascent in v. 30 (ודוד עלה במעלה הזיתים). The connection is further reinforced by the inclusion of the otherwise unnecessary phrase mentioning God, אשר־ישתוה שם לאלהים (v. 32, '[the place] where God was worshipped there'), and the frequent association of the presence of Yahweh with mountains. Thus the narrator gives a number of indications that Yahweh has sent Hushai to help deliver David, without stating it explicitly.

Moreover, Hushai's success in David's plan is explicitly declared the work of Yahweh in 17.14, ויהוה צוה להפר את־עצת אחיתפל הטובה ('the Lord commanded to defeat the good advice of Ahithophel'). The use of הטובה ('good') to describe Ahithophel's advice further emphasises that divine intervention was required to bring about victory for David. Despite this explicitness, there is ambiguity in the reason given by the narrator for God's defeat of Ahithophel's advice. Whereas we might expect its purpose to be rescuing David's place on the throne or an answer to his prayer, it is to bring harm upon Absalom (לבעבור הביא יהוה אל־אבשלום את־הרעה; 'in order that the Lord might bring evil to Absalom'). As we will see shortly, this foreshadows how the tension between God's punishment and deliverance might be resolved.

One final feature, which suggests that Yahweh is working for David's deliverance, is the role of the forest in the battle between the men of Absalom and David. 18.8 states that the forest consumed more men than the sword (וירב היער לאכל בעם מאשר אכלה החרב) and this impersonal force implies an indirect allusion to the intervention of God in the battle. It is a vague phrase that does not clarify whether

---

[144] E.g. Anderson, 2 Samuel, 204; Campbell, 2 Samuel, 149.

the trees consumed predominantly the men of Israel, whom we know
to have been defeated from the previous verse, or whether it consumed both sides equally. It therefore cannot be determined whether
this mysterious factor was working in favour of David or if it had an
even effect on both sides of the battle. Regardless, the trees ultimately
bring victory for David in 18.9 when Absalom's head is caught in the
branches of a terebinth tree. It may be a rare instance of the role of
chance in the book of Samuel but it can also be read as Yahweh's contribution towards the deliverance of David.

Thus, there is a significant tension within God's viewpoint of the
affair. It is implied that the events and actions of David's family are
a punishment from God for David's sins, yet God is also allied with
David against Absalom. The reader can hypothesise a number of different ways to resolve this tension. Perhaps God has mercy on David
and so delivers him from his own punishment. It is also possible that
the defeat of Absalom is a part of the curse against David's house—
David expresses greater grief at the death of Absalom than he does
at his rebellion. Perhaps God's punishment was not to take David's
kingship away but to bring conflict to his family and to have his wives
stolen before the eyes of Israel. Thus, he supports David's kingship
whilst these other punishments are taking place. There is not a simple
depiction of Yahweh in support of David, or against David but rather,
a complex exploration shaped by the viewpoints of other characters
and the narrator. In particular, the viewpoint of God offers no commentary on David's actions within II Sam 13–19 as he handles the
rebellions of his sons, only an overall evaluation through his judgment
and deliverance.

The viewpoints of David's servants and the Israelites

David's servants, with the exception of Joab, give little explicit evaluation of David and the events. However, they express a positive evaluation of his right to be king through their loyalty to him and, conversely,
a negative evaluation through disloyalty. They also give varying indications about why they hold such views, which add further dimensions
to their implied evaluation.

The use of structure in this section organises and highlights the
different attitudes towards David. Conroy has drawn attention to
the concentric structure of chapters 15–19. Chapters 15–16 feature
a sequence of David's encounters with loyal supporters (Ittai, Zadok
and Abiathar, and Hushai), then a questionable supporter (Ziba) and

finally a disloyal person (Shimei). In chapter 19, David encounters this sequence of people in reverse order: Shimei, Mephibosheth then Barzillai (a loyal supporter). At the centre of this concentric structure is the contention between the counselors Hushai and Ahithophel and, finally, the battle between Absalom and David.[145] The structure of David's encounters with his servants highlights the tension between their attitudes towards him. Some remain loyal whilst others see Absalom as the preferable king. These diverse viewpoints reflect the ambiguity of David's position.

Let us examine the set of servants who are loyal to David in 15.19–16.11 and 19.31–40. Firstly, Ittai the Gittite accompanies David as he leaves Jerusalem. David expresses surprise that Ittai is willing to accompany him even though he is a foreigner, but Ittai replies in v. 21 with words of unquestionable loyalty. He swears by Yahweh, despite his foreign origin, and this shows his full commitment to both David and David's God.[146] Abiathar and Zadok are not given any direct speech to express their loyalty but their symbolic act of accompanying David with the ark of God demonstrates their belief that Yahweh is with David. Similarly, Hushai does not express his loyalty with words but with his mourning garb of torn clothes and dust upon his head (15.32). Finally, at the conclusion of the concentric pattern in 19.31–40, David encounters Barzillai whom he previously met at Mahanaim in 17.27, when Barzillai and others brought him supplies, expressing their loyalty.

The intervening section in 16.15–19.15 is where these men's loyalty to David is proved most decisively. In particular, Hushai's loyalty is proved not only by his complicity in David's plot but also through his ambiguous words to Absalom in 16.16, יחי המלך ('May the king live'). Absalom naturally assumes that Hushai is referring to him as the king but the audience suspects Hushai has David in mind.[147] The double

---

[145] Conroy, *Absalom Absalom!* 89. See also Fokkelman, *King David*, 282, and Sacon, "Literary Structure," 31–34, for more extended although perhaps less tidy analyses of the structure.

[146] Polzin, *David and the Deuteronomist*, 151, even suggests that the name Ittai (אתי) is a wordplay (he is 'with' David) expressing his loyalty. The tenuous nature of this wordplay, and even more so, the wordplays he suggests for the names Zadok and Hushai, make their effectiveness somewhat doubtful.

[147] Brueggemann, *First and Second Samuel*, 309; Anderson, *2 Samuel*, 213. Brueggemann (pp. 311–12) also points out that Hushai indirectly praises David's courage as a warrior in his advice in 17.8ff.

meaning continues in v. 18 where Hushai says, כי אשר בחר יהוה והעם
הזה וכל־איש ישראל לו[148] אהיה ואתו אשב ('For whoever the Lord
and this people and all the men of Israel have chosen, I will be his
and I will remain with him'). This subtly suggests that Hushai believes
David to be Yahweh's chosen, despite the people having transferred
their choice to Absalom. These incidents, combined with the symbol-
ism of the ark in the hands of Zadok and Abiathar accompanying
David, suggest a reason for the loyalty of David's servants: they believe
God is with David despite the events turning against him. This point
of view reinforces the tension that Yahweh simultaneously punishes
and delivers David.

The positive evaluation by many of David's servants impresses
the reader that David is worthy of loyalty and that he remains God's
choice as king. Yet, these viewpoints do not comment specifically on
the morality of David's actions, only on his position as God's anointed.
It is also possible to interpret negative aspects to these interactions
that contribute to a negative evaluation of David or, at any rate, an
ambiguous one.

Firstly, Ittai's foreign status is emphasised in the narrative. He comes
amidst a list of foreigners in 15.18, the Cherethites, the Pelethites and
Gittites, and David mentions in v. 19 both that Ittai is a foreigner
(כי־נכרי אתה) and that he is in exile from his home (וגם־גלה אתה
למקומך). Several commentators have observed that Ittai's foreign status comments on David. He is now reliant on foreign help and, in
contrast to Ittai's loyalty, David's own people, including members of
his own family, have rejected him.[149] Gath, Ittai's origin, was a Philistine city and so it is only Israel's traditional enemies who now support
David. Ittai himself expresses a positive view of David but his foreignness highlights how many of David's own people disagree with this
evaluation.

David's isolation from his people is further suggested by the pattern among David's supporters of departing from him once they have
expressed their loyalty, albeit on friendly terms. Zadok and Abiathar
return with the ark to Jerusalem and Hushai soon follows so that he
can take part in the conspiracy against Absalom. In a lengthy episode in 19.31–40, the narrative focuses on Barzillai's decision to return

---

[148] Qere. Ketib is לא.
[149] Brueggemann, First and Second Samuel, 303; Anderson, 2 Samuel, 203.

home despite David's invitation to his table. Although Barzillai sends Chimham in his place, the interaction subtly alludes to the theme of distance between David and his supporters and hence also isolation from Israelites surrounding David.

Secondly, David meets people of questionable loyalty, namely Ziba and, after the conflict, Mephibosheth. Most scholars are uncertain from the evidence in the text whether it is Ziba or Mephibosheth who is lying,[150] although some have discerned implicit proof of Ziba's dishonesty.[151] As Campbell points out, the reader is given no more information than David himself[152] and so is placed in a position where he/she can evaluate David's action against his/her own assessment. Many readers have commented that David is not concerned with justice because he does not question Ziba further[153] and his final decision to halve the property indicates political expediency rather than desire for truth.[154] David does not wish to discover which man has been loyal to him and which is exploiting his weak position for his own advantage. The disloyalty in this section, more likely on the part of Ziba rather than Mephibosheth, is not due to disbelief that David is the Lord's anointed but rather, is an exploitation of David's weakness. Ziba goes to David directly after he leaves Jerusalem, showing that he anticipates that David will eventually be victorious against Absalom. Disloyalty in these episodes is not directed against David personally but it highlights David's weakness for politics over justice and the fragile position of his ignorance about who is loyal to him.

---

[150] See overview of scholarly positions in Jeremy Schipper, "'Why Do You Still Speak of Your Affairs?': Polyphony in Mephibosheth's Exchanges with David in 2 Samuel," *VT* 54 (2004): 355–51. Schipper himself concludes that there is evidence pointing both ways.

[151] E.g. Elie Assis, "Chiasmus in Biblical Narrative: Rhetoric of Characterization," *Prooftexts* 22 (2002): 279–80. Assis looks at chiasmus in Mephibosheth's words and concludes Mephibosheth's answer is well thought out and therefore indicative of his innocence. Noll, *The Faces of David*, 62, draws on David's broken promise to Jonathan by placing Mephibosheth under house arrest and so considers the fact that David does not cross examine Ziba and wrongly takes away Mephibosheth's property as a further indication of David's injustice towards Mephibosheth. However, the initially strange insertion of Ziba into the narrative of Shimei's men in 19.17 associates Ziba with the man who cursed David. The narrator subtly suggests that Ziba is not to be trusted and this emphasises the culpability of Ziba rather than David.

[152] Campbell, *2 Samuel*, 149.

[153] Noll, *The Faces of David*, 62.

[154] E.g. Campbell, *2 Samuel*, 163.

Finally, there are those who are disloyal towards David. Within the structure of David's encounters, he twice encounters Shimei, a relative of Saul. On the surface, Shimei's hostility originates from his loyalty towards the house of Saul. Whilst this is not an evaluation of David's most recent actions, it alludes to David's weakness that he has not completely silenced opposition against his succession to Saul. Moreover, his statements can be reinterpreted as referring to David's sin against Uriah, an event Shimei either did not know about or was not concerned with, but his accusations describe accurately. His repetition of the phrase אִישׁ הַדָּמִים ('man of blood') in 16.7 and 16.8 (with variation to אִישׁ דָּמִים) is reminiscent of David's guilt for the murder of Uriah and also refers to David's inaction after the shedding of Amnon's blood. Shimei's evaluation is correct, even if he gives inaccurate reasons for it. However, another aspect of Shimei's evaluation is proved incorrect. He says in 16.8 that Yahweh has taken the kingdom from David and given it to Absalom, a contrasting view from David's loyal servants who believe that God remains with David. Later Shimei reappears on the scene in chapter 19 and confesses that he sinned in his curses. Considering the events that have taken place in the intervening narrative it is presumably his belief in the divine favour of Absalom, rather than David's bloodguilt, that has altered.[155]

In addition to David's encounters on his way to and from Jerusalem, the narrator gives other indications of who was disloyal to David and why. In particular, כֹּל יִשְׂרָאֵל ('all Israel') or כָּל־אִישׁ יִשְׂרָאֵל ('all the men of Israel') are used to describe Absalom's supporters in the narrative.[156] The context suggests that כֹּל is intended hyperbolically, as David does have some supporters among Israel, but nevertheless, it emphasises the strength of Absalom's support. Furthermore, the narrative in 15.1–6 offers a reason why the people abandoned David in support of Absalom and thus had a negative evaluation of him. Firstly, we are told that Absalom acquired for himself a horse and chariot in which to ride about. Such actions are in contrast to David, who stayed at home when it was appropriate for him to be at war (II Sam 11.1).

---

[155] Cf. Ibid., 150. Campbell suggests that Shimei has realised he was wrong to shout abuse at the king (and thus he apologises for what he *did*) but he does not apologise for what he *said*. This reading is compatible with the analysis above because Shimei's cursing was only wrong because it was against the Lord's anointed.

[156] E.g. All Israel: 17.10, 11; 18.17; 19.11. All the men of Israel: 17.14; 17.24; see also 16.15 for a similar phrase.

Secondly, Absalom would sit at the gate and offer justice. Absalom is manipulative in his dispensation of justice through continual judgments in favour of the man before him (15.3).[157] Yet, as Brueggemann points out, Absalom has identified David's weak point and, in this way, finds his way into the hearts of Israel.[158] David's inaction after the illegal acts of Amnon and Absalom strongly suggests that the neglect of justice was a great failing of David. Furthermore, Absalom's success at gaining the people's favour through this method demonstrates that the people perceived this deficiency in David's kingship.[159]

In conclusion, after examining the loyalty and disloyalty of David's people, we discern a few themes in their evaluation of David. It is widely acknowledged that David remains God's chosen king. This is sufficient for his loyal supporters and they do not consider David's culpability. Among his other subjects, there are a number of criticisms of David. He does not dispense justice conscientiously, he has been a man of blood and he has dealt poorly with the sins of Amnon and Absalom. There is again a tension in the evaluation of David. God is with him yet his weaknesses are partly to blame for the ensuing events.

The viewpoint of Joab

Not only is there a tension between loyal and disloyal servants of David, there is a tension of loyalty and disloyalty within the one man Joab. Joab remains David's commander throughout this section but several moments of disloyalty to David's wishes emerge. In II Sam 13–19, this simmering disloyalty is manifested in three key incidents where Joab presents an opinion in opposition to David: he manipulates David to allow Absalom's return; he murders Absalom against David's wishes; and finally he rebukes David for his grief. The depiction of a fiercely loyal servant, who acts against his master at three

---

[157] See Robert M. Polzin, "Curses and Kings: A Reading of 2 Samuel 15–16," in *The New Literary Criticism and the Hebrew Bible*, ed. J. Cheryl Exum and David J.A. Clines (Sheffield: JSOT Press, 1993), 202.

[158] Brueggemann, *First and Second Samuel*, 301. Polzin, *David and the Deuteronomist*, 150, argues that the legal context for these actions shows that Absalom is not so much filling a gap in the justice system as doing something condemnatory. However, the response of the people of Israel demonstrates that they did not view it this way.

[159] Cf. I Sam 8.5 where it is precisely for the purpose of justice (מִשְׁפָּט) that Israel asked for a king in the first place.

key moments, is a contradiction that creates a fascinatingly complex characterisation of Joab and his relationship with David. Here we are interested in how Joab's viewpoint, at these moments of disloyalty, evaluates David's character and, in turn, how the characterisation of Joab affects our acceptance of his viewpoint. In other words, are Joab's defections against David appropriate or do they reflect his own private motivations or misguided notions?

The main cause of conflict between David and Joab is David's inaction and Joab's action. In all three incidents mentioned above, this issue arises. David does not act for or against his son Absalom in exile but finally Joab prompts him to allow his return. Joab murders Absalom when David had urged restraint. Finally Joab rebukes David for being inert with grief when his people wish to celebrate victory.

Throughout I and II Samuel, the characterisation of Joab and his brother Abishai is consistently as men of action, particularly violent action. Abishai, who is pointedly given the epithet of 'Joab's brother', first appears in I Sam 26.6 as a willing volunteer to accompany David into Saul's camp, where he wants to spear Saul in his sleep (I Sam 26.7–11).[160] From Joab's introduction in the narrative in II Sam 2, he is constantly in military action, performing duties for David. II Sam 14 is the first context in which we encounter Joab at home in Jerusalem and not at battle. Whilst Joab's actions are frequently characterised as violent, his decisive action also functions positively when he cuts short the civil wars at Gibeon in II Sam 2 and with Absalom in II Sam 18.[161]

Yet Joab's willingness for action is not always in the best interests of others. The most salient example of this is his obedience to David's command to murder Uriah. Joab's persuasion of David on behalf of Absalom is more ambiguous and scholars vary in their evaluation of this. Brueggemann and Fokkelman both assert that Joab's action is in the interest of the king, whereas Polzin suggests it may be for the interest of Israel. Bietenhard also admits ambiguity and proposes that Joab could be acting firstly as a statesman who wants Absalom in Jerusalem to keep him under control, secondly as a mediator out of love for the

---

[160] Abishai's characterisation is associated with that of Joab by their common designation, 'sons of Zeruiah' and David's frustration with them grouped as one entity in II Sam 19.21 and 19.22, 'what am I to do with you, you sons of Zeruiah'. The situations where David expresses frustration at Abishai, which also seems to include Joab, both consist of Abishai's willingness for action as he repeats a request to dispose of Shimei.

[161] Bietenhard, *Des Königs General*, 207.

king, or finally as an opportunist for his own political ends.[162] Unfortunately, an understanding of Joab's actions is obscured by the difficult translation of 13.39, which in turn complicates our understanding of 14.1.[163] Nevertheless, even if Joab's actions were not according to

---

[162] Brueggemann, *First and Second Samuel*, 291; Polzin, *David and the Deuteronomist*, 140; Bietenhard, *Des Königs General*, 174–9. Fokkelman, *King David*, 126, cites as evidence Joab's later effrontery towards Absalom as proof it is for David not Absalom. Bar-Efrat, *Das zweite Buch Samuel*, 139, 183, also notes that Joab's motivation is not communicated but proposes it is for the good of the kingdom rather than David. This motivation is then consistent with his violation of David's command not to harm Absalom later in the narrative.

[163] There are a number of problems with 13.39. The first is that the verb ותכל in the MT is third person feminine and so does not agree with David as the subject. Wellhausen long ago suggested רוח as a missing subject and simultaneously emended ותכל to the *qal* from the *piel*. Both of these changes are supported by LXX versions and later confirmed by 4QSamᵃ and so many scholars have followed these emendations. Driver, followed by Baldwin therefore translates v. 39 as 'And the spirit of the king longed to go forth unto Absalom' [S.R. Driver, *Notes on the Hebrew text and the Topography of the Books of Samuel*, 2nd ed. (Oxford: Clarendon Press, 1966), 305; Joyce G. Baldwin, *1 and 2 Samuel: An Introduction and Commentary*, Tyndale Old Testament Commentaries (Leicester: Inter-Varsity Press, 1988), 252]. This translation would suggest that Joab was taking this action for the sake of David's wishes. However, in response to this translation, Jongeling argues that it does not makes sense for Joab to resort to such cunning to encourage David to act on his own desire [K. Jongeling, "Joab and Tekoite Woman," *Jaarbericht ex oriente lux* xxx (1987–1988): 116]. Jongeling (p. 121), followed in Fokkelman, *King David*, 126–7, offers an alternative translation that has the advantage of not requiring any emendation of the text, 'And it [ie events above] made David, the king, long to set out on a military expedition against Absalom, because he still deplored Amnon's death' (note also the alternate translation of the root נחם). This translation goes to the other extreme and suggests that Joab in 14.1 is expressly going against David's desires by persuading him to bring back Absalom. The difficulty with this is that presumably if David had wanted to send out a military expedition against his son, he would have done so. Moreover, this desire does not fit with his later devotion to Absalom despite his attempted coup at the kingship. David is guilty not only of not responding to Absalom's act of murder, but of not *wanting* to respond to the crime, just as he was in the case of Amnon. There is a similar problem with the translation of P. Kyle McCarter, Jr., *II Samuel*, The Anchor Bible (New York: Double Day, 1984), 344. He emends ותכל to the *qal* with the stronger meaning of 'to cease' and understand the root יצא in a military sense, 'King [David's] enthusiasm for marching out against [him] was spent'. If David had actually wanted to march against Absalom all that time, again we assume he could have. The translations by Anderson, 'the king's anger ceased to be actively directed against Absalom' and Hertzberg, 'And David gradually began to lose his abhorrence of Absalom' follow a similar translation to McCarter, except they understand יצא in a less literal sense [Anderson, *2 Samuel*, 182, 84; Hans Wilhelm Hertzberg, *I & II Samuel: A Commentary*, trans. John Stephen Bowden, OTL (London: S.C.M. Press, 1964), 328]. These fit the context well for two reasons: firstly, David's response parallels his response to Amnon's sin against Tamar—he is angry yet he does not want to act against his son. Secondly, the abatement of David's anger but his lack of positive feelings towards Absalom creates an appropriate context for Joab to believe he has a chance at persuading David but that

David's wishes, it is possible that he was acting for David's sake even if the text gives no specific indications of this. Regarding the welfare of Israel, the parable of the woman of Tekoa suggests that the return of Absalom is in its favour (14.13). Yet subsequent events, particularly the slaughter of 20 000 men (18.7) in the war between Absalom and David, would favour the contrary. Regardless of Joab's good or self-serving intentions in this matter, hindsight reveals that this action was not in the interests of Israel. There is also ambiguity surrounding Joab's defiance of David by murdering Absalom. Here the tension is between the political good sense of disposing of the rebellious Absalom and David's heartfelt plea to deal gently with him.[164] Furthermore, the strange manner of Absalom's capture in a tree opens an opportunity for Joab to take him as prisoner without harming him, thus appeasing both David and political necessity.

Although Joab's own actions are at best ambiguous, there are indications in the text that Joab is justified in his criticism of David's inaction. Absalom's plot to kill Amnon is to some extent a result of David's inaction against Amnon for his violation of Tamar. In 13.21, David is angry (ויחר לו מאד), a passive state that produced no action.[165] The causal relationship between David's inaction and the murder of Amnon is subtly suggested by the juxtaposition of this statement of David's anger with a statement of Absalom's hatred towards Amnon in v. 22, which will later result in Amnon's death.

---

he must use cunning. It also fits well with David's partial admittance of Absalom to Jerusalem but not in his presence.

[164] Campbell and Perdue suggest that the text is ambiguous about whether David was commanding Joab to spare Absalom or to 'deal' with him albeit gently [Campbell, 2 Samuel, 156; Leo G. Perdue, "'Is There Anyone Left of the House of Saul': Ambiguity and the Characterization of David in the Succession Narrative," JSOT 30 (1984): 78]. However this is one section of the text which is not ambiguous. The unnamed soldier's paraphrase in 18.12, that David said to protect Absalom, and David's later lament in 19.1, 'If only I had died instead of you', conclusively show that it was on David's mind to spare Absalom's life.

[165] Cf. The LXX and probably the fragmentary text of 4QSam[a] which add 'but he did nothing to chasten his son Amnon for he loved him since he was his firstborn'. This version is favoured by McCarter, II Samuel, 319, who suspects the loss in the MT is due to homoioarkton. This version makes David's inaction even more stark although it does unfortunately subtract from the ambiguity of 13.37 where David mourns for his son but it does not specify whether it is Amnon or Absalom. An explicit statement of David's love for Amnon makes this later verse more likely to refer exclusively to Amnon.

David's inaction is also conveyed in the subtext of chapter 15 where the early stages of Absalom's conspiracy are described. Absalom's actions are very public, such as driving the streets in a chariot with fifty men and sitting at the city gate. Moreover, the narrator informs the reader that Absalom continued this for a considerable period,[166] sufficient time for his suspicious behaviour to come to David's attention. Despite the overt nature of Absalom's actions, David does nothing. Most critically, he does not stop Absalom going to Hebron where his rebellion gains momentum.

Therefore, there is tension between frustration at David's inaction and suspicion about the efficacy or morality of Joab's action. Neither David's inaction nor Joab's action fully appeals to the reader. However, the contrast between the two men contributes towards an evaluation of David. Joab acts as a counterpoint to David, which emphasises that David's inaction is inappropriate and to some degree responsible for the events. The narrator uses Joab's viewpoint to shape the reader's evaluation whilst highlighting the weaknesses in Joab's own character and actions.

This method of evaluation of David by the narrator reaches its pinnacle in the third incident of Joab's conflict with David. Joab rebukes David for mourning Absalom after their victory against him and urges him to sit at the city gate.[167] Scholars have tended to side with David in this interaction, describing Joab's words as unreasonable and exaggerated.[168] This demonstrates the effectiveness of the text in generating sympathy for David despite the long account of disastrous events that are, to some extent, due to his failings. An examination of Joab's statements reveals that there is great truth in his rebuke and it resonates well with the preceding events. Regardless of this, sympathy for David is sustained, as is doubt about the complete accuracy of Joab's speech.

---

[166] The LXX gives the time as four years in contrast to the MT 'forty years'. Forty years, unless it is a symbolic number of some sort, would be a remarkably long period, not only for Absalom to delay fulfilling his vow but also for the chronology of David's life. An additional suggestion is from two MT manuscripts which have 'forty days', a period of time probably too short for Absalom to have had a significant impact on the people of Israel. The LXX is thus preferred by most, if not all commentators [e.g. Anderson, *2 Samuel*; 193, McCarter, *II Samuel*, 355; Hertzberg, *I & II Samuel*, 335. An exception is Conroy, *Absalom Absalom!* 106, who prefers to remain undecided.]

[167] Although, as is pointed out in Fokkelman, *King David*, 274, David does not speak kindly to his servants as Joab suggests in 19.7, but remains stunned by grief.

[168] E.g. Fokkelman, *King David*, 277–8; and Anderson, *2 Samuel*, 227.

The first of Joab's statements is that David's servants have saved his life and the lives of his sons, daughters and wives and concubines (19.6; הממלטים את־נפשך היום ואת נפש בניך ובנתיך ונפש נשיך ונפש פלגשיך). The mortal threat to David's family implicit in this statement is supported by the urgency with which David removed his family from Jerusalem in 15.16 and is further illustrated by the fate of the ten concubines left behind by David to look after his house. Whilst the lives of David's family were not necessarily at risk,[169] his concubines were violated by Absalom. However, there is also a significant trace of irony in this statement when Joab mentions נפש בניך ('the life of your sons'). It was Joab and his armour bearers who took the life of the son, Absalom, whom David now grieves. Therefore, whilst it is true David's servants fought heroically for his safety, his servants also caused his current grief.

Secondly, Joab accuses David of loving those who hate him and hating those who love him, and that one son was more important to him that all his servants (19.7). David's inaction over the preceding chapters is plausibly attributed to his unceasing love of sons who 'hate' him. Furthermore, the paradoxical nature of David's love for those who hate him, as presented by Joab, resonates with the other reversals already alluded to in the chapter. There is mourning instead of rejoicing (19.3) and the victorious army act like fugitives (19.4).[170] Furthermore, it is reported in 18.7 that 20 000 men were lost that day and yet it is only Absalom's name that David repeats in his poignant lament, 'Absalom, Absalom, my son, my son'. Joab's point of view is not unreasonable to the reader.[171]

On the other hand, another evaluation of Joab's words is possible. Presumably Joab includes himself as one of David's commanders (שרים; also used of Joab in 18.5), but Joab's actions in defiance of David make it difficult for the audience to believe that he truly loves David. David's grief for Absalom is presented in such a sympathetic, heart-rending way that most readers will feel some measure of sympathy for David as he grieves his son. The lengthy messenger scene in

---

[169] As suggested in Anderson, 2 Samuel, 227.

[170] These reversals and others in 17.24–19.9 are observed by Conroy, Absalom Absalom! 51.

[171] The theme of David's disregard for those loyal to him is also highlighted in the list of David's mighty men in 23.8–39. Uriah's name is placed significantly last in the list, commenting on David's lack of appreciation for the men who risked their lives for him.

18.19–32 highlights David's intense anxiety for news of Absalom and the audience feels his suspense as each messenger arrives.[172] The vivid description of David's grief in 19.1 and his repeated cry for Absalom creates pathos in the scene. There is no explicit commentary in the text about whether David should be allowed to grieve for such a rebellious son and the reader is left to evaluate according to his/her own sensitivity to David's grief.

Joab's words also raise the theme of conflict between David's roles as father and as king. This has been traced by many scholars throughout the book of Samuel and, for this reason, will not be focused on here.[173] However we observe that the contrast between the public and private spheres functions similarly to the contrast between action and inaction. Joab is a man consistently concerned with public affairs in counterpoint to David, who is consumed by his family affairs.[174] The contrast between the attitude of Joab and David toward Absalom is highlighted through Bietenhard's study of the language they use to refer to him. Whilst Joab does not even refer to Absalom as David's son, David refers to him much more tenderly. He has an unambiguous focus on their familial relationship, 'my son', in chapter 19. According to Bietenhard, David's use of נער in chapter 18 does not indicate Absalom's military role but his status as a young man who needs protection.[175] Joab regards Absalom as the king's enemy; David regards him as a son. Although the audience may not entirely agree with Joab's heartless dismissal of family relationships, he provides a balance to David who succumbs to them.

The final statement of Joab is that all will be worse for David if he does not go out to his servants (v. 8): ‏ורעה לך זאת מכל־הרעה אשר־‏ ‏באה עליך מנעריך עד־עתה‏ ('this will be worse for you than all the evil which has come upon you from your youth until now'). This statement is similar to Joab's opening accusation that David has brought shame (‏הבשת‏; v. 6) on his servants. The threat that the people would revolt

---

[172] The other effect of this scene is to demonstrate how thoroughly David's concern lies with Absalom rather than the soldiers fighting for him.

[173] E.g. Kenneth R.R. Gros Louis, "Difficulty of Ruling Well: King David of Israel," *Semeia* 8 (1977): 15–33; Paul Borgman, *David, Saul, and God: Rediscovering an Ancient Story* (Oxford: Oxford University Press, 2008), 152–75. For its application in this chapter, see Fokkelman, *King David*, 281; and Conroy, *Absalom Absalom!* 49.

[174] Cf. Bietenhard, *Des Königs General*, 172, which describes the importance of the role of Joab for showing the public implications of David's private problems.

[175] Ibid., 172–73.

against David if he did not appear at the city gate carries considerable credence in light of Absalom's success at drawing on the people's discontent by sitting at the gate offering justice. On the other hand, the actions of the people in vv. 3–4 suggest that they respect David's grief and are willing to turn their victory into mourning for his sake.

We conclude that there are a number of tensions in Joab's evaluation of David. Initially we encounter the tension of Joab's constant loyalty yet occasionally disloyal acts. Joab's characterisation reveals ambiguity about his motivation for these criticisms of David, but their resonating truth forces the reader to consider this alternate point of view as a balance to David's weakness.

The viewpoint of the Narrator

Another way in which the narrator evaluates David is through his characterisation. Several studies on the characterisation of David in II Sam 13–19 have identified tensions in his character or comparisons with other characters. Among these, Gros Louis has studied the competing spheres of public and private David[176] and Gunn has observed the pattern that David's character is positive when he is giving, both in the political and familial spheres, and negative when he is grasping.[177] Jackson looks at the structure of the succession narrative and highlights the weakness of David in contrast to Uriah[178] and to Joab.[179] Perdue, after summarising these studies and others, demonstrates how many of David's actions can be read with both a positive and negative motive. David can be interpreted as the innocent bystander or as the culpable father and king.[180] Perdue comments insightfully on the ambiguity of David's character:

> We propose that the narrator's characterization of David is intentionally ambiguous so that two very different interpretations of David may emerge, depending on the reader's own assessment of the motives resting

---

[176] Gros Louis, "Difficulty of Ruling Well," 15–33.

[177] Gunn, *The Story of King David*, 101.

[178] See also Bar-Efrat, *Das zweite Buch Samuel*, 106, on the comparative analogy between Uriah and David in II Sam 11.

[179] Jared J. Jackson, "David's Throne: Patterns in the Succession Story," *CJT* 11 (1965): 183–95.

[180] Perdue, "'Is There Anyone Left of the House of Saul': Ambiguity and the Characterization of David in the Succession Narrative," 75–78.

behind the king's actions and speeches. We are not suggesting that the author is indifferent to the two different ways his character may be read. Rather, the storyteller's design is to demonstrate the complexity of David.[181]

Perdue's assessment of David's characterisation is very similar to our proposal for the complexity and ambiguity in the moral and critical evaluation of David in the events of II Sam 13–19. Complexity in characterisation is used to develop complexity in evaluation.

David's character in these chapters has many weaknesses. We have already examined his inaction and lack of proportion or control over his family. Yet David is not consumed by his weaknesses. There are glimpses of a David who can overcome them, particularly as he leaves Jerusalem. He strategically deploys his servants, Hushai, Zadok and Abiathar, to Jerusalem and concocts a plan for their sons to send messages to him in 15.24–37. Furthermore, his faith in God's deliverance in 15.31 recalls the David of I Samuel who is persecuted by Saul. This tension between David's positive and negative character traits complicates an evaluation of whether he is responsible for the events.

This complication occurs particularly through the depiction of David as passive and able to be manipulated. Jackson has observed the large number of people who lecture David throughout the narrative of II Samuel. He lists Michal, Uriah, Nathan, courtiers, Joab, Jonadab, the woman of Tekoa, Ittai, Shimei, and finally Bathsheba and Nathan in II Kings.[182] Such a list emphasises the passive position that David has reached. Furthermore, David is easily manipulated by Amnon in order to access Tamar, by Absalom in order to kill Amnon, and by Joab to bring back Absalom. David's reaction to the news Joab has killed Absalom is very different to the instant executions he orders after hearing of the deaths of Saul and Ishbosheth and this demonstrates that David has succumbed to Joab's manipulation.

Although David's own weak character is evaluated negatively, the text also highlights the culpability of those who are manipulating or taking advantage of David's weaknesses. We have previously examined Joab's inappropriate action and violence.[183] Similarly, Absalom

---

[181] Ibid.: 71.

[182] Jackson, "David's Throne," 187.

[183] Cf. Bietenhard, *Des Königs General*, 208. Whilst David and Joab share the guilt for the murder of Uriah, from the rebellion of Absalom onwards, Joab alone is responsible for the murders, in contrast to David's weakness and innocence.

is evaluated negatively, encouraging the reader to apportion blame towards him. The pericope of II Sam 13 introduces Absalom with some measure of defense for his later actions. The slow pace of the narrative focuses on the tragic details of Tamar's violation and generates sympathy for Absalom's desire for vengeance.[184] These circumstances are confirmed by the authoritative statement of the narrator in 13.22, that Absalom hated Amnon 'because he had violated his sister Tamar' (על־דבר אשר ענה את תמר אחתו). Yet, the wrong committed against Tamar is not the only plausible motivation for Absalom's murder plot against Amnon. Gunn and Fewell suggest that the frequent naming of David as 'king' reminds the reader of the political dimension to Absalom removing Amnon.[185] Such a reading is supported by Absalom's surprising advice to Tamar to hold her peace about her violation in 13.20. Punishment of Amnon by other means may not have served Absalom's political ends as effectively as his own course of action. Furthermore, Long observes that Absalom's language in 13.28, 'be courageous and valiant', is reminiscent of the commands of kings to their servants, such as in II Sam 2.7 and I Sam 18.17. This suggests that Absalom's political ambition influenced his actions as a secondary motive and therefore apportions blame to him even at this early stage in the narrative.

Absalom's culpability is developed more fully as he initiates his coup. When he manipulates justice to gain popularity, the root גנב ('to steal') is used in 15.6 to suggest that Absalom is immorally gaining support. A negative evaluation of Absalom in this scene continues in 15.11, where Absalom invites two hundred men, who were unaware that they were rebelling against David, to join him in Hebron. Finally, Absalom's rebellion is described as a קשר ('conspiracy') in 15.12. Absalom is deceiving the people to aid his opposition against David.

The scene in 16.20–22, where Absalom takes David's concubines, also reflects very negatively on him. This crime mirrors the crime of Amnon. Absalom commits a sexual crime with women who are a part

---

[184] Amit shows that the worse Amnon looks, the more positive Absalom appears [Yairah Amit, *Reading Biblical Narratives: Literary Criticism and the Hebrew Bible* (Minneapolis: Fortress Press, 2001), 130–31]. Unfortunately there is not space to explore in more detail the artful use of language in this pericope that evokes great feeling in the reader for Tamar. For a lengthy and perceptive analysis, see Bar-Efrat, *Narrative Art*, 239–82.

[185] Gunn and Fewell, *Narrative*, 151.

of his family. Furthermore, he is encouraged to commit this violation by his advisor Ahithophel, who performs a similar function in the narrative to Jonadab when he advises Amnon in 13.3–5. The parallel between Amnon and Absalom (and to some extent, David in II Sam 11) highlights the evil he is committing. By depicting Absalom as an agent of the disastrous events that befall David and Israel, David's guilty role is to some extent lessened. David is a victim, as well as a negligent party.

In summary, the narrator of II Sam 13–19 uses viewpoints to evaluate critically David's role in the civil war in Israel and the destruction of his family. David is presented as both undergoing punishment for his earlier crimes in II Sam 11 and being the beneficiary of God's deliverance. This tension demonstrates that the disasters befalling David are not a straightforward result of his sin. Some of David's servants believe David deserves loyalty and is the rightful king, whereas others are disloyal, representing the view that David has brought about his own dethronement. The criticisms of Joab are tainted by his ulterior motives, but at the same time they highlight David's weakness for his family and his lack discipline over them. These complex assessments of David are drawn together by the narrator to give a multifaceted evaluation of his strengths and weaknesses. David's weaknesses contribute towards the events of II Sam 13–19, but Absalom and Joab are also characterised as agents in this crisis.

Perdue suggests in his study of David's characterization that the complexity of David reflects, "ambiguity among many Israelites held about the institution of monarchy in general, an ambiguity reflected in many biblical texts." This analysis shows that different Israelites' views of King David are reflected even within this single narrative. The final form of this historiography contains contrasting and even contradictory viewpoints about David. The narratorial style and comments help the reader to weigh each of these points of view and understand their complexity and nuances.

4.3   CONCLUSION

In this chapter, we have examined some ways in which explicit and implicit commentaries on events in Samuel are drawn together to convey complex and critical evaluation. The narrative does not merely tell events but handles complex issues such as moral culpability, theological significance and political implications. At times the commentary appears contradictory or inconsistent, traits which are thought to derive from diverse original sources. Even taking into account such diachronic explanations, this study has demonstrated that the text in its final form achieves complexity and sophistication through these features.

This study of viewpoints and the juxtaposition of opposites in the text points to certain implications for reading the representation of the past in Samuel. Firstly, only the viewpoint of the narrator, and not of the characters, has authority. Thus, all the opinions expressed in the narrative do not represent a definitive evaluation of the events. Greater exertion is required from the reader than a mere acceptance of viewpoints as they are expressed. The reader must be sensitive to the narrator's explicit and implicit promptings that guide him/her through the process of assessing each viewpoint. Often a full appraisal cannot be made immediately and the reader must allow the narrative to take its course before certain characters are vindicated or proved false.

It is a significant feature of this historiography that multiple voices and opinions about events are heard. The narrator may unashamedly influence the reader about the level of trust or suspicion with which he/she should assess the viewpoint, but the viewpoint itself is not suppressed. This demonstrates an acknowledgement that the past has many perspectives and that they should not be excluded from historiography. However, this is different from postmodern conceptions of multiple voices in history because the narrative guides the reader through the viewpoints and suggests that there are right and wrong interpretations. It gives reasons why some viewpoints do not have the same authority as others and it influences the reader through the artful presentation and significantly placed narratorial comments.

This study demonstrates the power of narrative to present nuanced opinions without the use of extended propositional statements. Narrative has the advantage that it tolerates ambiguities in a way that exposition finds awkward. Ambiguous characterisation and motivation reflect genuine human experience, which is more complex than the extremes of black and white. By juxtaposing black and white views, the narrative forges the evaluation that neither extreme of right or wrong can fully capture all angles of the situation. This applies both to the viewpoints of individual characters and to the evaluation as a whole presented by the narrator.

In conclusion, the use of covert evaluation and the representation of diverse ideological perspectives imply that there is not one 'correct' reading of the evaluation of the past in Samuel. This portrait of evaluation as complex and open-ended sounds very modern and perhaps the overall effect of the various methods of evaluation on the reader is comparable to modern historiography because it reflects real life experience. However, this comparison must be qualified by the recognition that there are important differences in evaluation between modern historiography and Samuel's historiography.

Firstly, there are many methods of evaluation in the book of Samuel that are unlikely to be found in modern historiography. The use of unexplained gaps and contradictions in the narrative differs from the modern tendency to offer explanations of such features.

Secondly, there is a difference in the ideological underpinnings and therefore the nature of the evaluation. In Samuel, the Divine has ultimate authority, although explicit evaluation from Yahweh is sporadic and largely supplemented by the narrator and by characters within the text. Furthermore, even when Yahweh's evaluation is not prominent, moral and political evaluation is subsumed by theological concerns. The narrative of II Sam 13–19, where Yahweh is barely mentioned, is under the interpretative shadow of Nathan's oracle to David in II Sam 12. Once again, in this section we observe that different ideology between modern historiography and the book of Samuel results in a different representation of this integral feature of historiography.

CHAPTER FIVE

COHERENCE AND CONTRADICTIONS

The historical accuracy of the historiography in Samuel is one of the great concerns of modern scholarship. In modern historiography, accuracy requires strict adherence to the facts, and coherence and non-contradiction in the presentation. The purpose of this chapter is to examine whether these conventions for an accurate presentation also apply to the book of Samuel. This will not reveal whether the events of Samuel 'actually happened'. Rather, it will give an indication of which aspects of the historiography share a modern point of view for the need for accuracy, regardless of whether this accuracy was obtained.

According to the conventions of modern historiography, a work is only an accurate representation if it is based on the facts. Even amongst postmodern conceptions of historiography, which acknowledge the subjectivity of facts, there is an awareness that if an interpretation contradicts known physical facts, for example, location, time, participants, then it can be deemed an incorrect representation of history.[1] In an article titled, "The Truth of Historical Narratives," C. Behan McCullagh suggests a number of criteria by which a work of history can be considered a 'fair representation' of the past and, therefore, a truthful history, despite the subjectivity of a concept such as truth. First and foremost amongst these criteria is that all descriptions of the central subject must resemble what actually happened. He acknowledges this can never be known for certain and so, in reality, the descriptions can only cohere with our evidence and our other beliefs.[2] His second condition is a corollary of the first—the history must not imply facts about a subject that are false.[3]

---

[1] See John Passmore, "Narratives and Events," *History and Theory* 26 (1987): 71.

[2] C. Behan McCullagh, "The Truth of Historical Narratives," *History and Theory* 26 (1987): 33. He also points out (p. 34) that a work of history can have all true statements but still misrepresent or distort its subject. Thus he postulates a third criterion (p. 38), that all parts of the history should have the same degree of details.

[3] Ibid.: 37.

In modern conventions, there is also an emphasis on coherence in the overall historiography, not just with the known facts. Inconsistencies can arise in historical knowledge because its representation can be ambiguous and dependent on its context.[4] However, it is the work of the historian to resolve these inconsistencies, "either by zooming in or by zooming out on the historical reality to look for a context in which they disappear."[5] Thus, a 'good' representation of history is one in which there is coherence in the account, even if the coherence itself is not necessarily a justification of its truth. The idea that true 'facts' can be ambiguous and therefore incoherent without the appropriate context will be an important one in our analysis of Samuel.

The validity of Samuel as a reliable historical source has proved a difficult and controversial issue because of the absence of substantial external sources or archaeological evidence. Some scholars have rejected the book entirely as a historical source because of the uncertainties surrounding its historicity.[6] Other scholars have used criteria such as plausibility and coherency to determine which parts of the historiography may contain kernels of historical truth.[7] However, the criteria of plausibility and coherency have problems. Many implausible events have occurred in history and so there is danger of reducing history to something unremarkable if we accept only those events we deem likely. Nevertheless, reason is an important tool in modern historiography, especially in light of the minimal evidence available about the ancient past. Similarly, coherence and non-contradiction are problematic. As we have seen, it is the convention and even a requirement of modern historiography to explain context so that inconsistencies are smoothed away, but this is evidently not the convention

---

[4] Pollman describes the problems with using coherence as a justification for a particular representation of history. For example, there can be two versions of the past, which are internally consistent but which contradict eachother. This is because of the ambiguity of historical knowledge [Thijs Pollmann, "Coherence and Ambiguity in History," *History and Theory* 39 (2000): 175, 178].

[5] Ibid.: 179.

[6] E.g. Philip R. Davies, *In Search of Ancient Israel*, JSOTSup. 148 (Sheffield: JSOT Press, 1992); Thomas L. Thompson, *Early History of the Israelite People: From the Written and Archaeological Sources* (Leiden: Brill, 1992); Niels Peter Lemche, *The Israelites in History and Tradition* (London: SPCK, 1998); Giovanni Garbini, *History and Ideology in Ancient Israel* (London: SCM, 1988).

[7] E.g. J. Maxwell Miller, "Reading the Bible Historically: The Historian's Approach," in *Israel's Past in Present Research*, ed. V. Philips Long (Winona Lake: Eisenbrauns, 1999), 361.

of historiography in Samuel. The absence of this convention does not necessarily mean that the representation could not appear accurate for ancient readers.

Furthermore, historiography rarely presents us with simple statements of fact that logically contradict each other and are therefore conclusively false. As has been identified in modern historiography, facts can be ambiguous without the appropriate context. Even a contradiction such as the reports that both David and Elhanan killed Goliath can be given an explanation that is not textual. Perhaps David and Elhanan were the same person or perhaps there were two Goliaths. The events and processes of history are too complicated to be reduced to logic equations and therefore contradictions in the text do not necessarily represent an impossible set of events in the past. They demonstrate that the history is not written according to modern ideals but it may still be 'true' according to another culture's conventions.

The extensive use of imaginative narrative devices in Samuel has a significant impact on its conventions for accuracy. As Robert Alter writes:

> What we have in this great story, as I have proposed elsewhere, is not merely a report of history but an imagining of history that is analogous to what Shakespeare did with historical figures and events in his history plays. That is, the known general contours of the historical events and of the principal players are not tampered with, but the writer brings to bear the resources of his literary art in order to imagine deeply, and critically, the concrete moral and emotional predicaments of living in history, in the political realm…The writer does all this not to fabricate history but in order to understand it.[8]

Narrative historiography, by necessity, contains literary devices that stem from the imagination of the authors/redactors and so includes elements that a modern reader would consider unsupported by the evidence. Whilst many have understood the role of imaginative narrative strategies in the historiography of Samuel,[9] few have attempted to classify and analyse the extent and the nature of its deviation from a modern conception of what actually happened.

In light of these issues, we will explore the conventions of accuracy, coherence and contradiction in the historiography of Samuel. We will

---

[8] Robert Alter, *The David Story: A Translation with Commentary of 1 and 2 Samuel* (New York: W.W. Norton, 1999), xvii–xviii.

[9] See chapter 1: Introduction.

look at which features of the text were presented exactly as the authors/
redactors believed they occurred and which were elaborated or altered
according to the authors/redactors' imaginations. This question will be
investigated by determining which features in the text are presented
coherently and consistently, and which features are not. Moreover,
concerning the features that do not have consistency and accuracy by
modern standards, we will consider: firstly, what is the narrative effect
of these contradictions; and secondly, to what extent the 'accuracy' of
these features was compromised. Thus, the purpose of our study is not
to assert that the historiography in Samuel *is* necessarily accurate but
to explore which features it *presents* as accurate and consistent.

Some scholars assume that the authors/redactors did not notice the
contradictions and so consider them evidence of 'bad' or inaccurate
history. Others propose that the authors/redactors must have been
aware of these contradictions but included them because they arose
from competing traditions, all of which it was necessary to preserve.[10]
Either or even both of these theories may be correct. However, this
study will show that there are only contradictions in *certain* features
of the text. If either or both of these theories were the full story, then
we would presume that contradictions would have arisen in all of the
features of the historiography, not just some of them. Thus, the features that do *not* have contradictions would have been smoothed over
by the redactors because such contradictions were not acceptable in
historiography. The contradictions and incoherencies that remained
were not offensive to their concept of history or to the conventions of
their cultural milieu.

Our investigation into the book of Samuel's concept of accuracy
will begin by looking at inconsistencies within the MT version and
therefore, identifying the features that are not presented accurately by
a modern standard. Secondly, we will examine the contradictions and
inconsistencies between the MT and LXX version of the book. These
contradictions give an indication of which features of the text a translator or redactor felt at liberty to re-imagine or alter and which features it was necessary to keep constant. It is possible that changes took
place as a result of additional evidence available to the redactors of

---

[10] See Baruch Halpern, *The First Historians: The Hebrew Bible and History* (University
Park: Pennsylvania State University Press, 1988). Also, specific to I Sam 16–17, Charles
D. Isbell, "A Biblical Midrash on David and Goliath," *SJOT* 20 (2006): 259–63.

the later versions. However, the coexistence of these versions, possibly within the same community, point to a tolerance of such inconsistencies in historiography within that cultural milieu.

There are a number of different witnesses for the book of Samuel, including fragments of the book found at Qumran,[11] the Old Latin, Aramaic Targum Jonathan, Syriac Peshitta and Latin Vulgate. The group of manuscripts we will focus on in this chapter is the Septuagint. The Old Greek (OG) of the book of Samuel was probably translated somewhere between the 3rd and 2nd centuries BCE[12] and so reflects an even older Hebrew *Vorlage*. The OG of I Sam 1–II Sam 9 is largely accessible through the Codex Vaticanus (LXX[B]), with the Codex Alexandrinus (LXX[A]) and Lucianic manuscripts (LXX[L]) offering later recensions of this text. II Sam 10.1–I Kings 2.11 in LXX[B] is thought to be the *kaige* recension dating approximately to the 1st century CE and the OG is probably better represented by LXX[L].[13] I have selected the LXX for examination because of its completeness and antiquity.

One difficulty with analysing contradictions between the MT and LXX is that the differences can be attributed to two different causes— variant *Vorlagen* or the translator of the LXX. If the variations are the responsibility of the translator, then we gain information about the translator's conventions and conception of historiography. On the other hand, if the variations were already present in the LXX *Vorlage*, then the inconsistencies could reflect the philosophy of the scribes of the LXX *Vorlage* or the proto-MT, depending on which text was earlier. This conundrum limits our research because we do not know which of the texts we are learning about. The antiquity of the LXX allows us to generalise about the conception of history in the ancient milieu of the book of Samuel but not specifically the conventions of the MT authors/redactors.

What are the features of historiography?

The first step in this investigation is to delineate the various components of ancient historiography that could be presented contradictorily

---

[11] In the entire section of I Sam 16–18, 4QSam[a] contains only a few fragments of 17.3–8, 40–41, 18.4–5 [Frank Moore Cross et al., *Qumran Cave 4: 1–2 Samuel*, vol. XII, *DJD* (Oxford: Clarendon Press, 2005), 78–80].

[12] Emanuel Tov, *Textual Criticism of the Hebrew Bible*, 2nd ed. (Minneapolis: Fortress Press, 2001), 136–37.

[13] Hugo, "Text History," 6.

or incoherently within the MT or between the LXX and MT. Firstly, ancient historiography contains three features that have already been discussed in detail in this book: causation, critical evaluation and meaning. Even in modern historiography, these three qualities are considered subjective and abstract with many possible interpretations. They must not contradict the evidence but require the imagination and analysis of the historian for their discovery.

Furthermore, there are 'events' in history, the collections of 'stuff' that actually happened, which are being represented and explained in the historiography. Events are also subjective as the historian exercises his/her judgment in the selection of their contents, their boundaries and the way in which they will be represented in narrative.[14] Nevertheless, they are considered 'facts' that, according to modern historiography, should not be fabricated in any way. Either they happened or they did not. There is interpretation involved in their representation but not in whether they actually occurred. Yet in the book of Samuel, there is evidence to suggest that some of these 'facts' are fabricated or altered to some degree. In order to discover this degree, we will break down such events into their components.

Events themselves can be defined as "a perceived change in a given state of affairs" worthy of people's attention or interest.[15] Such changes in affairs usually comprise a number of minor changes such as actions, thoughts, changes in emotions and movements, or influences from the physical environment. In this section, we will refer to the changes that contribute to the overall shift in the state of affairs as 'changes of state'. These changes of state are connected to each other through the devices of narrative and given a chronological sequence. Thus, the first two components of an event are:

1. Changes in state
2. Chronology of these changes

---

[14] Robert F. Berkhofer, *Beyond the Great Story: History as Text and Discourse* (Cambridge, Mass.: Belknap Press of Harvard University Press, 1995), 53: "Evidence is not fact until given meaning in accordance with some framework or perspective. Likewise, events are not natural entities in histories, but constructions and syntheses that exist only under description."

[15] Michael Stanford, *A Companion to the Study of History* (Oxford: Blackwell, 1994), 170. See also Passmore, "Narratives and Events," 72.

The narrative is not just a series of changes in state, it is also a description of the static elements of the event.[16] These static elements are a series of 'facts' that could be observed about the event. The following is a comprehensive list of elements that are described in relation to any event in Samuel:

1. Time
2. Location
3. People (e.g. identity, appearance)
4. Objects
5. Sounds (e.g. speeches)

As we examine contradictions and inconsistencies in Samuel, we will observe closely the book's attitudes to the components of its 'events', along with their causation, critical evaluation and meaning. Based on the research of the previous three chapters, we expect these latter features of causation, critical evaluation and meaning to remain stable and consistent throughout the book and the versions. It is our hypothesis that the 'facts' or components of events lack precision in their description and that they are allowed to remain ambiguous in their context, contrary to the expectations of modern historiography. There is, however, some level of stability to them, some control on the variation or alteration that can occur, particularly in the way they contribute to causation, critical evaluation and meaning. This hypothesis will be tested in the story of David, Goliath and Saul in I Sam 17.

5.1   Coherence and Factual Precision in I Sam 17

Amongst popular audiences, the story of David and Goliath is famous as a heroic tale of the victory of the underdog. Amongst biblical scholars, the chapter is famous for blatant contradictions with its context and significant differences between the MT and LXX versions. It is therefore an ideal chapter for analysis in this section on coherency in the history of Samuel, as it presents the most obvious violations of our modern ideas of a logical representation of the past. This section will examine the contradictions of the MT version, analyse the chapter as a

---

[16] Passmore, "Narratives and Events," 72–73.

whole, and draw conclusions about the type of coherency or incoherency that can be found in its history. Then we will examine the differences between the LXX version and the MT and assess which details the authors, redactors or translators considered it important to keep stable and which were open to artistic license.

Contradictions in the Masoretic Text version of I Sam 17

Whilst there are a few contradictions within the MT story of I Sam 17, most contradictions are with the surrounding chapters. The most palpable are in the depiction of David's age, role, status and relationship to Saul.[17] In I Sam 16.1–13, David is a young shepherd boy who is anointed by Samuel as king. The depiction of David as shepherd continues in 16.14–23, but the additional information is given that he is 'a man of courage, a man of war' (וגבור חיל ואיש מלחמה). It is also reported in v. 22 that Saul is impressed by David and that he desires him to remain in his service.[18] However, in chapter 17, David is in Bethlehem looking after his father's sheep, not in the service of Saul. Verse 15 suggests that David commuted between the battlefield and his father's sheep but this verse is considered by many scholars to be a redactional attempt at harmonisation.[19] Regardless of whether this verse is redactional or original, David's place as Saul's armour bearer during a period of war was undoubtedly at Saul's side, not with his father's sheep or bringing provisions to his brothers.[20] In 18.6–7, the

---

[17] See Julius Wellhausen, *Prolegomena to the History of Ancient Israel* (Gloucester, Mass.: Smith, 1973), 263–64; Hans Joachim Stoebe, "Die Goliathperikope 1 Sam. XVII 1–XVIII 5 und die Textform der Septuaginta," *VT* 6 (1956): 410–13; P. Kyle McCarter, Jr., *I Samuel*, The Anchor Bible (New York: Doubleday, 1980), 295; Alexander Rofé, "The Battle of David and Goliath: Folklore, Theology, Eschatology," in *Judaic Perspectives on Ancient Israel*, ed. Jacob Neusner, Baruch A. Levine, and Ernest S. Frerichs (Philadelphia: Fortress Press, 1987), 210; John T. Willis, "Function of Comprehensive Anticipatory Redactional Joints in 1 Samuel 16–18," *ZAW* 85 (1973): 295–96; Antony F. Campbell, *1 Samuel*, FOTL (Grand Rapids: Eerdmans, 2003), 172. Even Fokkelman is willing to admit that these circumstances form some level of tension in the text [J.P. Fokkelman, *The Crossing Fates*, Vol. II of *Narrative Art and Poetry in the Books of Samuel: A Full Interpretation Based on Stylistic and Structural Analyses* (Assen: Van Gorcum, 1986), 201].

[18] Note the gap in the narrative that it only records Saul's request for David to remain permanently in his service (יעמד נא דוד לפני). It does not specify whether David would remain beyond the period of Saul's affliction by the evil spirit.

[19] E.g. McCarter, *I Samuel*, 303; Ralph W. Klein, *1 Samuel*, WBC (Waco: Word Books, 1983), 177; Campbell, *1 Samuel*, 173.

[20] Campbell, *1 Samuel*, 172.

women celebrate David along with Saul as if he were one of Saul's soldiers, not an unknown shepherd boy who had killed one giant. Then,
finally, in v. 10 David returns to his initial role of playing the harp for
Saul, suggesting continuity with the story of 16.14–23 not chapter 17.

These contradictions in David's role are further exacerbated by
apparent contradictions in Saul's recognition of David. Considering
David was Saul's armour bearer and greatly loved by him in 16.21, it is
remarkable that in vv. 55–58, Saul does not know the name of David's
father, nor does Abner. He does not use David's name in the question
and this may imply that he is asking who David is, not just the identity
of his father. Furthermore, it is difficult to believe that David's name
was not discussed at their recent meeting in 17.31–39, especially when
the fate of all Israel was balanced upon the outcome of the combat.[21]

A number of other contradictions in the unit have been observed.
These include: David is introduced in the narrative in vv. 12–15 as if
for the first time, despite appearing in chapter 16;[22] David kills Goliath twice, first by the sling and secondly by the sword;[23] David places
Goliath's armour in his tent in v. 54 despite having only arrived that
day and so he would be unlikely to have had a tent;[24] David takes
Goliath's head to Jerusalem in v. 54 but at this stage, Jerusalem was a
Jebusite city;[25] after this event, in v. 57, David still has Goliath's head
in his hand.[26]

Three more 'problems' with the MT version of David and Goliath
are worthy of mention. One, possibly the most straightforward contradiction of all, is with 2 Samuel 21.19 where it is stated that Elhanan
killed the giant Goliath.[27] The second and third are not contradictions
but rather implausible details. The height of Goliath, given in 17.4,
comes to approximately nine foot nine inches by today's measure-
ments.[28] This is implausibly tall especially as the text does not specifically term him a 'giant'. Furthermore, Goliath appears morning and

---

[21] Ibid., 173, 187.

[22] McCarter, *I Samuel*, 303.

[23] Campbell, *1 Samuel*, 173.

[24] Willis, "Redactional Joints," 304.

[25] Ibid.: 302; Klein, *1 Samuel*, 181; Fokkelman, *The Crossing Fates*, 207.

[26] Campbell, *1 Samuel*, 173.

[27] McCarter, *I Samuel*, 291; Leo Krinetzki, "Ein Beitrag zur Stilanalyse der Goliathperikope, 1 Sam 17:1–18:5," *Bib* 54 (1973): 200–01; Stanley Isser, *The Sword of Goliath: David in Heroic Literature* (Atlanta: SBL, 2003), 34–37; Azzan Yadin, "Goliath's
Armor and Israelite Collective Memory," *VT* 54 (2004): 377.

[28] McCarter, *I Samuel*, 291.

evening for forty days before the Israelites and it is implied that every time they flee in terror. This excessive number of times is somewhat farcical for a modern reader.[29]

Finally, there is another implausible aspect of the narrative that is not confined to this chapter: the record of direct speech. Direct speech in Hebrew narrative is widely acknowledged to be the invention of the authors/redactors' imaginations.[30] An invented speech would not be considered 'what actually happened' in modern historiography, even if it were based upon the 'gist' of what was said.

Similar to the present study, Barnhart suggests that speech and other literary devices are fabrications in the book designed to dramatise the story. He writes:

> I suspect the redactors of Samuel and Kings viewed some of their own fabrications as elements of good storytelling. At the same time, they regarded their work as attempts to disclose a greater truth that went beyond the mere facts. In some case [sic], the fabrications probably appeared to them to be trustworthy interpretations inserted to clarify and provide the fuller meaning. In other cases, the redactors perhaps believed they were providing the alleged 'voice' (i.e., deeper meaning) of the inherited story rather than always the actual 'words' spoken.[31]

In concluding his article, Barnhart suggests that these fabrications are designed to serve four interests: (1) to report, (2) to explain, (3) to justify, and (4) to entertain. The foundation for his argument is that the speech of Yahweh and other dialogue in the book must be invented because it is impossible that a writer would be privileged to this information. Furthermore, divine intervention, such as the plague of tumors against the Philistines or the plague of II Sam 24, is also the imposition of the writer who is attempting to explain the events.[32]

---

[29] Campbell, *1 Samuel*, 174.

[30] This assumption is influenced by the presence of this phenomenon in Greek historiography. According to Thucydides, *History of the Peloponnesian War (1.22)*, "With reference to the speeches in this history, some were delivered before the war began, others while it was going on; some I heard myself, others I got from various quarters; it was in all cases difficult to carry them word for word in one's memory, so my habit has been to make the speakers say what was in my opinion demanded of them by the various occasions, of course adhering as closely as possible to the general sense of what they really said."

[31] Joe E. Barnhart, "Acknowledged Fabrications in 1 and 2 Samuel and 1 Kings 1–2: Clues to the Wider Story's Composition," *SJOT* 20 (2006): 232.

[32] Ibid.: 235. Barnhart opens his article (p. 231) by referring to the number of lies that occur throughout Samuel which serve worthy purposes, suggesting that this also

There are two weaknesses in Barnhart's work. Whilst his foundation is justified, he extends his identification of fabrications to whole events in the narrative, such as David's refusing to take Saul's life in I Sam 24 and 26.[33] Whilst it may prove true that these are fabricated stories, it is a logical leap to assume that because the book fabricated dialogue, it has fabricated entire events. As we have seen, events are not single entities that are either completely fabricated or completely true. Rather, they are composed of different elements such as descriptions or meaning. It is possible that it is more acceptable to fabricate some of these elements than others, particularly as these elements involve varying degrees of interpretation.

A second disagreement flows from the first. Barnhart speculates that these are intentional fabrications in order to perform the four functions listed above. He writes, "The drive to justify the deeds of certain characters and political moves in the story encroached on the drive to report what actually happened."[34] However, he is applying a modern idea of 'what actually happened' to an ancient text without conclusive evidence that they had the same standards for this. If the known fabrications are restricted to matters of dramatisation of dialogue and interpretation of events, rather than whole events, the fabrications can be considered interpretation rather than a violation of what happened according to ancient conventions for historiography. As Barnhart writes concerning divine intervention:

> In the field of physics, scientists *fabricate* various entities invisible to the naked eye. Theories about the presumed entities expand and ideally are put to the test of falsification. If the theories not only continue to survive the tests but also appear to explain a vast spread of reality and prove useful in making predictions, they come to be regarded as more than fabrications.[35]

Elements that look like fabrications to our culture may yet be 'theories' or interpretation of the historiography and so they were acceptable in ancient historiography.

---

is a foundation for accepting known fabrications in the book. However, the fabricated stories, such as Nathan's oracle in II Sam 12 or the woman of Tekoa's deceptive story, are immediately acknowledged as fabrications once they have served their purpose. Similarly, Michal's lie to her father is found out. The other lies are not necessarily positively evaluated by the text.

[33] Ibid.: 236.
[34] Ibid.: 235–36.
[35] Ibid.: 235.

Now we will examine each of these contradictions and implausible details, and determine (a) what type of 'facts' they are; and (b) their contribution to the representation of the past and why this contribution was more important for the authors/redactors than resolving their incoherencies.

Components of description

1. *Goliath's appearance*

The first set of implausible descriptive details in I Sam 17 pertain to the physical appearance of Goliath the Philistine, thus falling under the category of 'description of persons' and 'description of objects'. Objections have primarily been made about Goliath's extraordinary height in v. 4. Tsumura has attempted to explain this height by looking at studies of other particularly tall people,[36] but ultimately no one in history is known to have approached nine foot nine inches in height. Yet, Goliath is not at any stage called a giant[37] nor is his height mentioned as the particular source of fear for the Israelites. It is more plausible that the text is not giving a precise measurement of his height but rather a measurement that gives an exaggerated impression of his stature.

The description of Goliath's armour and weaponry in vv. 5–7 is linked with the description of his appearance. Although the armour and the precise weights of its components are very impressive, they are not in themselves implausible.[38] Indeed, the Israelites would have had access to its precise specifications because David took it back to his tent and presumably it was kept as a trophy for a considerable period. Thus it is possible that it was recorded accurately in this historiography. Nevertheless, the probable inflation of Goliath's height and the extraordinary size of his armour suggest that this information is also

---

[36] David Toshio Tsumura, *The First Book of Samuel*, NICOT (Grand Rapids: Eerdmans, 2007), 441.

[37] Cf. The use of הרפה ('giant') in II Sam 21.16, 18, 20 and 22.

[38] Cf. Tsumura, *The First Book of Samuel*, 441. He suggests that, considering the great size of Goliath's weapons, it makes better sense for Goliath to have been nine foot nine. This assumes that, despite being such an unusually great height, Goliath suffered no health effects from gigantism. On the other hand, Hays claims to have a colleague under six foot who can fling weights much heavier than Goliath's armour and weaponry! See also his discussion on the practicality of Goliath's weaponry [J. Daniel Hays, "Reconsidering the Height of Goliath," *JETS* 48 (2005): 708–09].

a literary embellishment rather than an important factual record. In particular, his armour and weaponry are probably a conglomeration of weapons of different origins.[39] Further support is given by the discrepancy between this description in vv. 5–7, where Goliath has no sword, and v. 51, where David takes Goliath's sword (חרבו) and decapitates him.[40] The purpose appears to be literary effect rather than a reliable historical record of ancient Philistine armour and weapons.

The most palpable effect of this impressive description of Goliath's height and armour is to demonstrate that Goliath is a formidable enemy.[41] Indeed, Goliath's memorable height is undoubtedly responsible for this story entering the popular consciousness to such a great degree. It is a physical representation of the metaphorical 'great enemy'. However, the role of Goliath's appearance in the narrative is more sophisticated than merely a source of fear for the audience.

The concept of appearance is very significant in this narrative and the narratives preceding it. In 16.7, the Lord 'sees' (ראה) not as man 'sees' and he looks not at the outward appearance as man does, but at the heart.[42] This statement comments directly on the impressive height of Eliab (16.7) and indirectly on Saul (9.2, 10.23); both are rejected by God as king. Height is associated with deceptive outward appearance in this narrative. Therefore, when Goliath is reported as tall,[43] allusion is made to this theme. The allusion functions in two ways: firstly, it reminds the audience that outward appearances are deceptive and Israel should not consider Goliath's height an insurmountable obstacle;[44] secondly it draws a connection between Saul and Goliath

---

[39] Summarised in McCarter, *I Samuel*, 291–93.

[40] See Isser, *The Sword of Goliath*, 34–37, who explains this discrepancy as an appropriation of Elhanan's feat in order to explain the tradition of the sword of Goliath at Nob. There are also attempts to account for this by translating כידון in v. 6 as 'scimitar' [e.g. McCarter, *I Samuel*, 294]. Although this translation may be correct, there are still two different words used, indicating that technical precision and consistency of the description of weapons was not the highest priority in this narrative.

[41] E.g. McCarter, *I Samuel*, 292; A. Graeme Auld and Craig Y.S. Ho, "The Making of David and Goliath," *JSOT* 56 (1992): 130.

[42] Alter describes this whole pericope as an exercise in 'seeing' correctly [Robert Alter, *The Art of Biblical Narrative* (New York: Basic Books, 1981), 148]. Furthermore, 'seeing' and 'not seeing' recur constantly throughout the stories of Eli, Samuel and Saul (see chapter 2: Causation, pp. 60–61).

[43] This is highlighted by the use of the root גבה to describe all three men in 10.23, 16.7 and 17.4.

[44] Keith Bodner, *1 Samuel: A Narrative Commentary* (Sheffield: Sheffield Phoenix Press, 2008), 178.

and parallels them in the narrative.[45] Both of these themes are drawn out further in the narrative.

The theme of unnecessary intimidation by outward appearances is conveyed through the occurrence of the root ראה at key moments in the narrative. Furthermore, Fokkelman has pointed out that there is an opposition between seeing and hearing in this passage.[46] We will examine the concept of 'hearing' in rhetoric shortly, but presently we will look at how 'seeing' functions in this passage, in particular who sees what and their reactions.

The first instance of 'seeing' (using the root ראה) in chapter 17 is in vv. 24 and 25 when the Israelites 'see' Goliath and are frightened. The Israelites are deceived by Goliath's impressive height and armour and so flee in fear. Then, in v. 42, Goliath 'sees' David (וירא את דוד) and is deceived by appearances as he mocks David's youth and good looks but does not perceive David as a real threat.[47] The detailed description of David's appearance in this verse (כי היה נער ואדמני עם יפה מראה; 'for he was a young man, and ruddy with a handsome appearance') is a counterpart to Goliath's description in vv. 4–7. There is a significant contrast between the two men and this diametrically opposes Goliath and David.

David's defeat of Goliath produces a different type of 'seeing' in the narrative. No longer is 'seeing' deceptive, it now indicates comprehension. In v. 51, the Philistines see that Goliath is dead (ויראו הפלשתים כי מת גבורם) and flee, echoing Israel's own reaction to seeing Goliath in v. 24.[48] The Philistines are no longer deceived when they 'see' but they comprehend the danger to themselves.

A final instance of 'seeing' in the chapter takes places in v. 55 when Saul sees David going out against the Philistines (וכראות שאול את דוד) and he inquires who his father is. Saul is beginning to comprehend that David is someone he needs to observe closely.[49] This is expanded in 18.15 and 18.26 when Saul sees David again but in these instances it

---

[45] Diana Edelman, *King Saul in the Historiography of Judah*, JSOT Supp. 121 (Sheffield: JSOT Press, 1991), 126.

[46] Fokkelman, *The Crossing Fates*, 165.

[47] Edelman, *King Saul*, 131–32.

[48] This parallel is made clear in the text by the sequence of the roots ראה and נוס in both verses.

[49] Contrast Robert M Polzin, *Samuel and the Deuteronomist: A Literary Study of the Deuteronomic History; Part Two—I Samuel* (San Francisco: Harper and Row, 1989), 173. Polzin suggests that Saul seeing David mirrors Goliath seeing David because Polzin detects a mocking tone in Saul's reference to David. However, even if Saul

is coupled with explicit statements of Saul's jealousy. By this stage, he has comprehended to some degree the import of David's victory.

An important observation from this survey is that David never 'sees' Goliath throughout the encounter. He 'hears' him in v. 23 (וישמע דוד) and, in v. 28, Eliab suggests that David has come to the camp to 'see', but even here it is only the battle, not Goliath himself, to which Eliab refers (כי למען ראות המלחמה ירדת). Thus, David is the only character in the story who is not affected by appearances. Just as Yahweh does not look at the outward appearance in chapter 16, so also David does not look at Goliath's impressive exterior. Quinn-Miscall suggests that David's perception of Goliath, whilst not stated explicitly, might be of a large man encumbered by heavy armour.[50] Certainly this is what David's military strategy suggests. However, in terms of the motif of 'seeing', the significance in the narrative is that David is not intimidated by Goliath's external appearance. Whilst everyone is in awe of Goliath's height, David instead 'hears' what Goliath says, and he is the first (and only) to perceive that Goliath is defying Israel's God (v. 26; כי מי הפלשתי הערל הזה כי חרף מערכות אלהים חיים).[51] By considering Goliath a threat against Yahweh's integrity, he has confidence Yahweh will defend his name. It is a theological problem and, therefore, it will have a theological answer.

The lengthy description of Goliath's height, armour and weaponry follows the significance of 'seeing' in this chapter. It is important that the reader is impressed by Goliath's appearance—by his size, the weight of his armour and its exotic nature. This has the double function of helping the audience identify with Israel's fear and drawing the audience into the theme of the deceptive nature of appearances. This theme is important for the causation of the chapter as David is victorious precisely because he is *not* influenced by appearances.

The description of Goliath generates another layer of meaning through the parallels with Saul. Goliath's extraordinary size is reminiscent of Saul's above average height, although in the MT, even Saul

---

begins with mockery, his three-fold inquiry of David's identity suggests that he realises the importance of discovering who this David is.

[50] Peter D. Quinn-Miscall, *1 Samuel: A Literary Reading*, Indiana Studies in Biblical Literature (Bloomington: Indiana University Press, 1986), 60. See also McCarter, *I Samuel*, 292, who suggests that the description of Goliath's armour hints at a weak point in his helmet. Whilst the Israelites saw Goliath's armour as a threat, David saw it as an opportunity.

[51] Edelman, *King Saul*, 126.

is dramatically overshadowed by Goliath's nine foot, nine inches. One implication is that, externally, Saul is most suited to engaging in single combat with him. However, Saul trembles in fear with the rest of the Israelites in v. 11: וישמע שאול וכל ישראל את דברי הפלשתי האלה ויחתו ויראו מאד ('And when Saul and all of Israel heard these words of the Philistine, they were dismayed and very afraid'). Saul's height advantage, as well as his position as king, highlights his failure to defend Israel in this situation. A second implication is that it draws a similarity between the roles of Saul and Goliath roles in the narrative. This does not suggest Saul is an enemy of Israel in any way. Rather, they both represent figures who are outwardly impressive but are inwardly weak, and this in turn draws a contrast with David. The contrast between Saul and David is an ongoing device in Samuel for conveying the significance of the historiography.

The association of Saul with Goliath is again conveyed through the description of Saul's armour in v. 38: וילבש שאול את דוד מדיו ונתן קובע נחשת על ראשו וילבש אתו שריון ('And Saul clothed David in his garment and placed a bronze helmet on his head and clothed him in armour'). The words נחשת, קובע and שריון are also used in the description of Goliath's armour[52] and this creates a direct allusion. Like his height, Saul's armour is not quite the same standard as Goliath's, but it is comparable nevertheless. Note also that the detailed description of Saul's armour may be another example of details that are unlikely to be 'accurately' recorded from the past but they play a part in developing the meaning of the narrative.

Several suggestions have been made about the significance of Saul handing over his armour to David, and David rejecting it. Edelman has pointed out that the act of handing over clothing demonstrates a reversal in roles, again highlighting the theme that Saul is not properly fulfilling his role as king.[53] David's refusal of the armour foreshadows his refusal to take Saul's life in I Samuel 24 and 26. Furthermore, it is a strategic move on David's behalf not to wear cumbersome armour but to use a long-range weapon like a sling.[54] There is also significance in conjunction with the comparison between Saul's armour and Goliath. David specifically rejects an impressive outward appearance, symbolising his defeat over Goliath. Saul, who already had the armour and responsibility of king, had failed to fight Goliath. He was frightened

---

[52] Although notice the interchange of *quph* and *kaph* in the word קובע.
[53] Edelman, *King Saul*, 131.
[54] Campbell, *1 Samuel*, 188.

because his own appearance, whilst impressive, did not equal that of Goliath. On the other hand, David has not 'seen' Goliath and been overawed by his impressive appearance and so does not try to match that appearance by wearing armour. David will match Goliath's rhetoric because he has 'heard' Goliath, but in the battle itself, he will not attempt to match Goliath's impressive outward appearance.

Thus the theme of 'seeing' draws a connection from this event to God's words in 16.1–13 and starts to develop the difference in characterisation between Saul and David. Furthermore, it contributes to three other aspects of historiography: causation, critical evaluation, and meaning and significance. Goliath's impressive appearance 'causes' Saul and the rest of Israel to flee in terror. The comparison with Saul's armour contributes to an evaluation of Saul as weak and failing in his duties as king, despite his impressive outward appearance. This is compared to David who rises to this challenge and is not intimidated by appearance. The theme of 'seeing' conveys the significance of this event by relating it to the theme of appearance in 16.1–13, and, more generally, the story has significance within the overall structure of Saul's decline and David's rise. These three features of historiography are presented coherently in the text, even if the details of Goliath's height and armour are not plausible to a modern eye.

In conclusion, it appears that the authors/redactors felt free to invent or exaggerate the description of Goliath in the text, but there were limits to the extent of the invention. The importance of the meaning of this description for the overall representation of the past implies that the substance and impression created by Goliath's extraordinary appearance is purporting to be accurate, even if the precise details are not.

2. David or Elhanan

The contradictory statement that Elhanan killed Goliath in 2 Samuel 21.19 has been given a number of harmonising explanations. One possibility is that Elhanan was David's real name and 'David' his throne name.[55] Another is that there were two different Goliaths.[56] Tsumura

---

[55] Honeyman looks at Solomon's two names in II Sam 12.24–25 and suggests that David may also have had two names. He emends 'Jaare' to 'Jesse' in II Sam 21.19 which increases the similarity [A.M. Honeyman, "The Evidence for Regnal Names among the Hebrews," *JBL* 67 (1948): 22–24].

[56] Hertzberg suggests that the name 'Goliath' had come to designate a type [Hans Wilhelm Hertzberg, *I & II Samuel: A Commentary*, trans. John Stephen Bowden, OTL (London: S.C.M. Press, 1964), 387].

similarly points to all the differences between the accounts and concludes that they were not connected.[57] A third type of harmonisation
was attempted by the Chronicler in I Chronicles 20.5, which reads,
את לחמי אחי גלית הגתי ('Lahmi, the brother of Goliath, the Gittite').[58]
However, even if such harmonisations are possible, none are hinted at
by the text and evidently the contradiction was not of concern to the
ancient authors/redactors.

Scholars who do not accept these attempts at harmonising usually
suggest that the material in II Sam 21.19 is more original and that this
tradition was absorbed into I Sam 17. Some propose that the whole
story of David and Goliath was taken from a tradition about Elhanan
in order to glorify David,[59] or, more often, that the name of Goliath
has been taken and applied to another tradition of David engaging in
single combat.[60] It is more likely that Elhanan's victory was applied to
David than the reverse and, from the perspective of a modern historical reconstruction of the events, this is the best explanation if the two
stories cannot be harmonised.

However, for a reader of the book's final form, the responsibility
for the contradiction lies with II Sam 21.19. Not only does this verse
occur second, and therefore it is here that we could expect some sort
of explanation, but it is much shorter and disconnected from its context. I Sam 17 is explicit about who David and Goliath are, from where
they have come (both geographically and in terms of the story) and the
context for the battle. Furthermore, I Sam 17 is a key aspect of the causation for David replacing Saul as king over Israel. On the other hand,
II Sam 21.19 gives only geographical information and no other context
for this victory. Thus II Sam 21.19 is presented as an ambiguous fact
without sufficient context for a modern reader to consider it coherent
with I Sam 17, even if originally it was more accurate. The ambiguity
surrounding II Sam 21.19 may be designed to subvert David's victory

---

[57] Tsumura, *The First Book of Samuel*, 44.

[58] Note the similarity between 'Lahmi' and 'Bethlehemite' (בית הלחמי את גלית
הגתי) in II Sam 21.19. Alternatively, the book of Samuel may have suffered from
haplography.

[59] E.g. Rex Mason, *Propaganda and Subversion in the Old Testament* (London:
SPCK, 1997), 40.

[60] E.g. Campbell, *1 Samuel*, 177, and McCarter, *I Samuel*, 291. They both point out
that Goliath's name appears only twice in I Sam 17, suggesting a later addition.

or, alternatively, reinforce it through allusion and the association of David with victory over four other giants.[61]

As we do not know for sure if or how these two passages can be harmonised, we cannot say with any certainty that the identity of the participants in the historiography of Samuel could be changed. However, we propose that it was acceptable in this historiography for there to be ambiguity surrounding the identity of participants in a short note such as II Sam 21.19, which is not explicitly connected to any context or causal chains in the overall story.

3. *40 days*

Another detail in the text that is not plausible from a modern point of view is that Goliath appeared morning and evening before Israel for forty days (v. 16). As Campbell points out, it is a farcical image that Israel would align itself for battle twice a day for forty days, and every time flee in fear,[62] although it is only in v. 24 that Israel explicitly flees when they see Goliath. The description appears to be a stylised expression of the continued threat of Goliath rather than a literal account of the battle strategies of Goliath and Israel. In particular, the round number, forty, is very common in Hebrew narrative, suggesting it is used symbolically as a literary device.

Furthermore, this time designation has a function apart from being a record of the length of Goliath's challenge against Israel. Firstly, the great length of time and the ludicrous nature of the situation emphasises the cowardice of both Israel and Saul in not rising to the Philistine's challenge. David does not push ahead of more worthy contenders, but arrives on the battlefield after forty days of no response from Israel.

Secondly, the position of this verse immediately after v. 15 is important. Verse 15 describes David's commute between Bethlehem and the battlefield (וְדָוִד הֹלֵךְ וָשָׁב מֵעַל שָׁאוּל לִרְעוֹת אֶת צֹאן אָבִיו בֵּית לָחֶם; 'And David went back and forth from Saul to shepherding his father's flock at Bethlehem') and this gives the impression of a long period of repetitious movement to and fro. In this way, the actions of Goliath and David are paralleled and placed in opposition to each other. This

---

[61] See Isbell, "A Biblical Midrash on David and Goliath," 259–63. The four extra stones picked up by David in I Sam 17 symbolise the four further giants he will be involved in defeating.

[62] Campbell, *1 Samuel*, 174.

subtly foreshadows their future opposition on the battlefield. It is likely that 'accurate' chronological data has been sacrificed in the interests of creating a vivid background to David's battle with Goliath.

In modern historiography, if an exact time period is given, it is interpreted literally. In the book of Samuel, however, an exact number of days are given where modern literature might use the phrase 'for a long time'. This suggests that there is little intention of precision in its representation. It is acceptable for an approximation to be used without any explicit reference to its rough calculation or symbolic usage.

Throughout the historiography of Samuel, time designations tend to be used only where there is a literary effect, not as a record of a complete chronology. This is illustrated in I Sam 16–18, where the only time designation apart from '40 days' is the phrase ממחרת ('the next day') in 18.10. This exacerbates other problems with chronology for modern readers and, without any other designations in these chapters, these two references are of little help. In particular, there is no indication of the time gap between the pericopes in 16.13–14, 17.1 or 18.17. A sense of succession is only given in 18.1 and 18.6 through the use of temporal clauses כבלתו לדבר אל שאול ('when he finished speaking to Saul') and בבואם בשוב דוד מהכות את הפלשתי ('when they returned from David killing the Philistine'). Thus descriptions of time in events do not have the same level of precision we expect in modern historiography and this is due to their different purpose within the narratives. A specific time designation can be 'invented' in order to convey meaning in the pericope.

4. Speeches

Other features of I Samuel 17, which are not plausibly accurate in the narrative, are the speeches and dialogue.[63] Speech features particularly prominently in this chapter; as Brueggemann points out, the battle between David and Goliath itself is reported in just two verses (vv. 50–51) and the speeches form the focus of the chapter, not the action.[64]

---

[63] See Krinetzki, "Goliathperikope," 230, who mentions the artificiality of only ever having two people in dialogue at any one time in this chapter. This is also a characteristic of speech in Hebrew narrative more generally.

[64] Walter Brueggemann, *First and Second Samuel*, Interpretation (Louisville: John Knox Press, 1990), 133. Cf. According to Campbell, *1 Samuel*, 182, the speeches build up tension towards the battle. Whilst this effect is certainly evident, the speeches also develop meaning and causation.

Most of the direct speech in this chapter pushes forward the plot. Jesse, in vv. 17–18, provides the catalyst for David's arrival on the battle scene. The series of exchanges between the people[65] and David in vv. 25–27 introduce Saul's promised reward and this is an aspect of causation for David's involvement in the events. Eliab's exchange with David in vv. 28–29 reinforces David's unimpressive external appearance and unsuitability for engaging in battle with Goliath.[66] The dialogue between Saul and David in vv. 32–33 prepares for David's first significant speech in vv. 34–37 and finally David's words in v. 39 progress the story by indicating that he will not wear Saul's armour. This survey demonstrates the way in which dialogue is used to express causation, characterisation and the story's themes in the narrative.

Four more extensive and significant speeches in the narrative remain: Goliath's speech in vv. 8–10, David in vv. 34–37, Goliath in vv. 43–44 and David in vv. 45–47. We will examine the literary function of these speeches so that we can understand the purpose of dramatising and fabricating this dialogue.

Even by listing these speeches, the opposition between Goliath and David in these chapters is evident. Firstly, they are the only two characters given lengthy speeches, and secondly, they alternate in taking the rhetorical stage. As Dietrich writes, this chapter is just as much a battle of words as a physical battle.[67]

After the description of Goliath's impressive appearance in vv. 4–7, the audience is given a sample of his impressive battle rhetoric in vv. 8–10. Whilst he refers to Israel as 'Saul's servants' (v. 8; ואתם עבדים לשאול), it is to Israel as a whole that Goliath addresses himself (ויקרא אל מערכת ישראל; 'and he called to the battle lines of Israel'). Not even Goliath has confidence in Saul's ability to represent his nation in battle. Goliath's use of the phrase, ברו לכם איש ('choose for yourselves

---

[65] Notice particularly the artifice that the soldiers in Saul's army speak in one voice in the story. Again this is evidence that speech is used as a literary device rather than an accurate depiction of real-life speech.

[66] Bodner, *1 Samuel*, 183, describes another level of meaning conveyed by Eliab's speech. In I Sam 16 Eliab functions as a rebuke to Samuel not to judge by external appearances. Now, Eliab's voice doubles as a rebuke to David to be cautious about inward matters. He notes particularly that a number of words in Eliab's speech also occur in II Sam 11–12 (i.e. sheep, few, battle, see, wrath, evil, anger, kindle). Elsewhere, Bodner describes Eliab's words as 'double-voiced' [Keith Bodner, *David Observed: A King in the Eyes of His Court* (Sheffield: Sheffield Phoenix Press, 2005), 20].

[67] Walter Dietrich, "Die Erzählungen von David und Goliat in I Sam 17," *ZAW* 108 (1996): 175.

a man') further alludes to the theme of Saul's inadequacy. His command 'choose' recalls the description of Saul in 9.2 as 'choice'[68] and
again reinforces that he ought to be the one engaging in this combat.
Furthermore, the use of איש ('man') introduces the irony that Goliath will eventually be killed by a mere בן איש (v. 12; son of a man)
because all the real men of Israel were too afraid.

Whilst modern audiences generally remember Goliath as a man of
impressive stature and military might, his rhetoric has the greatest
effect on Israel in the story. It is only after 'hearing' (שמע) Goliath
speak in these verses that Israel is terrified in v. 11. Goliath threatens
with his rhetoric, not just his appearance.

The effect of Goliath's speech on Israel is powerfully conveyed by
its juxtaposition with a report of Israel's fear. This report immediately proceeds Goliath's speech in v. 11 and holds the position where
Israel ought to have responded with an answer to Goliath's challenge.
Instead, there is a resounding silence from Israel that is emphasised
by the repetition of ויאמר הפלשתי ('and the Philistine said') midway
through Goliath's speech at the beginning of v. 10. In the absence of
a response from Israel, Goliath must give his own response.[69] Overall, the use of Goliath's impressive speech in this section of the narrative creates causation for Israel's fear and critically evaluates Saul's
inadequacy.

The second extended speech in this narrative in vv. 34–37 belongs
to David, where he persuades Saul that he can go out to fight Goliath. Bodner's description of this speech is most apt, "In commercial
terms, David's presentation could be labeled as marketing genius." In
David's speech, he transforms his greatest weakness, his occupation as
a shepherd (highlighted by Saul in v. 33), into a strength. David begins
his marketing ploy with emphasis on this very circumstance by placing רעה ('shepherd') first in his opening statement. He then recounts
his impressive feats of strength as a shepherd against both lions and

---

[68] The root used to describe Saul in 9.2 is בחר whereas here in v. 8, Goliath uses
an otherwise unattested root, ברה. See however the entry in HALOT, which, although
drawing the connection with the noun ברית, points out that it is usually read as coming from בחר.

[69] Cf. Julio C. Trebolle Barrera, "The Story of David and Goliath (1 Sam 17–18):
Textual Variants and Literary Composition," *BIOSCS* 23 (1990): 16–30. He considers this repetition to be a 'resumptive repetition'. It indicates the positioning of two
sources alongside each other in the final form. However, here we observe that there is
also a literary effect of this repetition.

bears. In v. 36, David compares Goliath to these wild beasts and so simultaneously mocks his opponent and demonstrates the relevance of his résumé.

David does not match Goliath in appearance, but, in this first speech, David matches him in rhetoric.[70] Israel responds to 'hearing' Goliath with fear. David responds by delivering his own impressive speeches in reply.

David's speech not only establishes his credentials for fighting Goliath but he develops a theological dimension to the conflict. Although the description of his feats is initially an assertion of David's own strength, his account reaches its climax with the declaration that it was Yahweh who delivered him and Yahweh will therefore also deliver him from the Philistine (v. 37). David's designation of Goliath as 'uncircumcised' (ערל) and his description of Goliath as 'defying the armies of the living God' (כי חרף מערכת אלהים חיים) prepares for this climax. It is Yahweh's army that is being defied by this Philistine, and so Yahweh himself will bring victory for David. This is David's unique and powerful insight into the situation. Thus speech is very significant for our understanding of causation in this chapter because it combines the dual causes of David's strategy and Yahweh's intervention. David's speech is impressive in human terms, yet its climax is an affirmation that God will bring victory. It attributes his own physical achievements to the deliverance of God and firmly establishes that any victory will not belong to him alone.

David's ability to match Goliath rhetorically is further developed when they meet face to face and are given the opportunity for a pre-battle rhetorical confrontation. In these final speeches, David not only equals Goliath but surpasses him. In excellent rhetorical style, David takes each of the elements of Goliath's speech and addresses them in his own attack of words. Unlike Israel, which remains silent, David launches a counter attack.

There are three main elements to Goliath's speech in vv. 43–44. Firstly, he mockingly refers to himself as a dog; and already there is irony in this statement because David has just compared Goliath to an animal. Secondly, in v. 44, he threatens to give David's flesh to the birds of the air and beasts of the field (לעוף השמים ולבהמת השדה).

---

[70] Fokkelman, *The Crossing Fates*, 165.

Finally, not in direct speech but sandwiched between his other two statements is the report he cursed David by his gods.

In David's speech, he addresses the opposition created between Goliath's gods and Yahweh.[71] By repeating the participle בא ('coming') with the preposition ב ('with') in v. 45, David parallels Goliath's weapons with the name of the Lord as his own weapon. He makes explicit that the Lord himself will avenge the taunts of Goliath. The repetition of the root חרף ('to taunt') throughout the chapter culminates at this point. Previously, this verb is used of Goliath taunting Israel (ישראל; vv. 2, 25) or the battle lines of Israel (מערכת ישראל; v. 10). In his previous speeches, David implies it is Yahweh being defied by Goliath when he changes the object of this verb to 'the battle lines of the living God' (מערכת אלהים חיים; vv. 26, 36). Now for the first time in v. 45, David makes plain that it is God himself whom Goliath is defying (בשם יהוה צבאות אלהי מערכות ישראל אשר חרפת, 'in the name of the Lord of hosts, the God of the battle lines of Israel whom you have taunted'), although the grammar of this statement is ambiguous about whether he is referring to the army of Israel or Yahweh himself. Rofé describes David's overtly religious language in this speech as evidence that there are two different sources juxtaposed side by side. He says that the story has been transformed from a confrontation between David and Goliath into a confrontation between God and Goliath.[72] However, these statements are well integrated in the narrative because they respond to Goliath's introduction of his own gods into the conflict in v. 43. Furthermore, it is the climax of an escalating realisation that the battle belongs to Yahweh, and this is illustrated by the changing objects of the verb חרף.

Next, David addresses Goliath's taunt that David comes only with a stick. In both vv. 45 and 47, David states that he does not come with the outwardly impressive weapons of Goliath but with the far greater weapon: the name of Yahweh. The title צבאות ('hosts'), given to Yahweh in v. 45, particularly highlights Yahweh as a military weapon.

Finally, David addresses Goliath's threat of victory. He repeats Goliath's phrase לעוף השמים ולחית הארץ ('to the birds of the heavens and

---

[71] See also Bodner, *1 Samuel*, 186, who describes David's use of religious language as an attack on Goliath's curse by the gods.

[72] Rofé, "David and Goliath," 119.

to the beasts of the earth')[73] that he had used against David personally and applies it to the defeat of the entire Philistine army. He subtly 'trumps' Goliath's own threat by applying it to an even larger group of people.

Through the rhetoric of this speech, David effectively wins the battle of words in the chapter. The victory is achieved through two devices— irony and the relative length of their speeches. There is irony that Goliath refers to himself as a dog, when David himself has previously compared him to a beast. There is irony that David does *not* come only with a stick but has a sling hidden behind his back. Finally, there is irony in David's speech when he demonstrates that everything Goliath has mocked him for will be turned against Goliath himself. He will be struck with a greater weapon in the name of Yahweh and Goliath himself will become the pickings of wild animals. The comparative length of the speeches by David and Goliath indicates David's victory in the pre-battle rhetoric. David is given the longest stretch of direct speech in the chapter and so 'out-talks' Goliath. Goliath responds by advancing on David, thus mimicking the silence of Israel after Goliath's initial speech in vv. 8–10. This time it is Goliath who cannot give a response. Once again, speech in this chapter is used to express the characterisation of David responding to Goliath's rhetoric but not his appearance. It also combines the causation of David's personal charisma with an attribution of victory to Yahweh. In these ways, the speeches integrate a commentary on the story's meaning into the narrative. Although the imaginative reconstruction of speeches may not record precise facts in a modern sense, it records the meaning, causation and evaluation of the events.

Changes of state

The remaining contradictions in I Sam 17 are related to the changes of state that occur in the narrative. In other words, they are contradictions in the actions, acquisition of knowledge and changing roles of the characters. These contradictions have also received considerable attention from scholars who have attempted to resolve the tensions in

---

[73] Although, note the change from ולבהמת השדה ('to the beasts of the field') in Goliath's speech in v. 44 to ולחית הארץ ('to the beasts of the earth') in David's speech.

the narrative. Most frequently, these attempts at harmonisation have focused on re-understanding the chronology of the chapter.[74]

In modern historiography, narrative is expected to progress linearly unless some indication is given that the norm is being broken. However, in I Sam 17 the narrative appears to violate our expectation of linearity without giving any such explanation. The first way this occurs is between pericopes in the narrative. For example, there is no indication how chapter 16 and chapter 17 relate chronologically. As the narratives are juxtaposed, the modern reader assumes the events of chapter 17 follow on directly after chapter 16. Yet, the contradictions between the chapters can be overcome if we assume a different chronological progression. David's return to looking after his father's sheep and Saul's lack of memory of David could be explained if there were many years in between these two pericopes. These two contradictions could also be explained if 16.14–23 took place *after* chapter 17 and simultaneous to 17.55–18.2. Therefore, David is described as a man of war in 16.14–23 because of his heroics in the battle with Goliath and the routing of the Philistines afterwards. Saul would have taken David into his service both for his battlefield heroics and for his musical skills.[75] We do not know which, if any, of these chronological solutions may be correct because the text has not provided us with a time designation for either episode. However, all of the events in the text are in themselves plausible, just not in the position in which they have been placed in the narrative. The king's enquiry after David's father and David being all of shepherd boy, court musician, armour bearer and giant-killer are not unbelievable per se, only in the order they are presented in the narrative.

This suggests that a coherent chronology was not considered important to the ancient authors/redactors of Samuel and that it could be left

---

[74] See particularly Bodner, *1 Samuel*, 189, who finds coherence in the chapter through explaining sections of it as flashbacks. Also Gooding comments that the passage cannot be understood if one adheres to a pedantic timetable [D.W. Gooding, "An Approach to the Literary and Textual Problems in the David-Goliath Story " in *The Story of David and Goliath: Textual and Literary Criticism: Papers of a Joint Research Venture, OBO 73* (Fribourg: Editions Universitaires, 1986), 81]. An alternative explanation for David's changing role, however, is offered in Tsumura, *The First Book of Samuel*, 436, who suggests that the description 'man of war' in 16.18 could grammatically refer to Jesse or signify that David was from the ruling warrior class of society.

[75] The mention of David's role as court musician in 18.10 provides some evidence for this hypothesis as it suggests that the events of Goliath and Saul's struggle with the evil spirit were contemporaneous.

ambiguous. Let us now examine the effect of these contradictions and chronological impossibilities, and determine what alternate historiographic principles are governing the presentation of the material.

1. *David: Shepherd or warrior?*

One of the major contradictions in the MT version of I Sam 17 is that David is reintroduced as a shepherd boy after being reported as Saul's armour bearer in 16.21. His introduction in 17.12 gives his name and origin in a manner that is similar to the introduction of a new character. However, the depiction of David as a shepherd boy who goes into battle remains consistent throughout every scene of this chapter, even if it is in apparent contradiction with the chapter preceding it.[76] Laying aside the illogical chronological progression of David's roles in chapters 16 and 17, the primary effect of David as shepherd is to convey his characterisation and to attribute the causes of his victory to both calculation and faith.

David's role as shepherd presents him as young and unsuitable for battle, particularly in comparison to Goliath and Saul. This conveys the message that faith plays a large role in overcoming his physical disadvantage and lack of experience. David's military inexperience is made explicit in v. 33 but there is ambiguity whether he is actually the small shepherd boy most readers imagine him to be. Campbell describes a 'small boy' interpretation as unfounded in the text. He points out that this contradicts David's claim in vv. 34–35 that he could kill a lion and, furthermore, it would be nonsensical for Saul to offer his armour to David if there was such a disparity in size.[77] Whilst Campbell's arguments are convincing, there are also many elements of the text that project the image of David as small, particularly in conjunction with his role as shepherd. There is good reason for many readers to have made this assumption. The first suggestion of David's size comes from his designation as נער ('youth'). Although, as discussed previously, this word does not necessarily imply somebody young or small, its use is in contrast to the repetition of איש ('man') elsewhere in the chapter[78] to refer to all the other potential warriors: Goliath, the men

---

[76] Dietrich, "David und Goliat," 174.

[77] Antony F. Campbell, "Structure Analysis and the Art of Exegesis (1 Samuel 16:14–18:30)," in *Problems in Biblical Theology: Essays in Honor of Rolf Knierim*, ed. H.T.C. Sun, et al. (Grand Rapids: Eerdmans, 1997), 89.

[78] Verses 4, 8, 10, 12, 19, 23, 24, 25, 26, 27, 28, 33, 41 and 52.

of Israel, the one needed to kill Goliath and also the old man Jesse. Thus, the term נער is exploited for two of its meanings: attendant in contrast to experienced warrior; and young man in contrast to older man.[79] Furthermore, David's youth is implied in 17.13–14 where he is the youngest of Jesse's sons and only three sons are at war with Saul. The phrase, ודוד הוא הקטן ('But David was the youngest/small-est'), is both preceded and followed by the repeated statement, ושלשה הגדלים הלכו אחרי שאול ('and the three eldest/largest followed after Saul'). In particular, the inclusio of the adjective גדל surrounding קטן conjures up the image of a small David. Although the adjectives 'great' and 'small' are being used with reference to age, their physical mean-ings are subtly implied through the emphasis on the words. Moreover, David is the youngest of eight sons, implying that there are four sons who are older than him but not yet old enough for war with Saul.

David's role as a shepherd in the story also contributes to the image of David as small. It reinforces that David is the youngest member of the family and that he is not yet ready for battle. It emphasises that he is an outsider who is too young to be counted as one of the 'men' of Saul. It also conveys David's inexperience, which complements the image of David as a young and therefore small boy.

Whilst Campbell is correct that David is not explicitly physically small in size, the narrative sends subtle signals that he is young and inexperienced. In the imagination of the reader, this has the effect of depicting a diminutive physical size. By conjuring up an image of a small David in the imagination of the reader, the text emphasises the role of David's faith in God in his victory over Goliath. The odds were against him but these are overcome by faith in God. This is important both for his characterisation and for the causation in the pericope as the Divine overcomes David's personal unsuitability for battle. The exaggerated projection of David's 'smallness' conveys meaning in the text that the smaller overcomes the greater. The story of a shepherd boy overcoming a giant in battle is much more dramatic and evoca-tive of this meaning than the story of Saul's impressive young armour bearer achieving the same victory.

Furthermore, David as a young shepherd boy is an important device for conveying the contrast between him, and Goliath and Saul both of whom are experienced in war. The extraordinary height of both Goli-

---

[79] Edelman, *King Saul*, 130.

ath and Saul further inclines the reader to imagine David as small—
in contrast to these two men, particularly Goliath, everybody seems
small!

There are a number of other aspects of meaning in the text that rely
upon David's occupation as a shepherd boy for their representation in
the story. Firstly, David's role as shepherd creates the circumstances
through which David is commuting between Bethlehem and the battlefield. We have already demonstrated how this repetitive motion
mirrors Goliath's own repeated challenge to Israel. David leaving his
sheep with a keeper (v. 20) and his food supplies with a keeper (v. 22)
forms a parallel with Saul who also leaves his responsibility for Israel
with a keeper, that is, David. Furthermore, in v. 22, David forsakes his
baggage (ויטש דוד את הכלים) in stark contrast to Saul in 10.22, who
hides himself amongst the baggage (הכלים).[80] It has even been suggested that the common metaphor of a king as shepherd means that
this occupation for David has royal overtones.[81] These circumstances
all contribute to a critical evaluation of Saul as lacking the courage and
faith to fight Goliath himself. They also further highlight the depth of
David's faith in this passage.

The depiction of David in this chapter is not only as a man of faith
but also as a man of calculation. His position as shepherd is used to
convey this aspect of his character. This occurs in David's description
of himself striking down lions and bears in vv. 34–35. He may not
have had military experience but he has the calculation to know his
own strength and to convince Saul that he has a chance at victory.
In addition, David's role as his father's shepherd gives scope for his
repeated questioning about the reward for killing Goliath in vv. 25–30.
It is only because David is an outsider in the Israelite camp that, within
the narrative, he can ask repeatedly about the terms of the reward for
killing Goliath (vv. 26, 30). David's interest in the reward suggests an
additional motivation for entering the battle, alongside his outrage at
Goliath for defying Yahweh's army.

Therefore, the depiction of David as a shepherd is important for
his characterisation, for divine causation and for the critical evaluation of Saul. How and why he is a shepherd boy in this chapter is left

---

[80] Brueggemann, *First and Second Samuel*, 128.
[81] E.g. Mark K. George, "Constructing Identity in 1 Samuel 17," *Interpretation* 7
(1999): 404.

ambiguous but these other aspects of the historiography are explored in detail.

2. *Saul's recognition of David*

Another major contradiction within these chapters is Saul's questioning of David's identity in vv. 55–58, despite their previous interaction. Some have attempted to erase this contradiction from the story by examining the nature of Saul's question. Polzin argues that each time Saul asks the question 'Who is his father?' he is emphasising a different point. The first two times there are notes of derision and amazement. He wonders whether Saul seeing David in v. 55 mirrors Goliath seeing David in v. 42. He even suggests that when Saul saw David take off the armour, he assumed that he no longer intended to go into battle and could not see David's features when he went out. He also draws a parallel with chapter 14 where Saul was not aware that Jonathan had gone out to battle and concludes that he was not aware of David's activities either. Polzin's other suggestions include that Saul is asking David to renounce his paternity in favour of his own. When David calls himself the son of Jesse, he is refusing this demand.[82] This explanation has not received general acceptance from other scholars and Campbell describes the explanation as contrary to the use of plain words.[83] On the other hand, Fokkelman says that the question is not superficial but rather it is asking what the "essence or secret of David" is.[84] The diversity among these solutions and their assumption that Saul was either easily confused or implied more than the plain meaning of his words suggests that there is no completely satisfying solution.

If we take the question at its face value and assume that Saul was genuinely enquiring about the name of David's father, then there is a chronological contradiction with chapter 16. However, despite this contradiction, the question contributes to other aspects of the historiography and is coherent within the narrative if the chronology is ignored.

Behind this straightforward question there is ambiguity about *why* Saul wished to know who David's father is. As Edelman points out, on one level there is a pragmatic reason because he had earlier promised

---

[82] Polzin, *Samuel and the Deuteronomist*, 173–74.
[83] Campbell, "Structure Analysis," 95.
[84] Fokkelman, *The Crossing Fates*, 191.

to make the family of Goliath's slayer free (from taxes?)[85] in v. 25.[86] Analogy to the story of Saul in 10.10–12 offers another significant reason. In 10.10–12, Saul begins to prophesy and the people around him are amazed at Saul exhibiting such behaviour. In particular, it is remarked, ומי אביהם ('and who is their father?'), a curious question that has baffled scholars[87] but which creates a link with Saul's question in 17.55, 56 and 58.[88] Saul is watching a young shepherd boy go into battle with an armour clad giant and this context suggests that Saul is asking his question in response to his amazement at the young man. He is prompted by the remarkable sight, just as others were prompted earlier by Saul's prophesying, to find out more about this young man.[89]

Saul's delay in asking this question contributes to the characterisation of both his own character and that of David. Firstly, it augments the depiction of Saul's passivity when he ought to have been defending his people. It is not until he sees another man taking his place in the combat with Goliath that his interest is significantly aroused. The delayed question completes a picture of Saul's abrogation of responsibility with regards to Goliath. Secondly, the delayed question reinforces the remarkable nature of David's victory and again points to the role of the Divine. It emphasises that David was unknown when he went out into battle and increases the audience's amazement that such a young man could defeat Israel's enemy.

We have examined the purpose of this question within the context of chapter 17, but its relationship with chapter 16 is more complicated. This tension reveals a further effect of Saul's questions on the meaning of the narrative. The first meeting between Saul and David emphasises Saul's love for David. His affection for David is repeated within the narrative in v. 21 (ויאהבהו מאד) and v. 22 (כי מצא חן בעיני). In addition to this, David's relationship with Saul is structured according to

---

[85] For a summary of what this verse might mean, see Klein, *1 Samuel*, 178.

[86] Edelman, *King Saul*, 134.

[87] As McCarter says, "This cryptic question has no obvious meaning" [McCarter, *I Samuel*, 184].

[88] This parallel is explored in Edelman, *King Saul*, 134; and Auld and Ho, "The Making of David and Goliath," 30–31; and followed in Bodner, *1 Samuel*, 189.

[89] Similar to this, Fokkelman, *The Crossing Fates*, 191, suggests that Saul is seeking out the 'essence' of David in response to what he is saying. However, note that Fokkelman interprets this as the meaning of the question rather than as the reason for Saul asking it.

the appropriate hierarchy—David is Saul's court musician and provides a service for him. Even as a soldier in this chapter, he is Saul's
armour bearer and thus Saul's status is preserved. In the second meeting between Saul and David, these aspects are overturned. David now
functions in the role of king as he fights Israel's enemy. Although there
is no explicit conflict between Saul and David in vv. 34–37, their second meeting will develop into rivalry in 18.6–9. Thus the two meetings
between David and Saul reflect two different aspects to their relationship: love and rivalry. These will converge in 18.10 when Saul attacks
David whilst he is dutifully acting as court musician.

These two different angles on the relationship between Saul and
David suggest that the material in the two chapters has been arranged
thematically rather than strictly chronologically. The first account in
16.14–23 describes the close relationship between Saul and David and
the second account emphasises David's role as a warrior who presents himself as a potential rival to the throne. To some extent, these
themes align themselves with the other tension in David's character:
the work of divine providence and his own calculation bringing him
to the throne. In the first story, David is passive and finds his way into
Saul's court through the actions of Saul's favour. Then, in the second
story, David's ambition is explored more fully and his active role as a
soldier, not just musician, is presented. It is this second role that is a
threat to Saul.

3. *Goliath's head and armour*

In 17.54 there is an entire series of contradictions with the surrounding narrative: David takes Goliath's head to Jerusalem but has it in his
hand again in v. 57; there is a reference to Jerusalem that was still held
by the Jebusites in this period; and David places Goliath's weapons in
his tent despite only arriving there that day. Scholars have attempted
to solve the reference to Jerusalem in a number of ways. Tsumura
suggests that it refers proleptically to a suburb of Jerusalem or the
Jebusite walled city and that by the time of the author/narrator, this
area would have been called Jerusalem.[90] Gordon simply suggests that
the head was taken to Jerusalem at a later date.[91] Polzin also suggests

---

[90] Tsumura, *The First Book of Samuel*, 468.
[91] Robert P. Gordon, *1 & 2 Samuel: A Commentary* (Exeter: Paternoster, 1986), 158.

that Jerusalem is its ultimate destination but on his way there, David has it in his hand when he meets Saul.[92]

However, the problems in the verse would not be present if it took place some extended period of time after the other events of chapters 17 and even 18. In this case, they are anachronisms—events known from the hindsight of the authors/redactors that had not yet taken place at this chronological stage of the narrative. Again, this explanation cannot be verified because there is no time designation that confirms or denies a non-linear chronology.[93]

Apart from this chronological confusion, there is some level of coherency with the later narrative. Firstly, the reference to Jerusalem helps convey the significance of the episode by foreshadowing where David's victory will eventually lead.[94] It thus connects this episode with the greater structure of meaning in the book. The reference to Goliath's armour has less apparent meaning. It may function only as a preparation for the episode at Nob in chapter 21 but, if this is the case, the reference to David's tent is not explained.[95] A better explanation is that it continues the theme of 'seeing' in the narrative and David's earlier rejection of Saul's armour. Until this point, David's appearance deliberately contrasts the impressive armour of Goliath and this reaches its zenith when David takes off Saul's armour. This theme emphasises the divine role in David's victory as he is able to overcome the more impressive opponent. However, just as we saw a shift in vv. 49–51 from an emphasis on God's causation to David's causation, David taking the armour also indicates that David's outward appearance is becoming more impressive. David has progressed from a young shepherd boy to the possessor of such an extraordinary outfit for war. The role of David's strategy and calculation in his military successes is gradually increasing and, by taking the armour of Goliath, the narrative conveys this development. Thus, this reference

---

[92] Polzin, *Samuel and the Deuteronomist*, 161–62.

[93] Fokkelman, *The Crossing Fates*, 207, sees the necessity for the reader to imagine a time adjunct at the beginning of v. 54 and considers v. 54 to be a later addition. Note that this is one of the rare instances where Fokkelman is willing to admit that a verse is a later addition in the narrative. This is on the basis that it lies outside of other patterns in the chapter. Not even Fokkelman can find a chiasm that includes this verse!

[94] See Campbell, "Structure Analysis," 89–90, for a similar interpretation of this reference to Jerusalem. Also, Willis, "Redactional Joints," 304–05, lists these references amongst the anticipatory redactional joints in the chapter.

[95] Cf. Hertzberg, *I & II Samuel*, 145, who emends the text to read, 'the tent of the LORD'.

contributes to the characterisation of David as both strategic and full
of faith, and potentially contributes to the critical evaluation of David
as too calculating in later episodes.

Not only is 17.54 an unannounced break in the linear chronology, it
is an unusual position for such a break. As we have discussed, the following verses, vv. 55–58, also cause chronological problems in the narrative and therefore it is possible that the future looking v. 54 indicates
that the linear progression of the preceding narrative is now broken
and all that follows should not be considered a direct continuation.
The change of perspective, which occurs between v. 54 and v. 55, offers
evidence for this. From David's entry into the story in v. 12, the narrative has taken his perspective and he appears in every scene as the
main protagonist. Saul, on the other hand, has played a passive role
with only a few short speeches that are necessary for the main plot[96]
and provide a background to David's entrance on the scene.[97] Now, in
v. 55, the narrative shifts to Saul's point of view and David becomes
the passive object of observation. Verse 54 marks the end of the first
perspective and so it is appropriate that it offers a conclusion with a
reference to the future. Once again the problem is ambiguity in chronology and the effect of the features is the characterisation, causation
and meaning of the historiography.

4. David 'kills' Goliath twice

The final contradiction, David's double killing of Goliath in 17.50–51,
is a chronological problem of a different kind. In v. 49, the stone from
David's sling hits Goliath and he falls onto his face. In v. 50, it is stated
that David killed Goliath (וימיתהו) and that there was no sword in
David's hand (וחרב אין ביד דוד). Then, in v. 51, David takes a sword
in his hand and, once again, David kills Goliath (וימתתהו),[98] this time
by removing his head. Thus we have two accounts of David killing
Goliath.[99]

If we consider the phrases in v. 50, ויך את הפלשתי וימיתהו ('and
he smote the Philistine and he killed him') as a general statement of

---

[96] Verses 33 and 38.

[97] Verses 11 and 19.

[98] Note that the *polel* of מות is often translated 'to make a full end of' [see entry in
HALOT]. However, this does not lessen the finality of the hiphil in v. 50.

[99] Although, structurally, the two accounts are bound together in a chiasm. This
adds some level of unity to the contrasting accounts. See Fokkelman, *The Crossing
Fates*, 189.

David's victory referring to both past and future, then the contradiction is lessened. In other words, David overpowered Goliath without a sword in his hand, but he then used a sword to kill him. This whole series of events can be described as 'smiting and killing' Goliath. This is not the order in which the events are described in the narrative, but if we assume that the general statement of David killing Goliath is chronologically out of order, then the events are not implausible. Once again, we suspect that an illogical order of events does not affect the authors/redactors' conception of coherency in the passage.

Furthermore, the doubling in these verses has a significant effect on meaning and causation in the narrative. Both events fulfill an earlier prediction in the chapter and both events combine elements that suggest the Divine and David are causes for Goliath's death. However, the first account in vv. 49–50 emphasises David's faith and divine causation; and the second account in v. 51 emphasises David's own strategy as the primary cause.

The account in vv. 49–50 emphasises that Goliath was killed due to divine causes in two subtle ways and then in one explicit way. Firstly, we recall that David selects five smooth stones in v. 40 and places them in his pouch. Despite all his calculation, he thought it was likely that more than one stone would be needed. Yet, in v. 49, David's first stone hits its mark and overcomes Goliath. A second suggestion of divine causation comes in the manner of Goliath falling forward with his face to the ground in v. 49 (ויפל על פניו ארצה). This echoes the words used of the statue of Dagon, the Philistine god, who falls before the ark of God in I Sam 5.4: והנה דגון נפל לפניו ארצה ('and behold, Dagon fell before it to the ground'), and implies Yahweh acted to bring down the Philistine enemy. The most explicit reference comes at the end of v. 50 where it is stated, וחרב אין ביד דוד ('but there was no sword in the hand of David'), with the word 'sword' (חרב) in the emphatic position of the sentence. This statement demonstrates that David's prediction in v. 47, כי לא בחרב ובחנית יהושיע יהוה ('that the Lord does not save by sword or by spear') has been fulfilled and the Lord has saved by an alternative method. This again relates to the theme that David's appearance and weaponry are different from that of Goliath and Saul, and that David's faith in God brings about his victory.

Despite the strong element of divine causation in these two verses, David's own agency is also conveyed. As the sling was a powerful, long-range weapon that exploited David's mobility and allowed him to stay beyond Goliath's reach, the popular image of David with a toy slingshot is somewhat misleading.[100] Furthermore, his use of a sling undoubtedly utilised the skills he had developed as a shepherd boy. By refusing Saul's armour, David ensures his agility and this is a great advantage over the heavily-armoured Goliath. In v. 40, it is reported that David has both a stick and a sling in his hands but Goliath's comment in v. 43 reveals that Goliath noticed only the stick. He therefore also had the element of surprise on his side. David's accurate aim in v. 49 is the culmination of a pattern of David's calculation and strategy as a cause of Goliath's defeat.

The second account in v. 51 emphasises further David's causation in the narrative. This is primarily through his use of a sword. According to v. 47, the Lord does not use the sword to bring victory, but there is no reason why David cannot! Indeed, this final move is very strategic as it generates fear in the Philistine army and causes them to be routed back to Philistia. There is still a suggestion of divine intervention as the headless Philistine once again recalls the headless god Dagon in 5.4. However, this action is predominantly the initiative of David.

Thus, the ideology of causation in the two accounts of Goliath's death is a complex combination of David's strategy and the Divine. The two aspects are present in both accounts, but they each have a different emphasis. This indicates a level of consistency between the two accounts. However, apart from Goliath having two deaths, the second account introduces another contradiction—by David using a sword to kill Goliath, he negates the thrust of vv. 43 and 50, which say the Lord does not deliver with the sword. An examination of the verb נכה ('to smite'), a *Leitwort* in this passage,[101] illuminates this contradiction in two ways. Firstly, it draws attention to nuances within the story, which smooth the inconsistency, and secondly, it adds to our understanding of the emphases in each account.

The verb נכה is used repeatedly throughout chapter 17 to denote what must be done to Goliath in order for Israel to be released from the Philistine threat. Goliath uses this root twice in his challenge in v. 49. It is repeated by the Israelite men in v. 25, David in v. 26 and then the people in v. 27. David also uses the verb twice in v. 35 to

---

[100] Campbell, *1 Samuel*, 181. See also Jdg 20.16 for the effectiveness of the Benjaminites with their slings in war.

[101] This *Leitwort* is also noticed in Shimeon Bar-Efrat, *Das erste Buch Samuel: Ein narratologisch-philologischer Kommentar*, trans. Johannes Klein, BWANT 176 (Stuttgart: Kohlhammer, 2007), 237.

describe killing the lion and bear, and again in v. 46 as a threat against Goliath. Therefore, the dramatic tension running throughout this chapter is that somebody needs to smite Goliath. The cause of tension is not the threat of the Philistine army but of Goliath alone. In Goliath's challenge in v. 9, he suggests that the single combat will resolve the conflict immediately as Israel will become the Philistines' servants without any involvement of their army.

It is significant that the verb נכה is used twice in vv. 49 and 50 in the first account of David killing the Philistine but it is not used in the second account in v. 51. It is solely David's sling, not sword, which smites Goliath (i.e. נכה) and resolves the main tension of the narrative. God's deliverance of Israel without sword or spear pertains to the resolution achieved by Goliath falling to the ground. Indeed, David's predictions of how the Lord will act do not include the death of the Philistine. David mentions his own deliverance and that of Israel (v. 37: הוא יצילני; v. 47: יהושיע יהוה) and he says that the battle belongs to the Lord (v. 47; כי ליהוה המלחמה). Both of these aspects are fulfilled when David 'smites' Goliath and thus God delivers Israel from the tension of the chapter. From that point onward, Goliath is in David's hands, as is implied by a literal reading of David's statement in v. 47 ונתן אתכם בידנו ('and he will give you into our hands'). David uses the sword in v. 51, not as God's act of 'smiting' the Philistine, but as his own strategic flourish, to frighten the Philistine army into retreat. The use of the sword is primarily David's calculation. Again, the first account emphasises God's deliverance of Israel by smiting Goliath and the second emphasises David's strategy for routing the Philistine army.

In conclusion, each of these accounts demonstrates aspects of divine and human causation in the story and explores the interplay between these causes. The first account functions as a completion to the primary tension in the story, Goliath's personal threat against Israel, and the second account introduces the next stage of conflict as David overcomes the more general threat of the Philistine army.

Attributing these contradictions in 'changes of state' to chronological imprecision is speculation and does not prove the events actually took place. However, it constitutes evidence that I Sam 17 could have been read as coherent historiography provided the reader was not concerned with a strict chronology in the chapter. The absence and ambiguity of chronological markers in favour of a thematic and meaningful arrangement of material suggest that accuracy of chronology was not sought after in the historiography in Samuel.

Coherence amidst contradictions in the MT?

This survey has demonstrated that the contradictions and implausible details in the MT version of I Sam 17 contribute to the characterisation, causation, ideological evaluation or meaning and significance of the passage. Let us now draw together these contributions and examine whether there is coherence in these aspects of historiography.

1. *Causation:* There are two 'imbalances' created in this story that are restored to equilibrium. The first is established in v. 1 when the Philistines gather for battle against Israel and the second is established in vv. 8–11 when there is a need for an Israelite to meet Goliath's challenge. When the second imbalance is resolved and a man of Israel is willing to face Goliath, then the first imbalance of the Philistine threat can be addressed and brought to equilibrium by their defeat. Thus, there are two stages of causation in this chapter. Firstly there are the causes for David to present himself before Saul and for Saul to allow him to face Goliath—this brings resolution to the second imbalance. Then there are causes for David's victory over Goliath that bring resolution to the first imbalance of the Philistine threat.

Many of the features in this chapter point to the dual characterisation of David as full of faith and calculation[102] and this characterisation contributes to the resolution of both the first and second imbalances. David's faith plays a role in his presentation before Saul, despite being a mere shepherd. His calculation is conveyed through his repeated questioning about the reward and his convincing marketing ploy for Saul to allow him to go to battle.

In the defeat of Goliath, David's faith was suggested by the rejection of an impressive outward appearance and by his rhetoric about the defiance of Yahweh by Goliath and Yahweh's deliverance of his own army. David's calculation is conveyed through his choice of the sling as a weapon and his routing of the Philistines. Moreover, his speeches perform a double function by demonstrating that he can match Goliath's rhetoric even if he does not match his appearance.

---

[102] The two sides of David have been remarked upon by a number of scholars. Alter, *The David Story*, 110 and *The Art of Biblical Narrative*, 152–53, describe the two sides as spiritual and military. Campbell, *1 Samuel*, 186, traces them to two different accounts, one of David's courage and the other of his ambition. Quinn-Miscall, *1 Samuel*, 83, identifies a whole spectrum of portrayals of David.

His faith points to divine causation and his calculation corresponds to his own battle strategy. The dual causation is brought to a climax in the double account of Goliath's death.

Not only is this characterisation and causation consistent throughout the chapter but it is consistent with the portrayal of David and the causes for his victories in many battles later in the narrative. In 18.27–28, David uses his own strength to kill a hundred Philistines but Saul also attributes this victory to the presence of the Lord with David. In I Sam 23, David enquires of the Lord about whether he should attack the Philistines (vv. 2, 4) and Yahweh responds that he will bring him victory. Yet, in v. 5, David heroically fights the battle and the narrator states explicitly, וישע דוד את ישבי קעילה ('and David saved the inhabitants of Keilah'). In I Sam 24 and 26, Yahweh gives David two opportunities to encounter Saul, but David instead uses these opportunities to deter Saul from pursuing him. In I Sam 30, David again inquires with the ephod whether he will have success in rescuing his wives from the Amalekites, and the Lord gives an affirmative, implying his role in the success. Yet David then questions an Egyptian runaway in a strategic move to find the band of Amalekites and defeat them. David's success in these battles is consistently attributed to both divine causation and David's strategy or military strength.

2. *Critical evaluation*: As is common in Samuel, there is no explicit evaluation of the characters in this chapter. Goliath's status as a Philistine in conflict with Israel establishes his character unambiguously as the enemy. David's role as victor for Israel is therefore evaluated positively although his development as a 'round' character allows scope for negative actions. Saul's character is not given extended focus until the final verses of the MT (vv. 55–58) and, until this point, evaluation of his character and actions takes place through the lens of contrast with David and through allusions to his earlier exploits. Evaluation of the concept of kingship is tied to the evaluation of Saul and David. Overall, the battle against Goliath is portrayed as a battle on behalf of Yahweh and so victory is viewed as an unambiguously positive event.

The contradictions in I Sam 17 play a role in the critical evaluation, particularly concerning Saul as king. The similarity of Saul's armour to Goliath's armour forms a parallel and, in turn, it creates a contrast with David, who rejects Saul's armour. Goliath's repeated appearance for forty days highlights Saul's inaction on behalf of his people, as does his silence after Goliath's impressive speeches. This is placed in contrast with David who is a mere shepherd, whilst Saul is king. Finally, Saul's delayed question concerning David's identity reflects his inactivity in this Philistine crisis. This critical evaluation of Saul as a hesitant and ignorant king, particularly in contrast to David, is consistent with his depiction elsewhere in Samuel. In 14.1–23, Saul's victory is initiated by the bravery of Jonathan, who goes alone with his armour bearer into the enemy camp, just as David also goes forth in Saul's place in chapter 17. Furthermore, in both narratives Saul is ignorant in some way: he is ignorant of Jonathan's activity and he is ignorant of David's identity.[103] This analysis also coheres with the contrast between David and Saul in I Sam 24–26 and the subsequent negative evaluation of Saul. Thus the critical evaluation of Saul is consistent with the greater narrative of Samuel.

3. *Meaning and significance*: This chapter conveys political significance through its relation to the structure of succession of leaders. The significance is conveyed through the contrast of the declining King Saul with the recently anointed David, and their different levels of competence as Israel's leader. Theological significance emerges in David's rhetoric and Yahweh's confirmation of this rhetoric. The human significance is communicated by the rounded characterisation of David and its contrast with Saul's fear and abrogation of responsibility.

The contradictions of I Sam 17 convey aspects of meaning in the chapter that hold significance within the whole book. Saul handing his armour to David and David going to battle in his place foreshadow David's succession to Saul and demonstrate the significance of this narrative for the rivalry that will exist between them. This meaning is also generated through the final episode of the chapter where Saul watches David go in his place and he is amazed at such a shepherd boy. The reference to Jerusalem alludes to the significance of this narrative in David's journey towards the future capital of his kingdom and the armour in his tent can be seen as a symbol of the development in his character from shepherd to warrior.

Although the chronology in this chapter is left unexplained and the descriptions and speeches are not plausibly accurate for a modern

---

[103] Several commentators have observed the similarities between these two narratives, e.g. Polzin, *Samuel and the Deuteronomist*, 174; and Fokkelman, *The Crossing Fates*, 205–06.

audience, they contribute to another type of coherence in the narrative. They function within the narrative to generate meanings, causes,
characters and criticisms, which are both coherent and consistent with
the surrounding chapters. This suggests that coherency in these latter characteristics of historiography is more likely to be the guiding
structure for the representation of the past rather than accurate details
such as we demand in modern works of historiography. We now turn
to the LXX version of I Samuel 17 in search of further evidence for
this conclusion.

5.2   DIFFERENCES AND CONTRADICTIONS BETWEEN THE MT AND LXX OF I SAM 17

The text critical relationship between the MT and LXX

As discussed earlier, we will examine the LXX[B] text as representative
of the Septuagint in I Sam 17 and we will look at this text in its final
form, just as we have looked at the MT in its final form.

Before comparing and contrasting the LXX and MT versions of
I Sam 17, we will examine the relationship between these two texts.
Questions such as which text came first or whether one text is a harmonisation of the other will affect conclusions about how these ancient
authors/redactors/translators saw this work of historiography. In this
case, the source history of the story is intertwined with text critical
questions and so we will review these also. As the purpose of this study
is not to argue for any one stance on the textual history of Samuel,
the discussion will be directed towards highlighting the issues that we
must take into consideration in our discussion.[104] It is preferable that
our conclusions do not rest upon presuppositions about the chapter's
textual history that have not yet approached complete consensus.[105]

---

[104] For more detailed recent surveys of these issues, see John Van Seters, *The Biblical Saga of King David* (Winona Lake: Eisenbrauns, 2009), 137–57; Campbell, *1 Samuel*, 189–91; Isser, *The Sword of Goliath*, 28–34; A. Graeme Auld, "The Story of David and Goliath: A Test Case for Synchrony Plus Diachrony," in *David und Saul im Widerstreit—Diachronie und Synchronie im Wettstreit. Beiträge zur Auslegung des ersten Samuelbuches*, ed. Walter Dietrich (Fribourg: Academic Press, 2004), 119–22.

[105] As our survey of this question will show, the proto-MT tends to be considered later but there remain influential dissenters from this consensus and so the debate can still be considered open [see also Hugo, "Text History," 8].

Whilst there are many different formulations of the tradition and textual history of I Sam 17, they fall into two general categories: those arguing for the priority of the LXX *Vorlage* and those arguing the priority of a proto-MT.[106]

The multiplicity of contradictions in the MT has suggested to scholars that the LXX *Vorlage* is the more original tradition of the David and Goliath story and that the MT constitutes an expansion. McCarter suggests that the MT contains two previously independent narratives, one of which corresponds to the LXX, and these were combined with minimal redactional attempts at harmonisation in vv. 14b–15 and v. 31.[107] Other scholars do not agree that the additional material in the MT constituted an independent narrative but rather see it as a series of expansions based on one or more alternative traditions.[108]

The debate on the textual and literary history of I Samuel 17 has gained momentum with the publication of a joint research venture by Lust, Tov, Barthélemy and Gooding. Both Lust and Tov argue for the priority of the LXX using significantly different approaches. In an argument similar to McCarter, Lust suggests that epic stories often attract additional material (for example the flood narrative) and that the sections of the MT that are not found in the LXX (vv. 12–31, 55–58) are not necessary for the sense of the story. Furthermore, he draws attention to the tensions in the MT story that could be explained as expansions from the LXX.[109] Tov, on the other hand, analyses the translation method of the LXX and concludes that the translator remained loyal to the conjectured Hebrew *Vorlage*. He considers it inconceivable that the translator in this section would so radically alter the Hebrew when there are no parallel instances in Samuel. He does not comment on the likelihood of the redactor of the Hebrew *Vorlage* making the omissions. Finally, he points out that the LXX version does not appear

---

[106] Note that there is a third argument in Simon J. De Vries, "David's Victory over the Philistine as Saga and as Legend," *JBL* 92 (1973): 23–36. The LXX and MT are the results of two different recensions of the same text and therefore they are both the product of a combination of sources.

[107] McCarter, *I Samuel*, 306–08.

[108] E.g. Stoebe, "Die Goliathperikope," 397–413; Klein, *1 Samuel*, 174.

[109] J. Lust, "The Story of David and Goliath in Hebrew and in Greek," in *The Story of David and Goliath: Textual and Literary Criticism: Papers of a Joint Research Venture*, OBO 73 (Fribourg: Editions Universitaires, 1986), 5–18.

to be a harmonised version of the MT because there are still many inconsistencies remaining.[110]

In response to Lust's study in particular, Auld and Ho proposed the theory that the LXX version was more original and that the MT represents a re-composition of the original story in order to create a parallel structure with the Saul story.[111] Their study makes a compelling case by demonstrating the large number of parallels between the stories of Saul and David. Significantly, the elements of the story that draw these parallels are found in the MT pluses, suggesting that these sections were added to enhance the literary effect of these parallel leaders.[112]

Two final contributions to this side of the debate that we will mention here come from Krinetzki and Trebolle Barrera. Krinetzki suggests that there are two recensions in the MT: the first, corresponding to the LXX in 17.10–11, 32–54, is theologically oriented, whereas the second, in 17.12–31, 17.55–18.5, is more interested in David's relationships with his brothers and with Jonathan. It is therefore likely that the former is connected with the cult and the latter with kingly circles.[113] In a different approach, Trebolle Barrera's detailed study has pointed to a number of 'resumptive repetitions' in the MT, for example vv. 13a and 14b, which may be traces of editorial work. The additional material may be as old as the original material, although some verses, such as vv. 41 and 48a, appear to be sutures of the final composition.[114]

In summary, arguments for the originality of the LXX tend to regard the additions in the MT to have drawn from alternate tradition(s) about David and Goliath. The additional material is not necessarily younger than the LXX material and may even have constituted an independent narrative. However, this side of the argument maintains that the LXX material also stood as an independent tradition prior to the incorporation of the MT additions.

---

[110] Emanuel Tov, "The Nature of the Differences between MT and the LXX in 1 Sam. 17–18," in *The Story of David and Goliath: Textual and Literary Criticism: Papers of a Joint Research Venture*, OBO 73 (Fribourg: Editions Universitaires, 1986), 19–46.

[111] Auld and Ho, "The Making of David and Goliath," 19–39. See also Auld, "The Story of David and Goliath," 124–25, where he points out that the additions in the MT do not have a stock of words distinctive from the rest of the chapter. Rather, he suggests, these sections are drawn both from I Sam 9–11 and II Sam 21.

[112] Auld and Ho, "The Making of David and Goliath," 19–39.

[113] Krinetzki, "Goliathperikope," 197–99.

[114] Trebolle Barrera, "The Story of David and Goliath (1 Sam 17–18): Textual Variants and Literary Composition," 16–30.

The alternative to the priority of the LXX material is the priority of
the proto-MT. This view denies that the proto-MT came about as an
expansion of an earlier account corresponding to the LXX.[115] However, arguments against the priority of the LXX *Vorlage* differ significantly amongst scholars. Firstly, there are those who make a case
for the unity of the chapter, and, secondly, those who maintain that
the proto-MT is a composition of sources but refute that any of these
sources correspond directly with the account in the LXX.

Gordon,[116] Polzin,[117] Fokkelman[118] and Gooding[119] have all argued
for the priority of the MT based on literary arguments. They have
each sought to demonstrate that there is literary integrity in the final
MT version and that there is coherence between the sections found in
the LXX and those found only in the MT. These scholars differ over
whether all the inconsistencies of the MT can be smoothed over but
they are united in their arguments that there is some level of internal
consistency in the chapter.[120] We will look at the precise details of
these studies shortly when we examine the coherency of the final form
of the MT in contrast to the LXX. However, as Auld has pointed out,
this does not necessarily imply the priority of the MT. The MT version
may be the result of a skillful and deliberate expansion of the LXX

---

[115] Wellhausen is often credited with this view but, as has been pointed out in
Lust, "The Story of David and Goliath," 5, Wellhausen's view oscillates among his
publications.

[116] Gordon, *1 & 2 Samuel*, 66.

[117] Polzin's work is particularly noted for his harmonisation of vv.55–58 with the
rest of the chapter. He writes, "Why would some guiding intelligence take care in
verse 15 to make David's situation there consistent with the events of the preceding
chapter, but then allow to stand, or worse still incorporate, a conclusion that is inconsistent not only with chapter 16 but also with Saul's and David's meeting in the middle
of chapter 17?" [Polzin, *Samuel and the Deuteronomist*, 172].

[118] Fokkelman admits that there are some inconsistencies but argues for an overall
cohesion. He writes, "Having reached the end of my analysis, I am of the opinion that
our text has a great internal cohesion. In my literary experience, the unity of this story
is substantially unaffected by the contribution of v. 15, which is in contradiction with
the reading that the Saul of vv. 55–58 (and hence also of 33–37) meets David for the
first time, and the glaring achrony of v. 54 which still awaits treatment here." [Fok-
kelman, *The Crossing Fates*, 201].

[119] Gooding argues that the MT has "the best thought flow" [Gooding, "Literary
and Textual Problems," 75].

[120] Cf. Campbell, *1 Samuel*, 172, who acknowledges the art of the MT but attributes
this to a skillful and intelligent editor. The large number of dualities are best explained
in his opinion by the interweaving of two sources, one of which corresponds to the
LXX material. One of the sources attributes David's rise to courage and the other to
ambition (p. 186).

Vorlage drawing on material elsewhere in Samuel. He writes, "Each version was successful in its own terms—looking for the better one has always proved unnecessarily subjective."[121] The practicality of this is demonstrated by the conflicting arguments surveyed here, each claiming a different text has greater coherence.

On the other hand, many scholars have argued that there is a lack of cohesion in the MT due to its literary history, but the LXX does not correspond to any of its sources.[122] Barthélemy believes the MT is composed of a number of stories but points out that 17.32–54 presupposes 17.12–31 and therefore was written after it.[123] Gronbaek suggested that there were two stories combined in the MT: the first was about Saul's victory over the Philistines (vv. 1–3, 19, 20b-21, 52–53) and the second, David's combat with Goliath.[124] Van der Kooij suggests that the MT contains an older story in vv. 12–58 about a shepherd boy who overcomes a giant. This story was then dramatised and theologised by a redactor who added the introduction in vv. 1–11. Finally vv. 37, 35 and 47 were added in a second redaction.[125]

A number of scholars have based their source analysis on contrasting depictions of David in the story. Rofé, later followed by Van Seters, suggests that there are two contrasts in the story: the first is between an unknown shepherd boy and a heroic giant, and the second between Yahweh and Goliath. In the first, David has a fairy tale victory over a more powerful enemy whereas in the second he trusts, not in his shepherd's weapons, but his faith.[126] The folkloric nature of David's victory in the MT suggests it is original.[127] On the other hand, Dietrich assumes a more complex and extensive work of the editor in combining essentially two sources: in the first David is an unknown soldier

---

[121] Auld, "The Story of David and Goliath," 124–25.

[122] See particularly Arie van der Kooij, "The Story of David and Goliath: The Early History of its Text," *Ephemerides Theologicae Lovanienses* 68 (1992): 126. He points out that it is an assumption in Tov's work that the LXX should coincidently agree with one of the MT sources. His point is that the LXX may not be a clue at all for the literary history of the chapter.

[123] D. Barthélemy, "Trois Niveaux D'analyse (A Propos de David et Goliath)," in *The Story of David and Goliath: Textual and Literary Criticism: Papers of a Joint Research Venture*, OBO 73 (Fribourg: Editions Universitaires, 1986), 49.

[124] Jakob Gronbaek, *Die Geschichte vom Aufstieg Davids (1 Sam. 15–2 Sam. 5)*, vol. X, Acta Theologica Danica (Copenhagen: Prostant Apud Munksgaard, 1971), 80–100.

[125] Kooij, "The Story of David and Goliath," 128.

[126] Rofé, "David and Goliath," 117–18. See also Van Seters, *The Biblical Saga*, 157.

[127] Rofé, "David and Goliath," 119.

with a sling, while the second is a legendary tale about David the shepherd boy who kills Goliath and is brought before the king. These were
combined and theological commentary added.[128]

Most scholars who argue for the priority of the MT suggest that
the LXX edition came about as a harmonisation of a proto-MT. The
changes were made to smooth out the difficulties with chapter 17 as
well as create consistency with the preceding chapter.[129] The main
argument leveled against the LXX as a harmonisation is that there are
still a number of inconsistencies present in this shorter text.[130] These
inconsistencies have been explained in a number of ways. Rofé suggests that the editor was hesitant to remove details that were fundamental to the structure of the story.[131] Pisano assumes a less intelligent
editor and writes, "In performing its harmonising surgery, LXX has
ended up with fragments of different sources which were not originally intended to go together."[132] Van der Kooij argues the shortening
in the LXX indicates a later interest in the chapter that he attributes
to the Greek period. He draws parallels with the book of 1 Maccabees
and suggests that the new edition may have been made for pro-Macca-
bean propaganda or other political interests.[133] Barthélemy argues that
the Greek smoothes the inconsistency that David is a shepherd boy in
vv. 32–54 through its translation choice. He also explains the omission of non-contradictory sections in the LXX by suggesting the har-
moniser continued to omit material until he/she came to a verse that
linked with the proceeding section. For example, 18.1–6a was omitted
because 18.6b linked best with 17.54.[134]

As mentioned earlier, the purpose of this study is not to propose a
particular textual and literary history of I Sam 17. Indeed, this survey

---

[128] Dietrich, "David und Goliat," 184.
[129] E.g. Barthélemy, "Trois Niveaux D'analyse," 50–54; Rofé, "David and Goliath,"
120; Stephen Pisano, *Additions or Omissions in the Books of Samuel: The Significant
Pluses and Minuses in the Massoretic, LXX and Qumran Texts*, vol. 57, Orbis Biblicus
et Orientalis (Freiburg: Universitatsverlag, 1984), 84; Dietrich, "David und Goliat,"
177.
[130] E.g. Bar-Efrat, *Das erste Buch Samuel*, 234.
[131] Rofé, "David and Goliath," 121.
[132] Pisano, *Additions or Omissions*, 84.
[133] Kooij, "The Story of David and Goliath," 130. In contrast to other theories, van
der Kooij believes the shortening of the LXX was performed by the translator rather
than in the Hebrew *Vorlage*. Earlier in his article (p. 124) he criticises Tov's methodology in ascertaining that the LXX translator is unlikely to have made changes.
[134] Barthélemy, "Trois Niveaux D'analyse," 50.

has further highlighted the problematic nature of doing so. Most of the contradictions highlighted in our analysis of the MT appear in its additional material.[135] The contradictions remain in the MT, even if the additional material originates from a different source, because the authors/redactors saw no need for consistency in certain aspects of description and chronology of events. On the other hand, causation, critical evaluation and meaning are consistent in the MT but this could be the work of a clever author/redactor who has chosen his/her source material based on these criteria. Finally, even though the presence of at least two sources in the MT is highly probable, there is no certain evidence to suggest that the LXX version corresponds to one of them. It may have been a later harmonisation that was similar to one of the original sources but had no direct genetic connection to it.

Our primary interest in this chapter is the coherence of the final form of the MT compared to the LXX, and this survey is useful for demonstrating the number of contrasting ways in which coherence has been interpreted in the versions. Among those who consider the LXX to have greater coherence than the MT, this observation can be used to argue, on the one hand, that it is more original, and on the other, that it represents a harmonisation and is therefore later than the proto-MT. Among those who consider the LXX to have less coherence, it is argued on the one hand, that it is therefore not a harmonisation and so is original, and on the other, that coherence is irrelevant evidence as both the LXX and the MT have inconsistencies. Although inconsistencies have been used extensively to argue for a particular literary history of the text, in themselves they do not solve the issue one way or the other.

Finally, with a lack of consensus about the priority of the MT or the LXX, we must be cautious in the following comparison of the two texts. As the direction of change between the texts is uncertain, their differences cannot be definitively attributed to the authors/redactors/translators of either text. Our conclusions pertain only to the ancient context of both texts, rather than the final form of the MT specifically. Secondly, this survey highlights that the textual histories of the MT and LXX were probably complex and we do not know at what stage

---

[135] These include Goliath's unrealistic height, the period of time 40 days, David's retroversion to a shepherd for his father's flock, David killing Goliath twice, and Saul's enquiry after the identity of David.

in their textual histories the changes took place. As there are probably many authors, redactors and scribes of the MT and LXX and translators of the LXX, the changes could have been caused by different hands at different times, sometimes accidentally and sometimes purposefully. Again, our conclusions apply to the broad ancient context of all these authors, redactors, scribes and translators.

A comparison of the final forms of the MT and LXX of I Sam 17[136]

In order to determine the degree of change in facts between the MT and the LXX, we will once again examine the different components of 'events': their changes of state and their chronology; and descriptive details. Through these categories, we will determine which 'facts' were altered between the MT and LXX.

1. Changes of state within events

Our first observation about the differences between the MT and LXX is that the content of the changes of state do not differ, but some are omitted or added. Most significantly, the chronology of these 'changes of state' is varied but their order of presentation remains the same.

The LXX version of I Sam 17 follows smoothly after chapter 16 with the absence of MT vv. 12–31 and vv. 55–58. David's entrance in LXX v. 32 requires that 16.21 is chronologically prior to this chapter as it explains David's presence at the location of the battle. In the LXX, there is no indication that David is still a shepherd boy and so Saul's request in 16.22 that David stay permanently in his service is unambiguously granted. David's reference to his days as a shepherd in LXX vv. 34–36 refers to his past, not the present. The absence of Saul's questioning about David's identity also allows the LXX version to flow smoothly and sequentially from the close relationship of Saul and David in chapter 16. This linear chronology is not stated explicitly in the LXX, but it is assumed because a linear structure can be understood coherently, and there is no reason to speculate that the chronology is otherwise. The chronologies of the MT and LXX versions do not explicitly contradict each other, but their implications suggest

---

[136] A further problem that we encounter comparing the MT and LXX is which differences are intentional and which are due to scribal error. We will attempt to restrict our examples to intentional differences, and where this is any question of this, comment will be made.

two different conclusions about the order of events. The LXX offers a simpler understanding of how the main events of chapters 16–18 fit together, through the absence of the material that complicates such an understanding. The MT includes extra material that creates a non-chronological structure. Thus the LXX lacks precision in chronology like the MT but has less ambiguity in its presentation.

Significantly, the events in each version are presented in the same order in the narrative, despite their implied chronology being different. Furthermore, as the chronology in each is not stated explicitly, it is difficult to assert that historians felt at liberty to 'change' the chronology of the events of the past, especially as the changes could be due to textual variations. However, the evidence suggests that the precise chronological order was unimportant and could be manipulated by the addition or omission of events from the narrative.

2. Descriptive details

Secondly, analysis of the LXX confirms that descriptive details in the text are a means to an end in the narrative rather than an accurate record of facts. The descriptive details are among many of the variations between LXX and MT.

a) Participants and objects

The identities of the participants in the events of I Sam 17 are not altered between the versions, but there are significant variations in the descriptions of their appearances and associated objects.

One of the most significant variations is Goliath's height and appearance. Goliath's height in the LXX is a much more plausible four cubits and a span (approx. 6 foot 7 inches)[137] and there are small variations in the description of his armour. In v. 5, the MT describes Goliath's helmet as bronze (נחשת) whereas this word is absent in the Greek. On the other hand, the MT describes Goliath's chain mail as 5000 shekels of bronze (נחשת) whereas the LXX describes it as bronze and iron (χαλκοῦ καὶ σιδήρου).[138] In MT v. 6, Goliath has some sort

---

[137] 4QSamᵃ is damaged where this number should appear. On the basis of the size of the gap, it is generally agreed that ארבע not שש is the more likely reconstruction [see Cross et al., Qumran Cave 4: 1–2 Samuel, 79].

[138] Note that 4QSamᵃ contains neither bronze nor iron [Ibid., 78].

of scimitar between his shoulders (כידון)[139] whereas the LXX mentions a shield (ἀσπίς).[140] A similar variation can be found in v. 38 where the MT includes the additional information that Saul clothed David in his armour (וילבש אתו שריון) as well as his cloak and helmet. These variations confirm our earlier proposition that such details were included for their effect in the narrative and not as historical 'facts'. Whilst some of these details could be attributed to scribal error or translational problems, their cumulative effect is that the description is altered and this must have been observed by the scribes/translators.

In most of the examples above, variations in descriptions involve omission or expansion rather than an actual change of a particular detail. However, the alteration in Goliath's height demonstrates that details could also be changed so that they form a contradiction with each other between the versions.

b) *Location*

The fluidity of geographical details was not overtly apparent when we examined the MT alone, but comparison between the LXX and MT shows that they could be altered to some degree. MT v. 52 says that the Israelites pursued the Philistines, עד בואך גיא ועד שערי עקרון ויפלו חללי פלשתים בדרך שערים ועד גת ועד עקרון ('as far as [the] valley and as far as the gates of Ekron and the slain Philistines fell on the road of Shaarayim and as far as Gath and as far as Ekron'). The Greek on the other hand says, ἕως εἰσόδου Γεθ καὶ ἕως τῆς πύλης Ἀακαλῶνος καὶ ἔπεσαν τραυματίαι τῶν ἀλλοφύλων ἐν τῇ ὁδῷ τῶν πυλῶν καὶ ἕως Γεθ καὶ ἕως Ακκαρων ('as far as the entrance to Geth and as far as the Gate of Ascalon, and the wounds of the allophyles fell on the way of the gates, even as far as Geth and as far as Akkaron').[141] The interchange

---

[139] See G. Molin, "What is a *Kidon*?," *JSS* 1 (1956): 334–37, for a justification of this translation. 4QSamᵃ here agrees with MT [Cross et al., *Qumran Cave 4: 1–2 Samuel*, 78] suggesting that it is a translational difference rather than a different *Vorlage*. The translator may have had the same difficulty we have in translating this word. However, as noted above, at times 4QSamᵃ agrees with neither LXX or MT and so it is also possible that the Greek's *Vorlage* was variant from both 4QSamᵃ and MT.

[140] There is an additional variation between the LXX and the *Ketib* in the MT. In v. 7 the MT *Ketib* describes the *arrow point* of Goliath's spear (חץ) as like a weaver's beam and the LXX describes the *shaft* of his spear (κοντὸς) as like a weaver's beam. However, the Greek κοντὸς could reflect the Hebrew *Qere* עץ.

[141] All translations of the LXX are from Albert Pietersma and Benjamin G. Wright, eds., *A New English Translation of the Septuagint* (New York: Oxford University Press, 2007), unless otherwise stated.

between 'Shaarayim' and 'the gates' could be explained as the result of translating Hebrew to Greek. Although there is some significant difference between גת (Hebrew transliteration of Geth) and גיא ('valley'), a translation error is also possible here. However, the interchange of Ekron and Ashkelon, another Philistine city, indicates a conscious flexibility of geography.[142] Ekron and Ashkelon were both Philistine cities and, therefore, there is little change in the overall meaning of the verse. The change demonstrates a lack of precision in geographical locations such as required in modern historiography.[143]

c) *Speech*

In our analysis of the MT, we proposed that it was not plausible that the speeches of the characters were the actual words said by these people. This is confirmed by the variations in direct speech between the MT and the LXX. There are subtle variations in vv. 8, 32, 35–37, 43 and 45–46. Some of these variations can be attributed to the process of translation or transmission. In LXX v. 8, Εβραῖοι can be reconstructed as a translation of עברים ('Hebrews'), which could have been corrupted from עבדים ('servants'), as is found in the MT, or vice versa. Translation of technical military equipment could explain the interchange of LXX 'shield' and MT 'sword' in v. 45, and this reflects a similar interchange of these words in v. 6. Others are additions or omissions, such as the extra material in LXX v. 36 ('Shall I not go and smite him and take away today a reproach from Israel? For who is this uncircumcised one…') and v. 43 ('and stones'). Indeed, there is only one variation that creates a contradiction between the two texts. In MT v. 32, David speaks generally, 'let no man's heart fail on account

---

[142] If the change occurred from the LXX to MT, the cause could be a harmonisation with the second half of the verse or unfamiliarity with the place name Ashkelon. However, it is unlikely that a scribe or editor would be unfamiliar with Ashkelon because it existed continually throughout this period. If the change occurred from the MT to LXX, it could be to avoid redundancy. Note also that the MT adds the place name 'Elah' in v. 2 (האלה), which is not present in the Greek. The Greek adds the word αὐτοί ('that'), possibly a translation of אֵלֶּה ('these') which shares the same consonants as הָאֵלָה ('Elah'). Thus the variation could be due to a transposition of האלה and ויערכו either in the MT or in the Hebrew *Vorlage* of the LXX.

[143] For a study of the literary function of geography in this chapter, see John A. Beck, "David and Goliath, a Story of Place: The Narrative-Geographical Shaping of 1 Samuel 17," *WTJ* 68 (2006): 321–30. He writes (p. 327), "All the geographical details in the exposition slow the reading process and draw the informed reader to the conclusion that this battle is over an absolutely critical piece of land with overwhelming economic and security implications."

of [Goliath]' (אל יפל לב אדם עליו), whereas in the LXX he directly
addresses Saul, 'On no account let the heart of my lord collapse upon
him' (μὴ δὴ συμπεσέτω ἡ καρδία τοῦ κυρίου μου ἐπ᾽ αὐτόν). However,
it is possible that even this variation is due to scribal or translational
error. Assuming κυρίου was translating אדני, the connection between
this word and אדם is more apparent. The quantity of variations suggests that the authors/redactors employed creative license in the recreation of these dialogues, even though a number of them appear to
have been the result of scribal or copying errors.

Whilst this conclusion is not surprising, our hope is for the comparison also to reveal the *extent* to which the speech could be changed.
As many of the variations can be attributed to different readings rather
than conscious changes, it is difficult to draw major conclusions here.
However, from the data available, we can suggest that overall the sense
of the speech is unchanged despite changes, additions or omissions of
wording. There may have been greater license for altering speech than
was exercised here. However, in this particular case, it is evident that
there was respect for the general meaning but not for the particular
words.

Coherency amidst contradictions?

Overall, these categories of historical representation tend not to
require the same level of consistency and reliability as in modern historiography. In our study of the MT, we proposed that such features
contribute towards the representation of causation, critical evaluation
and significance in the historiography and in turn, these latter qualities had consistency and coherency in the book. However, if the chronology, descriptive details and speeches vary between the texts, might
not their meaning also change? Furthermore, there are many other
variations between the versions that could radically alter the meaning
of the story. Let us now examine the categories of causation, critical
evaluation and significance in this story and determine if and how they
could be altered.

1. *Causation*
In the MT version of I Sam 17, we identified two different threads of
causation for the defeat of Goliath and the Philistines in this chapter. These include divine causation and the characterisation of David.
David is characterised as a man of great faith and this reliance on

Yahweh implies divine causation in the chapter. However, he is also characterised as a man of strategy and ambition. Other causes for his success are the rewards motivating this ambition and his personal strategic plan that exploits Goliath's weaknesses. Whilst the LXX also depicts divine causation and David's strategy, David's ambition is absent from this version.

Firstly, we will examine whether the difference in descriptive details about Goliath has an affect on the exposition of causation in this chapter. Goliath's increased height in the MT increases the impressiveness of David's victory.[144] However, the more plausible height found in the LXX represents a more realistic image of Goliath than the 'larger than life' aspect of the MT. Although the different heights will have slightly different effects on the audience, they both exceed average height to the extent that they can contribute to the theme of 'appearance', which we have discussed with respect to the MT. Furthermore, Goliath's height in the LXX is more similar to that of Saul[145] and this maintains the parallels between their impressive exteriors. Similarly, the small changes in description of Goliath's armour do not affect the message that Goliath's appearance was impressive. In the LXX, Goliath's chain mail is made not only of bronze, but also 'of iron' (σιδήρου), and this increases the effect because iron is an even stronger metal than bronze. Another variation occurs in v. 49, where the LXX includes an additional statement that the stone penetrated 'through the helmet' (διὰ τῆς περικεφαλαίας) of Goliath. This reinforces that David's sling has overcome Goliath's impressive armour. Thus, Goliath's height is more impressive in the MT but his armour is to some extent more impressive and emphasised in the LXX. Overall, the versions use these slightly different emphases to contribute to the same theme: Goliath has an impressive exterior in contrast to David. The constancy of this theme ensures that divine causation is represented in both versions.

Variations in David's speeches also convey a slightly different effect to the audience but, overall, contribute in a similar way to the causation of the chapter. In our analysis of the MT, David's rhetoric conveyed his understanding of the theological dimension of the combat and his

---

[144] Auld and Ho, "The Making of David and Goliath," 30.

[145] Based on 1 Sam 9.2, Saul was a head taller than any of the other people. This is still unlikely to have been a height of six feet seven inches, but it was closer than in the MT.

own personal ability to match Goliath's rhetoric. These contributed to the depiction of the causation of the Divine and David.

A key element of David's speeches is that Goliath's challenge is really a challenge against Yahweh and so Yahweh will bring Israel victory. In the MT, this theme is initiated in v. 26, but this verse is absent in the LXX. However, the LXX contains an additional statement in v. 36 that reinforces the circumstance of Goliath's 'reproach' (ὄνειδος) and his status as 'uncircumcised' (ἀπερίτμητος). The Hebrew equivalent of these two words both appear in MT v. 26 and so the omission of v. 26 in the LXX is balanced by the addition in v. 36. For good measure, ἀπεριτμήτου is repeated in v. 37 in the LXX where it does not appear in the MT. There is also a subtle translation choice in the LXX of v. 46 that reinforces the theme of the divine battle: the LXX has chosen to translate the Hebrew פגר ('dead body') as κῶλά, which means 'limbs' outside the LXX and New Testament but which can mean both 'limbs' and 'dead bodies' in the LXX.[146] Furthermore, it adds that David will give, not only the limbs of the Philistine army, but the limbs of Goliath himself (δώσω τὰ κῶλά σου) to the birds and wild animals. This subtle reference to Goliath's limbs being removed once again recalls I Sam 5.4 where the statue of Dagon is found with only his trunk remaining. This enhances the other allusion to this story in v. 49 in both the MT and LXX where Goliath falls on his face. David's recognition that Goliath is an insult to Yahweh is thus present in both MT and LXX, with special emphasis in these verses of the LXX to balance the absence of vv. 12–31. In both texts, David does not respond to the impressive sight of Goliath but rather responds to his speeches with equal rhetorical skill. David is following the divine example from 16.7 by not looking on outward appearance. He relies on God's defense of his own name for victory.

Secondly we examine David's ability to match Goliath's rhetoric and how this reflects on his own personal qualities. In the MT we saw that it is David's 'marketing genius' that convinces Saul to allow him to face Goliath in combat. In v. 5 there is a variation in the LXX where David says he caught the lion (or bear) by the 'throat' (φάρυγγος) rather

---

[146] See entry in Frederick William Danker, *A Greek-English Lexicon of the New Testament and other Early Christian Literature* (Chicago: University of Chicago, 2000). Elsewhere, פגר (often in plural) is translated as σώματα in Gen 18.1; σώματα νεκρά in 2 Kg 19.35, Is 37.36; νεκροί in Is 34.3, 14.19 and 2 Chron 20.24; ὀστᾶ in Ezek 6.5; κῶλά in Lev 26.30, Num 14.29–33, Is 66.24.

than the 'beard' (בזקנו) in the MT. The LXX reads more smoothly after David's reference to both a lion and a bear because it is difficult to understand the latter as having a beard. An advantage of the MT reading is that it draws an even closer parallel between Goliath (who presumably *would* have had a beard) and the wild animals and dehumanises him. Once again, this absence is balanced in the LXX by an additional speech by David in v. 43, where he answers Goliath's rhetorical question, 'Am I like a dog?' with 'No, but worse than a dog' (οὐχί ἀλλ᾽ ἢ χείρω κυνός). David's rhetoric is important for causation because it demonstrates that he has great courage in responding to Goliath.[147] This is connected to divine causation because he attributes this courage to his faith. However, it is also connected to the depiction of David as a man of strategy and calculation because he has the ability to engage with Goliath on the battlefield, a personal quality that will contribute to his victory.

Variations in David's tactics for killing Goliath also have a minimal impact upon causation between the versions. Overall, the description of David going unarmoured into battle with only a staff, a sling and five stones is not significantly changed between the two versions. One difference occurs in v. 41 of the MT, which is absent in the LXX, 'Then the Philistine came and approached David, with the shield bearer in front of him'. Auld and Ho suggest that the addition of the shield bearer in the MT forms an additional contrast between the well-equipped Goliath and the scantily equipped David.[148] On the other hand, as Quinn-Miscall points out, the shield bearer may also be considered a weakness for Goliath because a shield is precisely the piece of armour Goliath could have employed to protect himself from David's stone. However, as his armour bearer was carrying the shield, he remained unprotected.[149] Both effects of this detail are relevant because together

---

[147] Cf. Gooding, "Literary and Textual Problems," 69, who claims that this statement is a clumsy inclusion. Either it is a joke in an inappropriate moment, David is downplaying his own victory, or he is interrupting Goliath's speech. Regardless of the clumsiness of David's quip, it demonstrates his effort at mocking Goliath in return when the rest of Israel ran in fear.

[148] Auld and Ho, "The Making of David and Goliath," 30.

[149] Quinn-Miscall, *1 Samuel*, 60. A third suggestion is that Goliath suffered from vision impairment and so he relied on the armour bearer to guide him in the right direction [Vladimir M. Berginer and Chaim Cohen, "The Nature of Goliath's Visual Disorder and the Actual Role of his Personal Bodyguard: נשא הצנה (I Sam 17:7,41)," *ANES* 43 (2006): 27–44]. This however is not the most obvious implication of the mention of Goliath's armour bearer in the MT.

they illustrate the message of the chapter—whilst Goliath was outwardly impressive, he was ultimately ineffective. Although this verse is
not present in the LXX, in David's speech of v. 4 he mentions Goliath's
shield (ἀσπίδι), whereas the MT uses a word that can be translated as
'scimitar' (כידון). David's reference to Goliath's shield in v. 45 reminds
the reader that Goliath has the equipment to counteract David's sling
but yet he does not use it. Thus, the use of this word in LXX v. 45 has
a similar effect to MT v. 41, although perhaps with a lesser degree of
emphasis in the LXX.

A second difference between the accounts is that, in v. 43 of the
LXX, Goliath comments not only on David's staff but also on his stones
(λίθοις). Both Gordon and Gooding suggest that the LXX has missed
the point that the stones were unseen by Goliath and therefore were
a part of David's strategy for exploiting Goliath's weaknesses.[150] The
effect of this additional word in the LXX is that there is less emphasis
on the cunning nature of David's strategy. It attributes more credit for
the victory over Goliath to the Divine because, in this version, Goliath
did not use his shield, despite being reminded of it in v. 45 and despite
knowing that David had stones.

There may be less emphasis on David's strategy in v. 43 but, again,
this is balanced in the LXX by the absence of v. 50. Earlier, we examined vv. 49–51 in the MT and observed that there is a combination
of causes by Yahweh and David in Goliath's death. Without v. 50,
the LXX reads more smoothly with respect to Goliath's physical death
but it also creates a contradiction with v. 47 as Goliath is killed by
the sword. This can be resolved in the same way as the MT—Yahweh
delivers Israel by Goliath falling to the ground and then David completes the task with a sword. However, the absence of v. 50 obscures
the distinction. There is less emphasis on David's use of a sword in
v. 51 through the absence of the MT phrase וישלפה מתערה ('and he
drew it out of its sheath') but it is still evident that a sword is used.
Overall, by omitting v. 50, the LXX lacks the explicit allusion to Yahweh's deliverance, which was promised in v. 47, so there is slightly less
emphasis on divine causation.

Until this point, the variations between versions have had little
effect on the presentation of causation in the narrative. However, we
now turn to the absence of MT vv. 12–31 in the LXX. There are several

---

[150] Gordon, *1 & 2 Samuel*, 157; Gooding, "Literary and Textual Problems," 67–68.

aspects of causation that are created in the MT in this section. These include: David's characterisation as a shepherd, as the youngest in his family, as hearing but not seeing Goliath and his interest in Saul's promised reward.

The LXX version of I Sam 17 does not state explicitly that David is no longer a shepherd, but his immediate presence at the battle with the Philistines and Saul's request in 16.22 strongly suggest to the reader that David is permanently in Saul's service. On the other hand, David still refers to being a shepherd in LXX vv. 34–35, implying it is in the recent past. Both LXX and MT v. 33 suggest that David is still a young man who is more accustomed to being a shepherd than to being a war-rior. Without the simultaneity of shepherd and armour bearer roles, the LXX does not highlight to the same extent David's unsuitability for contesting the Philistine champion and, therefore, the divine causa-tion in his victory. This message is present in the LXX version but the contrast between David and Goliath is not so stark.

Secondly, without vv. 12–31, the LXX version contains less impli-cation that David was a small young man. Nevertheless, the audience is informed in 16.1–13 that David is the youngest of eight sons and the omissions in the LXX version result in a closer proximity between these two stories. In LXX 17.39, there is additional information that David 'grew tired walking once and twice' in Saul's cloak, helmet and sword (ἐκοπίασεν), implying that he was too small for its great weight. Furthermore, in the LXX, David is mocked by Goliath in v. 42 for being a mere boy (παιδάριον) just as he is in the MT. Again, the ele-ments of the size contrast between David and Goliath are present in the LXX, but the effect is not as strong without the additional material represented in the MT.

Thirdly, the themes of 'hearing' and 'seeing' are not explored to the same extent in the LXX with the absence of vv. 12–31. The LXX does not include any of the references to Israel 'seeing' Goliath, only Goliath 'seeing' David once in v. 42. There is a trace of wordplay on 'seeing' as the same level of detail is devoted to Goliath's appearance in vv. 4–7 and David's appearance in v. 42. In v. 42 of the MT, the word for appearance (מראה) is based on the root to see (ראה) and this allusion is preserved through the rather loose translation of this whole phrase into the Greek, μετὰ κάλλους ὀφθαλμῶν ('with beautiful eyes'). Furthermore, the LXX of 16.1–13 preserves the wordplay on seeing and the deceptiveness of appearance, so there is some preparation for the theme. Similarly, there are no overt references to David 'hearing'

Goliath, but subtle traces of this theme are present. None of Goliath's speeches are absent and so, similar to the MT, David responds to Goliath's rhetoric and not to his impressive appearance. The resulting causation for David's victory is therefore essentially the same: he has faith in God rather than an impressive appearance. However, the same depth of analysis of this cause is not given in the LXX.

A final aspect of causation found in the MT vv. 12–31 is David's ambition as he repeatedly asks the nature of the reward for killing Goliath. This cause for David's victory has no counterpart in the LXX. Indeed, no causation is given for him approaching Saul about the combat in the narrative at all. In the MT, David is driven by great courage, an understanding of the combat's theological dimension and a personal ambition to obtain the reward. David's later rhetoric in the LXX presumes the first two of these reasons but the third is dependent on his repeated questioning in MT vv. 12–31. Furthermore, the section in vv. 55–58 where Saul asks David's father's name (possibly because he is now eligible for tax exemption) is absent, as is the section in 18.17–19 where Saul offers David his daughter Merab. Thus the reward for David is completely absent in the LXX version.[151] The resolution to the imbalance that no one is willing to fight Goliath has only two causes in the LXX, not the three found in the MT.

Thus, there has been either simplification in the LXX or amplification in the MT of the causes for David fighting Goliath. The causation is not *changed* but it has either been added to or subtracted from, to alter the depiction of David's motives. The LXX version is therefore more positive about the character of David than the MT, altering the depiction of his ambition and calculation.

2. *Critical evaluation*

The variations between the MT and LXX also affect the critical evaluations of Saul and David in the narrative. Let us first examine David. As the LXX is a shorter text, there is significantly less scope for critically evaluating David throughout the unfolding narrative. In particular, David's victory over Goliath is not perceived in such miraculous terms in the LXX as it is in the MT. The character of Goliath is not

---

[151] Note also that David's ambitious doubling of Saul's request for one hundred Philistine foreskins in 18.27 is omitted in the LXX with David acquiring only the one hundred Saul asked for. There is a consistent lack of emphasis on David's ambition in the LXX version of events.

developed so extensively in the LXX, as he is not as tall and there is no report that he appeared unchallenged morning and evening for forty days. Furthermore, David's past (or present) as a shepherd and his youth are less emphasised in the LXX. The disparity between him and his enemy is lessened, making his victory slightly less impressive. The absence of Saul's wonder about David in vv. 55–58 also contributes to a more moderate victory.

With the diminishing of the theme of 'seeing' and 'hearing' in the LXX, there is less contrast between the responses of David and the Israelites to the threat of Goliath. This contrast is particularly lessened by the absence of v. 24 (וכל איש ישראל בראותם את האיש וינסו מפניו וייראו מאד; 'And all the men of Israel, when they saw the man, fled from him and were very afraid') and v. 48b (וימהר דוד וירץ המערכה לקראת הפלשתי; 'And David ran quickly toward the battle line to meet the Philistine'). We saw in our analysis of the MT version that these verses form a contrast between Israel, who fled from Goliath in fear because of what they 'saw', and David, who runs towards Goliath to fight him. Another variation between the texts, which affects this theme, is the absence of the word 'armour' (שריון) in the LXX of v. 38. Without this part of the verse, the parallel to Goliath's armour is significantly lessened and there is less significance in David's rejection of the outwardly impressive armour. The final sentence of v. 39 in the LXX also diminishes David's deliberate rejection of the appearance of Saul and Goliath as others remove the clothing for him (καὶ ἀφαιροῦσιν αὐτὰ ἀπ᾽ αὐτοῦ; 'And they removed them from him'). By contrast, the MT places David as the subject and he not only removes the clothing, but actually turns them away from himself in a physical act of rejection (ויסרם דוד מעליו; 'And David turned them away from himself'). The variations in the LXX contribute to a less dramatic depiction of David's victory and so reduce this aspect of David's faith in God.

In our analysis of the MT, the theme of 'seeing' and the disparity between David and Goliath developed the depiction of David's courage and faith respectively and therefore implied a positive evaluation of him. The absence of some of these elements reduces the impact of the positive evaluation. Nevertheless, David's extensive speeches, which express his faith in Yahweh's deliverance and his courage in facing Goliath rhetorically, remain in the LXX and so the positive evaluation can be observed in this version.

Whilst the positive evaluation of David is lessened, the aspects of
negative evaluation are completely absent in the LXX version. Primarily, David's self-ambition is not present in the LXX version as it omits
vv. 12–31. Another variation that places David in a subtly better light
is the use of the word κατεπάτουν ('they trampled') in the LXX v. 53
in place of the MT וישסו ('and they plundered'). Whilst plundering
was not forbidden, it could recall for some readers a parallel with Saul
sparing the king and best livestock of the Ammonites in 15.9, an act
which cost him the kingship. In the LXX version there is no possibility
of drawing this comparison. Through the absence of the negative elements found in the MT, the LXX balances the less developed positive
evaluation. Yet, similar to the results of our analysis of causation, we
see that critical evaluation of David has either been simplified in the
LXX or amplified in the MT. The two accounts are not contradictory
but one presents a more complex representation than the other.

Let us now turn to the critical evaluation of Saul in this chapter. Saul
is repeatedly evaluated negatively by contrast with the actions of David
and in parallel with the appearance of Goliath. This contrast is also
conveyed in the LXX, for example, through their differing responses
to Goliath's rhetoric. Similar to the MT, Saul responds with fear and
David with his own rhetoric. Within the structure of the LXX, Saul's
fear in v. 11 and David's speech in v. 32 are juxtaposed giving the
contrast particular emphasis. However, there are also variations that
result in some of the points of contrast in the MT being absent in the
LXX. Notably, v. 55 is absent where Saul passively watches and David
bravely fights the battle for him.

The parallel between Saul and Goliath is present in the LXX but,
again, it is not as developed as in the MT. In the LXX, there is height
similarity and, therefore, comparison: between Saul who was chosen
as king for his impressive exterior and Goliath who is feared for his
impressive exterior. We have already observed that Saul's armour in
LXX v. 38 is not described in similar terms to Goliath's armour as
in the MT. Saul's helmet in LXX v. 38 (περικεφαλαίαν) recalls v. 5
to some degree but the parallel is much less pronounced without the
addition of the armour. Furthermore, the absence of v. 50 and the
reminder that Yahweh saves 'not by sword or spear' give less emphasis to the difference between Saul's armour and weapons, and David's
faith in Yahweh.

On the other hand, there is a variation between the LXX and MT
that generates additional evaluation in the LXX over the MT. In v. 32

of the MT, David's words to Saul speak only indirectly of Saul's fear in v. 11, אל יפל לב אדם עליו ('Do not let anyone's heart fall on his account'). In the LXX, David explicitly refers to Saul's fear of the Philistine, μὴ δὴ συμπεσέτω ἡ καρδία τοῦ κυρίου μου ἐπ' αὐτόν ('On no account let the heart of my lord collapse upon him'). The juxtaposition of the word 'lord' (κυρίου) with David's claim that 'your servant' (ὁ δοῦλός σου) will fight the Philistine highlights the reversal of roles. Thus, this variation between the LXX and MT balances the other aspects of critical evaluation of Saul absent in the LXX. Overall, the evaluation of Saul is largely unchanged between the two texts.

3. *Meaning and Significance*

The character of leaders, politics and theology are the three main areas of significance in this story. We will examine each of these categories for change between the LXX and MT versions of the story.

The character of leaders in the book of Samuel is conveyed predominantly through the structure of parallels between their selection, rise and fall. Auld and Ho have shown that most of the parallels between the selection and rise of Saul in I Sam 9–11 and David in I Sam 17 are found in the additional material of the MT and are therefore not present in the LXX.[152] Amongst these parallels in chapter 17, they cite from Lust: the introduction of each man's father before the introduction of the future leader; the setting of a minor task for Saul and David by their respective fathers; and meeting with the current leader of the nation whilst fulfilling this task.[153] They add the parallel that Saul hides amongst the baggage in 10.22, whilst David runs from the baggage to the battlefield in 17.22.[154] All of these parallels occur in MT 17.12–31 and 55–58 and so do not appear in the LXX. Therefore, there is less emphasis on these parallels in the LXX than in the MT.

On the other hand, some parallels between the selection and rise of Saul and David are present in chapters 16–17 as a whole. The LXX version contains the introduction to David through his father in 16.1–13 and so retains the parallel with Saul in 9.1–2. David is sent by Jesse

---

[152] Auld and Ho, "The Making of David and Goliath," 19–31. Auld and Ho use this evidence in support of the priority of the LXX version, arguing that the MT material was added in order to strengthen these parallels. Whilst this argument is persuasive, it does not completely exclude the possibility that the LXX *Vorlage* was disinterested in these parallels or even ideologically opposed to them and so omitted this material.

[153] Ibid.: 24; Lust, "The Story of David and Goliath," 13.

[154] Auld and Ho, "The Making of David and Goliath," 28.

with food provisions to be musician in the court of Saul in 16.20 and
this parallels Saul's commission to find his father's donkeys. Saul's reticence in 10.22 is contrasted with David's forthrightness in chapter 17,
even without the word parallel הכלים ('baggage'). Finally, the LXX
retains the structure of David's selection in chapter 16 followed by a
military victory in chapter 17 and this echoes Saul's selection in chapter 9–10 and military victory in chapter 11. The structure of parallels
is not absent in the LXX, but there is considerably less emphasis on it.
The political significance of the chapter is also affected by variations
between the versions. We have discussed the role of vv. 55–58 in the
MT for developing the political rivalry between Saul and David. However, the absence of this material in the LXX juxtaposes chapter 17
with the explicit statement of Saul's jealousy in 18.6–9, so the political
rivalry is implied. The cause of jealousy is not as developed in the LXX
because Saul does not watch David take his place in the combat with
Goliath. Nevertheless, the women's songs of praise imply this theme
by attributing to David a greater victory than Saul.

One element of Saul's jealousy that is present in the MT and not the
LXX is David's personal political ambition. Rather, the LXX presents
a one sided rivalry between Saul and David. David piously performs
his duty for his nation and Saul responds to this with jealousy. There
is no indication that David has personal ambitions that are inciting
Saul's jealousy.

Finally, we examine the theological significance of the variations
between the versions. Many scholars have observed that the material
common to both LXX and MT is more overtly theological than the
additional material in the MT.[155] All of David's theological speeches
are present in the LXX except for his brief statement in v. 26, the
sentiment of which is present in vv. 36 and 45 in the LXX. Therefore, the most explicit theological significance of the chapter remains
unchanged between the texts.

However, the MT conveys additional theological meaning through
subtle narrative methods and these are not represented in the LXX.
The theme of 'seeing' draws the connection between this chapter and
the theological message of 16.7, that Yahweh sees not as man sees.
Moreover, the extensive depiction of David as a young shepherd

---

[155] Stoebe, "Die Goliathperikope," 404; Krinetzki, "Goliathperikope," 199; Rofé,
"David and Goliath," 118; Kooij, "The Story of David and Goliath," 128; Van Seters,
The Biblical Saga, 157.

overcoming a powerful giant connects with the theological meaning of Hannah's song in I Sam 2, that the mighty will be brought low and the humble lifted up. Once again, there is more complexity in the MT version of this chapter. The theological meaning of the MT does not contradict the LXX but the additional material in the MT offers additional significance for the events.

In summary, these three features of historiography: causation, critical evaluation and meaning and significance, are simplified or made more complex in the narrative but do not contain contradictions between versions.

5.3   CONCLUSION

In this chapter we sought to ascertain how the concepts of accuracy and coherence in the historiography of Samuel are similar or different from the ideals of modern historiography. In modern historiography, a history is considered 'accurate' if it is in accord with all the available evidence, if it is coherent within itself and if it does not have unnecessary ambiguity of facts without context. Furthermore, it must not invent 'facts' for which there is no evidence. Thus, there are two important requirements: coherency in all aspects of the history and immutability of 'facts'.

The well-known contradictions within Samuel and the dubious nature of many of its 'facts' demonstrate that the same type of accuracy was not necessary in order to present a plausible historiography. Furthermore, the fluidity of the representation between versions indicates that there was freedom to alter the 'facts' and interpretation of the history in ways that would constitute a contradiction or inaccuracy in modern historiography. This chapter has systematically studied these contradictions in order to discover which aspects of the historiography required coherency and the type and extent of literary imagination used in the representation of facts. In particular, there are many explanations that could resolve the tensions from the contradictions but these cannot be found in the text.[156]

---

[156] Concerning the contradictions in the MT of I Sam 17, Bar Efrat writes that presumably the MT editors saw solutions but they have not included them. This suggests that they have a different view of the sense of writing to us [Bar-Efrat, *Das erste Buch Samuel*, 235].

In order to conduct this study, we divided the aspects of history into different components so we could determine which of these components were presented coherently and have the appearance of accuracy. On the one hand, there are the events of history, which, in modern historiography, normally comprise the facts about what happened. These events can be divided into two components: changes of state and description. On the other hand, there are analytical aspects of historiography: causation, critical evaluation and meaning and significance. As we review the extent and nature of coherency and accuracy in each of these components, we will draw in examples from elsewhere in Samuel in order to support the generalisations we are making about them.

Events

1. *Description*

This study has demonstrated that descriptive details in the text have a high level of fluidity and variation between versions and, therefore, are unlikely to have been considered important for their own sake; rather they are significant for the effect they produce. This tendency was exhibited in all of the components of description identified.

Firstly, specific time designations are almost entirely absent from the text and the one instance, '40 days', is implausible. As we look elsewhere in Samuel, there is often variation between the MT and LXX of such periods of time. In I Sam 4.15, Eli lives to 98 years in the MT but only 90 years in the LXX. In 4.18, he judges 40 years in the MT and only 20 years in the LXX. In the MT of I Sam 27.7, David lives amongst the Philistines for a year and four months rather than four months in the LXX. The problematic verse in MT I Sam 13.1, where Saul becomes king at one year old and remains king for only two years, is absent entirely from the LXX. Whilst these variations can be explained by scribal error, the frequency of number variation suggests that they were relatively fluid, even if the numbers had symbolic significance. Another variation of this type can be found in II Sam 15.7. Here the MT reads a highly implausible '40 years' for Absalom's time in Jerusalem, whereas the LXX^L reads a more realistic '4 years'. These variations can be attributed either to a harmonising tendency (or scribal error) or to an approximation of the time period. In cases of the latter, it would seem that the authors/redactors were satisfied with using a specific number, even though its precise accuracy was not known.[157]

Secondly, there is fluidity in the location of events, particularly their geographical place names. In I Sam 17.1–2 there was minor variation between the LXX and MT and this can be found elsewhere throughout Samuel. Examples include I Sam 9.4,[158] 14.23,[159] 22.5–6[160] and 25.1,[161] which are unlikely to be the result of translation. When there is no obvious textual or harmonising reason for these variations, the alternate place names tend to be located close together. This suggests that the general locality was kept stable but precision within this locality was not important. If a specific location is not known precisely in modern historiography, then a more general place designation is usually given. However, in the historiography of Samuel, this evidence points to the acceptability of specific locations that are only approximate to where the event is thought to have taken place. Alternatively, the changes could have occurred because the new place name was better known to the readers. In this case, precision would have been sacrificed in order to make the text more contemporary for its readers.

A third component in events is the description of people. Apart from David and Elhanan, the only other example of an interchange of identities is Merab and Michal in II Sam 21.8. In the MT, the occurrence of Michal as the husband of Adriel forms a contradiction and, furthermore, the LXX (and some Hebrew manuscripts) have a variant reading 'Merab'. The contradiction within the MT can be attributed

---

[157] The implausibility of numbers has frequently been observed in the Hebrew Bible. On the hyperbolic numbers of Samuel, Kings and Chronicles, see David M. Fouts, "The Incredible Numbers of the Hebrew Kings," in *Giving the Sense: Understanding and Using Old Testament Historical Texts*, ed. David M. Howard, Jr. and Michael A. Grisanti (Leicester: Apollos, 2003), 283–299. On the symbolic value of numbers in the Hebrew Bible, see J.B. Segal, "Numerals in the Old Testament," *JSS* 10 (1965), 2–20.

[158] LXX 'Selcha' for MT 'Shalishah'. On the difficulties with the MT place names, see Rachelle Gilmour, "Suspense and Anticipation in I Sam. 9:1–14," *JHS* (2009): 9–11.

[159] LXX[B] 'Mount of Ephraim' and LXX[L] 'Beth-Horon' for MT 'Beth-Aven'. Note that Beth-Horon and Beth-Aven (Bethel) both lie in the Hill country of Ephraim [see map in McCarter, *I Samuel*, 231].

[160] LXX 'City of Saric' for MT 'forest of Hereth' and LXX 'the hill below the field that is in Rama' for MT 'Gibeah, under the tamarisk tree'. Benjaminite Ramah and Gibeah are also closely located.

[161] LXX 'Maon' for MT 'Paran'. This change may be the result of harmonisation with 25.2, which also mentions Maon. Paran is apparently in the southern Sinai peninsula [Klein, *1 Samuel*, 245] and so is too far away to be plausible in this story.

either to scribal error or a lack of context for the inconsistency. Whilst
scribal error or harmonisation are the most common explanations for
variation between the MT and LXX, it is also possible that it was a
deliberate editorial decision in the MT to characterise Michal negatively.[162] Ultimately, as with David and Elhanan, it is difficult to use
this example as evidence of the fluidy of identities. Michal/Merab herself does not actually feature in the narrative but rather her name is
a part of the description of the five grandsons of Saul. Therefore, it is
not a variation or contradiction in identities but a description of other
characters. Similar to the mention of Elhanan, very little information
is given about this figure apart from this one contradictory detail and
this does not affect the causation of the surrounding narrative.

On the other hand, there is variation and implausibility in the
appearance or general description of people, for example Goliath's
appearance in I Sam 17. Another example from Samuel is in I Sam
21.8 [LXX v. 7]. In the MT, Doeg is described as an Edomite but in
the LXX, he is Aramean. In this case, Doeg's foreignness is preserved
but his precise country of origin is changed. It is possible that this is
due to scribal error (האדמי 'the Edomite' could easily have been confused with הארמי 'the Aramean') but it may also reflect some sort of
anti-Edomite or anti-Aramean bias. Overall, there are few examples
of descriptions of people in Samuel and so the potential for variation
is minimal. However, from our limited evidence, we may conjecture
once again that these descriptions are approximately accurate but lack
precision.

Fourthly, we examine the description of objects in the narrative,
such as Goliath's armour. Another example is in I Sam 22.19 where
Saul slaughters different animals at Nob in the two versions: oxen,
donkeys and sheep in the MT and calves, oxen and sheep in the LXX.
None of the variations in these descriptions of objects make a material
difference to our understanding of the story, yet they demonstrate a
different attitude to precision in the text.

The final components of events are speeches and dialogue. Another
example of significant variation in a speech is in I Sam 8.11–18 where
four of the eight verses contain differences between the LXX and MT.

---

[162] Robert Rezetko, *Source and Revision in the Narratives of David's Transfer of the
Ark: Text, Language, and Story in 2 Samuel 6 and 1 Chronicles 13, 15–16* (New York:
T & T Clark, 2007), 273–274.

These variations rarely affect the meaning of the speeches but their presence indicates that there was not a concern for preserving the precise words said by people in the past. This conclusion is unsurprising as it is highly implausible that the historian could gain such information.

In summary, there is significant evidence that these descriptions do not conform to modern historiographic standards of accuracy. In modern historiography, when a detail is not known precisely, it is important to avoid contradiction with what 'actually happened' and to give only a general description. In other words, facts should not be invented. In the historiography of Samuel it is acceptable to give specific details, which approximate the evidence, even if their specificity means they contradict it. Facts can still be 'accurate' despite lacking precision. We do not know if the evidence used by the authors/redactors had any connection to what 'actually happened' but the variations and inconsistencies in descriptions in this presentation of the past suggests that they did not affect the work's historical integrity. The authors/redactors were free to invent descriptions provided they were appropriate for the surrounding events and meaning in the story.

2. *Changes of state and their chronology*

In our study of I Sam 17, it was observed that the 'changes of state' that take place in events tend to be added or omitted between versions rather than altered entirely. The large section of material in I Sam 17.12–31, which is absent in the LXX, is the most significant example of such an omission/addition along with further sections in I Sam 18.1–5. 9–11, 17–19 and 30. Other additions and subtractions throughout Samuel tend to be on a smaller scale.

It is difficult to establish contradictions of 'changes of state' within the MT because such contradictions can be attributed to chronology or other ambiguity in the text. An example from elsewhere in Samuel concerns the sons of Absalom. There is a contradiction between II Sam 14.27, where it is reported that Absalom had three sons (ויולדו לאבשלום שלושה בנים), and II Sam 18.18, where Absalom says that he had no sons by whom his name could be remembered (אין לי בן בעבור הזכיר שמי). There are possible explanations for this contradiction—perhaps Absalom's sons died young or II Sam 18.18 took place before the birth of Absalom's sons—but these intervening events are not explained. The context is ambiguous.

In I Sam 17, there are 'changes of state', such as David's meeting with Saul, that do not fit coherently in their present order of occurrence. The types of contradictions we have identified can be resolved by proposing a non-chronological order of events, repetition of events, or omission of events that would resolve the contradictions. Even if the contradiction is present in the text because of an inaccuracy of sources, or fabrication by the authors/redactors, such inconsistencies in the sequence of events did not violate the expectations for a work of historiography as it appears in the final form. Furthermore, the LXX reads more smoothly as a linear progression, demonstrating the fluid nature of the chronology of the story.

Other examples of thematic rather than chronological arrangement of material have been explored in previous chapters of this book. I Sam 9–11 is arranged according to a pattern of selection, designation and confirmation of Saul as king, without time designations to indicate how these events fit together chronologically. This creates 'cumulative' causation for Saul's succession to the throne. I Sam 24–26 contains repeated events in sequence without any acknowledgement of the repetition. This conveys the development of Saul and David as characters but does not explain how these two sets of events relate to each other chronologically or logically.[163] The report of Solomon's birth in II Sam 12 is reported before the siege at Rabbah, even though it is unlikely that Rabbah was held for the number of years that it took for Bathsheba to bear two children. Instead, Solomon's birth gives thematic closure to II Sam 11.1–12.25, which is framed by reports of war with the Ammonites.[164]

In summary, contradictions between 'changes of state' were acceptable in the historiography of Samuel and it was not necessary to explain the chronological context of these events. Although causal chains were important for connecting large-scale events, smaller 'changes of state' were not necessarily logically connected with their surrounding mate-

---

[163] For a study of intentional violations of chronological order in biblical narrative, see David A. Glatt, *Chronological Displacement in Biblical and Related Literatures* (Atlanta: Scholars Press, 1993). Although he does not give any examples from Samuel, he mentions some features of chronological displacement in other historical books that we also observe here. These include avoidance of explicit details and chronological dates, ambiguous chronological formulas, topical links and blurring of precise event sequences (see summary on pp. 184–85).

[164] Shimeon Bar-Efrat, *Das zweite Buch Samuel: Ein narratologisch-philologischer Kommentar*, trans. Johannes Klein, BWANT 181 (Stuttgart: Kohlhammer, 2009), 122.

rial. The placement of material in an order that highlights the meaning of the events was more important than resolving the ambiguity.

Were the authors/redactors free to invent 'changes of state' in the story, as they were free to invent descriptions? Our comparison between the LXX and MT versions suggests that the authors/redactors were indifferent to, and possibly even free to invent the chronology of events, or at least the implied chronology of events because few time designations are given. This freedom to invent is bound by the stability of causation, meaning and critical evaluation in the text.

Whether the actual 'changes of state' could be invented is more difficult to determine because we do not know the source of the additional material found in the MT. On one hand, we have observed that there are no alterations in the 'changes of state' between the MT and LXX versions, only additions or omissions. On the other hand, if descriptions could be invented, then it is possible that actions could likewise, in order to increase the dramatic effect of the story. Moreover, for many of the reported actions in Samuel, it is implausible that an historian had access to this information. The authors/redactors/translators of the MT and LXX may have considered it important not to alter the 'changes of state' but it is probable that at some stage in their sources or their redaction, creative license was employed to dramatise the events of Samuel with additional actions. The contribution of this section on these issues is that there were boundaries to the extent to which such 'changes of state' were invented or imagined. The overall event remained constant even if the 'changes of state' within it could be created. In other words, the causation, critical evaluation and meaning and significance of the overall event could not change or needed to remain coherent with the surrounding story.

Analytical aspects of historiography

1. Causation

Despite the contradictions in I Sam 17, we have demonstrated that the causation remains coherent and consistent with the surrounding chapters of Samuel. The variations between the LXX and MT affect this causation considerably but the two versions do not contradict one another. Rather, the MT offers a more complex combination of divine causation, David's faith and David's ambition but the LXX emphasises only David's faith and the subsequent work of the Divine.

Another example of a contradiction in the MT of Samuel, which leads to coherent causation, is in I Sam 14.18 where it is said that Saul had the ark of the Lord with him. From the statements of I Sam 7.2 and II Sam 6.2, it would seem unlikely that Saul could have had the ark with him; therefore, there is either an inaccuracy or an omission of necessary explanation.[165] The LXX has 'ephod' instead of ark, which eliminates this contradiction. Although the physical cause of Saul's victory is altered, the divine causation conveyed by it remains unchanged.

Elsewhere in Samuel, there are less dramatic variations between the LXX and MT and, therefore, less dramatic differences in causation. In most cases, the variation is one of intensification. The LXX contains additional description of David's feigned madness before Achish in I Sam 21.13, intensifying Achish's reasons for not wanting David to remain in his presence. Tamar's 'appearance was very beautiful' (καλὴ τῷ εἴδει σφόδρα) in the LXX[166] of II Sam 13.1, compared to the MT where she is just 'beautiful' (יפה). The additional description in the LXX intensifies the causation that Amnon was driven to his sin by lust for her beauty.

Other more significant examples in Samuel support our findings. In I Sam 1, there are two variations between the LXX and MT that affect the causes for Hannah's distress, prayer and promise to give Samuel to the priesthood. In v. 5 of the LXX it is stated explicitly that Elkanah loved Hannah more than Peninah (ὅτι τὴν Ανναν ἠγάπα Ελκανα ὑπὲρ ταύτην), whereas in the MT it is only implied through the type scene of a barren woman and a rival fertile wife. Then, in v. 6, the MT adds that Peninah provoked Hannah because of her misfortune (וכעסתה צרתה גם כעס בעבור הרעמה). Thus, in the MT, rivalry with Peninah is an important personal cause, whereas in the LXX her grief is portrayed more intensely as the failure to have a child for her loving husband. Ultimately, the variation in causation is minimal. Hannah's personal feelings are still responsible for Samuel's future role as leader in Israel but there is a shift in emphasis on the cause of these feelings.

---

[165] See Philip R. Davies, "Ark or Ephod in 1 Sam 14:18," *JTS* 26 (1975): 82–87. Davies attributes this contradiction to the historical inaccuracy of the ark narrative and proposes that the ark has been systematically replaced by the ephod elsewhere in the text to avoid such contradictions. Cf. Rezetko, *Source and Revision*, 97 n. 58. He argues that the oracular consultation and other language in the passage suggests the originality of 'ephod'.

[166] Both LXX^B and the *kaige* recension in LXX^L.

I Sam 14.15 offers another example where variation shifts the emphasis in causation. The LXX includes a statement that the confusion in
the Philistine camp came from the Lord (καὶ ἐγενήθη ἔκστασις παρὰ
κυρίου). Divine causation is acknowledged elsewhere in the MT in
vv. 6, 10 and 12 and so the LXX additional material does not represent
a change in the causation, only makes it more explicit.

2. *Critical Evaluation*

In our analysis of I Sam 17, the LXX version offers a less complex
evaluation of David, who is untainted by ambition, and a less negative
evaluation of Saul. On the other hand, another example of change in
the critical evaluation of Saul between the MT and LXX demonstrate
a reverse where the LXX is more explicitly negative. In I Sam 14.25,
the LXX states that Saul's oath was an act of ignorance (καὶ Σαουλ
ἠγνόησεν ἄγνοιαν μεγάλην).

There are other examples of variation in the evaluation of David
between the two versions. The evaluation is more positive in the LXX of
1 Sam 21.2 where Ahimelech is only confused or amazed (ἐξέστη) not
trembling with fear (ויחרד) at David's presence at Nob. This reduces
the implication that David is taking the sanctuary bread by force. The
evaluation of David is more negative in the *kaige* recension of LXX[B] in
II Sam 12.7 where there is a more complete statement, σὺ εἶ ὁ ἀνὴρ ὁ
ποιήσας τοῦτο ('you are the man who did this') echoing v. 5, compared
to the more ambiguous MT אתה האיש ('you are the man').[167]

Other characters are evaluated in varying degrees between the MT
and LXX. Wevers writes concerning Joab: "his will power, directness of
speech and vengeful character are hinted at somewhat more strongly"
in the Greek than the Hebrew in II Sam 14.21, 18.7 and 19.7.[168] The
narrator in the *kaige* recension of LXX[B] emphasises Amnon's wickedness in II Sam 13.15 by the addition of the phrase ὅτι μείζων ἡ κακία
ἡ ἐσχάτη ἢ ἡ πρώτη ('for the last wickedness was greater than the
first').[169]

---

[167] For a number of other variations in the evaluation of David, see also John W.
Wevers, "A Study in the Exegetical Principles Underlying the Greek Text of 2 Sam
11:2—1 Kings 1:11," *CBQ* 15 (1953): 40–42.
[168] Ibid.: 39.
[169] Translation from Lancelot C.L. Brenton, "The Septuagint in English." (London:
Samuel Bagster & Sons, 1851). Note that this addition is thought to be the result of a
marginal annotation to v16 [P. Kyle McCarter, Jr., *II Samuel*, The Anchor Bible (New
York: Double Day, 1984), 317].

In each of these cases, the evaluation of the characters is not changed qualitatively but rather, there is a change in emphasis or explicitness.

3. *Meaning and Significance*

There is little change in the overall meaning and significance of I Sam 17 despite the variations between the MT and LXX. The overall structure of the rise and fall of leaders is not affected by the LXX omissions and there are no other apparent variations that alter this structure in any major way. The comparison between David and Saul is perhaps lessened by the absence of David and Jonathan's covenant in 18.1–5 in the LXX and therefore the absence of any juxtaposition between this account and Saul's jealousy in 18.6–29. Essentially both versions contain the significance of the rise and fall of successive leaders.

In our analysis of meaning and significance, we pointed to the role of the beginning and ending of the book for highlighting its main themes. There are a number of variations, particularly in the poetry of these sections. One significant absence in the LXX of I Sam 2.1–10 is the description of God as 'rock', as in the MT this passage draws a close connection with II Sam 22.2–3 where the imagery is also used. However, the overall theme of reversal is present in both poems and so a connection can be made without this verbal link.

A difference in meaning is observed by Hugo, who argues that there is a pro-temple bias in the MT by analysing variations from the LXX. He examines II Sam 15.25, where the Antiochian text adds 'let it [the ark] lodge in his own place'. This may have been omitted in the MT because only Yahweh can designate the place for the temple.[170] Further, II Sam 15.8 adds in the LXX, '[I will serve] in Hebron', again theologically problematic for a divinely chosen temple in Jerusalem.[171] Moreover, he re-examines II Sam 24.25, suggesting that it would have been inappropriate for Solomon to enlarge the altar and therefore this was omitted in the MT version.[172]

---

[170] Philippe Hugo, "The Jerusalem Temple seen in Second Samuel according to the Masoretic Text and the Septuagint," in *XIIIth Congress of the International Organization for Septuagint and Cognate Studies 2007 Ljubljana*, ed. J.K.H. Peters (Atlanta: SBL, 2008), 187–89.

[171] Ibid., 192–94.

[172] Ibid., 190–92.

In contrast, Schniedewind assumes the priority of the MT and suggests that there is a bias towards the temple in the LXX.[173] He points out that the dynastic promise of II Sam 7 is turned into a promise for a temple in the LXX through the alteration of pronouns in v. 7 (MT 'Yahweh' becomes LXX 'you' and MT 'you' becomes LXX 'him'). Moreover, v. 5 is posed as a statement not a question in the LXX, so the MT ambiguity about Yahweh's opposition to the concept of a temple is absent and it is made clearer that he is only opposed to David building it. In v. 16, the change in possessive pronouns from MT 'your' to LXX 'his' implies in the LXX it is the temple that will last forever, not David's dynasty. Finally, the addition in the LXX II Sam 24.25 of the tradition that Solomon built an altar on the threshing floor of Araunah (καὶ προσέθηκεν Σαλωμων ἐπὶ τὸ θυσιαστήριον ἐπ' ἐσχάτῳ ὅτι μικρὸν ἦν ἐν πρώτοις; 'and Solomon made an addition to the altar afterwards, for it was little at first') demonstrates a further interest in the significance of the temple. Overall, these variations suggest a pronounced *tendenz* in the LXX.[174] The significance of these passages is made either more complex or more simple but the two versions are not in contradiction with each other. The MT also contains the promise that Solomon will build a temple (v. 13: הוא יבנה בית לשמי) and the LXX contains the promise that the Lord will establish a dynasty for David (v. 12: καὶ ἀναστήσω τὸ σπέρμα σου μετὰ σέ ὃς ἔσται ἐκ τῆς κοιλίας σου καὶ ἑτοιμάσω τὴν βασιλείαν αὐτοῦ).

If we lay aside questions of priority, we are able to harmonise the variations observed by these two scholars. The LXX has a greater interest in the temple but it also contains a more complex depiction. It casts suspicion on Solomon for adding to the altar, and on David for usurping Yahweh's role for designating the location and for allowing Absalom to worship in Hebron. There is a difference in complexity but not a contradiction.

---

[173] William M. Schniedewind, "Textual Criticisim and Theological Interpretation: The Pro-Temple *Tendenz* in the Greek Text of Samuel-Kings," *HTR* 87 (1994): 107–16.

[174] Cf. Tryggve N.D. Mettinger, *King and Messiah: The Civil and Sacral Legitimation of the Israelite Kings* (Lund: CWK Gleerup, 1976), 58. In his reading of II Sam 7, he perceives a bias towards Solomon in the LXX and considers the MT a later dynastic redaction.

The conventions of historiography in Samuel

With such limited outside evidence for this period of Israel's history, and a lack of scholarly consensus on the date and nature of Samuel's sources, we cannot determine with certainty the accuracy of this historiography. In contrast, this section has analysed the conventions for the presentation of accuracy in the book of Samuel: which features are coherent and non-contradictory and which features exhibit elements of invention and creative license.

In modern historiography, the accuracy of every 'fact' is important for the 'truthfulness' of the representation. In the historiography of Samuel, contradictions, implausible details and incoherencies abound both within the MT and between the MT and LXX. The different components of 'events' in Samuel could contain additions and omissions, and some could be altered entirely. In particular, the chronology of events is less important than its thematic arrangement, which draws out the meaning of the historiography.[175] All of the descriptions and 'changes of state' that are implausible or inconsistent contribute in some way to the causation, critical evaluation or meaning and significance, which in turn are coherent and consistent within the book as a whole.

Whilst these 'facts' could be changed, added or omitted, there were set boundaries on the alteration. Usually the details are approximate and specific details have been used where modern historiography might admit to not having the precise information. These 'invented' facts contribute to the causation, critical evaluation and meaning of the narrative; therefore, it is likely the consistency of these three features of historiography form the boundary for the amount of alteration that can take place in the events. In other words, facts can be invented or altered so long as they do not change the way that the history would be interpreted. By changing or inventing a fact, the authors/redactors could not change or interpret the meaning of the narrative, only enhance or withdraw emphasis from it.

---

[175] Cf. McCullagh, "The Truth of Historical Narratives," 31, on modern historiography, "An absolutely minimal requirement of historical narratives which have a central subject is that they recount events in the history of their subject in roughly chronological order, making them both credible and intelligible. This is relatively uncontroversial."

This indicates a very different attitude from modern historiography towards 'facts' and their relationship to causation, critical evaluation and meaning and significance. Whereas in modern historiography, 'facts' are used as evidence to *prove* a particular interpretation, in the historiography of Samuel they are used to *express* the interpretation. Therefore, if a particular interpretation of history could be expressed better by inventing a speech to dramatise the narrative, then this was acceptable within the conventions of this historiography. The authors/ redactors were free to use literary techniques that invented or altered facts provided they conveyed coherent causation, critical evaluation and meaning.

Throughout this study we have focused on differences from modern historiography. The ideals of modern historiography suggest that 'facts' represent objective reality, but there is also a recognition that this reality is more complex. Interpretation plays a large role in the description of events as it relies on the perception of the historian and therefore his/her interpretative sense of how the world operates. Moreover, the historian has the privilege of selectivity from the vast quantity of 'facts' and so can also exercise interpretation in this respect. Thus, the approach to 'facts' in the historiography of Samuel as an expression of, rather than evidence for, interpretation shows some similarities to recent acknowledgement of their subjective nature. Pre-modern and postmodern conceptions of history are united in their rejection of the modern immutability of facts.

Secondly, contradictions in Samuel often appear to be the result of ambiguity in the context for events within the book. The ideal of modern historiography is to resolve contradictions through sufficient context. However, all of the context can never be given and therefore some ambiguity is inevitable. The context is complex and infinite, and so only that which is necessary for giving coherence to modern historiography needs to be included. In a sense, the contradictions allowed to remain in the historiography of Samuel are also an expression of this complexity. The contradictions may be the result of multiple sources and/or the invention of the author. The absence of any thorough attempt to resolve these contradictions by the authors/redactors/ translators indicates that they were aware of the complexity of the past and understood that contradictions could arise where sufficient context was either not known or otherwise irrelevant.

Whilst this study does not address the accuracy of the representation of the past in the book of Samuel, it proposes the historiographical features in which we can expect a modern concept of accuracy. It provides a guide for judging the 'historicity' of the representation on its own terms and according to its own conventions, helping to understand why it violates our modern requirements for accuracy so blatantly.

CHAPTER SIX

CONCLUSION

At the beginning of this study, historiography was defined as a representation of the past. This definition highlighted the fundamental similarity between the book of Samuel and modern works of historiography. In particular, we have examined four characteristics of historiography found in Samuel: causation, meaning and significance, evaluation and coherence. These concepts are central to the interpretation of the past as they give it order, relevance and shape the reader's understanding and perception of people and events. In this way these concepts overlap with modern historiography. However, there are also important differences between the book of Samuel and modern historiography. We have examined both similarities and differences in order to contribute to two areas of scholarly endeavour: the poetics of Hebrew narrative and the conception of historiography in this ancient source for the history of Israel. We will now summarise our findings.

The historiography of Samuel uses narrative to merge information and interpretation about the past and this dramatisation generates both interest and significance. This study has contributed to the area of poetics by examining the ways in which narrative devices can convey concepts normally expounded explicitly in modern historiography. In our study of causation we identified three main ways in which causation was developed. Firstly, there were chains of causation where the narrative shifts between states of imbalance and equilibrium. The agents and circumstances of each shift are the causes in the narrative chains. Secondly, there is cumulative causation. Juxtaposed episodes are not related by causal chains but each offer a different cause for a final outcome, which in turn draws the disparate episodes together. Finally, there is causation expounded through the speech of characters. This type of causation is given depth and complexity through the surrounding narrative, characterisation and subtle devices, such as key words, within the speech. All three types of causation can be developed simultaneously in the narrative, increasing the number of causes and their complexity in the narrative.

There is meaning and significance in historiography when the events and details are connected to the course of history and have relevance for later times. Connection with the narrative is primarily achieved through causal chains and major themes such as the kingship of Israel. However, there are also many literary devices that highlight the themes, deepen the connections and relevance, and extend them to the smallest details in the text. The beginning and end of the book establish the main themes, particularly through verbal repetitions and the abstract medium of poetry. The structure of the rise and fall of leaders connects many aspects of the book and unites them into a pattern recurring in the course of history. Comparative analogies generate meaning in the narrative using details in the text, such as repetitions of events and individual words.

In our study of moral, political and theological evaluation, we overviewed the numerous covert devices that shape the reader's perception of people and events. Complexity is achieved in the narrative through different voices and perspectives, which can be adjudicated by attention to characterisation. Furthermore, opposing viewpoints are often juxtaposed, creating a gap that the reader must imaginatively fill. These devices occur in many sections of Samuel, including both those commonly thought composite and those thought unified.

Despite contradictions and inconsistencies in the events and descriptions in Samuel, there is a significant measure of coherence achieved in the causation, meaning and significance, and evaluation in the narrative. Furthermore, imaginatively reconstructed dialogues and visual descriptions create important effects in the narrative, and they contribute coherently to the interpretation of the history. Comparison with the literary structure of the LXX version illuminated several additional literary features in the MT story of David and Goliath.

The historiography of Samuel may share the features of causation, meaning and significance, evaluation and coherence with modern historiography but it also demonstrates some sharp differences in its conception of them. In addition to political, public and social causation, which is common in modern historiography, the book of Samuel also contains divine and personal causes. These additional two types of causes feature prominently in the narrative, perhaps surpassing the others. In particular, political results can have private causes and private events can have public causes. The dichotomy between the two spheres is significantly less pronounced than in the modern day. This is also demonstrated by the complex way in which the causes interrelate. Contrary to the popular perception that different pericopes in Samuel focus on one or another type of cause, in most cases they are closely connected and even interdependent. In particular, other types of causation always accompany divine causation.

The book of Samuel conveys the *political* meaning and significance of its subject matter, similar to modern historiography, but it adds two additional areas of significance for the reader. The first is *theological* significance and this corresponds to studies of Jewish thought that suggest its theology is understood through remembering the past.[1] The second is *human* significance, particularly lessons from the lives of great leaders. The multitude of themes that occur in the book of Samuel can all be placed in one of these three categories. Moreover, we observed that meaning in the history of Samuel is conceived as both linear and cyclic, in contrast to the common focus on linearity in modern historiography. This is expressed through patterns that can either repeat or be broken.

Not only is evaluation in the book of Samuel implicit rather than explicit, conclusive evaluation is often left for the reader's own judgment. The narrative guides the reader through different perspectives, shaping and limiting the possible evaluation but not providing one 'correct' solution. Another important difference is the authority of the Divine. His authoritative evaluation is not domineering but incompletely depicted in the narrative; and this allows scope for more complex assessments provided there is no contradiction.

Contradictions and inaccuracies within the MT version and between the MT and LXX reveal a very different conception of historicity and accuracy in Samuel from modern historiography. Modern historiography aims to resolve ambiguity in the context of events in order to achieve a smooth and consistent account. By contrast, the final form of the book of Samuel retains contradictions and allows ambiguity, particularly of chronology. 'Facts', such as descriptions, lack precision and dialogue can be dramatized and reconstructed. This suggests that these features are used to express the interpretation of history rather than to provide evidence and justification. It was observed that the contradictions and inaccuracies made a literary contribution towards causation,

---

[1] See the study in Yosef Hayim Yerushalmi, *Zakhor, Jewish History and Jewish Memory* (Seattle: University of Washington Press, 1982); Also, Yairah Amit, *History and Ideology: Introduction to Historiography in the Hebrew Bible* (Sheffield: Sheffield Academic Press, 1999), 16–19.

meaning and significance, and evaluation in the narrative and these concepts were presented coherently despite the other inconsistencies.

The final way in which the historiography of Samuel is different to modern conceptions is its use of narrative. Most of the literary devices are foreign to modern historiography; some are peculiar to Hebrew narrative and others would be considered inappropriate for history. Devices that have recurred throughout our analysis, are: the use of a thematic structure rather than linear chronological order of events; patterns of parallels and comparisons; repetition of events; *Leitwörter*; dramatized dialogue; and type scenes. These devices are not familiar to modern historians. It is nonsensical for our modern conception of history that an historian would confuse the chronological progression of the narrative or leave it ambiguous for the sake of conveying cumulative causation, complex evaluation or meaning through juxtaposition. It is unimaginable for a modern historian to invent a dialogue or description in order to depict the event more 'truly'. Yet, these devices are used creatively to produce the gripping, insightful and, for many, satisfying account of Israel's past in the book of Samuel.

The context for our discussion of Samuel's conception of history is the use of Samuel as a source for writing the history of Israel. There are a number of implications from this study that bear directly upon the ongoing debate. Firstly, this study provides arguments against either a maximalist or minimalist position towards the book of Samuel when reconstructing Israel's history. This study has shown that the main concerns of the book of Samuel are different from the concerns of modern historiography in several fundamental ways; consequently there is a significant gap between the historiography of Samuel and the goal of a modern historian. For example, efforts to resolve contradictions and create coherence in Samuel will always remain speculative and contrary to the purposes of the book, which has preferred to use gaps, achronology and unexplained context to convey interpretation. Regardless of the historicity of Samuel, the nature of its historiography dictates that use of this text alone will be insufficient for a satisfactory modern historiography. On the other hand, this study has also highlighted the similarities between historiography in Samuel and the modern day, indicating that it should be considered useful in a modern study of ancient Israel. The main features of historiography: causation, meaning and significance and evaluation are presented coherently, and political, public and social causes and significance are frequently addressed. The significant overlap and other similarities highlighted in this study point to the indispensability of the book of Samuel as a source. These implications have been argued many times by scholars but they bear repetition here in light of our detailed study of the similarities and differences between Samuel and modern historiography. Each similarity and difference specified in this study can be used as a guide for which aspects of Samuel correspond to a modern conception of history.

However, a second implication from our study suggests that the process of distinguishing useful history in Samuel is not as straightforward as identifying the similarities and differences (laying aside the currently unsolvable question of historicity). This study has demonstrated that aspects of historiography in Samuel unacceptable to modern historians are frequently bound up with aspects that are closer to modern conceptions of history. Thus, when reconstructing the history of ancient Israel, whole pericopes ought not be rejected because they contain elements unacceptable for modern historians, as often these pericopes contribute to aspects of historiography that are of interest. Several examples will explain this more clearly.

In the series of pericopes that describe Saul's accession as king, it was noted that I Sam 11.1–11 is frequently thought the most appropriate explanation from a modern point of view. However, our study of causation suggests that, not only does this pericope have a strong element of divine causation, the previous pericopes contain elements of political causation. A rejection of I Sam 9.1–10.27 will overlook Saul's initial political reticence and the grudging transference of power directly from Samuel to Saul before the public become involved. Source critical considerations may lead a scholar to consider I Sam 11.1–11 older than the other narratives and therefore, justifiably to prioritise this section. However, where such source critical arguments are not accepted, the preceding narratives should not be rejected for their non-political emphasis alone.

Similarly, in the story of David's rise, it is common to disregard David's occupation as shepherd boy when he fights Goliath, due to contradictions and implausibility. However, this carries important political interpretation. David is an outsider to Saul and the Israelite army and he brings a new approach of piety and calculation to the Philistine threat.

Hannah's song, commonly thought to be falsely attributed to Hannah, is also easily ignored in historical reconstruction. However, our study has shown that it has an important role in introducing the meaning and significance of the whole book, in particular the political significance of the rise and fall of leaders.

Conversely, the succession narrative is often favoured in historical reconstruction because it appears political and secular to modern readers. Closer analysis reveals its entire structure is dependent upon the divine oracle in II Sam 12 and has been shaped by these theological beliefs. Throughout Samuel the theological, political and human are all incorporated, even if some sections place more emphasis on one particular aspect.

Through our investigation of the conception of history in Samuel, we have discovered the purpose of many features unacceptable for modern historians. This warns against taking pericopes out of their interpretative context. As events and facts are used to express, rather than give evidence for, interpretation, we do not necessarily have to disregard the interpretation conveyed by a pericope if we find its contents implausible. Political sections of the narrative are shaped by theological concerns and theological sections are in turn shaped by the political. Attempts to distinguish based on this criteria alone will overlook the subtleties of the text's complex interpretation. Although the literary devices or subject matter within the narrative may not be acceptable to modern historians, the interpretation they convey may be more useful when we understand that book's mode of representing the past.

The significant differences between modern and ancient historiography require that we ask the right questions of historiography in Samuel rather than make demands of the book foreign to its own conception of history. The emphasis on theological interpretation and the significance of the characters of leaders naturally lends itself to questions of a religious or didactic nature and this has been the main use of the book for generations in a religious context. However, what are appropriate historical questions? We consider two important concerns of modern historiography: political interpretation and facts.

Our analysis suggests that political questions are appropriate because there is political causation, meaning and evaluation. However, the world-view of the book will result in an unsatisfying answer. Political causes, significance and evaluation of political outcomes are given in the text but these are deeply entwined with theological and private character concerns. The politics will inevitably be less sophisticated than what we expect in modern historiography because complexity in politics in Samuel arises from interaction with characterisation and theology rather than from the political situation alone.

Our study of 'facts' in Samuel, such as events and descriptions, suggests that questions of their historicity should only be approximate and not precise. The purpose of such facts is not to record them for their own sake but to dramatise the events and convey interpretation. Therefore, a fact can be inaccurate or approximate from a modern point of view, but in the historiography of Samuel, it is included because it successfully conveys the desired meaning, causation or characterisation. The interpretation itself may be legitimate even if the 'facts' used to convey it are imprecise or even invented. The gap between the modern and the ancient conception of facts will inevitably lead to an unsatisfying answer for modern questions of historicity and so questions are better directed to the resulting interpretation, which has greater overlap with modern conceptions of historiography.

Finally, our study of the nature and conception of history in the book of Samuel can persuade us to broaden our own conception of history in the modern day. The creative use of narrative to convey the past in an interesting and compelling way in the book of Samuel ought to challenge modern conventions for straightforward explanation. The potential for story to convey life's ambiguities and complexity demonstrates its usefulness for historiography. Modern historiography may surpass Samuel in its sophisticated political, economic and social analysis of causes, meaning and evaluation. However, the breadth of concern in the book of Samuel, and the perception that private and personal matters can affect public affairs, can challenge modern historians to consider this type of analysis of the past.

BIBLIOGRAPHY

Accordance version 8. Oaktree Software Inc., 2009.

Abbott, H. Porter. *The Cambridge Introduction to Narrative.* 2nd ed. Cambridge: Cambridge University Press, 2008.

Aberbach, David. "mnh ʿcht ʿpym (1 Sam. I 5): A New Interpretation." *VT* 24, (1974): 350–53.

Ackerman, James S. "Knowing Good and Evil: A Literary Analysis of the Court History in 2 Samuel 9–20 and 1 Kings 1–2." *JBL* 109, (1990): 41–60.

Ahlström, Gösta W. "The Role of Archaeological and Literary Remains in Reconstructing Israel's History." In *The Fabric of History: Text, Artifact and Israel's Past*, edited by Diana Edelman, 116–41. Sheffield: JSOT Press, 1991.

Aiken, D. Wyatt. "History, Truth and the Rational Mind: Why it is impossible to Separate Myth from History." *TZ* 47, (1991): 226–53.

Alonso Schökel, Luis. "Narrative Art in Joshua-Judges-Samuel-Kings." In *Israel's Past in Present Research*, edited by V. Philips Long, 255–78. Winona Lake: Eisenbrauns, 1999.

Alter, Robert. "Sacred History and Prose Fiction." In *The Creation of Sacred Literature: Composition and Redaction of the Biblical Text*, edited by Richard Elliott Friedman, 7–24. Berkeley: University of California Press, 1981.

———. "Samson Without Folklore." In *Text and Tradition*, edited by S. Niditch, 47–56. Atlanta: SBL, 1990.

———. *The Art of Biblical Narrative.* New York: Basic Books, 1981.

———. *The David Story: A Translation with Commentary of 1 and 2 Samuel.* New York: W.W. Norton, 1999.

Amit, Yairah. *History and Ideology: Introduction to Historiography in the Hebrew Bible.* Sheffield: Sheffield Academic Press, 1999.

———. *Reading Biblical Narratives: Literary Criticism and the Hebrew Bible.* Minneapolis: Fortress Press, 2001.

———. " 'The Glory of Israel Does Not Deceive or Change His Mind': On the Reliability of Narrator and Speakers in Biblical Narrative." *Prooftexts* 12, (1992): 201–12.

Anderson, A.A. *2 Samuel*, WBC. Waco: Word Books, 1989.

Ap-Thomas, Dafydd R. "Saul's 'Uncle'." *VT* 11, (1961): 241–45.

Appleby, Joyce Oldham, Lynn Avery Hunt, and Margaret C. Jacob. *Telling the Truth about History.* New York: Norton, 1994.

Arnold, Bill T. "Necromancy and Cleromancy in 1 and 2 Samuel." *CBQ* 66, (2004): 199–213.

———. "Review of 'The Turn of the Cycle'." *JBL* 124, (2005): 533–36.

Assman, Jan. *Religion and Cultural Memory.* Translated by Rodney Livingstone. Stanford: Stanford University Press, 2005.

Assis, Elie. "Chiasmus in Biblical Narrative: Rhetoric of Characterization." *Prooftexts* 22, (2002): 273–304.

Auld, A. Graeme. "1 and 2 Samuel." In *Eerdmans Commentary on the Bible*, edited by James D.G. Dunn, 213–45. Grand Rapids: Eerdmans, 2003.

———. *Kings without Privilege: David and Moses in the Story of the Bible's Kings.* Edinburgh: T&T Clark, 1994.

———. "Re-reading Samuel (Historically): 'etwas mehr Nichtwissen'." In *Origins of the Ancient Israelite States*, edited by Fritz Volkmar and Philip R. Davies, 160–69. Sheffield: Sheffield Academic Press, 1996.

——. "The Story of David and Goliath: A Test Case for Synchrony Plus Diachrony." In *David und Saul im Widerstreit—Diachronie und Synchronie im Wettstreit. Beiträge zur Auslegung des ersten Samuelbuches*, edited by Walter Dietrich, 118–28. Fribourg: Academic Press, 2004.

Auld, A. Graeme, and Craig Y.S. Ho. "The Making of David and Goliath." *JSOT* 56, (1992): 19–39.

Bach, Alice. "Signs of the Flesh: Observations on Characterization in the Bible." *Semeia* 63, (1993): 63–79.

Baldwin, Joyce G. *1 and 2 Samuel: An Introduction and Commentary*, Tyndale Old Testament Commentaries. Leicester: Inter-Varsity Press, 1988.

Banks, Diane. *Writing the History of Israel*. New York: T&T Clark, 2006.

Bar-Efrat, Shimeon. *Das erste Buch Samuel: Ein narratologisch-philologischer Kommentar*. Translated by Johannes Klein, BWANT 176. Stuttgart: Kohlhammer, 2007.

——. *Das zweite Buch Samuel: Ein narratologisch-philologischer Kommentar*. Translated by Johannes Klein, BWANT 181. Stuttgart: Kohlhammer, 2009.

——. *Narrative Art in the Bible*, JSOTSup. 70. Sheffield: Almond Press, 1989.

Barnhart, Joe E. "Acknowledged Fabrications in 1 and 2 Samuel and 1 Kings 1–2: Clues to the Wider Story's Composition." *SJOT* 20, (2006): 231–36.

Barr, James. *History and Ideology in the Old Testament: Biblical Studies at the End of a Millennium*. Oxford: Oxford University Press, 2000.

Barstad, Hans M. "History and the Hebrew Bible." In *Can a 'History of Israel' Be Written?*, edited by Lester L. Grabbe, 37–64. Sheffield: Sheffield Academic Press, 1997.

Barthélemy, D. "Trois Niveaux D'analyse (A Propos de David et Goliath)." In *The Story of David and Goliath: Textual and Literary Criticism: Papers of a Joint Research Venture*, 47–54. Fribourg: Editions Universitaires, 1986.

Barton, John. "Historical Criticism and Literary Interpretation: Is There Any Common Ground?" In *Israel's Past in Present Research*, edited by V. Philips Long, 427–38. Winona Lake: Eisenbrauns, 1999.

——. "Historiography and Theodicy in the Old Testament." In *Reflection and Refraction: Studies in Biblical Historiography in Honour of A. Graeme Auld*, edited by R. Rezetko, T. H. Lim and W. B. Aucker, 27–33. Leiden: Brill, 2007.

——. *Reading the Old Testament: Method in Biblical Study*. Louisville: Westminster John Knox Press, 1996.

Beck, John A. "David and Goliath, a Story of Place: The Narrative-Geographical Shaping of 1 Samuel 17." *WTJ* 68, (2006): 321–30.

Becker, C.L. *Detachment and the Writing of History*. New York: Cornell University Press, 1967.

Berginer, Vladimir M., and Chaim Cohen. "The Nature of Goliath's Visual Disorder and the Actual Role of his Personal Bodyguard: נשא הצנה (I Sam 17:7,41)." *ANES* 43, (2006): 27–44.

Berkhofer, Robert F. *Beyond the Great Story: History as Text and Discourse*. Cambridge, Mass.: Belknap Press of Harvard University Press, 1995.

Berlin, Adele. *Poetics and Interpretation of Biblical Narrative*, Bible and Literature Series. Sheffield: Almond, 1983.

Berman, Joshua. *Narrative Analogy in the Hebrew Bible: Battle Stories and Their Equivalent Non-Battle Narratives*, VTSup. 103. Leiden: Brill, 2004.

Biddle, Mark E. "Ancestral Motifs in 1 Samuel 25: Intertextuality and Characterization." *JBL* 121, (2002): 617–38.

Bietenhard, Sophia Katharina. *Des Königs General: Die Heerführertraditionen in der vorstaatlichen und frühen staatlichen Zeit und die Joabgestalt in 2 Sam 2–20; 1 Kön 1–2*. Freiburg, Schweiz: Universitätsverlag, 1998.

Birch, Bruce C. "Development of the Tradition on the Anointing of Saul in 1 Sam 9:1–10:16." *JBL* 90, (1971): 55–68.

Blum, Erhard. "Historiography or Poetry: The Nature of the Hebrew Bible Prose Tradition." in *Memory in the Bible and Antiquity*, Wissenschaftliche Untersuchungen zum Neuen Testament vol. 212, edited by L.T. Stuckenbruck, S.C. Barton & B.G. Wold, 25–45. Tübingen: Mohr Siebeck, 2007.

Bodner, Keith. *1 Samuel: A Narrative Commentary*. Sheffield: Sheffield Phoenix Press, 2008.

——. *David Observed: A King in the Eyes of His Court*. Sheffield: Sheffield Phoenix Press, 2005.

Boeker, Hans Jochen. *Die Beurteilung der Anfänge des Königtums in den deuteronomistischen Anschnitten des I. Samuelbuches*. Neukirchen-Vluyn: Neukirchener Verlag, 1969.

Bolin, Thomas M. "History, Historiography, and the Use of the Past in the Hebrew Bible." In *The Limits of Historiography: Genre and Narrative in Ancient Historical Texts*, edited by C.S. Kraus, 113–40. Leiden: Brill, 1999.

Booth, Wayne C. *The Rhetoric of Fiction*. Chicago: University of Chicago Press, 1961.

Borgman, Paul. *David, Saul, and God: Rediscovering an Ancient Story*. Oxford: Oxford University Press, 2008.

Brenton, Lancelot C.L. "The Septuagint in English." London: Samuel Bagster & Sons, 1851.

Brettler, Marc Zvi. *The Creation of History in Ancient Israel*. London: Routledge, 1995.

Brown, Francis, S.R. Driver, and Charles A. Briggs. "A Hebrew and English Lexicon of the Old Testament." Massachusetts: Hendrickson, 2005.

Brueggemann, Walter. "2 Samuel 21–24: An Appendix of Deconstruction?" *CBQ* 50, (1988): 383–97.

——. *First and Second Samuel*, Interpretation. Louisville: John Knox Press, 1990.

——. "Narrative Coherence and Theological Intentionality in 1 Samuel 18." *CBQ* 55, (1993): 225–43.

Budde, Karl. *Die Bücher Samuel*. Tübingen: J.C.B. Mohr, 1902.

——. *Geschichte der althebräischen Literatur*. Leipzig: Amelang, 1909.

Burke, Peter. "History of Events and the Revival of Narrative." In *New Perspectives on Historical Writing*, edited by Peter Burke, 233–48. Cambridge: Polity Press, 1991.

——. "Overture: The New History, its Past and its Future." In *New Perspectives on Historical Writing*, edited by Peter Burke, 1–23. Cambridge: Polity Press, 1991.

Campbell, Antony F. *1 Samuel*, FOTL. Grand Rapids: Eerdmans, 2003.

——. *2 Samuel*, FOTL. Grand Rapids: Eerdmans, 2005.

——. "Structure Analysis and the Art of Exegesis (1 Samuel 16:14–18:30)." In *Problems in Biblical Theology: Essays in Honor of Rolf Knierim*, edited by H.T.C. Sun, K.L. Eades, J.M. Robinson and G.I. Moller, 76–103. Grand Rapids: Eerdmans, 1997.

Carlson, R.A. *David, the Chosen King*. Stockhom: Almqist & Wiksell, 1964.

Carr, E.H. *What is History?* London: Penguin Books, 1964.

Chepey, Stuart. *Nazirites in Late Second Temple Judaism: A Survey of Ancient Jewish Writings, the New Testament, Archaeological Evidence and Other Writings from Late Antiquity*. Leiden: Brill, 2005.

Childs, Brevard S. *Introduction to the Old Testament as Scripture*. Philadelphia: Fortress Press, 1979.

Clements, Ronald E. "Deuteronomistic Interpretation of the Founding of the Monarchy in 1 Sam 8." *VT* 24, (1974): 398–410.

Cohen, Ralph. "History and Genre," *NLH* 17 (1986): 203–18.

Collingwood, R.G. *The Idea of History*. Oxford: Oxford University Press, 1961.

Collins, John Joseph. "The 'Historical Character' of the Old Testament in Recent Biblical Theology." In *Israel's Past in Present Research*, edited by V. Philips Long, 150–69. Winona Lake: Eisenbrauns, 1999.

Conkin, Paul K. "Causation Revisited." *History and Theory* 13, (1974): 1–20.
Conroy, Charles. *Absalom Absalom! Narrative and Language in 2 Sam 13–20*. Rome: Biblical Institute Press, 1978.
Corfield, P.J. *Time and the Shape of History*. New Haven: Yale University Press, 2007.
Craig, Kenneth M., Jr. "The Character(ization) of God in 2 Samuel 7:1–17." *Semeia* 63, (1993): 159–76.
Cross, Frank Moore. *Canaanite Myth and Hebrew Epic: Essays in the History of the Religion of Israel*. Cambridge, Mass.: Harvard University Press, 1973.
Cross, Frank Moore, Donald W. Parry, Richard J. Saley, and Eugene Ulrich. *Qumran Cave 4: 1–2 Samuel*. Vol. XII, *DJD*. Oxford: Clarendon Press, 2005.
Crüsemann, Frank. *Der Widerstand gegen das Königtum*. Neukirchen-Vluyn: Neukirchener Verlag, 1978.
Danker, Frederick William. *A Greek-English Lexicon of the New Testament and other Early Christian Literature*. Chicago: University of Chicago, 2000.
Davies, Philip R. "Ark or Ephod in 1 Sam 14:18." *JTS* 26, (1975): 82–87.
——. *In Search of Ancient Israel*, JSOTSup. 148. Sheffield: JSOT Press, 1992.
De Vries, Simon J. "David's Victory over the Philistine as Saga and as Legend." *JBL* 92, (1973): 23–36.
Deist, Ferdinand. "*'APPAYIM* (1 Sam 1:5) < **PYM?*" *VT* 27, (1977): 205–09.
——. "Contingency, Continuity and Integrity in Historical Understanding: An Old Testament Perspective." In *Israel's Past in Present Research*, edited by V. Philips Long, 373–90. Winona Lake: Eisenbrauns, 1999.
Derow, Peter. "Historical Explanation: Polybius and his Predecessors." In *Greek Historiography*, edited by Simon Hornblower, 73–90. Oxford: Clarendon Press, 1994.
Diamond, Eliezer. "An Israelite Self-Offering in the Priestly Code: A New Perspective on the Nazirite." *JQR* 88, (1997): 1–18.
Dietrich, Walter. "Die Erzählungen von David und Goliat in I Sam 17." *ZAW* 108, (1996): 172–91.
Driver, S.R. *Notes on the Hebrew text and the Topography of the Books of Samuel*. 2nd ed. Oxford: Clarendon Press, 1966.
Dus, Jan. "Die Geburtslegende Samuels, I. Sam. 1: Eine traditionsgeschichtliche Untersuchung zu 1 Sam 1–3." *RSO* 43, (1968): 163–94.
Edelman, Diana. "Clio's Dilemma: The Changing Face of Historiography." In *Congress Volume, 1998*, edited by A. Lemaire & M. Saebø, VTSup. 80, 247–255. Leiden: Brill, 1999.
——. "Doing History in Biblical Studies." In *The Fabric of History: Text, Artifact and Israel's Past*, edited by Diana Edelman, 13–25. Sheffield: JSOT Press, 1991.
——. *King Saul in the Historiography of Judah*, JSOT Supp. 121. Sheffield: JSOT Press, 1991.
——. "Saul ben Kish in History and Tradition." In *Origins of the Ancient Israelite States*, edited by Fritz Volkmar and Philip R. Davies, 142–59. Sheffield: Sheffield Academic Press, 1996.
——. "Saul's Rescue of Jabesh-Gilead (1 Sam 11:1–11): Sorting Story from History." *ZAW* 96, (1984): 195–209.
——, ed. *The Fabric of History: Text, Artifact, and Israel's Past*, JSOTSup. 127. Sheffield: JSOT Press, 1991.
Edenburg, Cynthia. "How (Not) to Murder a King: Variations on a Theme in 1 Sam 24; 26." *SJOT* 12, (1998): 64–85.
Eliade, Mircea. *Cosmos and History: The Myth of the Eternal Return*. New York: Harper, 1959.
Eslinger, Lyle M. *Into the Hands of the Living God*, JSOTSup. 84. Sheffield: Almond Press, 1989.
——. *Kingship of God in Crisis: A Close Reading of 1 Samuel 1–12*. Decatur: Almond Press, 1985.
——. "Viewpoints and Point of View in 1 Samuel 8–12." *JSOT* 26, (1983): 61–76.

Exum, J. Cheryl. *Tragedy and Biblical Narrative: Arrows of the Almighty.* Cambridge: Cambridge University Press, 1992.

Flanagan, James W. "Court History or Succession Document: A Study of 2 Samuel 9–20 and 1 Kings 1–2." *JBL* 91, (1972): 172–81.

Fohrer, Georg. *Introduction to the Old Testament.* Translated by David Green. London: S.P.C.K., 1970.

Fokkelman, J.P. *King David*, Vol. I of *Narrative Art and Poetry in the Books of Samuel: A Full Interpretation Based on Stylistic and Structural Analyses.* Assen: Van Gorcum, 1981.

——. *The Crossing Fates*, Vol. II of *Narrative Art and Poetry in the Books of Samuel: A Full Interpretation Based on Stylistic and Structural Analyses.* Assen: Van Gorcum, 1986.

——. *Throne and City*, Vol. III of *Narrative Art and Poetry in the Books of Samuel: A Full Interpretation Based on Stylistic and Structural Analyses.* Assen: Van Gorcum, 1990.

——. *Vow and Desire*, Vol. IV of *Narrative Art and Poetry in the Books of Samuel: A Full Interpretation Based on Stylistic and Structural Analyses.* Assen: Van Gorcum, 1993.

Fouts, David M. "The Incredible Numbers of the Hebrew Kings." In *Giving the Sense: Understanding and Using Old Testament Historical Texts*, edited by David M. Howard, Jr. and Michael A. Grisanti, 283–99. Leicester: Apollos, 2003.

Fowler, Alistair. *Kinds of Literature: An Introduction to the Theory of Genres and Modes.* Oxford: Clarendon, 1982.

Frolov, Serge. *The Turn of the Cycle: 1 Samuel 1–8 in Synchronic and Diachronic Perspectives.* Berlin: Walter de Gruyter, 2004.

Garbini, Giovanni. *History and Ideology in Ancient Israel.* London: SCM, 1988.

Garsiel, Moshe. *Biblical Names: A Literary Study of Midrashic Derivations and Puns.* Ramat Gan: Bar-Ilan University Press, 1991.

——. *The First Book of Samuel: A Literary Study of Comparative Structures, Analogies and Parallels.* Ramat-Gan: Revivim, 1985.

Gelston, A. "A Note on II Samuel 7¹⁰." *ZAW* 84, (1972): 92–94.

George, Mark K. "Constructing Identity in 1 Samuel 17." *Interpretation* 7, (1999): 389–412.

——. "Fluid Stability in Second Samuel 7." *CBQ* 64, (2002): 17–36.

Gilmour, Rachelle. "Suspense and Anticipation in I Sam. 9:1–14." *JHS* (2009).

Glatt, David A. *Chronological Displacement in Biblical and Related Literatures.* Atlanta: Scholars Press, 1993.

Gooding, D.W. "An Approach to the Literary and Textual Problems in the David-Goliath Story " In *The Story of David and Goliath: Textual and Literary Criticism: Papers of a Joint Research Venture*, 55–86. Fribourg: Editions Universitaires, 1986.

Gordon, Robert P. "Who Made the Kingmaker? Reflections on Samuel and the Institution of the Monarchy." In *Faith, Tradition, and History: Old Testament Historiography in its Near Eastern Context*, edited by Alan R. Millard, James K. Hoffmeier and David W. Baker, 255–69. Winona Lake: Eisenbrauns, 1994.

——. *1 & 2 Samuel: A Commentary.* Exeter: Paternoster, 1986.

——. "David's Rise and Saul's Demise: Narrative Analogy in 1 Samuel 24–26." *TB* 31, (1980): 37–64.

——. "Word-Play and Verse-Order in 1 Samuel 24:5–8." *VT* 40, (1990): 139–44.

Gould, Stephen Jay. *Time's Arrow, Time's Cycle: Myth and Metaphor in the Discovery of Geological Time*, The Jerusalem-Harvard lectures. Cambridge, Mass.: Harvard University Press, 1987.

Green, Barbara. "Enacting Imaginatively the Unthinkable: 1 Samuel 25 and the Story of Saul." *BI* 11, (2003): 1–23.

——. *How are the Mighty Fallen? A Dialogical Study of King Saul in 1 Samuel*, JSOTSup. 365. Sheffield: Sheffield Academic Press, 2003.

Gressmann, Hugo. *Die älteste Geschichtsschreibung und Prophetie Israels (von Samuel bis Amos und Hosea): übersetzt, erklärt und mit Einleitungen versehen.* Göttingen: V & R, 1910.

Gronbaek, Jakob. *Die Geschichte vom Aufstieg Davids (1 Sam. 15-2 Sam. 5).* Vol. X, Acta Theologica Danica. Copenhagen: Prostant Apud Munksgaard, 1971.

Gros Louis, Kenneth R.R. "Difficulty of Ruling Well: King David of Israel." *Semeia* 8, (1977): 15–33.

Gunkel, Hermann. *Das Märchen im Alten Testament.* Tübingen: Mohr, 1921.

——. *Genesis.* Translated by Mark E. Biddle. Macon: Mercer University Press, 1997.

Gunn, D.M. "Entertainment, Ideology, and the Reception of 'History': 'David's Jerusalem' as a Question of Space." In *"A Wise and Discerning Mind": Essays in Honor of Burke O. Long,* edited by S.M. Olyan and R.C. Culley, 153–61. Providence: Brown Judaic Studies, 2000.

——. *The Fate of King Saul: An Interpretation of a Biblical Story,* JSOTSup. 14. Sheffield: JSOT Press, 1980.

——. *The Story of King David: Genre and Interpretation.* Sheffield: JSOT Press, 1978.

Gunn, D.M., and Danna Nolan Fewell. *Narrative in the Hebrew Bible.* Oxford: Oxford University Press, 1993.

Hagan, Harry. "Deception as Motif and Theme in 2 Sm 9–20; 1 Kgs 1–2." *Bib* 60, (1979): 301–26.

Halpern, Baruch. *David's Secret Demons: Messiah, Murderer, Traitor, King.* Grand Rapids: Eerdmans, 2001.

——. *The Constitution of the Monarchy in Israel.* Chico: Scholars Press, 1981.

——. "The Construction of the Davidic State: An Exercise in Historiography." In *Origins of the Ancient Israelite States,* edited by Fritz Volkmar and Philip R. Davies, 44–75. Sheffield: Sheffield Academic Press, 1996.

——. *The First Historians: The Hebrew Bible and History.* University Park: Pennsylvania State University Press, 1988.

Hays, J. Daniel. "Reconsidering the Height of Goliath." *JETS* 48, (2005): 701–14.

Herodotus. *The Histories.* Translated by Aubrey De Selincourt and John Marincola. London: Penguin Books, 2003.

Herrmann, Siegfried. "Die Königsnovelle in Ägypten und in Israel." *Wissenschaftliche Zeitschrift der Karl-Marx-Universität* 3, (1953): 51–62.

Hertzberg, Hans Wilhelm. *I & II Samuel: A Commentary.* Translated by John Stephen Bowden, OTL. London: S.C.M. Press, 1964.

Hill, Andrew E. "On David's 'Taking' and 'Leaving' Concubines (2 Samuel 5:13; 15:16)." *JBL* 125, (2006): 129–50.

Hobsbawm, E. "Marx and History." *NLR* 143, (1984): 39–50.

Honeyman, A.M. "The Evidence for Regnal Names among the Hebrews." *JBL* 67, (1948): 13–25.

Hornblower, Simon. "Narratology and Narrative Techniques in Thucydides." In *Greek Historiography,* edited by Simon Hornblower, 131–66. Oxford: Clarendon Press, 1994.

Hugo, Philippe. "Text History of the Books of Samuel." In *Archaeology of the Books of Samuel: The Entangling of the Textual and Literary History,* edited by Philippe Hugo and Adrian Schenker, 1–19. Leiden: Brill, 2010.

——. "The Jerusalem Temple seen in Second Samuel according to the Masoretic Text and the Septuagint." In *XIIIth Congress of the International Organization for Septuagint and Cognate Studies 2007 Ljubljana,* edited by J.K.H. Peters, 183–06. Atlanta: SBL, 2008.

Humphreys, W. Lee. "The Tragedy of King Saul: A Study of the Structure of 1 Samuel 9–31." *JSOT* 6, (1978): 18–27.

Hurowitz, Victor (Avigdor). *I Have Built You an Exalted House: Temple Building in the Bible in Light of Mesopotamian and Northwest Semitic Writings,* JSOTSup. 115. Sheffield: JSOT Press, 1992.

Iggers, Georg G. *Historiography in the Twentieth Century: From Scientific Objectivity to the Postmodern Challenge*. Hanover, NH: Wesleyan University Press, 1997.

Isbell, Charles D. "A Biblical Midrash on David and Goliath." *SJOT* 20, (2006): 259–63.

Ishida, Tomoo. *The Royal Dynasties in Ancient Israel: A Study on the Formation and Development of Royal-Dynastic Ideology*. Berlin: Walter de Gruyter, 1977.

Isser, Stanley. *The Sword of Goliath: David in Heroic Literature*. Atlanta: SBL, 2003.

Jackson, Jared J. "David's Throne: Patterns in the Succession Story." *CJT* 11, (1965): 183–95.

Jenkins, Keith. *Re-thinking History*. London: Routledge, 1991.

Jensen, Hans Järgen Lundager. "Desire, Rivalry and Collective Violence in the 'Succession Narrative'." *JSOT* (1992): 39–59.

Jobling, David. *1 Samuel*, Berit Olam. Collegeville: Liturgical Press, 1998.

Jongeling, K. "Joab and Tekoite Woman." *Jaarbericht ex oriente lux* xxx, (1987–1988): 116–22.

Kafalenos, Emma. *Narrative Causalities*. Columbus: Ohio State University Press, 2006.

Kessler, John. "Sexuality and Politics: The Motif of the Displaced Husband in the Books of Samuel." *CBQ* 62, (2000): 409–23.

Klein, Ralph W. *1 Samuel*, WBC. Waco: Word Books, 1983.

Klement, Herbert H. *II Samuel 21–24. Context, Structure and Meaning in the Samuel Conclusion*. Frankfurt am Main: Peter Lang, 2000.

Knauf, Ernst Axel. "Does 'Deuteronomic Historiography' (DH) Exist?" In *Israel Constructs Its History: Deuteronomistic Historiography in Recent Research*, edited by Albert de Pury, Thomas Römer and Jean-Daniel Macchi, 388–98. Sheffield: Sheffield Academic Press, 2000.

Koch, Klaus. *The Growth of the Biblical Tradition: The Form-Critical Method*. London: A. & C. Black, 1969.

Koehler, Ludwig, Johann Jakob Stamm, M.E.J. Richardson, and Walter Baumgartner. *The Hebrew and Aramaic Lexicon of the Old Testament*. Leiden: E.J. Brill, 1994.

Kofoed, Jens Bruun. *Text and History: Historiography and the Study of the Biblical Text*. Winona Lake: Eisenbrauns, 2005.

Kooij, Arie van der. "The Story of David and Goliath: The Early History of its Text." *Ephemerides Theologicae Lovanienses* 68, (1992): 118–31.

Krieger, Leonard. *Ranke: The Meaning of History*. Chicago: University of Chicago Press, 1977.

Krinetzki, Leo. "Ein Beitrag zur Stilanalyse der Goliathperikope, 1 Sam 17:1–18:5." *Bib* 54, (1973): 187–236.

Kruger, Paul A. "The Symbolic Significance of the Hem (*kanaf*) in 1 Samuel 15:27." In *Text and Context: Old Testament and Semitic Studies for F.C. Fensham*, edited by W. Claasen, 105–16. Sheffield: JSOT Press, 1988.

Lawton, Robert B. "Saul, Jonathan and the 'Son of Jesse'." *JSOT* 58, (1993): 35–46.

Lemche, Niels Peter. *The Israelites in History and Tradition*. London: SPCK, 1998.

Levenson, Jon D., and Baruch Halpern. "The Political Import of David's Marriages." *JBL* 99, (1980): 507–18.

Levenson, Jon D. "1 Samuel 25 as Literature and as History." *CBQ* 40, (1978): 11–28.

Levich, Marvin. "Interpretation in History: Or What Historians Do and Philosophers Say." *History and Theory* 24, (1985): 44–61.

Licht, Jacob. "Biblical Historicism." In *History, Historiography and Interpretation*, edited by Hayim Tadmor and Moshe Weinfeld, 107–20. Jerusalem: Magnes Press, 1983.

Long, Burke O. "Wounded Beginnings: David and Two Sons." In *Images of Man and God: Old Testament Short Stories in Literary Focus*, edited by Burke O. Long, 26–34. Sheffield: Almond Press, 1981.

Long, V. Philips. *The Reign and Rejection of King Saul: A Case for Literary and Theological Coherence*, SBL Dissertation Series. Atlanta: Scholars Press, 1989.

Longman, Tremper. *Literary Approaches to Biblical Interpretation*, Foundations of Contemporary Interpretation. Grand Rapids: Academie Books, 1987.

Loretz, O. "The Perfectum Copulativum in 2 SM 7, 9–11." *CBQ* 23, (1961): 294–96.

Lowenthal, David. *The Past is a Foreign Country*. Cambridge: Cambridge University Press, 1985.

Lust, J. "The Story of David and Goliath in Hebrew and in Greek." In *The Story of David and Goliath: Textual and Literary Criticism: Papers of a Joint Research Venture*, 5–18. Fribourg: Editions Universitaires, 1986.

Macdonald, John. "The Status and Role of the *na'ar* in Israelite Society." *JNES* 35, (1976): 147–70.

Martin, Ged. *Past Futures: The Impossible Necessity of History*. Toronto: University of Toronto Press, 1996.

Mason, Rex. *Propaganda and Subversion in the Old Testament*. London: SPCK, 1997.

Mauchline, John. *1 and 2 Samuel*, NCBC. London: Oliphants, 1971.

Mayes, A.D.H. "Rise of the Israelite Monarchy." *ZAW* 90, (1978): 1–19.

McCarter, P. Kyle, Jr. *I Samuel*, The Anchor Bible. New York: Doubleday, 1980.

———. *II Samuel*, The Anchor Bible. New York: Double Day, 1984.

———. "The Apology of David." *JBL* 99, (1980): 489–504.

McCarthy, Dennis J. "2 Samuel 7 and the Structure of the Deuteronomic History." *JBL* 84, (1965): 131–38.

———. "Inauguration of Monarchy in Israel: A Form-Critical Study of 1 Samuel 8–12." *Interpretation* 27, (1973): 401–12.

McCullagh, C. Behan. "The Truth of Historical Narratives." *History and Theory* 26, (1987): 30–46.

McKane, William. *I & II Samuel: Introduction and Commentary*, TBC. London: S.C.M. Press, 1975.

McKenzie, Steven L. *King David: A Biography*. Oxford: Oxford University Press, 2000.

———. "The Trouble with Kingship." In *Israel Constructs its History: Deuteronomistic Historiography in Recent Research*, edited by Albert de Pury, Thomas Römer and Jean-Daniel Macchi, 286–314. Sheffield: Sheffield Academic Press, 2000.

McLellan, David. *The Thought of Karl Marx: An Introduction*. 2nd ed. London: Macmillan, 1980.

Mettinger, Tryggve N.D. *King and Messiah: The Civil and Sacral Legitimation of the Israelite Kings*. Lund: CWK Gleerup, 1976.

Miller, J. Maxwell. "Reading the Bible Historically: The Historian's Approach." In *Israel's Past in Present Research*, edited by V. Philips Long, 356–72. Winona Lake: Eisenbrauns, 1999.

———. "Saul's Rise to Power: Some Observations Concerning I Sam 9:1–10:16; 10:26–11:15 and 13:2–14:46." *CBQ* 36, (1974): 157–74.

Molin, G. "What is a *Kidon*?" *JSS* 1, (1956): 334–37.

Moore, Megan Bishop. *Philosophy and Practice in Writing a History of Ancient Israel*. New York: T&T Clark, 2006.

Morley, Neville. *Writing Ancient History*. Ithaca: Cornell University Press, 1999.

Murray, D.F. *Divine Prerogative and Royal Pretension: Pragmatics, Poetics and Polemics in a Narrative Sequence about David (2 Samuel 5.17–7.29)*, JSOTSup. 264. Sheffield: Sheffield Academic Press, 1998.

Nicholson, Ernest. "Story and History in the Old Testament." In *Language, Theology and the Bible*, edited by Samuel E. Balentine and John Barton, 135–50. Oxford: Clarendon Press, 1994.

Nicholson, Sarah. *Three Faces of Saul: An Intertextual Approach to Biblical Tragedy*, JSOTSup. 339. Sheffield: Sheffield Academic Press, 2002.

Noll, K.L. *The Faces of David*. Sheffield: Sheffield Academic Press, 1997.

Nordheim, Erckhard von. "König und Tempel: Der Hintergrund des Tempelbauverbotes in 2 Samuel vii." *VT* 27, (1977): 434–53.

Noth, Martin. *The Deuteronomistic History*, JSOTSup. 15. Sheffield: JSOT Press, 1981.

——. *The History of Israel*. 2nd ed. London: A. & C. Black, 1960.

Oldfield, Adrian. "Moral Judgments in History." *History and Theory* 20, (1981): 260–77.

Ota, Michiko. "A Note on 2 Sam 7." In *A Light unto My Path: Old Testament Studies in Honor of Jacob M. Myers*, edited by Howard N. Bream, Ralph D. Heim and Carey A. Moore, 403–7. Philadelphia: Temple University Press, 1974.

Passmore, John. "Narratives and Events." *History and Theory* 26, (1987): 68–74.

Perdue, Leo G. "'Is There Anyone Left of the House of Saul': Ambiguity and the Characterization of David in the Succession Narrative." *JSOT* 30, (1984): 67–84.

Pietersma, Albert, and Benjamin G. Wright, eds. *A New English Translation of the Septuagint*. New York: Oxford University Press, 2007.

Pisano, Stephen. "2 Samuel 5–8 and the Deuteronomist: Textual Criticism or Literary Criticism?" In *Israel Constructs its History: Deuteronomistic Historiography in Recent Research*, edited by Albert de Pury, Thomas Römer and Jean-Daniel Macchi, 258–85. Sheffield: Sheffield Academic Press, 2000.

——. *Additions or Omissions in the Books of Samuel: The Significant Pluses and Minuses in the Massoretic, LXX and Qumran Texts*. Vol. 57, Orbis Biblicus et Orientalis. Freiburg: Universitatsverlag, 1984.

Pollmann, Thijs. "Coherence and Ambiguity in History." *History and Theory* 39, (2000): 167–80.

Polzin, Robert M. *David and the Deuteronomist: A Literary Study of the Deuteronomic History; Part Three—II Samuel*. San Francisco: Harper and Row, 1993.

——. *Samuel and the Deuteronomist: A Literary Study of the Deuteronomic History; Part Two—I Samuel*. San Francisco: Harper and Row, 1989.

——. "Curses and Kings: A Reading of 2 Samuel 15–16." In *The New Literary Criticism and the Hebrew Bible*, edited by J. Cheryl Exum and David J.A. Clines, 201–26. Sheffield: JSOT Press, 1993.

Porter, J.R. "Review of 'Second Samuel 21–24: Context, Structure and Meaning in the Samuel Conclusion'." *JSOT* 94, (2001): 66–67.

Preston, Thomas R. "The Heroism of Saul: Patterns of Meaning in the Narrative of the Early Kingship." *JSOT* 24, (1982): 27–46.

Prouser, O. Horn. "Suited to the Throne: The Symbolic Use of Clothing in the David and Saul Narratives." *JSOT* 71, (1996): 27–37.

Provan, Iain W., Tremper Longman, and V. Philips Long. *A Biblical History of Israel*. Louisville: Westminster John Knox Press, 2003.

Quinn-Miscall, Peter D. *1 Samuel: A Literary Reading*, Indiana Studies in Biblical Literature. Bloomington: Indiana University Press, 1986.

——. *The Workings of Old Testament Narrative*, Semeia studies. Philadelphia: Fortress Press, 1983.

Rezetko, Robert. *Source and Revision in the Narratives of David's Transfer of the Ark: Text, Language, and Story in 2 Samuel 6 and 1 Chronicles 13, 15–16*. New York: T & T Clark, 2007.

Richardson, Brian. *Unlikely Stories: Causality and the Nature of Modern Narrative*. Newark: University of Delaware Press, 1997.

Rofé, Alexander. "The Battle of David and Goliath: Folklore, Theology, Eschatology." In *Judaic Perspectives on Ancient Israel*, edited by Jacob Neusner, Baruch A. Levine and Ernest S. Frerichs, 117–51. Philadelphia: Fortress Press, 1987.

Rose, Martin. "Deuteronomistic Ideology and Theology of the Old Testament." In *Israel Constructs its History*, edited by Albert de Pury, 424–55. Sheffield: Sheffield Academic Press, 2000.

Rost, Leonhard. *The Succession to the Throne of David*. Translated by Michael D. Rutter and David M. Gunn. Sheffield: Almond Press, 1982.

Rüsen, Jörn. "Introduction: What does 'Making Sense of History' Mean?" In *Meaning and Representation in History*, edited by Jörn Rüsen, 1–5. New York: Berghahn Books, 2006.

Sacon, Kiyoshi K. "A Study of the Literary Structure of 'The Succession Narrative'." In *Studies in the Period of David and Solomon and Other Essays*, edited by Tomoo Ishida, 27–54. Winona Lake: Eisenbrauns, 1982.

Savran, George W. *Telling and Retelling: Quotation in Biblical Narrative*. Bloomington: Indiana University Press, 1988.

Schaper, Joachim. "The Living Word Engraved in Stone." In *Memory in the Bible and Antiquity*, Wissenschaftliche Untersuchungen zum Neuen Testament vol. 212, edited by L.T. Stuckenbruck, S.C. Barton & B.G. Wold, 9–23. Tübingen: Mohr Siebeck, 2007.

Scheffler, E.H. "Saving Saul from the Deuteronomist." In *Past, Present, Future*, edited by Johannes C. De Moor and H.F. Van Rooy, 263–71. Leiden: Brill, 2000.

Schipper, Jeremy. "'Why Do You Still Speak of Your Affairs?': Polyphony in Mephibosheth's Exchanges with David in 2 Samuel." *VT* 54, (2004): 344–51.

Schmidt, Ludwig. *Menschlicher Erfolg und Jahwes Initiative: Studien zu Tradition, Interpretation und Historie in Überlieferungen von Gideon, Saul und David*. Vol. 38, WMANT. Neukirchen-Vluyn: Neukirchener Verlag, 1970.

Schniedewind, William M. *Society and the Promise to David: The Reception History of 2 Samuel 7:1–17*. New York: Oxford University Press, 1999.

——. "Textual Criticisim and Theological Interpretation: The Pro-Temple *Tendenz* in the Greek Text of Samuel-Kings." *HTR* 87, (1994): 107–16.

Schwartz, Regina M. "The Histories of David: Biblical Scholarship and Biblical Stories." In *Not in Heaven: Coherence and Complexity in Biblical Narrative*, edited by Jason P. Rosenblatt and Joseph C. Sitterson, 192–209. Bloomington: Indiana University Press, 1991.

Segal, J.B. "Numerals in the Old Testament." *JSS* 10, (1965): 2–20.

Seow, C.L. *Myth, Drama and the Politics of David's Dance*. Atlanta: Scholars Press, 1989.

Simon, László T. *Identity and Identification: An Exegetical and Theological Study of 2Sam 21–24*. Rome: Gregorian University Press, 2000.

Smith, Henry Preserved. *A Critical and Exegetical Commentary on the Books of Samuel*. Edinburgh: T & T Clark, 1899.

Stähli, Hans-Peter. *Knabe-Jüngling-Knecht: Untersuchungen zum Begriff נער im Alten Testament*. Frankfurt am Main: Peter Lang, 1978.

Stanford, Michael. *A Companion to the Study of History*. Oxford: Blackwell, 1994.

——. *An Introduction to the Philosophy of History*. Malden: Blackwell, 1998.

Stern, Fritz Richard. *The Varieties of History: From Voltaire to the Present*, London: Macmillan, 1970.

Sternberg, Meir. *The Poetics of Biblical Narrative: Ideological Literature and the Drama of Reading*. Bloomington: Indiana University Press, 1985.

Stoebe, Hans Joachim. "Die Goliathperikope 1 Sam. XVII 1–XVIII 5 und die Textform der Septuaginta." *VT* 6, (1956): 397–413.

Tadmor, H. "Autobiographical Apology in the Royal Assyrian Literature." In *History, Historiography and Interpretation*, edited by Hayim Tadmor and Moshe Weinfeld, 36–57. Jerusalem: Magnes Press, 1983.

Thomas, David Winton. "Consideration of Some Unusual Ways of Expressing the Superlative in Hebrew." *VT* 3, (1953): 209–24.

Thompson, J.A. "The Significance of the Verb Love in the David-Jonathan Narratives in 1 Samuel." *VT* 24, (1974): 334–38.

Thompson, Thomas L. *Early History of the Israelite People: From the Written and Archaeological Sources*. Leiden: Brill, 1992.

Thucydides. *History of the Peloponnesian War*. Translated by Rex Warner. Harmondsworth: Penguin Books, 1972.

Tosh, John. *The Pursuit of History: Aims, Methods and New Directions in the Study of Modern History*. 3rd ed. Harlow: Longman, 1999.

Tov, Emanuel. *Textual Criticism of the Hebrew Bible*. 2nd ed. Minneapolis: Fortress Press, 2001.

——. "The Nature of the Differences between MT and the LXX in 1 Sam. 17–18." In *The Story of David and Goliath: Textual and Literary Criticism: Papers of a Joint Research Venture*, 19–46. Fribourg: Editions Universitaires, 1986.

Trebolle Barrera, Julio C. "The Story of David and Goliath (1 Sam 17–18): Textual Variants and Literary Composition." *BIOSCS* 23, (1990): 16–30.

Tsevat, Matitiahu. "Die Namengebung Samuels und die Substitutionstheorie." *ZAW* 99, (1987): 250–54.

——. "Studies in the Book of Samuel III: The Steadfast House: What was David Promised in II Sam. 7:11b-16." *HUCA* 34, (1963): 71–82.

——. "The Biblical Account of the Foundation of the Monarchy in Israel." In *The Meaning of the Book of Job and Other Essays*, 77–99. New York: KTAV, 1980.

——. "The House of David in Nathan's Prophecy." *Bib* 46, (1965): 353–56.

——. "Was Samuel a Nazirite?" In *"Sha'arei Talmon": Studies in the Bible, Qumran, and the Ancient Near East Presented to Shemaryahu Talmon*, edited by Michael Fishbane and Emanuel Tov, 199–204. Winona Lake: Eisenbrauns, 1992.

Tsumura, David Toshio. *The First Book of Samuel*, NICOT. Grand Rapids: Eerdmans, 2007.

Tucker, Gene M. *Form Criticism of the Old Testament*. Philadelphia: Fortress Press, 1971.

Van der Toorn, Karel. "Saul and the Rise of Israelite State Religion." *VT* 43, (1993): 519–42.

Van Seters, John. *In Search of History: Historiography in the Ancient World and the Origins of Biblical History*. New Haven: Yale University Press, 1983.

——. *The Biblical Saga of King David*. Winona Lake: Eisenbrauns, 2009.

Van Zyl, A.H. "1 Sam 1:2–2:11 - A Life-World Lament of Affliction." *JNSL* 12, (1984): 151–61.

Vann, Richard T. "Historians and Moral Evaluations." *History and Theory* 43, (2004): 3–30.

Vannoy, J. Robert. *Covenant Renewal at Gilgal: A Study of I Samuel 11:14–12:25*. Cherry Hill: Mack Pub. Co., 1977.

Veijola, Timo. *Die Ewige Dynastie: David und die Entstehung seiner Dynastie nach der deuteronomistischen Darstellung*. Helsinki: Suomalainen Tiedeakatemia, 1975.

Walsh, Jerome T. *Style and Structure in Biblical Hebrew Narrative*. Collegeville: Liturgical Press, 2001.

Walsh, W.H. "'Meaning' in History." In *Theories of History*, edited by Patrick Gardiner, 296–307. New York: The Free Press, 1959.

Watson, W.G.E. "Hebrew Poetry." In *Text in Context*, edited by A.D.H. Mayes, 253–85. Oxford: Oxford University Press, 2000.

Watts, James W. *Psalm and Story: Inset Hymns in Hebrew Narrative*, JSOTSup 139. Sheffield, England: JSOT Press, 1992.

Weinfeld, Moshe. *Deuteronomy and the Deuteronomic School*. Oxford: Clarendon Press, 1972.

Weiser, Artur. *Introduction to the Old Testament*. London: Darton, Longman & Todd, 1961.

——. *Samuel: Seine geschichtliche Aufgabe und religiöse Bedeutung*. Göttingen: Vandenhoeck & Ruprecht, 1962.

Wellhausen, Julius. *Prolegomena to the History of Ancient Israel*. Gloucester, Mass.: Smith, 1973.

Wesselius, J.W. "Joab's Death and the Central Theme of the Succession Narrative (2 Samuel IX—1 Kings II)." *VT* 40, (1990): 336–51.

Westbrook, Raymond. "1 Samuel 1:8." *JBL* 109, (1990): 114–15.

Westermann, Claus. "The Old Testament's Understanding of History in Relation to That of the Enlightenment." In *Israel's Past in Present Research*, edited by V. Philips Long, 220–31. Winona Lake: Eisenbrauns, 1999.

Wevers, John W. "A Study in the Exegetical Principles Underlying the Greek Text of 2 Sam 11:2 – 1 Kings 1:11." *CBQ* 15, (1953): 30–45.

Whedbee, J. William. "On Divine and Human Bonds: The Tragedy of the House of David." In *Canon, Theology and OT Interpretation*, edited by G.M. Tucker, D.L. Peterson and R.R. Wilson, 147–65. Philadelphia: Fortress, 1988.

White, Hayden V. "Anomalies of Genre: The Utility of Theory and History for the Study of Literary Genres," *NLH* 34 (2003): 597–615.

——. *The Content of the Form: Narrative Discourse and Historical Representation*. Baltimore: Johns Hopkins University Press, 1987.

White, Marsha. "Saul and Jonathan in 1 Samuel 1 and 14." In *Saul in Story and Tradition*, edited by Carl S. Ehrlich and Marsha White, 119–38. Tübingen: Mohr Siebeck, 2006.

Whitelam, Keith W. "The Defence of David." *JSOT* 29, (1984): 61–87.

Whybray, Roger N. *The Succession Narrative: A Study of II Samuel 9–20; I Kings 1 and 2*, SBT. London: SCM, 1968.

——. "What Do We Know About Ancient Israel." In *Israel's Past in Present Research*, edited by V. Philips Long, 181–87. Winona Lake, Ind: Eisenbrauns, 1999.

Wilcoxen, Jay A. "Narrative." In *Old Testament Form Criticism*, edited by John Haralson Hayes. San Antonio: Trinity University Press, 1974.

Williams, Ronald J. *Hebrew Syntax: An Outline*. Toronto: University of Toronto Press, 1967.

Willis, John T. "Cultic Elements in the Story of Samuel's Birth and Dedication." *ST* 26, (1972): 33–61.

——. "Function of Comprehensive Anticipatory Redactional Joints in 1 Samuel 16–18." *ZAW* 85, (1973): 294–314.

Yadin, Azzan. "Goliath's Armor and Israelite Collective Memory." *VT* 54, (2004): 373–95.

Yerushalmi, Yosef Hayim. *Zakhor, Jewish History and Jewish Memory*. Seattle: University of Washington Press, 1982.

Younger, K. Lawson, Jr. *Ancient Conquest Accounts: A Study in Ancient Near Eastern and Biblical History Writing*, JSOTSup. 98. Sheffield: JSOT Press, 1990.

Zakovitch, Yair. "A Study of Precise and Partial Derivations in Biblical Etymology." *JSOT* 15, (1980): 31–50.

——. "Juxtaposition in the Abraham Cycle." In *Pomegranates and Golden Bells: Studies in Biblical, Jewish, and Near Eastern Ritual, Law, and Literature in Honor of Jacob Milgrom*, edited by David P. Wright, David Noel Freedman and Avi Hurvitz, 509–24. Winona Lake: Eisenbrauns, 1995.

——. *The Concept of the Miracle in the Bible*. Tel Aviv: MOD Books, 1990.

AUTHOR INDEX

SCRIPTURE INDEX

SUBJECT INDEX

SUPPLEMENTS TO VETUS TESTAMENTUM

95. Vos, J.C. DE. *Das Los Judas*. Über Entstehung und Ziele der Landbeschreibung in Josua 15. ISBN 90 04 12953 7

96. LEHNART, B. *Prophet und König im Nordreich Israel*. Studien zur sogenannten vor klassischen Prophetie im Nordreich Israel anhand der Samuel-, Elija- und Elischa-Überlieferungen. 2003. ISBN 90 04 13237 6

97. Lo, A. *Job 28 as Rhetoric*. An Analysis of Job 28 in the Context of Job 22-31. 2003. ISBN 90 04 13320 8

98. TRUDINGER, P.L. *The Psalms of the Tamid Service*. A Liturgical Text from the Second Temple. 2004. ISBN 90 04 12968 5

99. FLINT, P.W. and P.D. MILLER, JR. (eds.) with the assistance of A. Brunell. *The Book of Psalms*. Composition and Reception. 2004. ISBN 90 04 13842 8

100. WEINFELD, M. *The Place of the Law in the Religion of Ancient Israel*. 2004. ISBN 90 04 13749 1

101. FLINT, P.W., J.C. VANDERKAM and E. Tov. (eds.) *Studies in the Hebrew Bible, Qumran, and the Septuagint*. Essays Presented to Eugene Ulrich on the Occasion of his Sixty-Fifth Birthday. 2004. ISBN 90 04 13738 6

102. MEER, M.N. VAN DER. *Formation and Reformulation*. The Redaction of the Book of Joshua in the Light of the Oldest Textual Witnesses. 2004. ISBN 90 04 13125 6

103. BERMAN, J.A. *Narrative Analogy in the Hebrew Bible*. Battle Stories and Their Equivalent Non-battle Narratives. 2004. ISBN 90 04 13119 1

104. KEULEN, P.S.F. VAN. *Two Versions of the Solomon Narrative*. An Inquiry into the Relationship between MT 1 Kgs. 2-11 and LXX 3 Reg. 2-11. 2004. ISBN 90 04 13895 1

105. MARX, A. *Les systèmes sacrificiels de l'Ancien Testament*. Forms et fonctions du culte sacrificiel à Yhwh. 2005. ISBN 90 04 14286 X

106. ASSIS, E. *Self-Interest or Communal Interest*. An Ideology of Leadership in the Gideon, Abimelech and Jephthah Narritives (Judg 6-12). 2005. ISBN 90 04 14354 8

107. WEISS, A.L. *Figurative Language in Biblical Prose Narrative*. Metaphor in the Book of Samuel. 2006. ISBN 90 04 14837 X

108. WAGNER, T. *Gottes Herrschaft*. Eine Analyse der Denkschrift (Jes 6, 1-9,6). 2006. ISBN 90 04 14912 0

109. LEMAIRE, A. (ed.). *Congress Volume Leiden 2004*. 2006. ISBN 90 04 14913 9

110. GOLDMAN, Y.A.P., A. van der Kooij and R.D. Weis (eds.). *Sôfer Mahîr*. Essays in Honour of Adrian Schenker Offered by Editors of *Biblia Hebraica Quinta*. 2006. ISBN 90 04 15016 1

111. WONG, G.T.K. *Compositional Strategy of the Book of Judges*. An Inductive, Rhetorical Study. 2006. ISBN 90 04 15086 2

112. HØYLAND LAVIK, M. *A People Tall and Smooth-Skinned*. The Rhetoric of Isaiah 18. 2006. ISBN 90 04 15434 5

113. REZETKO, R., T.H. LIM and W.B. AUCKER (eds.). *Reflection and Refraction*. Studies in Biblical Historiography in Honour of A. Graeme Auld. 2006. ISBN 90 04 14512 5

114. SMITH, M.S. and W.T. PITARD. *The Ugaritic Baal Cycle*. Volume II. Introduction with Text, Translation and Commentary of KTU/CAT 1.3–1.4. 2009. ISBN 978 90 04 15348 6

115. BERGSMA, J.S. *The Jubilee from Leviticus to Qumran*. A History of Interpretation. 2006. ISBN-13 978 90 04 15299 1. ISBN-10 90 04 15299 7

116. GOFF, M.J. *Discerning Wisdom*. The Sapiential Literature of the Dead Sea Scrolls. 2006. ISBN-13 978 90 04 14749 2. ISBN-10 90 04 14749 7

117. DE JONG, M.J. *Isaiah among the Ancient Near Eastern Prophets.* A Comparative Study of the Earliest Stages of the Isaiah Tradition and the Neo-Assyrian Prophecies. 2007. ISBN 978 90 04 16161 0

118. FORTI, T.L. *Animal Imagery in the Book of Proverbs.* 2007. ISBN 978 90 04 16287 7

119. PINÇON, B. *L'énigme du bonheur.* Étude sur le sujet du bien dans le livre de Qohélet. 2008. ISBN 978 90 04 16717 9

120. ZIEGLER, Y. *Promises to Keep.* The Oath in Biblical Narrative. 2008. ISBN 978 90 04 16843 5

121. VILLANUEVA, F.G. *The 'Uncertainty of a Hearing'.* A Study of the Sudden Change of Mood in the Psalms of Lament. 2008. ISBN 978 90 04 16847 3

122. CRANE, A.S. *Israel's Restoration.* A Textual-Comparative Exploration of Ezekiel 36–39. 2008. ISBN 978 90 04 16962 3

123. MIRGUET, F. *La représentation du divin dans les récits du Pentateuque.* Médiations syntaxiques et narratives. 2009. ISBN 978 90 04 17051 3

124. RUITEN, J. VAN and J.C. VOS DE (eds.). *The Land of Israel in Bible, History, and Theology.* Studies in Honour of Ed Noort. 2009. ISBN 978 90 04 17515 0

125. EVANS, P.S. *The Invasion of Sennacherib in the Book of Kings.* A Source-Critical and Rhetorical Study of 2 Kings 18-19. 2009. ISBN 978 90 04 17596 9

126. GLENNY, W.E. *Finding Meaning in the Text.* Translation Technique and Theology in the Septuagint of Amos. 2009. ISBN 978 90 04 17638 6

127. COOK, J. (ed.). *Septuagint and Reception.* Essays prepared for the Association for the Study of the Septuagint in South Africa. 2009. ISBN 978 90 04 17725 3

128. KARTVEIT, M. *The Origin of the Samaritans.* 2009. ISBN 978 90 04 17819 9

129. LEMAIRE, A., B. HALPERN and M.J. ADAMS (eds.). *The Books of Kings.* Sources, Composition, Historiography and Reception. 2010. ISBN 978 90 04 17729 1

130. GALIL, G., M. GELLER and A. MILLARD (eds.). *Homeland and Exile.* Biblical and Ancient Near Eastern Studies in Honour of Bustenay Oded. 2009. ISBN 978 90 04 17889 2

131. ANTHONIOZ, S. *L'eau, enjeux politiques et théologiques, de Sumer à la Bible.* 2009. ISBN 978 90 04 17898 4

132. HUGO, P. and A. SCHENKER (eds.). *Archaeology of the Books of Samuel.* The Entangling of theTextual and Literary History. 2010. ISBN 978 90 04 17957 8

133. LEMAIRE, A. (ed.). *Congress Volume Ljubljana.* 2007. 2010. ISBN 978 90 04 17977 6

134. ULRICH, E. (ed.). *The Biblical Qumran Scrolls.* Transcriptions and Textual Variants. 2010. ISBN 978 90 04 18038 3

135. DELL, K.J., G. DAVIES and Y. VON KOH (eds.). *Genesis, Isaiah and Psalms.* A Festschrift to honour Professor John Emerton for his eightieth birthday. 2010. ISBN 978 90 04 18231 8

136. GOOD, R. *The Septuagint's Translation of the Hebrew Verbal System in Chronicles.* 2010. ISBN 978 90 04 15158 1

137. REYNOLDS, K.A. *Torah as Teacher.* The Exemplary Torah Student in Psalm 119. 2010. ISBN 978 90 04 18268 4

138. VAN DER MEER, M., P. VAN KEULEN, W. TH. VAN PEURSEN and B. TER HAAR ROMENY (eds.). *Isaiah in Context.* Studies in Honour of Arie van der Kooij on the Occasion of his Sixty-Fifth Birthday. 2010. ISBN 978 90 04 18657 6

139. TIEMEYER, L.-S. *For the Comfort of Zion.* The Geographical and Theological Location of Isaiah 40-55. 2011. ISBN 978 90 04 18930 0

140/1. LANGE, A., E. TOV and M. WEIGOLD (eds.). *The Dead Sea Scrolls In Context.* Integrating the Dead Sea Scrolls in the Study of Ancient Texts, Languages, and Cultures. 2011. ISBN 978 90 04 18903 4

141. HALVORSON-TAYLOR, M.A. *Enduring Exile.* The Metaphorization of Exile in the Hebrew Bible. 2011. ISBN 978 90 04 16097 2

142. JOACHIMSEN, K. *Identities in Transition.* The Pursuit of Isa. 52:13-53:12. 2011. ISBN 978 90 04 20106 4

143. GILMOUR, R. *Representing the Past.* A Literary Analysis of Narrative Historiography in the Book of Samuel. 2011. ISBN 978 90 04 2034 02